THE SPIRIT OF LIFE

JÜRGEN MOLTMANN

The Spirit of Life

A UNIVERSAL AFFIRMATION

FORTRESS PRESS   MINNEAPOLIS

THE SPIRIT OF LIFE
A Universal Affirmation

First Fortress Press edition published 1992.
Second impression 1993.

Library of Congress Cataloguing-in-Publication data available
ISBN 0–8006–2737–7

Manufactured in Great Britain   1-2737
96   95   94   93   92   1   2   3   4   5   6   7   8   9   10

CONTENTS

PART THREE: THE FELLOWSHIP AND PERSON OF THE SPIRIT

Contents   ix

PREFACE

The simple question: when did you last feel the workings of the Holy Spirit? embarrasses us. The Spirit's 'holiness' fills us with religious awe. We are conscious that the Spirit is something apart from secular life, and sense our own remoteness from God. Religious experiences, as we all know, are not everyone's line of country.

It is a different matter if we are asked: when were you last conscious of *'the spirit of life?'* Then we can answer out of our own everyday experiences and can talk about our consolations and encouragements. Then 'spirit' is the love of life which delights us, and the energies of the spirit are the living energies which this love of life awakens in us.

The Spirit of God is called *the Holy Spirit* because it makes our life here something living, not because it is alien and estranged from life. The Spirit sets this life in the presence of the living God and in the great river of eternal love. In order to bring out the unity between the experience of God and the experience of life, I shall be talking in this book about *'the Spirit of life'*, and I should like to invite readers to open themselves for their own experiences, and to look at them for what they are.

For me this book has turned into a voyage of discovery into an unknown country. I expected something, and sought for something, and experienced it: the presence of eternity. For this pneumatology there are both objective grounds and external reasons.

The objective grounds are to be found in the logic of trinitarian thinking. I began this series in 1980 with *The Trinity and the Kingdom of God*, and the social doctrine of the Trinity I put forward there draws the christocentricism familiar to us from Protestant and dialectical theology into the wider trinitarian framework of the doctrine of God, giving the appropriate relative independence both to the person and efficacy of the Father in the creation of being, and to the person and efficacy of the Spirit in the living energy of life. I tried to develop this in the context of creation in 1985, in the book

God in Creation. The present book on 'the Spirit of Life' is designed
to move in the same direction, in the context of life's quickening and
its sanctification. My starting point is that the efficacy of Christ is
not without the efficacy of the Spirit, which is its goal; but that the
efficacy of the Spirit is nevertheless distinguishable from the efficacy
of Christ, and is not congruent with that or absorbed by it. As the
Old Testament shows, the operations of God's Spirit precede the
workings of Christ; and the New Testament tells us that they go
beyond the workings of Christ. They relate Christ's liberating and
redemptive efficacy to the life which streams everywhere from its
source and is moved by 'the Spirit of life'; for it is this life which is
to be liberated and redeemed. The operations of God's life-giving
and life-affirming Spirit are universal and can be recognized in
everything which ministers to life and resists its destruction. This
efficacy of the Spirit does not replace Christ's efficacy, but makes it
universally relevant.

I was led to follow up this theme of the relative independence of
the living Spirit of God partly because of the interests and work of
my doctoral students, a noticeable number of whom, ever since 1980,
have chosen pneumatological subjects for their theses. I have learnt
as much from my work with them as they may have done from me.
I should like to mention Lyle Dabney, 'Die Kenosis des Geistes.
Kontinuität zwischen Schöpfung und Erlösung im Werk des Heiligen
Geistes' (1989), Lin, Hong-Hsin, 'Die Person des Heiligen Geistes
als Thema der Pneumatologie in der Reformierten Theologie (1990),
Peter Zimmerling, 'Zinzendorfs Trinitätslehre' (1990), Adelbert
Schloz-Dürr, 'Der Ausgang des Geistes vom Vater. Kriterien einer
ökumenischen Pneumatologie' and Duncan Reid, 'Die Lehre von
den ungeschaffenen Energien. Ihre Bedeutung für die ökumenische
Theologie'. An earlier contribution, dealing with my own approach
to pneumatology, is Donald A. Claybrook, *The Emerging Doctrine
of the Holy Spirit in the Writings of Jürgen Moltmann*, Louisville
1983. All those I have mentioned, alone and together with myself,
have tried to enter into theological dialogue with Orthodox theology.
For that reason this pneumatology is in its theological structure
(which is particularly evident in chs II and III, and XI and XII), a
further contribution to trinitarian doctrine – the crown of Christian
theology. I have published my essays on the doctrine of the Trinity
written during the last ten years in the thematically arranged volume
History and the Triune God: Contributions to Trinitarian Theology

(1991). Since that book and the present volume are related, there are a number of cross-threads. My contribution to the Seventh Assembly of the World Council of Churches in Canberra, 1991, 'Come Holy Spirit – Renew the Whole Creation', is to be found in the essay volume, not in the present book. Anyone who finds particular themes missing here, may look for them in the other volume.

The theological understanding of God the Holy Spirit is only one path of access to this book, however. The other is to be found in the experience of affirmed and loved life. Experiences of this kind provide the external occasion for this book. Human life – and surely not human life alone – only becomes living, and happy in its livingness, if it affirms other life and is itself affirmed. To say this sounds like a cliché. Yet it is by no means a matter of course. In view of the destruction which men and women are inflicting on nature, and in the face of the collective suicide to which human beings are leading humanity, it is in fact difficult to believe this simple statement, and more difficult still to live accordingly. Whether humanity has a future, or whether it is going to become extinct in the next few centuries, depends on our will to live – and that means our absolute will for our one, indivisible life. Whether humanity *ought* to live, or ought to become extinct, is a question which cannot be answered through the dictates of rational expediency, but only out of a love for life. Even now we experience personally and jointly so much blighted and ruined life that to affirm life whole-heartedly is difficult. We have got used to death, at least to the death of other creatures and other people. And to get used to death is the beginning of freezing into lifelessness oneself. So the essential thing is to affirm life – the life of other creatures – the life of other people – our own lives. If we do not, there will be no rebirth and no restoration of the life that is threatened. But anyone who really says 'yes' to life says 'no' to war. Anyone who really loves life says 'no' to poverty. So the people who truly affirm and love life take up the struggle against violence and injustice. They refuse to get used to it. They do not conform. They resist.

We have experienced the catastrophes, and have read the writing on the wall which calls us to be converted from death to life: Chernobyl in 1986 and the Gulf War in 1991. But we have experienced revolutions for life too, and have seen the miracle that after forty years of humiliation, people could take to the streets and break the spell that bound them. They acted out of self-respect. That was the non-violent, democratic revolution which took place in East Germany and Eastern Europe in 1989. We have experienced the forces which deny life, but we also experience the energies that affirm it.

In this question about life, the world religions are not unequivocal. It is not clear whether they want this world to go on existing, and whether they really affirm life here on earth at all. Everywhere we can also see the apocalyptic annihilation of the world being adorned with a religious nimbus. We can detect frightening signs of religious self-hate and, not least, an 'other-worldly' indifference towards life and death here. Where can we find the religion which Albert Schweitzer sought for, the religion of an unconditional affirmation of life, and a comprehensive 'reverence for life'? I have in mind a theology which springs from the experience of life, a theology similar to the one which Friedrich Christoph Oetinger conceived in 1765, when he wrote his *Theologia ex idea vitae deducta* as a counter-blast to the mechanistic philosophy of the Enlightenment.

This book on 'the Spirit of Life' can be described as 'a holistic pneumatology' and, as a way of deepening the concept of life, I have drawn less on the *Zeitgeist* than on the early 'philosophy of life' developed by Wilhelm Dilthey, Henri Bergson, Georg Simmel and Friedrich Nietzsche. I have learnt even more from the psycho-social work of feminist theology, and from philosophical attempts to 'bring back the body' and to rediscover the senses. In this respect too, this book grew out of shared work. In my seminar on 'The Rebirth and Sanctification of Life' (summer semester 1990) I was able to learn from groups of Methodist, charismatic, feminist and ecology-concerned students, and no less so in my seminar on 'The Spirituality and Ethics of Creation' (winter semester 1990–91). Most chapters in this book are based on lectures given during the summer semester of 1990. These were then developed, and discussed with a smaller group. I should like to thank Carmen Krieg, Thomas Kucharz, Claudia Rehberger and Dr Miroslav Volf for their critical comments and suggestions, which I have incorporated into the manuscript in my own way.

Tübingen, April 2, 1991   Jürgen Moltmann

ABBREVIATIONS

AV	Authorized Version of the Bible (1611, King James Version)
BKAT	Biblischer Kommentar, Altes Testament, ed. S. Herrmann et al., Neukirchen-Vluyn
BSt	Biblische Studien, Neukirchen
CD	K. Barth, *Church Dogmatics*, ET Edinburgh and Grand Rapids 1936–69
EK	*Evangelische Kommentare*, Stuttgart
ET	English translation
EvTh	*Evangelische Theologie*, Munich
FZPhTh	*Freiburger Zeitschrift für Philosophie und Theologie*, Fribourg, Switzerland
HWP	*Historisches Wörterbuch der Philosophie*, ed. J. Ritter, Basel etc., 1971ff.
JAAR	*Journal of the American Academy of Religion*, Philadelphia
JBTh	*Jahrbuch für Biblische Theologie*, Neukirchen
KuD	*Kerygma und Dogma*, Göttingen
LThK	*Lexikon für Theologie und Kirche*, Freiburg 1957ff.
MThZ	*Münchener theologische Zeitschrift*, Munich
NHThG	*Neues Handbuch theologischer Grundbegriffe*, ed. P. Eicher, Munich 1984–85
NTD	Das Neue Testament Deutsch, Göttingen 1932ff.
PG	J. P. Migne, Patrologia Graeca, Paris 1857ff.
PhB	Philosophische Bibliothek, Hamburg
PL	J. P. Migne, Patrologia Latina, Paris 1844ff.
RGG[3]	*Die Religion in Geschichte und Gegenwart*, 3rd ed., Tübingen 1957–1965
SC	Sources chrétiennes, ed. H. Lubac et al., Paris
TDNT	*Theological Dictionary of the New Testament* (trans. of *ThWNT* by G. W. Bromiley), Grand Rapids and London 1964–76

TDOT	*Theological Dictionary of the Old Testament* (trans. of *ThWAT* by J. T. Willis and G. W. Bromiley), Grand Rapids 1974–
THAT	*Theologisches Handwörterbuch zum Alten Testament*, ed. E. Jenni et al., Munich etc., 1971–76
ThEx	Theologische Existenz heute, Munich
ThLZ	*Theologische Literaturzeitung*, Leipzig
ThWAT	*Theologisches Wörterbuch zum Alten Testament*, ed. G. J. Botterweck and H. Ringren, Stuttgart 1970ff.
ThWNT	*Theologisches Wörterbuch zum Neuen Testament*, ed. G. Kittel et al., Stuttgart 1933–79
ThZ	*Theologische Zeitschrift*, Basel
TRE	*Theologische Realenzyklopädie*, ed. G. Krause and G. Müller, Berlin 1974ff.
WA	M. Luther, *Werke*, Weimarer Ausgabe, Weimar, 1883ff.
ZKG	*Zeitschrift für Kirchengeschichte*, Stuttgart etc

Translator's Note

Biblical quotations have as a rule been taken from RSV, except where changes of wording were necessary to bring out the author's point. Where English translations of books referred to exist, references to these have been given, but in many cases quotations have been translated directly from the German. The absence in the relevant note of a page reference to the existing English translation will make this clear.

A few very minor changes have been made to the German text for the benefit of the English-speaking reader. These were made in consultation with Professor Moltmann. For his generosity and patience in entering into discussion, elucidating difficulties, and considering particular translation problems I am deeply grateful.

Margaret Kohl

Introduction: Approaches in Pneumatology Today

About twenty years ago it was usual to introduce studies on the Holy Spirit with a complaint about 'forgetfulness of the Spirit' at the present day generally, and in Protestant theology in particular. The Holy Spirit was said to be the Cinderella of Western theology. So it had to be specially cherished and coaxed into a growth of its own.[1] This was undoubtedly a reaction against a particular kind of 'neo-orthodoxy' in the Protestant churches, as well as a counterweight to the christocentricism of Karl Barth's theology, and the theology of the 1934 Barmen Declaration of the Confessing Church. So one of Barth's own last words was always quoted: he dreamed, he said, of a new theology which would begin with the third article of the creed and would realize in a new way the real concern of his old opponent, Schleiermacher.[2]

This criticism of contemporary theology, and this reminder of the master's blessing, initiated a whole flood of writings about the Holy Spirit and its special efficacies.[3] 'Forgetfulness of the Spirit' gave way to a positive obsession with the Spirit. But if we look critically at the actual results, we are bound to conclude that in sober fact, although light has been thrown on a whole number of individual aspects, a new paradigm in pneumatology has not yet emerged.[4] Most studies are no more than prolongations of the traditional doctrines, either pursuing further the Catholic doctrine of grace, or expanding the Protestant pattern 'Word and Spirit'. It is only hesitantly that the very foundation of the Western church's pneumatology is even put forward for discussion – by which I mean the doctrine about the Spirit's origin *a patre filioque*, the doctrine which led to the division of the church in 1054.[5] No less hesitant is recognition of the new pentecostal and charismatic movements, and reflection about their special experiences of the Spirit.[6]

Between the patristic pneumatology of the Orthodox church on the one hand, and the pentecostal experiences of the young churches on the other, there are also the still unsettled questions of modern European times – the age of 'subjectivity' and 'experience'. Fired by Joachimite expectation, the classic German philosophers, Lessing, Kant, Fichte and Hegel, interpreted 'Enlightenment' as 'the third age' – that is to say, 'the age of the Spirit'.[7] So there can be no question of the Spirit's 'being forgotten' in modern times. On the contrary: the rationalism and pietism of the Enlightenment was every bit as Enthusiastic as pentecostal Christianity today.

It was the established churches' fear of the religious, as well as the irreligious, 'free thinking' of the modern world which led to more and more reserve in the doctrine of the Holy Spirit. In reaction against the spirit of the new liberty – freedom of belief, freedom of religion, freedom of conscience and free churches – the only Spirit that was declared holy was the Spirit that is bound to the ecclesiastical institution for mediating grace, and to the preaching of the official 'spiritual pastors and teachers'. The Spirit which people experience personally in their own decision of faith, in believers' baptism, in the inner experience of faith in which 'they feel their hearts strangely warmed' (as John Wesley put it), and in their own charismatic endowment, was declared 'unholy' and 'enthusiastic'. Even today, in ecclesiastical discussions about the Holy Spirit, people like to turn first and foremost to 'the criterion for discerning the spirits' – even when there do not seem to be any spirits to hand.

On the other hand, the continual assertion that God's Spirit is bound to the church, its word and sacraments, its authority, its institutions and ministries, impoverishes the congregations. It empties the churches, while the Spirit emigrates to the spontaneous groups and personal experience. Men and women are not being taken seriously as independent people if they are only supposed to be 'in the Spirit' when they are recipients of the church's ministerial acts and its proclamation. God's Spirit is more than merely the being-revealed of his revelation in human beings, and more than simply the finding of faith in the heart through the proclaimed word. For the Spirit actually brings men and women to the beginning of a new life, and makes them the determining subjects of that new life in the fellowship of Christ. People do not only experience the Holy Spirit outwardly in the community of their church. They experience it to a much greater degree inwardly, in self-encounter – as the experience that 'God's love has been poured into our hearts through the Holy Spirit' (Rom. 5.5). Many people express this personal experience of the Spirit in the simple words: 'God loves me'. In this experience of God they also experience their own indestructible and inalienable dignity, so that they can get up out of the dust. They find themselves, and no longer have to try despairingly to be themselves – or despairingly not to be themselves.[8] Don't the words of the Bible which have come down to us over the centuries, and the words of proclamation which we hear from Christians today, spring from experiences of the Spirit like this?

There are no words of God without human experiences of God's Spirit. So the words of proclamation spoken by the Bible and the church must also be related to the experiences of people today, so that they are not – as Karl Rahner said – merely 'hearers of the Word', but become spokesmen of the Word too.

But this is only possible if Word and Spirit are seen as existing in a *mutual relationship*, not as a one-way street. The Spirit is the subject determining the Word, not just the operation of that Word. The efficacies of the Spirit reach beyond the Word. Nor do the experiences of the Spirit find expression in words alone. They are as multifarious and protean as sensory reality itself. The Spirit has its non-verbal expressions too. The indwelling of the Spirit 'in our hearts' goes deeper than the conscious level in us. It rouses all our senses, permeates the unconscious too, and quickens the body, giving it new life (I Cor. 6. 19f.). A new energy for living proceeds from the Spirit. To bind the experience of the Spirit solely to the Word is one-sided, and represses these dimensions. The non-verbal dimensions for their part show that the Word is bound to the Spirit, but that the Spirit is not bound to the Word, and that Spirit and Word belong in a mutual relationship which must not be conceived exclusively, or in merely intellectual terms.

1. *The Ecumenical and Pentecostal Invitation to the Fellowship of the Holy Spirit*

The ecumenical movement has come up against questions of pneumatology in different ways: (*a*) in the motivation to ecumenical fellowship; (*b*) in the encounter of churches with differing experiences and theologies of the Holy Spirit.

(*a*) the motivation towards ecumenical fellowship with the other churches, the overcoming of painful divisions between churches, and the prospect of a conciliar union of divided churches was often ascribed by the pioneers of the movement to God's Spirit. After centuries of Western division in matters of belief, and following generations of denominational absolutism, the ecumenical movement is without doubt the most important Christian event of the twentieth century. For the first time, there is a revolution of feeling. The other churches are no longer viewed as opponents or competitors. They are taken seriously as partners on a shared path.[9] But this is possible only if we see 'the fellowship of the Holy Spirit' as something that transcends the denominational frontiers, and throws them open, so that we view Christians belonging to other churches as members of this great community of God. At the moment people are no longer interested in laying down demarcation lines, as a way of safeguarding their own territory. Their concern is to discover mutual complement-ariness, as a means of arriving at a greater unity. This ecumenical experience of the Spirit seems to me more important than the highly-charged expectations which some theologians (with Oscar Cullmann's help) have brought to the ecumenical movement, inter-preting it in the context of salvation history as a transition to the epoch of the Spirit, or as entry into the third age of 'the Johannine church' – which is to say the church of the Spirit.[10]

(*b*) If we encounter the other churches as partners, parallel to our own church in the all-embracing 'fellowship of the Holy Spirit', we inevitably enter once more into the disputes which once led to church division. In the context of pneumatology, there are two points to be mentioned here: 1. The question of the *filioque*, with the canon-law and symbolic significance of this Western interpolation into the 381 version of the Nicene Creed, as well as the consequences for trinitarian theology of the subordination of the Spirit to the Son, which was the practical result; 2. The question about the charismatic experiences of God's Spirit and their importance for personal, shared and political life, and for the life of nature. In 1961 the Orthodox churches joined the ecumenical movement, and a number of pentecostal churches came in later. So it is in these two problem complexes that ecumenical ventures in pneumatology are being made. The successful growth of pentecostal churches outside the ecumenical movement is also a serious challenge to all the old, mainstream churches. And not least, return to the common confession of faith in the words of the Nicene Creed led to theological work on its third article in the Commission on Faith and Order, and at congresses in Rome.[11] With or without the addition of the *filioque*, this article leaves so many questions open that it is essential to work towards common answers which will take us beyond the solutions of the church Fathers.

2. *Overcoming the False Alternative between Divine Revelation and Human Experience of the Holy Spirit*

The dialectical theology of Barth, Brunner, Bultmann and Gogarten led to an alternative which today is proving to be unfruitful. The dialectical theologians began by reproaching nineteenth-century liberal and pietistic theology with starting from human consciousness of God, not from the divine Word to men and women; this, they said, was theology 'from below', not theology 'from above'. In the German tradition, Friedrich Schleiermacher was regarded as the founder of the modern theology of consciousness and experience. If God-consciousness is always already inherent in a human being's immediate self-consciousness (since he knows that he is 'simply dependent'), then there is continuity between the human spirit and the Spirit of God. But if God-consciousness only comes into being at all because the Wholly Other God reveals himself, then the Spirit of God is the being-revealed of this self-revelation of God in us; and it remains for us just as inexperienceable, hidden and 'other' as God himself. In this case there is a permanent discontinuity between God's Spirit and the spirit of human beings. For then the Holy Spirit is not a modality of our experience of God; it is a modality of God's revelation to us. If the Spirit is a modality of our own experience, then human experience of God is the foundation of human theology. But this can be at the cost of the qualitative difference between God and human beings. If the Spirit is viewed as a modality of the divine revelation, then the foundation of theology is God's revelation of himself. But in this case the qualitative difference between God and human beings makes every immediate relation of human beings to God impossible. And so there can be no natural human theology either.[12]

Hendrik Berkhof and Alasdair Heron believe that this alternative is the main problem in pneumatology today. Berkhof even thinks that it is 'the determining question in the whole history of the Western church'. I do not myself see this question as a problem, because I cannot see that there is any fundamental alternative between God's revelation to human beings, and human experience of God. How is a man or woman supposed to be able to talk about God if God does not reveal himself? How are men and women supposed to be able to talk about a God of whom there is no human experience? It is only in the narrow concepts of modern philosophy that 'revelation' and 'experience' are antitheses. But theology ought not simply to take over modern epistemological and scientific conceptualizations of experience, and then look round for alternatives. It ought to determine these conceptions themselves. God's revelation is always the revelation of God to others, and is therefore a making-itself-experienceable through others. The experience of God is always a suffering of the God who is Other, and the experience of fundamental change in the relationship to that Other.

In 1929, in his lecture 'The Holy Spirit and Christian Life', Karl Barth settled accounts with Idealist notions about the continuity between the Spirit of God and the spirit of human beings.[13] He employed three arguments: 1. God's Spirit is not the spirit of human beings, because there is no continuity between Creator and what he has created, not even in the soul's remembrance of its divine origin (as Augustine had once said). The relationship between Creator and creature in the Holy Spirit is conferred by the Creator alone. 2. The human being does not simply *differ* from the Creator because of his 'creatureliness'. He is actually at variance with God much more fundamentally than that, because he is a sinner. So the 'Holy' Spirit encounters him in utter contradiction to his own sinful spirit. It is the Holy Spirit as reconciler who contravenes this human enmity towards God, and in that very way is on the true side of human beings, in the name of God's grace contraverting human hostility towards grace.[14] Sanctification through the Holy Spirit therefore coincides with the justification of the sinner through God's grace. Sinful men and women remain dependent on this 'alien', external grace. Christian life is nothing other than 'a receiving of God's revelation'.[15] 3. Finally, the Holy Spirit is holy because 'it is *eschatologically* present to the human spirit in God's revelation, and in no other way'.[16] But 'the Holy Spirit as redeemer' is 'eschatological' because it belongs to eternity, and therefore to God, whereas human beings exist here in time and in the shadow of death.

Barth undoubtedly thinks that by saying this he has formulated the Spirit's 'true continuity to the human spirit'. But his eschatology is not linked with the future of the new creation of all things; it is related to God's eternity, over against the temporality of human beings.[17] Consequently the Holy Spirit reveals nothing to human beings which they could see, hear, smell or taste, and so experience through their senses; on the contrary, it reveals something which human beings can never experience: God's eternity and the life which lies beyond the frontier of death, as eternal life. Barth therefore calls the Holy Spirit 'the Spirit of promise', because it places human beings in expectation of the 'Wholly Other', and can hence never be experienced. As the subjective reality of God's self-revelation, the Holy Spirit remains entirely on God's side, so it can never be experienced by human beings at all. Even the faith which the Spirit effects does not know itself. It remains hidden and inexperienceable to itself, so that the believer has to believe in his belief.

By setting up this antithesis between revelation and experience, Barth merely replaced the theological immanentism which he complained about by a theological transcendentalism. But the real phenomenon is to be found neither in the Spirit's immanence nor in its transcendence, neither in the continuity nor in the discontinuity. It is to be found in God's *immanence* in human experience, and in the *transcendence* of human beings in God. Because God's Spirit is present in human beings, the human spirit is self-transcendently aligned towards God. Anyone who stylizes revelation and experience into alternatives, ends up with revelations that cannot be experienced, and experiences without revelation.[18] The new foundation of the eschatology which takes its bearings from the future by way of the 'theology of hope', does away with the Platonic time-eternity pattern which Barth and his brother, the philosopher Heinrich Barth, maintained in 1930. The new approach now develops eschatology as the horizon of expectation for the historical experience of the divine Spirit. The Holy Spirit is not simply the subjective side of God's revelation of himself, and faith is not merely the echo of the Word of God in the human heart. The Holy Spirit is much more than that. It is the power that raises the dead, the power of the new creation of all things; and faith is the beginning of the rebirth of human beings to new life.

But this means that the Holy Spirit is by no means merely a matter of revelation. It has to do with life and its source.[19] The Holy Spirit is called 'holy' because it sanctifies life and renews the face of the earth.

3. The Discovery of the Cosmic Breadth of the Divine Spirit

In both Protestant and Catholic theology and devotion, there is a tendency to view the Holy Spirit solely as *the Spirit of redemption*. Its place is the church, and it gives men and women the assurance of the eternal blessedness of their souls. This redemptive Spirit is cut off both from bodily life and from the life of nature. It makes people turn away from 'this world' and hope for a better world beyond. They then seek and experience in the Spirit of Christ a power that is different from the divine energy of life, which according to the Old Testament ideas interpenetrates all the living.[20] The theological textbooks therefore talk about the Holy Spirit in connection with God, faith, the Christian life, the church and prayer, but seldom in connection with the body and nature.[21] In Yves Congar's great book on the Holy Spirit, he has almost nothing to say about the Spirit of creation, or the Spirit of the new creation of all things. It would seem as if the Spirit of God is simply and solely the Spirit of the church, and the Spirit of faith. But this would restrict 'the fellowship of the Holy Spirit', and make it impossible for the church to communicate its experience of the Spirit to the world.[22] Some theologians have discovered a new love for the charismatic movements; but this can also be an escape, a flight from the politics and ecology of the Spirit in the world of today.

What is behind this trend, which must undoubtedly be termed purely individualistic? One reason is certainly the continuing Platonization of Christianity. Even today this still puts its mark on what is termed 'spirituality' in the church and religious groups. It takes the form of a kind of hostility to the body, a kind of remoteness from the world, and a preference for the inner experiences of the soul rather than the sensory experiences of sociality and nature.

Another reason, I believe, is the far-reaching decision in favour of the *filioque*. This has meant that the Holy Spirit has come to be understood solely as 'the Spirit of Christ', and not at the same time as 'the Spirit of the Father'. As *the Spirit of Christ* it is *the redemptive Spirit*. But the work of creation too is ascribed to the Father, so *the Spirit of the Father* is also *the Spirit of creation*. If redemption is placed in radical discontinuity to creation, then 'the Spirit of Christ' has no longer anything to do with Yahweh's *ruach*. According to this notion, the soul is saved from this vale of tears, and from this frail husk of the body, and is carried up into the heaven of the blessed spirits. But these notions of redemption are not Christian. They are gnostic. It was in order to contravert them that the ancient church introduced '*the resurrection of the body*' into the third article of the Apostles' Creed, and confessed the Spirit 'who spake by the prophets', as the Nicene Creed puts it. But if redemption is the resurrection of the body and the new creation of all things, then the redeeming Spirit of Christ cannot be any Spirit other than Yahweh's creative *ruach*. If Christ is confessed as the reconciler and head of the whole cosmos, as he is in the Epistle to the Colossians, then the Spirit is present wherever Christ is present, and has to be understood as the divine energy of life animating the new creation of all things.

But this brings us up against the question about the continuity and discontinuity of the redemptive and the newly creating Spirit on the one hand, and the creative and all-animating Spirit on the other – the relation between the *Spiritus sanctificans* and the *Spiritus vivificans*.[23] This is not a special problem of pneumatology, however. It is the question about the unity of God's work in the creation, redemption and the sanctification of all things. In both the Old and the New Testaments, the words used for the divine act of *creating* are also used for God's *liberating* and *redeeming* acts (e.g., Isa. 43.19). Redemption is the final new creation of all things out of their sin, transitoriness and mortality, for everlasting life, enduring continuance and eternal glory. The new creation is not without any presuppositions, like creation-in-the-beginning. It presupposes what is old, and is therefore seen pre-eminently in *the raising of the dead* (Ezek. 37; I Cor. 15). But if the redeeming Spirit is the Spirit of the resurrection and new creation of all things, then to employ Platonic and gnostic conceptions is simply to misunderstand it. To experience the power of the resurrection, and to have to do with this divine energy, does not lead to a non-sensuous and inward-turned spirituality, hostile to the body and detached from the world. It brings the new vitality of a love for life.

The new approaches to an 'ecological theology',[24] 'cosmic christology',[25] and the rediscovery of the body,[26] start from the Hebrew understanding of the divine Spirit and presuppose that the redeeming Spirit of Christ and the creative and life-giving Spirit of God are one and the same. So experience of the life-giving Spirit in the faith of the heart and in the sociality of love leads of itself beyond the limits of the church to the rediscovery of the same Spirit in nature, in plants, in animals, and in the ecosystems of the earth.

To experience the fellowship of the Spirit inevitably carries Christianity beyond itself into the greater fellowship of all God's creatures. For *the community of creation*, in which all created things exist with one another, for one another and in one another, is also *the fellowship of the Holy Spirit*. Both experiences of the Spirit bring the church today into solidarity with the cosmos, which is so mortally threatened. Faced with 'the end of nature', the churches will either discover the cosmic significance of Christ and the Spirit, or they will share the guilt for the annihilation of God's earthly creation. In earlier times, contempt for life, hostility towards the body, and detachment from the world was merely an inward attitude of mind. Now it has become an everyday reality in the cynicism of the progressive destruction of nature. Discovery of the cosmic breadth of God's Spirit leads in the opposite direction – to respect for the dignity of all created things, in which God is present through his Spirit. In the present situation this discovery is not romantic poetry or speculative vision. It is the essential premise for the survival of humanity on God's one, unique earth.

4. *The Question about the Personhood of the Holy Spirit*

From the very beginning, the personhood of the Holy Spirit was an unsolved problem, and the problem is as difficult as it is fascinating. To start from the *experience* of the Spirit meant finding largely non-personal words and phrases to describe it: the Spirit is a divine energy, it is wind and fire, light and a wide space, inward assurance and mutual love. Because of what the Spirit effects, its nature was often described through analogies of this kind, drawn from other experiences. Yet in prayer, direct address has to take the place of paraphrases like these. But addresses to the Holy Spirit in prayer are rare, compared with the many ways of addressing God the Father, and the appeals to Christ the Lord and to Jesus. Prayers to the Holy Spirit are always *epikleses* – pleas for the coming of the Spirit: *veni Creator Spiritus*. They seldom include thanksgiving or cries for help.

Theological assertions about the personhood of the Holy Spirit were made in the patristic church in the dispute with the Pneumatomachi. These people interpreted the general Christian subordinationism to mean that the Spirit is subordinated to the Son as the Son is subordinated to the Father. 'The Spirit of the Son' then means the Son's mode of efficacy – a way in which the Son exercises his power – but not an independent divine person, over against the Son; just as 'the Spirit of the Father' means the Father's mode of efficacy, but not an independent divine person, over against the Father. Tertullian's famous trinitarian formula, *una substantia – tres personae*, asserts the divine personhood of the Holy Spirit, and puts it on the same level as the personhood of the Father and the Son. It secures for the Holy Spirit the same worship and glorification as that given to the Father and the Son; and it is this that is stated in the third article of the creed. This divine personhood of the Spirit is really only asserted, however, not demonstrated. But for all that, to assert the personhood of the Spirit in the theology of the Trinity leads in a different direction from statements based on the experience of the Spirit. What the Spirit *effects* allows its subjectivity to be discerned (as the effector of a work), but not its personhood. Its personhood becomes comprehensible only from that which the Spirit *is*, in relation to the Father and the Son.[27] For personhood is always being-in-relationship. But the relationships which constitute the personhood of the Spirit must be looked for within the Trinity itself, not in the Spirit's outward efficacies.

If we proceed from the experience of the Spirit, then we must not start with a hard and fast definition of experience, but must keep the concept open for the transcendent origin of experiences. People call what they 'experience' about God 'the power of God' or 'the Spirit of God'. Do they mean by this a *characteristic* of the eternal God's essential being? Then it would have to be 'the powerful God, the spiritual God'. By making the power or Spirit of God a substantive, more is evidently meant than merely a divine attribute. This is a reality in which God himself is present according to his will. So 'Yahweh's *ruach*' is described as 'confronting event of the efficacious presence of God'.[28] It is not a characteristic of God's being. It is *a mode of his presence* in his creation and in human history. But if we were to term this 'God in action',[29] we should be rashly setting bounds to the perception of the Holy Spirit. The mode of God's presence in human history comprehends not merely God in action but God in passion too; and this touches both God's suffering with his people, in whom he desires to be present, and also 'the descent of the Spirit'. If we take up later Jewish insights into the nature of the Shekinah, when we talk about the Holy Spirit we can talk about

'God's indwellings'.[30] It is characteristic of these divine indwellings to be hidden, secret and silent. In everyday life they are perceived as God's inexpressible closeness. They are experienced as God's companionship. In experiences of suffering they often lead to the assurance of God's nearness.

Because of these modes of descent, self-emptying, and participation in the situation of men and women, some theologians have talked about an 'anonymity of the Spirit',[31] about an 'unknown' or 'unacknowledged God',[32] or about 'the shy member of the Trinity'. So when experience of the Spirit leads us to talk about 'the power' of God, about wind, fire, light, or a wide space, we are talking about the *kenotic forms* of the Spirit, forms of his self-emptying. They are not objectifications of the Spirit, but as kenotic forms actually presuppose the personhood of the Spirit, as the determining subject of these forms.

The subjectivity of the Spirit becomes more clearly discernible still if we see God's Shekinah not only as a *mode of his presence*, but also as *God's counterpart in God* himself. According to late Jewish writings, the Shekinah in its earthly history of suffering turns to God himself; and it is in the same way that in his descent the indwelling and co-suffering Spirit of God also turns to God himself (Rom. 8.23; Rev. 22.17). Just as in the Wisdom literature Wisdom is by no means merely thought of as 'one of God's attributes', but is also seen as 'God's daughter', so the Holy Spirit too has to be understood as a counterpart of God in God himself.

I have deliberately avoided the terms 'hypostasis' and 'person' at this point, because I do not wish to blur the differences between the personhood of the Father, and the personhood of the Son, and the personhood of the Spirit, by using a term for person common to them all.[33] The Holy Spirit has a wholly unique personhood, not only in the form in which it is experienced, but also in its relationships to the Father and the Son. We should be losing sight of this if we expected the Spirit to have the same kind of personhood as the Father. We should be losing sight of it if we presupposed that the Spirit has a personhood like that of the Son. In praying to the Father, to Christ and to the Spirit, these differences can immediately be noticed in the different form of intercession, invocation and adoration.

Among more recent outlines of pneumatology, the work of Hendrik Berkhof and Heribert Mühlen may be mentioned, as opposite poles.

In his brief *Theology of the Holy Spirit* (1964), Berkhof puts forward a modalist pneumatology. He takes up Karl Barth's early modalistic trinitarian doctrine about the 'One God in three different modes of existence' and uses the three modes of God's existence for three ways of divine movement (*modi motus*): a unified creative movement proceeds to the world from God the Father through Christ in the energies of the Holy Spirit. 'Spirit' is to be interpreted as a predicate of the subjects 'God' and 'Christ', and is simply the name for 'the efficacious God'.[34] The Spirit of the Father means the efficacious Father, the Spirit of the Son the efficacious Christ. This means that, unlike Barth, Berkhof surrenders the three divine modes of existence. Instead of a Trinity, he asserts a binity of Father and Son. The Spirit is nothing other than their efficacy. It is then only possible to talk about a 'personhood' of the Spirit to the extent in which this divine efficacy has 'person-like features',[35] and can make itself felt, for example, in 'personal encounter'. But this is determined by our human personhood, not by personhood in its divine form. In his dogmatics, *Christelijk Geloof* (1973, ET *Christian Faith*, 1979), Berkhof then drew the appropriate conclusions, and went over to a unitarian pneumatology. Like Israel, Jesus Christ is God's partner in the covenant, and the Holy Spirit is the divine bond in this covenant between God and human beings. As the perfect partner to the covenant, Christ is both the work of the Spirit and the sender of the Spirit into the world. For Berkhof, God the Father is 'the One God, who is Person'. The Holy Spirit is the mode of efficacy of the one God, who creates his human partner to the covenant in the Spirit-imbued Christ, and through Christ's mediation draws human beings into this divine covenant.

Berkhof's sequence of ideas is consistent, and makes it clear that to surrender the personhood of the Holy Spirit does not result merely in the dissolution of the doctrine of the Trinity. It leads to the dissolution of christology as well. Trinity turns into binity, and binity becomes monism. All that is left is the divine monarch of the world.

We have to thank Heribert Mühlen, on the Catholic side, for his endeavours to find a new foundation for the personhood of the Spirit.[36] After Karl Barth, Karl Rahner too, in German Catholic theology, had departed from the concept of person in the doctrine of the Trinity, on the grounds that in modern times this term has become open to misunderstanding. He talked instead about 'One God in three distinct modes of subsistence'.[37] But both Barth and Rahner misunderstood the modern concept of person because they interpreted it individualistically. The modern philosophical personalism of Hölderlin, Feuerbach, Buber, Ebner and others defines person as 'primal distance and relationship' (Buber's phrase). To be a person means 'being-in-relationship'. These thinkers did not see even 'subjectivity' in isolation, but viewed it in the social network of 'inter-subjectivity'. Mühlen is one of the first to draw on these conceptual possibilities in order to develop a 'personalist' doctrine of the Trinity in which 'person', 'relation' and 'sociality' are used as complementary terms. If the Father is the divine 'I', then the Son is the divine 'THOU', and the Holy Spirit, as the bond of love and peace between the two, is the divine 'WE'.

This is an interesting conceptual attempt, but it has limitations. For the divine 'WE' has no inward relation such as the divine 'I' and 'THOU' have to one another; it merely represents the community of the two outwardly. It therefore still has to look for its personal counterpart. What exists in God is really a binity, which merely appears outwardly as a unity, thus representing a trinity. This is a modern personalistic variant of the Western doctrine of the Trinity, according to which the Spirit 'proceeds from the Father and the Son'. It does not yet provide a new starting point for trinitarian doctrine itself. Like the Western trinitarian doctrine that follows Augustine, this attempt too shows its weakness in its pneumatology.

Over against Berkhof's modalism and Mühlen's personalism, I shall try here to develop *a trinitarian pneumatology* out of the experience and theology of the Holy Spirit.

PART ONE

EXPERIENCES OF THE SPIRIT

I

Experience of Life – Experience of God

In volume one of this series, *The Trinity and the Kingdom of God*, I presented the Holy Spirit in its trinitarian communion with the Father and the Son. In volume two, *God in Creation*, I looked at the Spirit as the power and life of the whole creation. In volume three, *The Way of Jesus Christ*, I developed a Spirit christology designed to be a necessary complement – not an alternative – to Logos christology. These being the presuppositions, it will be justifiable to start volume four on *The Spirit of Life* with the personal and shared *experience of the Spirit*, instead of with the objective word of the proclamation, and the spiritual institutions of the church; and I hope that I can do this without being at once put down as a modernist, liberal, or pietistic 'experiential' theologian. The theology of revelation is church theology, a theology for pastors and priests. The theology of experience is pre-eminently lay theology. To begin with experience may sound subjective, arbitrary and fortuitous, but I hope to show that it is none of these things. By experience of the Spirit I mean an awareness of God in, with and beneath the experience of life, which gives us assurance of God's fellowship, friendship and love.

I am also choosing the phrase 'experience of the Spirit' as a way of understanding appropriately the intermediate state of every *historical experience* between remembered past and expected future. The experience, life and fellowship of God's Spirit come into being when Christ is made present and when the new creation of all things is anticipated. These things are resonances of Christ, and a prelude to the kingdom of God. The experience of the Spirit is never without the remembrance of Christ, and never without the expectation of his future. But in the harmony between this expectation and this remembrance, experience of the Spirit acquires a stature and a dignity which is so much its own, and so entirely without substitute, that it is rightly called *experience of God*. In this sense pneumatology presupposes christology, and prepares the way for eschatology. But the experience of life can also be so intensive that remembrances and expectations are forgotten, and all there is is pure present. We then talk about life's ecstasies. Experiences of God can be so intensive that, as Parmenides said, 'the beginnings are obliterated and the ending vanishes' and the eternal present fills everything. Then we talk about mystical or 'eschatological' moments. In this sense christology leads to pneumatology, and eschatology is its consummation.

We shall begin with a brief phenomenology of experience in the form of a meditation on the world in which we live, drawing on the language of everyday. This should allow us to make an initial appraisal of the many strata and different dimensions of experience. We shall then look at the modern methodization and subjectification of the concept of experience in the empirical sciences, since it is these that have led science to declare that God is in principle 'inexperienceable'. In the third part of the chapter we shall draw on the concept of immanent transcendence, and shall break open and expand the modern concept of experience, so as to discuss dimensions of the experience of God in, with and beneath the experience of life.

§1 DIMENSIONS OF EXPERIENCE

H. G. Gadamer points out that experience is one of the least explained concepts in philosophy.[1] This may be said even more emphatically about theology, which ever since the beginning of modern times has taken over the concept of experience with particular enthusiasm. Just because experience is not apparently a hard and fast concept, and is not already 'given' to experience itself, it rouses our curiosity, impelling us to start from specific experiences. The reason why the conceptuality is unexplained is not any lack of effort to understand it. The reason is the simple fact that although from primary experiences we arrive at concepts, concepts do not lead us to these experiences. Of course in experiences which are socially mediated, concepts and experiences influence one another mutually. But in this case the experiences are generally secondary. Primary experiences are the source of the ideas and concepts with which we try to comprehend them. They therefore remain paramount, and above the concepts.

But these experiences for their part point us towards the ideas and concepts with which we try to grasp them; for experiences which are not understood are like experiences that have never existed. They are repressed experiences, which probe and throb in the subconscious. Every experience of life thrusts towards its expression in the people affected, whether it be expression through their Gestalt, their attitude to life, or through their thoughts, words and deeds, images, symbols and rituals. Without the expression that corresponds to it, an experience 'sticks fast' in the human being, so to speak. It oppresses him – or he suppresses it. We should not see the relation between experience and concept too narrowly, or in merely intellectual terms. If instead of concepts we talk in a wider sense about 'expression', we can modify Kant's famous dictum and say: experiences without expression are blind, expressions without experience are empty. Experiences can be expressed through the body or the spirit, through art or through the intellect. There are bodily and emotional, spontaneous and ritual modes of expression.

'The universe belongs to the dancer', says one of the New Testament apocryphal writings, talking about the experience of grace: 'The person who does not dance does not know what is coming to pass.'[2] The important thing is the expression, not the concept, for it is in expression that life is classified and structured, unfurled and heightened. Expression is the creative achievement of living.[3]

If we leave mystical ecstasies on one side for the moment, experiences depend on *sensory impressions*. But we do not call every sensory impression an 'experience'. Of course we notice and practise regular, accustomed acts, like washing our hands or cleaning our teeth, but these seldom become 'experiences' worth mentioning – unless, for example, we have had to do without them for a long time. But then what do we mean when we talk in a more emphatic sense about experiences, or even 'experiences of life'? One definition says: 'Experience is the term used to describe in the widest sense the totality of that which a person encounters in the life of his consciousness.'[4] It is lasting expansions of the consciousness that are meant here, not fleeting impressions. 'Experience accordingly comprehends the totality of everything which the understanding acquires in the exercise of its activity,' explains J.-P. Jossua.[5] So by experience he means a perception which touches the person at the centre of his personhood, a centre which Jossua believes is constituted by consciousness and reason; and at this centre, perceptions affect us in such a way that they turn into experiences.

This identification of the true centre of human beings with consciousness and reason is Western, modern and, not least, typically male. According to the Western view – and especially the modern Western view – the human being (which pre-eminently means the man) is the subject of reason and will. His bodily nature plays no part. The life of his senses is subordinate.[6] But we acquire most of our experiences neither through our consciousness, nor through our reason, nor as the result of any deliberate intention. We perceive the happenings that affect us by way of our senses. They affect our bodies. They penetrate the unconscious levels of our psyche. And it is probably only a small segment of our experiences of which we are conscious, and which is 'acquired' by the reason in the exercise of its reflective and interpretative activity. When people arrive at tranquillity, they know what a wealth of experiences overwhelms them, experiences that have happened to them, and to which they have not actively contributed at all.

Of course consciousness and reason and the understanding, will all belong to experience and the working-over of experience. But our bodies as a whole experience in another manner too, and work on experience in other ways. When we allow experiences which burden us to lie fallow for a while, or suppress them, or are even able to forget them, we sense how the unconscious energies have worked on these experiences in the meantime. It therefore seems too narrow and too 'ego-centric' to relate experience merely to 'the life of the consciousness' and 'the activity of the reason', and to exclude whatever does not belong to these contexts.

The transition from perceptions to experiences is certainly so fluid that it is pointless to try to define the frontier between them in hard and fast terms. Any such definition would lead only to the impoverishment of experience, and would mean imposing a straitjacket on the way experience is received. But it is helpful to look at the other side too – at those *limit situations* for which we at all events use the language of experience. In the elemental experiences of life, love and death we are touched by perceptions of a sensory kind which overpower us to such a degree that we are not master of them. They mould us, and become our companions. There are events in the past which never become 'past', but are continually present to us. We repress them, we work on them, we puzzle over them and interpret them, for we have to live with them. Our biographies are moulded by experiences like this, experiences which affect us in this elemental way.

Even today I can still feel shaken by the terror of early *experiences of death*, even if I am no longer consciously aware of them, and even though 'the activity of my reason' tells me that these experiences are forty-seven years old, and go back to the fire-storm that raged through Hamburg in 1943. But for all that, these experiences are present with me still. I can feel myself back into them, and they still plunge me into the same terror as they did then. Ever since, my life has been hung over by the tormenting, insistent questions: 'Where is God?' and 'Why am I not dead too?' In the depths of experiences like this, there is apparently no such thing as 'time the great healer', and no merciful forgetting. So we can never say about an experience of this kind 'I had it' as if it were finished and done with, something past and gone. We are continually still involved in experiencing confronting events* like these, because they continually, over and over again, press for an answer.

The happiness of *experiencing deep love* has a similar effect on us. It becomes lastingly and permanently present, and in its way abolishes the transience of time, for – as Nietzsche said – 'all delight longs for eternity, for deep, deep eternity'. The events with which love begins mould the present, because they are the beginning of a new life story. They are overwhelming, as we say, because the overspill of happiness is so unexpected and so incredibly abundant. They penetrate the depths of soul and body, so that the awareness and the activities of the reason discover this overflowing happiness when they open themselves for it, and relate themselves to it. We can never say about the happiness of love either, that we have *had* this experience. For we never *had* it at all, never *acquired* it for ourselves. The experience found us. We do not 'make' it, as German says we do. It makes something out of us; and moreover we are never finished with the experience of this happiness in such a way that the process of experiencing turns into the closed event of an 'experience'.

Anyone who says that he has 'had' an experience like this is also

---

* The phrase 'confronting event' has been chosen to translate the German word *Ereignis* in order to bring out its dynamic and challenging element. The word 'happening' – otherwise a possibility – has meanwhile acquired a different connotation [Trans.].

saying that he is no longer living in it, and that it is no longer present to him – or is present only as something past. That is why, in everyday speech, the wise saws drawn from experience sound so resigned. Past experience may make us wise, but it does not make us live again, or make us happy either. It is therefore inappropriate and completely mistaken to talk about 'commanding' experiences. It is wrong to try 'to master' the past. Nor can we 'grasp' elemental experiences of pain and happiness in order to 'get them under control'. This language of domination is not suited to the experience of life. On the contrary, it induces people to let life pass them by, because they are unwilling to let it touch them any more, for fear of no longer being able to control it, and because they are afraid of losing themselves. We can neither master nor grasp elemental experiences of death and love. But we can give them expression, and we can express ourselves in them. We can find the form, configuration or Gestalt which will allow us to live from them and with them. There is no way of defining or conceptualizing grief; it is lament that lends sorrow an expression which allows people to live in it and with it. There is no way of defining overpowering happiness either. It is the exultation which makes lovers happy. 'The rose flowers without a why', says Rilke.

And as for the ultimate questions of life and existence, we shall never grasp why there *is* anything at all, and why we – we, of all people – should exist. But if we have kept anything of the pristine awareness we had as children, we shall be able to marvel at the uniqueness of every moment, just as, when we were children – when we were born and woke to life – we were astonished because life itself was new and for-the-very-first-time.

Out of its fathomless source, life thrusts forward to expression, expression through living. That is why the deeper experiences of life remain uncompleted. We discover ourselves in them again and again, each time in a different way. This is the charm of re-membrance. We experience life with these experiences, and they travel with us.

The elemental experiences which we have described make it clear that we have to talk about experiences in both the *active* and the *passive*. We 'have' and 'acquire' experiences. Experiences 'happen' to us and 'befall' us.[7] The modern concept of experience is one-sided, because it is purely active. So here we shall stress the passive side of experiences, as everyday language does too. For primary experience is something that 'happens to us', something that overpowers us without our intending it, unexpectedly and suddenly. When something like this happens to us, the centre of the determining subject is not in us – in our consciousness or our will: it is to be found in the event that 'befalls' us, and in its source. The person who experiences is changed in the process of experiencing. So although in German one talks about 'making' an experience, it is not I who 'make' the experience. It is the experience that 'makes' something of me. I perceive the external happening with my senses, and notice that it has brought about a change in my own self.

Experience has an *outward reference*, in the perception of the happening, and an *inward reference*, in the perception of the change in the self. The inward changes can also alter the previous structure of the perceiving subject, strengthening that structure or destroying it. At all events, the experience of the self is largely dependent on outward experiences. Perceptions on these two levels, outward and inward, do not have to take place simultaneously, although they are mutually related. Perception of the change in one's own self is often delayed, and usually comes too late for people who are committed only to active life. But there are no elemental experiences in life without receptivity – that is to say, without the preparedness for inward change and the risk that involves. Without the pain of this change, we shall hardly experience life at all; nor shall we arrive at any new experiences. There is no experience without jeopardy.

If we leave the spheres of objects and events, and turn to social relationships, then the mutual conditioning of experience of the self and the experience of other people is stronger still. The way a child experiences itself depends on the way it is accepted, loved and experienced by its parents. If confidence is placed in it, the child acquires self-confidence; if it is rejected, it begins to hate itself. In adult I-Thou relationships things are no different: the more we are trusted, the more we trust ourselves; and conversely, the more we trust ourselves, the more we are able to trust other people. We love our neighbour as ourselves, and ourselves as our neighbour. Self-love and love of our neighbour condition one another mutually. The same is true of self-hate and misanthropy. If people's dignity is disregarded and belittled, either individually or collectively, it is easy for these judgments to become internalized, so that they turn into self-contempt and persecution complexes. Our experience of ourselves is always woven into a network of social relationships, on which it is dependent.

Of course there are also relatively autonomous personalities, the

'inner-directed types' who are always marked out by their sovereignty
and egocentricism. And at the other extreme there are the 'other-
directed types', who are characterized by their capacity for participation, and by uncertainty of themselves and their values.[8] But in the
broad area between these extremes, most people try to find a
harmonious balance between their experience of others and their
experience of their own selves. The livingness of life comes into play
in the reciprocity between word and answer, action and reaction, the
discovery of others and the discovery of oneself in relationships.
Goethe offers an early testimony to this I-Thou philosophy in his
Westöstlichen Diwan:

Zuleika: The slave, the lord of victories,
              The crowd, whene'er you ask, confess
          In sense of personal being lies
              A child of earth's chief happiness.

          There's not a life we need refuse
              If our true self we do not miss.
          There's not a thing one may not lose
              If one remains the man he is.

Hatem: So it is held, so well may be,
              But down a different track I come;
          Of all the bliss earth holds for me
              I in Zuleika find the sum.

          Does she expend her being on me,
              Myself grows to myself of cost;
          Turns she away, then instantly
              I to my very self am lost.[8a]

This means: we see with the eyes of other people. We experience
ourselves in the experience of other people. We are in ourselves
dependent on the knowledge and recognition of other people. It
follows that our experience of ourselves and our empirical awareness
of ourselves is always a 'mediated' and never an 'immediate' self-
awareness.[9] Apparently human beings cannot find themselves in
themselves, or hold fast to what they are in themselves, without self-
division or self-dissolution. It sounds paradoxical, but it is none the

less true to say that it is only the person who goes out of himself who comes to himself. It is only in other people that we find the way to ourselves. No one can every say 'I am who I am', for no one is God. We say 'I am because you are: you are because I am', for as human beings we are aligned towards other human beings, and as created beings we are aligned towards other created beings.[10] Because from the time we are born, being human means being-in-relationship, human subjectivity is only possible in inter-subjectivity.

On the level of the relationship between subject and object, there is a certain subjective solitariness in the experience of objects, and the way we shape them and work on them. There are events too which affect us individually and make us lonely, such as experiences of death, pain and grief. But on the social levels, where relationships between subject and subject come into play, experiences are shared experiences. Some experiences actually confer community between people. Exclusively individual experiences are not communicable at all, for 'the individual is ineffable'. But shared experiences put their stamp on the community experienced. An important way of communicating shared experiences is narrative.[11] The community experienced can be understood as essentially a narrative community.

The experiences that confer community and the experiences shared in community have to be told again and again in ever new ways, and in accordance with the new situation, because they create a bond and open up opportunities for experience that is both mutual and personal. Every generation in Israel should see itself as if it had come out of Egypt, says the midrash. Narrative communities are shaped by the re-calling and making-present of their common origin, and by the shared voyage of discovery into memories. An astonishing fact here is that we do not merely relate shared experiences over and over again in ever new ways; community is built up over the generations too, by way of the continually repeated telling of stories about family and folk. The social community existing at any one time is only one side of the narrative community. Community in the temporal sequence of the generations is the other side. A world which stresses only the horizontal social links threatens to erase tradition, and this also means demolishing the ties binding the generations together. If only two generations – parents and children – live together, and if even they are separated in space and time, then humanity's memory will be lost, and all that will be left will be ephemera – people of the moment.

Finally, beyond the shared experiences of individuals and generations in personal relationships, there are also *collective experiences*,
which acquire fixed form in external institutions and in psychological
attitudes. These shape the individual's experience of his own self
(though generally unconsciously), and anonymously regulate a
society's collective behaviour and assumptions. These patterns can
serve the common life, but they can also be blind and criminal. There
are collective experiences which people cannot rid themselves of,
even if they dissociate themselves from them personally, because
these experiences continually catch up with them. For Germans this
is Auschwitz, for Americans Vietnam, for Russians Chernobyl, for
Koreans the division of their country; and so forth. For all human
beings it is, not least, the poisoned environment and all the people
who are living with it today, and who will have to live with it in the
future.

In normal times, we are unable to do anything about collective
experiences. People conform to them because they are involuntarily
determined by them. It is only in times of danger and upheaval that
people become aware of these patterns, and discover ways of changing
them. Prolonged dictatorships have anonymous effects like this.
Once they crumble, people suddenly become publicly aware of
the patterns the dictatorship has imposed. The matter-of-course
capitalism of the northern industrial world makes the people living
in it incapable, through an ingrained turn of mind, of seeing the
victims it claims in the Third World. The matter-of-course culture of
human domination makes the people who enjoy its benefits incapable
of sympathy for the spoilations of nature caused by industry, modern
communications and the refuse of our consumer society.

These collective patterns of outward and inward living only
become part of the experience and awareness of the 'insiders' by way
of the people 'outside'. It is only the victims who make the perpetrators
aware for the first time of what they are doing. That is why it is a
vital part of collective self-experience for Germans to see themselves
and their own world through the eyes of the Auschwitz victims. That
is why it is essential for northern industrial society to see itself through
the eyes of the hungry children in the Third World. And that is why
one should see one's own car and one's own refuse with the eyes of
the groaning earth and dying nature. We then experience our world
as others experience it, and wake up out of our self-complacent
illusions to the realization of our own reality. The perpetrators are

dependent on their victims' experiences, if they wish to know themselves, for the memory of suffering does not end, whereas our remembrance of what we have done ourselves is short-lived. The victims' recollections of suffering are stronger than the perpetrators' recollections of what they did, because the remembrance of suffering outlasts time, and is not subject to oblivion. So truth is in the hands of the victims, and it is from them that deliverance from delusion to reality comes.[12]

The final dimension of experience goes beyond things, events and people. It is in this dimension that we find *the bacic trust*[13] with which people commit themselves to this life, the *expectation* with which they lay themselves open for the experiences that come to meet them, the *interest* they have in other people, and the way in which – overreaching their needs and drives – they thrust beyond every fulfilment and every disappointment into what is wide and open. We can call this the religious dimension of experience, if by 'religious' we are not thinking of some special enclave, cut off from everyday secular life, but mean something that is present in, with and beneath all our experiences of things, events and people. But this is then rather a hidden and, generally speaking, a tacit dimension, which is not to be emphasized on its own, but in which all experiences find their echo.[14] It is true that this dimension provides the preconditions for all the various experiences of life, but the preconditions are hardly discernible in themselves. They can be perceived only from the experiences. Moreover, the preconditions for experience are not hard and fast either. They shift and waver, because they are highly vulnerable. Every severe disappointment in life diminishes the basic trust with which life is affirmed, and restricts a person's interest in life as such. Every despair constricts expectations about living, and diminishes the openness for new experiences. Whether through fulfilment or through frustration, vital impulses can swing over from eager desire to melancholy, and can be self-destructive.

In each case these are transcendent conditions which make experience possible. But they are self-transcendencies, not transcendence itself. In his Large Catechism, expounding the first commandment, Luther wrote: 'The trust and faith of the heart make God and idol . . . That on which thou hast set thy heart and they reliance, that is in truth thy God.' By saying this he set the standard for modern times by assigning the religious category largely to the subjectivity of 'the heart'. But he was not establishing a metaphysical category. He was

describing a primal human phenomenon: the person whose God is
Mammon has different experiences in life from the person whose
heart is set on the God whose kingdom belongs to the poor. 'Our
ultimate concern' (as Paul Tillich paraphrases Luther's idea) can be
many things which have to be called idolatry and superstition. In
every case this ultimate concern either opens up experiences of life,
or restricts them; and it is according to its judgment that the
experiences are already assessed.

§2 EXPERIENCE SUBJECTIFIED AND METHODOLOGIZED IN MODERN TIMES: GOD IN THE DETERMINING SUBJECT

The scientific and technological civilization of modern times began
with a radical breach with the accepted understanding of truth.
Earlier, tradition had been paramount, the mind and spirit being
cultivated by the texts of the Fathers. This now changed. Now the
mind was cultivated through personal experience and experiment.
When Galileo wanted to show his opponents Jupiter's satellites, they
refused even to look through the telescope, because they believed –
as Bertolt Brecht makes them say – 'that no truth can be found in
nature – only in the comparison of texts'.[15] Up to the beginning of
modern times, tradition handed down the wisdom garnered from
experience, and in order to demonstrate the truth of a proposition it
was sufficient to say πάλαι λέγεται – it was said long ago. When
empiricism supported by experiment took the field, modern times
began. Pascal aptly deplored the conflicts with scripture and tradition
which arose as a result: 'If we see the difference clearly, we shall
lament the blindness of those who in physics desire only tradition to
enjoy authority, instead of reason and experiment, and shall be
horrified at the wrongness of those others who in theology use only
the arguments of reason in place of the tradition of scripture and the
Fathers.'[16]

The concept of *method* developed in scientific theory at the same
time as the first scientific experiments. The term stood for the
verifiable way of arriving at secure knowledge. Petrus Ramus was
one of the first to introduce 'method' into the discussion, through his
pragmatic and empirically reformed Aristotelianism.[17] In 1692 René
Descartes then wrote his classic *Discourse on the Method of Rightly
Conducting the Reason in the Search for Truth in the Sciences*. His
intention was to arrive at a practical philosophy 'by means of which,

knowing the force and the action of fire, water, air, the stars, heavens and all other bodies that environ us, as distinctly as we know the different crafts of our artisans, we can in the same way employ them in all those uses to which they are adapted, and thus render ourselves the masters and possessors of nature'.[18] For this purpose, Descartes introduced the fundamental distinction between *res cogitans* and *res extensa* (which is also known as the 'subject-object relationship'), understanding the perceiving human subject to be the constitutive condition which makes objective experience possible – whereas the objects of that experience are supposed to be characterized solely by the spatial category of extension.

This epistemological schematization means an enormous curtailment of the primal dimensions of experience. No historical dimensions are then available to the human subject of experience, nor do they belong to the object of experience (which is merely spatially constituted). Experience as it is secured by scientific method is now objectified to such a degree that it no longer has any historically contingent aspects. The objectivity of methodologically secured experience is to be found in its *verifiability*, and this is based on the *repeatability* of the experiment itself, and the experience involved.

The premise of this theory is that the structure of the human subject of scientific experience is given and fixed. The perceiving subject can expand his knowledge and his skills, but he is never passively exposed to experience, or fundamentally changed by experience. The self-consciousness of the human subject actively constitutes his world of possible experiences. That is, the consciousness is never passively formed by any experience on the human side. There is therefore nothing – no world, and no possible experience – outside the experience of the perceiving subject himself. The reason for this is that only *active experiences* are selected, together with the deliberate expansion of these experiences through experiment. 'Experience' is now considered to be merely 'remembered practice'. Experiences are 'acquired' – 'made', as German says – through experiment, in that nature is compelled to submit to the inquisitorial questions of the human being.[19] Experiment puts nature on the rack, in order to extort her secrets from her and make her compliant. The concept of experience is reduced to the domination of nature, and nature is dominated so that she may be of utility for human life. So as part of the practice of perception, 'experience' becomes part of the practice of human life.

The methodological objectification of experience raises the fundamental question about the conditions which make experience possible, and about the mode in which objects of possible experience exist. Here we can do no more than refer to the discussion about this question which continued from Descartes to Kant by way of Locke and Hume.[20] In our present context, the important point is the *homogeneity* that is presupposed, 'the unified character of the way in which things exist', and the passivity of all objects of possible experience, whether they are now thought to be determined by extension, or by space, time and causality. The result is an enormous uniformization of the world accessible to men and women, experienced by them, and therefore practised. Whether things, events or persons, all are 'objects of the possible experience of the conscious subject'. The methods for acquiring verifiable and repeatable knowledge must always and everywhere be the same. Experiences that are fortuitous, unique, unrepeatable, and for which there is no warranty are no longer perceived at all; they are filtered out. They are excluded from the technological reconstruction of the world, because they are bound to count as unreasonable. The abundant wealth of life and experience is stifled through the eternal return of the same thing in the mechanism of rational demonstrability.

The controllable verifiability of experiences is a gain bought at the price of a desolate erosion of life. The construction of the world according to the ideas of geometry means its complete loss of sensuousness,[21] and if 'reason perceives only that which it brings forth itself according to its own design', as Kant says,[22] then we are confronted with the critical question: is there any experience at all which is not projected experience of the self? If there is no experience of something other, which modifies the self, then there is really no experience at all. The self which knows no difference in itself, is to itself a matter of indifference. The ego which sees its own reflection in its projections and productions, is merely bored in the hall of mirrors of its own self.

At the time of Descartes, Locke and Kant, this was initially no more than a question of scientific theory. But in the technological world of today it is palpable everywhere. From the very beginning, the intention of the methodological experience of nature was that nature should be appropriated by human beings for human use.

Today this has led to the irreversible 'end of nature' – at least the nature accessible to human beings. All that is left is human environment and technological nature. In the mass cities, human beings encounter only their own products. If the immediate self-consciousness is constitutive for the space of all possible experience, then *narcissism* is the logical and practical consequence of this anthropocentric view of the world.[23]

§3 IMMANENT TRANSCENDENCE: GOD IN ALL THINGS

If we view the philosophy of modern subjectivity in the light of its contemporary influence, we have to say that the scientific and technological domination of nature has destroyed as much nature as it has made accessible. Human experience of nature has expanded to an unparalleled degree. But at the same time nature has come to experience human beings as unparalleled destroyers. This fact forbids us to adapt theology uncritically to the ideology of the modern world. It enjoins us to see the modern world in the light of its victim, nature. The modern concept of experience, which takes its bearings from the experiencing subject, and has domination as its lodestone, would otherwise degenerate into the illusion of the modern world.

Is God an object of possible experience? According to the pattern of the modern constitution of experience, this is out of the question: God can be objectively neither known nor experienced. A God who 'exists' in this objective sense does not exist at all, at least not as God. The modern empirical sciences are in principle agnostic. According to Kant's *Critique of Pure Reason*, God is as hidden and unknowable as the *Ding an sich*. He is not only unknowable because he is not an object of possible experience. The limits of reason itself have actually made it impossible for him to reveal himself and to manifest himself in the world of experience. In the human world of experience he can never make himself known.

Although according to the modern constitution of reason there neither can nor may be any objective experience of God, it is, for all that, still possible to talk about the experience of God. We can do so in the non-objective context of human experience of the self. Descartes put forward the proof of God's existence in the framework of the human subject's certainty of his own self. For Kant, God – like freedom and immortality – was a postulate of practical reason, in the framework of the moral self-respect of human beings. For

Schleiermacher, 'immediate self-consciousness' always in itself implied 'the feeling of absolute dependence'. Even if God is not an object of the general experience of the world and life, the experience of God can still be present as transcendental constitution of the human self-consciousness, which is at the centre of the world in which the human being lives. So today the presence of the divine Spirit in human beings is often identified with human beings' special position in the cosmos – their openness to the world (Max Scheler's phrase), their self-transcendence (Karl Rahner's description), their ecstatic self-transcendence (Wolfhart Pannenberg) or their ex-centric position (Helmut Plessner).

Eilert Herms has once again consistently presented this viewpoint, but without being prepared to see its limitations.[24] Like Schleiermacher, he starts from an 'immediate self-consciousness', meaning by this that 'in all the acts of the self-conscious subject, the consciousness of the self is already "given" '.[25] He distinguishes the immediacy of the self-consciousness from the immediacy of the impressions, and thinks that this distinction provides the foundation which makes the actively self-conscious transference of perception into objective knowledge possible. This is 'the theory of the subject who is enabled through direct discovery of the self to arrive at active determination of the self, and hence to *create* [the German word is *machen*, 'make'] experience'.[26]

But consciousness of the self is only already existent and 'immediate' in reference to objective consciousness. Where the experience of God's Spirit is concerned, it is mediated. Herms thinks that at this point he can link the Reformers' version of what is meant by experience of the Spirit with the modern concept of experience. And he believes that he can do this in such a way that the Protestant belief in justification enters into a covenant with modern reason, so that belief in justification constitutes modern reason, and modern reason interprets the belief in justification. God's revelatory act takes place in the believer's encounter with himself. The operation of God's Spirit 'can be remembered [by the human being] as a particular happening in the world through which God reveals himself in Jesus Christ'.[27] But in faith the act of the Spirit becomes 'the present of the world of the human being', for the present event of justification manifests the self-demonstration of the Creator in his Word, and gives the present world in general its particular quality. So experience of the presence of God's Spirit does not merely qualify the immediate self-consciousness. It gives the world of human beings its special quality too. For the experience of faith also teaches that, as Luther says in his exposition in the Small Catechism, 'God created me, together with all other creatures'. Like Schleiermacher, Herms thinks that Catholic theology is unable to link God's revelation successfully with the modern sense of truth, because it is bound to maintain that God's revelation is independent of the awareness of truth in the believer.

The critical questions that arise here touch especially on the exclusiveness of the correlation between experience of God and experience of the self, and the modern definition of this self-experience. Human consciousness of the self is not as absolute as has been claimed, ever since Descartes. Particularly, if one starts from the assumption that the consciousness is constituted by 'the ground of the whole existence of the world, including itself', then consciousness does not differ essentially from the other elements that make up the world. The transcendental constitution would then have to be discernible from the 'other elements in the world' too, not only from the individual self.

If we abandon the narrow subject-object pattern, however (which may well be applicable to possible 'objects' of experience), and if we adopt the social pattern of inter-subjectivity, it then immediately becomes clear that from birth onwards, awareness of the self is something that is *constituted*; it is by no means solely constituting in character. Social experience displays the same characteristics that modern subjectivism has assigned to the personal consciousness of the self. The experience of God's Spirit is always also the experience of what Schleiermacher calls 'the common spirit', the God who is sociality (Hölderlin's 'gemeinschaftliche Gottheit'), who binds together I and Thou and Us, as Feuerbach said.[28] If, furnished with these richer relationships in the pattern of inter-subjectivity, we turn back to the relationship between human beings and the world, we shall then here too find that the world experienced in nature is more fertile and abundant than the small segment of it which human beings contrive to experience by way of their sciences; and we shall discover transcendence even in nature's immanence. A. N. Whitehead's non-subjectivist but relativist metaphysics would seem particularly well equipped to fit the subject-centred world of modern men and women into the wider processes of reality, depriving that world of its absolutist and narrow attitude to nature, so that in this very way

human beings can be installed in their proper rights and responsibility.[29]

If, finally, we go even beyond the pattern of inter-subjectivity and
perceive the bodily character of human beings in the framework of
the world as nature, it becomes completely clear that the modern
European concept of experience is not wide enough to embrace real
experiences and the potentialities for experience; for this concept is
related solely to the consciousness, and is interpreted in purely active
terms.

I would therefore propose that, while holding fast to this sector of
experience – i.e., active experience, which takes its bearings from the
experiencing subject – we should expand it, so that it can embrace
the dimensions we described in § 1. For we must abandon the notion
that 'all experienceable objects are of the same, unified kind'. Objects,
events, persons and socialities can be 'unified' only at the cost of their
violation. We are living in a pluralist, polycentric world of many
dimensions, and if we are to participate in reality we need a many-
dimensioned concept of experience. Nor must the frontiers of potential experience be laid down *a priori* any longer. They have to be
thrown open for the future, and kept flexible.

As far as the dimension of theology is concerned, I would suggest
abandoning the narrow reference to the modern concept of 'self-
consciousness', so that we can discover transcendence in every
experience, not merely in experience of the self. For this, the term
immanent transcendence offers itself.[30]

Every experience that happens to us or that we have, can possess
a transcendent, inward side. *The experience of God's Spirit* is not
limited to the human subject's experience of the self. It is also a
constitutive element in the experience of the 'Thou', in the experience
of sociality, and in the experience of nature. 'God's spirit fills the
world and he who holds all things together knows every sound'
(Wisd. 1.7). It is therefore possible to experience God *in, with and
beneath* each everyday experience of the world, if God is in all things,
and if all things are in God, so that God himself 'experiences' all
things in his own way. If experiences of God embrace experiences of
life (and every existential interpretation says that they do), then –
seen in reverse – experiences of life can also embrace experiences of
God. The experience of God found in human experience of the self
has its inalienable and indestructible character; and the experience
of God in the experience of sociality has its own particular character

too. If experience of God is related to the experience of the whole world and the whole of life, this by no means implies that all possible experiences have to be turned into the same thing and pantheistically made a matter of indifference; for according to Christian understanding, this experience of God is the experience of the presence of God the Creator in the protean variety of his creation. In the community of creation, human beings have their unique character and assume their own responsibility. Given the premise that God is experienced in experience of the world and life, it once again becomes possible to talk about special experiences of God in the contingent and exceptional phenomena which are called 'holy', without having to declare everything else profane.

The possibility of perceiving God in all things, and all things in God, is grounded theologically on an understanding of the Spirit of God as the power of creation and the wellspring of life.[31] 'The spirit of God has made me, and the breath of the Almighty gives me life', says Job 33.4. And Job. 34.13f. is prompted by the same idea as Ps. 104.29f.: 'Who has commanded what is on earth? or who has disposed over the whole world? If he thought only of himself, and took back to himself his spirit and his breath, all flesh would perish together, and man would return to dust.' Every experience of a creation of the Spirit is hence also an experience of the Spirit itself. Every true experience of the self becomes also an experience of the divine spirit of life in the human being. Every lived moment can be lived in the inconceivable closeness of God in the Spirit: *Interior intimo meo*, said Augustine – God is closer to me than I am to myself.[32] Calvin says that the Holy Spirit is the *fons vitae*, the well of life; and if this is so, then every experience of life can be a discovery of this living source.

To experience God in all things presupposes that there is a transcendence which is immanent in things and which can be inductively discovered. It is the infinite in the finite, the eternal in the temporal, and the enduring in the transitory. The active and forceful 'getting to know' something generally discerns only that side of things which is related to human beings, and which they can make use of. It perceives nothing of things as they are in themselves, with their own value, and their own inward dimension. But even if I ask quite simply: 'what do the things of nature which I perceive, mean for God their Creator?' this question makes me aware of the relativity and limitation of human perception. If we can call what for us is nature, 'God's creation', we have already invoked its immanent transcendence. We have then recognized the Creator's right to what he has created. And in so doing we have also acknowledged the rights of our fellow creatures themselves, rights which exist quite apart from their value for us. We become aware of what they mean for God. We sense that God 'feels' and 'experiences' what he has created in his own way: the way of his eternal love.

To experience all things in God means moving in the opposite direction. It means passing from the all-embracing horizon of the world and perception to the individual things which appear against this background. Perception that is related to the perceiving subject asks: 'what does it mean for me?' This is now replaced by the perception which takes its bearings from the all-embracing horizon. Things then appear in the light of the boundary encircling them. If this boundary is not annihilating Nothingness, but is God the Creator, then things do not fade into that horizon; on the contrary, their contours become sharply distinct. We then perceive the finite in the infinite, the temporal in the eternal, and the evanescent in what endures. We carry experiences of the world into the experience of God. 'Reverence for life' is absorbed into reverence for God, and the veneration of nature becomes part of the adoration of God. We sense that in everything God is waiting for us.

Like the anthropocentricism of the modern Western world, the mode of experience which is related to the perceiving subject can be traced back to the biblical anthropology according to which only human beings are made in the image of God (Gen. 1.26), and in which man is king over nature (Ps. 8). But tradition history has increasingly overlooked the fact that human beings enjoy this distinction only in the framework of the community of creation (Ps. 104), and that it is only the person who is aware that he is a created being that is meant. The attribute does not apply to anyone who concludes from this mark of honour that he is the god and lord of his world. What H. E. Richter calls the modern 'God complex' cannot find any justification in the biblical idea that human beings are made in the image of God, for that idea puts an end to the God complex altogether.

It is true that mediaeval tradition already prepared the way for modern anthropocentricism when it distinguished between 'traces of God' in the body and in all other created things, and 'the image of God' in the reasonable human soul. God can be more clearly perceived in his image than in any traces of himself. Consequently self-knowledge leads to a clearer knowledge of God than does knowledge of the world. Inward self-knowledge is not mediated through the senses, and is hence not open to doubt. I can doubt everything except that it is I who doubts.[33]

In the preface to his *Meditations*, Descartes tells us that he has merely taken up Augustine's ideas about 'God and the soul', carrying through philosophically what Augustine had begun in theology. 'Look within, truth dwells in the inner man . . . The most excellent of all mirrors for seeing God is our reasonable soul, if that can be found.'[34] Luther's theology was concentrated on the encounter between the justifying God and sinful human beings in the event of Word and faith. In this way he gave the content of Western theology a new definition, but not its framework; for its framework revolves round 'God and the soul'.[35] But in the circle comprehending God and the soul there is no place for the human body, which Paul says is intended to be 'the temple of the Holy Spirit', or for nature, which God has already made his temple, according to Isa. 66.1 and Acts 7.48f. It is true that Luther too was convinced that God is present in all things. But 'all things' are filtered out and excluded from the foundation of the believing person on the justifying Word.

The elevation of the soul above nature and the body has induced human beings to seize power over nature and progressively to destroy her.[36] Since this is the outcome of these ideas, a revision of anthropocentric pneumatology is also required – the pneumatology which is not only anthropologically concentrated, but in its anthropology is related solely to the consciousness, and even there only to the immediate consciousness. A doctrine of God which leads to a cleavage in reality is not a doctrine of God the Creator. An experience of God restricted to the immediate self-consciousness is not an experience of the God whom Wisdom calls 'the lover of life'. This brings us to the conclusion that it is literally essential for us to develop *a holistic doctrine of God the Holy Spirit*. It must be holistic in at least two ways. On the one hand, it must comprehend human beings in their total being, soul and body, consciousness and the unconscious, person and sociality, society and social institutions. On the other hand it must also embrace the wholeness of the community of creation, which is shared by human beings, the earth, and all other created beings and things. If this holistic view is critically related to the existing cleavages in human beings themselves, to the divisions between human beings, and to the disjunction between human beings and nature, its effect can be therapeutic. And it is then by no means a romantic illusion.

II

Historical Experience of the Spirit

By a historical experience of God we mean an experience of God which happens to people in the medium of history through historical events, and which is perceived in terms of time. But we mean the reverse too: we can also mean an awareness of reality as history which emerges from experiences of God like this. Israel always linked its experiences of God with historical persons and historical happenings. The formulation 'the God of Abraham, the God of Isaac and the God of Jacob' recalls the one God of the patriarchs, and this remembrance is at the same time a recollection of the various experiences of God associated with their names. Through historical remembrance, the God of the Exodus, the covenant and the promised land becomes present to such a degree that as the Creator of the world and the Lord of human liberty he determines the present. The historical experience of God is always tensed between the remembrance and the expectation which frame that experience. Remembrances of God and expectations of God make the experienced presence of God a historical present. We perceive the uniqueness of the moment and the irreversibility of the times. Historical present is comprehended as a path determined by remembrances which leads towards a goal. But as the present of the eternal God it is so profound that both beginning and goal are also contemporary and immediate.

'Present' was originally not a temporal term at all; it was a spatial one. And this is still so essentially. The word denotes the 'there-ness' of something or someone. In the temporal sense it can mean the present of the past in remembrance, or the present of the future in expectation. In its emphatic sense, present means the *nunc stans*, the eternal Now; and it is then a category of eternity, for the eternal has only one time: present. Eternity is found in the depths of the experienced moment, not in the extension of time.

In this chapter we shall be asking about the special experience of God's Spirit in Israel. In the first section we shall discuss the difficulties of translating the Hebrew word *ruach*. In the second section we shall look at the mediations of the Spirit between God and his people, by way of charismatic judges, ecstatic and literary prophets, and anointed kings. To these we shall add the individual experiences of the Spirit 'in the heart', and the universal experience of God's Spirit in the whole creation. In a third section we shall compare the experience of God's Spirit with the experience of the Shekinah.

First of all let us look at the prophetic expectations associated with the Spirit and the Shekinah – expectations of the messiah, expectations for the people, and expectations for the 'End-time' – that is, for the beginning of the new creation of all things.

§1 SPIRIT – THE DIVINE ENERGY OF LIFE

If we wish to understand the Old Testament word *ruach*, we must forget the word 'spirit', which belongs to Western culture. The Greek word $\pi\nu\epsilon\tilde{\upsilon}\mu\alpha$, the Latin *spiritus*, and the Germanic *Geist*/ghost were always conceived as antitheses to matter and body. They mean something immaterial.[1] Whether we are talking Greek, Latin, German or English, by the Spirit of God we then mean something disembodied, supersensory and supernatural. But if we talk in Hebrew about Yahweh's *ruach*, we are saying: God is a tempest, a storm, a force in body and soul, humanity and nature.[2] The Western cleavage between spirit and body, spirituality and sensuousness is so deeply rooted in our languages that we must have recourse to other translations if we want to arrive at a more or less adequate rendering of the word *ruach*.

In the Old Testament, the word *ruach* occurs about 380 times. The phrase *ruach Yahweh* is used in 27 passages. The meaning of the word is so complex, and the periods from which the relevant writings date are so widely separated, that it is impossible to find a simple semantic pattern for the word's usage, or to construct a single, unified concept for what is meant.[3] *Ruach* was probably originally an onomatopoeic word for a gale[4] – for example, the strong wind which divided the Reed Sea for Israel's Exodus from Egypt (Ex. 14.21). The word always means something living compared with something dead, something moving, over against what is rigid and petrified. In the transferred sense, when the word is applied to God, the tempest becomes a parable for the irresistible force of the Creator's power, God's killing wrath and life-giving mercy (cf. Ezek 13.13f.; 36.26f.).

Because people saw the livingness of life in the inhaling and exhaling of air, *ruach* was also the breath of life and the power to live enjoyed by human beings and animals (Eccles. 12.7; 3.21).[5] Since life was seen too in the movement of the blood, a distinction was also made between 'the blood soul' (*nepesh*) and 'the personal soul' (*ruach*). In Ps. 51.10, the psalmist prays for 'a new, steadfast *ruach*'. In Ps. 31.5, the psalmist commits his *ruach* into God's hands (cf. Luke 23.46). When Yahweh's *ruach* is mentioned in this context, a distinction is often made between God's own creative power to give life, and the created ability to live enjoyed by all the living. We find this in Ps. 104.29f., for example: 'When thou takest away *their ruach* they die. When thou sendest forth *thy ruach* they are created; and thou renewest the face of the ground.'

According to the general spiritualist world-view of the times and civilizations which are the background of the Old Testament writings, there was both *good* and *evil ruach* everywhere. Judges 9.23 says that 'God sent an *evil ruach* between Abimelech and the men of Schechem'. I Sam. 16.14 tells us that 'an *evil ruach* from the Lord' tormented Saul. According to I Kings 22.22, God allowed the prophet Ahab to be enticed by 'a *lying ruach*'. The special point about the early Israelite view is evidently that sovereignty was not thought to be exercised by many gods and demons, but that the one God was seen as Lord over these good and evil forces.

If the *ruach* is associated with God, and God with the *ruach*, then Yahweh's *ruach* and Yahweh's *dabar* – his word – are very close to one another. *Ruach* is thought of as the breath of God's voice. So in the early period the prophets owe their call to Yahweh's *ruach*, while later they are generally called by Yahweh's *dabar*. If this unity of breath and voice is carried over to God's creative activity, then all things are called to life through God's Spirit and his Word. We may think of Ps. 33.6: 'By *the word* of the Lord the heavens were made, and all their host by the *ruach* of his mouth.' It is not by chance either when the creation story in the Priestly Writing talks about the *ruach elohim*, which 'vibrated' over the chaos (Gen. 1.2).[6] The God who according to the story that follows creates everything through the

Word, speaks in the creative energies of the *ruach*. Remembering the analogy of breath and voice, we might even say that the words of creation specify and define, but that they are spoken in the same breath, so that all creatures come to life through the one same *ruach*; and it is this that constitutes the community of creation. The masculine Word (*dabar*) and the feminine life force (*ruach*) necessarily complement one another.

How, then – after these few leads – ought we to translate Yahweh's *ruach*?

1. It is the confronting event of God's efficacious presence 'which reaches into the depths of human existence'.[7] Yahweh's *ruach* is his 'divine presence', as Ps. 139.7, 23f. brings out so impressively: 'Whither shall I go from thy spirit? Or whither shall I flee from thy presence? . . . Search me, O God, and know my heart! Try me and know my thoughts! And see if I am on a wicked way, and lead me in the way everlasting!' But if we interpret *ruach* as the 'confronting event of God's presence', then the converse must be true too: we have to understand the happenings of God's presence as *ruach*. In the creative power of life, God is present. Every efficacious presence of God is determined by the *ruach* and, as Calvin said, has to be interpreted pneumatologically.

2. But this theological person-formula for the *ruach* as God's presence is not a sufficient way of naming the power from which everything that has life lives. The *creative power* of God is communicated to the beings he has created in such a way that in talking about *ruach* we are talking about the energy of *their* life too. It is not wrong to talk about the Spirit as the 'drive' and 'instinct' awakened by God.[8] The *ruach* as Yahweh's *ruach* is of course transcendent in origin; but it is equally true to say that as the power of life in all the living it is immanently efficacious.[9] The creative power of God is the transcendent side of the *ruach*. The power to live enjoyed by everything that is alive is its immanent side. The *ruach* is certainly present only when and where God wills it to be so; but with his will towards creation it is also present in everything, and keeps all things in being and in life.[10] When we think about the *ruach* we have to say that God is in all things, and all things are in God – though this does not mean making God the same as everything else.

3. But though we may call *ruach* the confronting event of the personal presence of God, and the life force immanent in all the living, this is still not enough to exhaust the full meaning of the word.

'The term is probably related to *rewah* = breadth. *Ruach* creates space. It sets in motion. It leads out of narrow places into wide vistas, thus conferring life.'[11] To experience the *ruach* is to experience what is divine not only as a person, and not merely as a force, but also as *space* – as the space of freedom in which the living being can unfold. That is the experience of the Spirit: 'Thou has set my feet in a broad place' (Ps. 31.8). 'You also he allured out of distress into a broad place where there is no cramping' (Job 36.16). According to Kabbalistic Jewish tradition, one of God's secret names is MAKOM, the wide space.[12] If God's Spirit is experienced as this broad, open space for living conferred on created beings, then it is easy to understand the spatial designations which declare that people live '*in*' God's Spirit, and experience God spatially as 'breadth'.

§2 GOD'S PRESENCE IN THE SPIRIT AMONG HIS PEOPLE

In its account of Israel's early period, the Book of Judges tells about the historical activity of the divine Spirit in Israel's charismatic leaders.[13] The people possessed and led by the Spirit act in God's stead and in his name, and lead his people to liberty. It is charismatic endowments that are being talked about here. That is to say, these are spontaneous and temporally limited gifts conferred on individuals *for* the whole people. In so far they are corporate endowments *belonging to* the whole people itself, since Israel is as such intended to be 'a royal priesthood' for the nations (Ex. 19.6; I Peter 2.9). Of course we find parallels in the history of religion, in the shamanism which was part of the spiritualism that was originally common to the different peoples. But from early on, Israel traced these phenomena back to the one God, not to a multiplicity of spirits and demons. Charismatic endowment generated seers, sages, prophets and leaders. In the century and a half between the conquest of the promised land and the establishment of the monarchy in Israel, charismatic 'judges' led Israel's tribes, and saved them in critical situations. In these stories, the real, active and determining subject is always Yahweh's *ruach*. 'Yahweh's *ruach* came upon Othniel' (Judg. 3.10) and upon the saviour Gideon (6.34). 'Yahweh's *ruach* began to stir Samson' (13.25) and gave him such strength that he 'tore the lion asunder' with his bare hands (14.6) and 'killed thirty men' on the way to Ashkelon (14.19).

Once the monarchy had been established with Saul, the last of the 'judges' and the first of the kings, this spontaneous and temporally limited charisma came to an end. Now Yahweh's *ruach* becomes a permanent gift conferred on God's anointed one, for the abilities required of a ruler are given to him indefinitely. Because God makes a special covenant with *the king* in the people of the covenant, Yahweh's *ruach* is expected to take the form of a special divine presence which will accompany Israel's kings. Because the king represents God among the people, and the people before God, his charisma is also one of the corporate gifts conferred on the people of the covenant.

Israel's early prophets were evidently itinerant preachers possessed by the divine Spirit. We are told about Samuel that 'he who is now called a prophet was formerly called a seer' (I Sam. 9.9). Unlike the shamanistic seers and the Islamic dervishes, Israel's prophets are inspired with insight into *the will* of the Lord, and are given to know *what has to be done* as a consequence. This becomes clear from Samuel's encounter with Saul, which we are told about in I Sam. 10: 'The spirit of the Lord will come mightily upon you, and you shall prophesy with them and be turned into another man' (v.6). And so 'Saul also [came to be] among the prophets' (v.12). Even as king he is still dependent on the flashes and fortuities of the Spirit. It is only after David has been anointed by Samuel (16.13) that 'the Spirit of the Lord came mightily upon [him] from that day forward' – that is, the Spirit remained with him permanently.

In Israel's early period, ecstasies (I Sam. 10.5f.; 19.20–24), unusual wisdom (Gen. 41.38, describing Joseph), and right judgment are all put down to God's Spirit. The Nicaeno-Constantinopolitan creed (381) acknowledges the Holy *Spirit* 'who spake by the prophets', and this corresponds to the way the Jewish targum talks about 'the spirit of prophecy'. But in fact it is only the early pre-exilic prophets who appeal solely to the inspiration of Yahweh's *ruach*, and they are not really specifically Israelite in character. The later, 'classical' pre-exilic prophets – Amos, Hosea, Micah, Isaiah and Jeremiah – proclaim Yahweh's *dabar*, or word. The call through God's word now takes the place of enthusiastic 'in-spiration' through God's Spirit: 'Thus says the Lord . . .' is the formula of their authority. That is why Amos says: 'I am no prophet, nor a prophet's son; I am a herdsman. But the Lord took me from following the flock, and said to me, "Go, prophesy to my people Israel". Now therefore hear the word of the Lord . . .' (Amos 7.14–16). 'The Lord God has spoken;

who can but prophesy?' (3.8) That is his legitimation formula. The 'literary' prophets are moulded by call, not inspiration, by the word of God, not by exceptional ecstasies. In the exilic period we then again find in Ezekiel and Deutero-Isaiah an emphatic appeal to Yahweh's *ruach* and its inspiration in visions and prophecies, even if the unusual phenomena that accompanied Israel's early prophets and seers are now missing.

When Saul is anointed king by the prophet Samuel (I Sam. 10), the *king's endowment with the Spirit* is ritualized in Israel. Nathan's prophecy to King David (II Sam. 7) gives Israel's monarchy a messianic perspective: 'I will establish the throne of his kingdom for ever' (v.13). God's mercy will remain with him and God will be 'his father' and he will be 'my son' (v.14). It is the future king's endowment with the Spirit which will constitute God's fatherhood and the king's sonship – hence the promise given to the king in Ps. 2.7: 'You are my son, today I have begotten you.' Because the people of Israel can also be called God's 'first-born son' (Ex. 4.22), this intimate relationship to God on the part of Israel's kings must be understood as a representative one, and *pars pro toto*.

Israel, then, was corporately endowed with the Spirit through the medium of her judges, prophets and kings. But the psalms show that there was an individual, *inward experience of the Spirit* too. Psalm 51 is a typical example: 'Create in me a clean heart, O God, and put a new and steadfast spirit within me. Cast me not away from thy presence, and take not thy holy Spirit from me' (vv.10f.). Here, as in Psalm 139, God's *Spirit* and God's *face*, turned towards what he has created, are seen together, so that when he talks about the Spirit the psalmist also means the commitment of God's own person. On the other hand, in the human being the spirit is associated with the heart, so that what is meant is God's commitment to the human person. When God withdraws his Spirit, it is the same as if he turns away, and hides his face. It means death for the human being, and for everything else that God has created (Ps. 104).[14]

The gift of the Spirit comes from the countenance of God when it is turned towards human beings and shines on them. It is a gift that brings inward assurance in living, and new vital energies. What the petitioner experiences in the prayer in Psalm 51 is intended to be experienced by the whole people, according to Ezek. 36.26f.: the 'new heart' and the 'new spirit'. In both the individual and the corporate perspective, this means the fulfilment of *God's Torah:*

'Through *ruach* – and that means through God's presence right into the depths of human existence – God's commandments come to be truly kept.'[15] But the keeping of God's commandments brings about a lived and living harmony between human beings and God, for their happiness and his glory.

What the psalms have to say about the presence of the Spirit in the depths of the human heart is developed by Wisdom literature in the wider context of the natural cosmos. In the three great didactic poems Proverbs 8, Job 28 and Ecclesiasticus 24, the Wisdom of God is presented as an ordering power immanent in the world.[16] This Wisdom is certainly transcendent in origin, and was with God before the creation of the world, 'playing before him always' (Prov. 8.30). As 'God's daughter', Wisdom is described as if she is a separate person, with a self-confident utterance of her own. But at the same time God's Wisdom is 'poured out upon all his works' (Ecclus. 1.9). It fills the whole world (Wisd. 1.7), for it is through his Wisdom that God has 'made' all his works (Ps. 104.24). In Wisdom he founded the earth (Prov. 3.19). God's Wisdom speaks to human beings out of creation, so as to bring them into harmony with that creation, and in this way to make them wise. That is why the heavens 'tell', the firmament 'proclaims', and all his works 'praise' God.

> But ask the beasts, and they will teach you;
> the birds of the air, and they will tell you;
> or the plants of the earth, and they will teach you;
> and the fish of the sea will declare to you.
> Who among all these does not know that the hand of the Lord
>   has done this?'
>
> (Job 12.7–9)

As The Wisdom of Solomon shows, *ruach* and *ḥokmā*, Spirit and Wisdom, are so close to one another that they are actually inter-changeable. 'The Spirit of the Lord has filled the world' (1.7); 'Thy immortal Spirit is in all things' (12.1); 'I know everything that is hidden and manifest, for Wisdom, the fashioner of all things, taught me. For in her there is a spirit that is intelligent . . .' (7.21f.). So what this chapter says about Wisdom can be said about God's Spirit too: it is the 'breath of God's power', 'a pure emanation of the Almighty's glory', 'a reflection of eternal light' and 'an image of his righteousness'. Some of the church Fathers have therefore seen this divine Wisdom as prefiguration, not of the Logos, but of the Holy Spirit.[17] If this is possible, then we have to ascribe to the divine Spirit an 'immanent transcendence'. In the form of Wisdom, the Spirit is a kind of counterpart in God himself, and is at the same time the divine presence in creation and history. Where the later apocryphal and rabbinic literature of Palestinian Judaism is concerned, the following may be said: 'The way the spirit takes on independent form in Judaism is striking. In rabbinic literature, the spirit is very often talked about in personal categories . . . The essential point is that here the human being is face to face with a reality that comes to him from God, and in some sense represents God's presence, although the two are not identical.'[18]

§3 GOD'S SPIRIT AND HIS SHEKINAH

The Old Testament talks about Yahweh's *ruach* on many different levels, and in association with other concepts. But 'Holy Spirit' is a term used only at a relatively late period (Ps. 51.11; Isa. 63.10f.), and then with a restricted meaning. In early rabbinic literature, 'Holy Spirit' means rather 'spirit of the sanctuary'.[19] It is not a term for God. It means a medium of revelation and a qualification for a sanctified ministry.[20] But when Christian theologians talk about 'the Holy Spirit', they always mean God himself, never merely one of his gifts. The Spirit is the giver in what he gives. He gives himself. The descriptions of Yahweh's *ruach* which we have cited as 'God's presence' or 'the confronting event of God's presence', are descriptions put forward by Christian theologians, and they cannot appeal to the special Israelite use of the term 'Holy Spirit'. What these phrases describe is actually much more closely related to the idea of the Shekinah, the descent and indwelling of God in space and time, at a particular place and a particular era of earthly beings and in their history. It is therefore useful at this point to compare the divine spirit with the divine indwelling, so as to elicit the full spectrum, and in order to grasp the relevance of the presence of God's Spirit in the desolation of the beings he has created.

The idea of the Shekinah developed out of cultic language, and originally meant God's 'tabernacle', or tent, and his 'dwelling' among his people, first in the transportable Ark, and then, after the entry into the temple, on Zion. In the temple the God of Israel finds his 'rest'.[21] God is present in the sanctuary. The destruction of Jerusalem, and the deportation of a section of the people into Babylonian exile, raised the question about the other presence of God among his people. There came to be a notion that God has his dwelling among his people in the Shekinah, and through the Shekinah accompanies the people into exile. The Shekinah is present in the worshipping community. It is present in the synagogues, among the judges, with the wretched, the sick, and so forth. The Shekinah shares Israel's joys and sufferings. It is more especially Israel's divine 'companion in suffering'. This leads on to the expectation that the exiled Shekinah will return to Jerusalem from the foreign land together with the people. When God delivers his people and brings them home again, his Shekinah, which has travelled with them, will also be delivered from its wanderings, and will return home.[22]

The Shekinah is not a divine attribute. It is the presence of God himself. But it is not God in his essential omnipresence. It is his special, willed and promised presence in the world. The Shekinah is God himself, present at a particular place and at a particular time. 'When two sit down together to study the Torah, the Shekinah is in their midst.'[23] The descent and habitation of God at a particular place and a particular time among particular people must therefore be distinguished from the very God himself whom even the heavens are unable to contain. The Shekinah is certainly the present God, but this presence is distinguished from his eternity. If the Shekinah is the earthly, temporal and spatial presence of God, then it is at once identical with God and distinct from him. Because of this, later rabbinic and kabbalistic scholars tried to think of the Shekinah as a hypostasis, as an intermediary or go-between, or a divine emanation. But if the Shekinah is God himself and yet distinct from God himself, then the Hegelian expression 'God's self-distinction' (which Franz Rosenweig used for it) is more appropriate, because it preserves the sovereignty of God above the suffering history of his Shekinah.[24] If we talk about a divine 'self-distinction' of this kind, then we are assuming a difference in God between what distinguishes and what is distinguished, between the self-surrendering and the self-surrendered God; but we are still at the same time holding fast to the identity of the One God.

Israel's God is 'the Lord', and yet he is simultaneously experienced as 'Israel's servant':[25] he carries the torch ahead of Israel in the wilderness; he provides for Israel's needs like a slave; he bears Israel with all her sins; he offers himself up for Israel. 'He lifted them up and carried them all the days of old' (Isa. 63.9). He binds himself so closely to Israel that he becomes one heart and one soul with her, as if he were her 'twin brother'. So Israel's shame is God's shame too, Israel's exile is God's exile, Israel's sufferings are God's sufferings; for everyone who attacks Israel attacks God's honour and the name which God allows to be sanctified in his people. 'In all their affliction he was afflicted' (Isa. 63.8f.). 'I am with him in trouble' (Ps. 91.15). The knowledge that *God was suffering with them* will have been the one consolation in the people's hopeless suffering, and is often so even today.[26] The midrash tells: 'And the Holy One, blessed be He, said to the children of Israel: When I saw that you left my dwelling place, I left it also, so that I might return home with you.'[27] When a human being suffers torment, what does the Shekinah say? 'My head is heavy, my arm is heavy.'[28] Psalm 23.4 also talks about the Shekinah's consoling companionship in 'the valley of the shadow of death'.

This idea about *the God who suffers with us* then inevitably leads to the bold concept that God's self-deliverance goes together with the deliverance of Israel. When Israel is delivered, God's Shekinah will return home from its wanderings. The divine deliverance lies in the event in which the Eternal One will be united with his Shekinah. It was Franz Rosenzweig who called the way of suffering taken by the Shekinah its 'wanderings', a kind of odyssey.[29] If its return and reunification with the exalted God means God's deliverance, then every 'Sh'ma Israel' prayer does not only confess God's unity as his eternal attribute; it also creates that unity: through the prayer, God's Shekinah in the person who prays returns to the exalted God. 'To acknowledge God's unity – the Jew calls it *uniting* God. For this unity is, in that it becomes; it is a Becoming Unity. And this Becoming is laid on the soul of man and in his hands.'[30]

Through his 'self-distinction', God can humiliate and lower himself, be with his people, and identify himself with his people's fate. But through his 'self-distinction' God is also able to identify himself with himself and, with his self-distinction, to be one. Ideas about the accompanying Shekinah and the indwelling Spirit of God certainly do not require a theological interpretation of this kind, but they do permit it. To say that the Shekinah is a divine attribute or a divine emanation (interpretations also found), does not permit the full and real presence of God in his Shekinah and his Spirit to be thought. But the idea of 'God's self-distinction' makes this entirely possible.[31]

Adopting this interpretation, let us now expand the idea about 'the Shekinah's odyssey' and its 'becoming-unity with God', now applying it to creation and to ourselves personally. This interpretation of the experience of the Shekinah was developed in my seminar during the winter semester 1989/90.

God loves his creation. God is bound to every one of his creatures in passionate affirmation. God loves with creative love. That is why he himself dwells empathically in every created being, feeling himself into them by virtue of his love. The love draws him out of himself, so to speak, carrying him wholly into the created beings whom he loves. Because he is 'the lover of life', his eternal Spirit is 'in all things' as their vital force. In the self-distinction and the self-giving of love, God is present in all his creatures and is himself their innermost mystery.

The moment a created being turns away from this divine love, from which it nevertheless lives, it becomes anxious, aggressive and destructive, because it becomes self-seeking. Its will cuts it off from God's will, and its life turns away from the love of God, to self-hate. The whole misery of men and women comes from a love for God that has miscarried. And the result is on God's side what Martin Buber called a 'de-selfing' (*Entselbung*) – a kind of self-emptying of God. His Shekinah indwells every one of his creatures; but this Shekinah is now alienated from God himself. It is grieved and hurt, but it does not leave these lost beings to themselves. It suffers in the victims and is tormented in the perpetrators. It goes with sinners on the wanderings of their estrangement. The Shekinah does not leave us. Even in our most frightful errors, it accompanies us with its great yearning for God, its homesickness to be one with God. We sense its pain in the 'drawing' of the Spirit.

With every bit of self-seeking and self-contradiction which we surrender to the will of the Creator who loves us, the Shekinah comes close to God. If we live entirely in the prayer 'Thy will be done', the Shekinah in us is united with God himself. We live again wholly, and can undividedly affirm life. The wanderings are over. The goal has been reached. We are conscious of God's happiness in us, and are conscious of ourselves in God's bliss.

When does this happen? It happens when we encounter overwhelming joy: we become selflessly happy and come wholly to ourselves. It happens when we encounter bitter suffering: we experience ourselves in the pain, and trust ourselves wholly to God. It need not happen once and for all. It can also happen briefly, for a time. When we once more break asunder and become inwardly disunited, the Shekinah sets off with us again on our odyssey. If we become one with ourselves, the Shekinah comes to rest. But the intense approaches to God himself of the Shekinah which is our driving force are linked with indescribable joy. We become sensitive to the Shekinah in us, and equally sensitive to the Shekinah in other people and in all other creatures. We expect the mystical union of the Shekinah with God in every true encounter. That is why we long for the love in which we forget ourselves and at the same time find ourselves. We encounter every other created being in the expectation of meeting God. For we have discovered that in these other people and these other creatures God waits for our love, and for the homecoming of his Shekinah: 'As you did it to one of the least of these my brethren, you did it to me' (Matt. 25.40).

What does the theology of the Shekinah contribute to an understanding of the divine Spirit? Although in rabbinic literature the expression 'Holy Spirit' has a particular, restricted meaning, the parallel to the idea of Yahweh's *ruach* is nevertheless unmistakable. 'The radiant brightness' of the Shekinah could also be described by kabbalistic thinkers as 'Holy Spirit'.[32]

1. The doctrine of the Shekinah makes the personal character of the Spirit clear. The Spirit is the efficacious presence of God himself. The Spirit is the presence of God in person. The Spirit is more than one of God's attributes, and more than a gift of God to what he has created. The Spirit is *God's empathy*, his feeling identification with what he loves.

2. The concept of the Shekinah also draws attention to *the sensibility of God the Spirit*. The Spirit indwells. The Spirit suffers with the suffering. The Spirit is grieved and quenched. The Spirit rejoices when we rejoice. When it descends and takes up its habitation and indwelling in wandering and suffering created beings, the Spirit thrusts forward with intense longing for union with God, and sighs to be at rest in the new, perfected creation.

3. The idea of the Shekinah points towards *the kenosis of the Spirit*.[33] In his Shekinah, God renounces his impassibility and becomes able to suffer because he is willing to love. The theophany of the Spirit is not anthropomorphism, but is made possible through his indwelling in created being.

§4 MESSIANIC EXPECTATIONS OF THE SPIRIT

The rise of messianic hopes in Israel has been put down to disappointment over the fall of Jerusalem, the holy city, and the destruction of God's temple on Zion.[34] Scholars have seen these hopes arriving at their full flowering during the sufferings of the prisoners in Babylonian exile. It is quite true that the messianic idea is a 'theory explaining a catastrophe',[35] and that hope for a homecoming can keep prisoners alive. But why was it Israel particularly that developed the messianic hope, and not all other repressed and imprisoned peoples? The reason for that lies deeper. It is only out of hope that we can be disappointed. To despair – *de-sperare* – presupposes that very *spes*, or hope, from which despair departs. Where there is no hope, there are no disappointments either. The close bond between faith in God and hope for the future exists in historical experiences of God. Because these experiences have to be remembered, they are also expected, and the telling of them awakens hope for similar experiences in the future too. In mystical experiences of God, time and the hour are forgotten. In the eternal present of Being, life's remembrances and life's expectations vanish. In the cosmic experience of God, remembrances and expectations turn towards the eternal return of the same thing in the rhythms and cycles of nature. But in the historical experience of God, God is perceived in unique and contingent events, and is hoped for with the expectation of eternal and necessary present. From the very beginning, Israel's experience of God 'the Lord' was indissolubly bound up with the expectation of 'the Day of the Lord'. An expectation of the parousia like this is an organic component in the historical experience of God.[36] Only narrative is able to preserve the historical character of such experiences. Only hope is able to maintain their divine character.

If we call the *experiences* of God encountered by Abraham, Isaac and Jacob 'historical', then these experiences necessarily imply the *expectation* of God for the people of succeeding generations. The first commandment holds fast the remembrance of Israel's 'seminal experience' in the Exodus event; and the remembrance is historical because this unique event of Israel's past is the reason for her present in the divine covenant, and her hope for the promised land. The messianic expectations of God certainly arrived at their flowering because of the destruction of the temple and the new experience of oppression in Babylonian exile. But these expectations had their historical foundation in Israel's primal and pristine experiences of God, and are the same experiences, reborn and in a new guise. The expectations of the messianic saviour-king in Isaiah go back to the Nathan promise. Hope for the new, final Exodus actualizes the first Exodus from Egypt and implants new trust in the liberating God. Ezekiel's expectation of the raising and rebirth of dead Israel takes up the remembrances of earlier, similar experiences of the Spirit. In

Jeremiah, the fulfilment of the Torah through the Spirit who moves the hearts of men and women from within, is an expectation founded on recollections of God's covenant and God's faithfulness, in the face of the rovings and apostasies of his people. Israel's religion was from the very outset a religion based on *the expectation of God*. Waiting for God must undoubtedly be viewed as the foundation for the different horizons of hope for the messiah and for the Spirit. Let us look at the role of Yahweh's *ruach* in what are called Israel's messianic expectations of God.

1. *The Messiah of the Spirit*

The rebuilding of Zion has as its premise the renewal of the people. This can come about only when sins are laid bare and sinners are cleansed. This is apparently viewed as the special work of the Spirit. 'Then the Lord will wash away the filth of the daughters of Zion and cleanse the bloodstains of Jerusalem from its midst by a spirit of judgment and by a spirit of burning' (Isa. 4.4; Zech. 13.1; Matt. 3.11). The fire is purificatory, not punitive, as Isa. 6.6f. also makes plain. The messianic promise in Isaiah 9 only indirectly intimates that the king will be endowed with the Spirit (9.6). But Isa. 11.2 gives the ancient royal formula new force and validity: 'The Spirit of the Lord shall rest upon him, the spirit of wisdom and understanding, the spirit of counsel and might, the spirit of knowledge and the fear of the Lord.' To say that the Spirit 'rests' on the messianic king is a way of expressing God's faithfulness to him, and his own reliability for God. It is also, and not least, a way of describing the divine Shekinah in the messiah. In his Servant songs, Deutero-Isaiah lays particular stress on the link between *Spirit and justice:* 'Behold my servant and my chosen, in whom my soul delights; I have put my Spirit upon him, he will bring forth justice to the nations' (Isa. 42.1). Trito-Isaiah, finally, sees the coming messiah as quintessential bearer of the Spirit: 'The Spirit of the Lord God is upon me, because the Lord has anointed me' (61.1) He too joins together the messiah's endowment with the Spirit and the justice of compassion which the messiah brings the poor, the wretched and the imprisoned; and he links this with the proclamation of the End-time sabbath, which from time immemorial has been held to embrace social and ecological justice. The ultimate and eternal sabbath of the End-time is the reason why the messiah brings justice among the nations, and why he will initiate the rebirth of all the living for God's new creation (Isa. 11.6ff.; 65.17; 66.22ff.).

Isaiah 66.2 clarifies and makes explicit the connection between the new creation of nature and justice for the poor and wretched: 'All these things my hand has made, and so all these things are mine, says the Lord. But this is the man to whom I will look, he that is wretched and of a contrite spirit, and trembles at my word.' The new creation of nature out of God's Spirit will bring the Creator's justice and righteousness to the earth itself: 'Until *the Spirit from on high* is poured upon us, and the wilderness becomes a fruitful field, and the fruitful field is deemed a forest. Then justice will dwell in the wilderness, and righteousness abide in the fruitful field, and the fruit of righteousness will be peace' (Isa. 32.15–17).

The expectation of God grounded on history, then, has cosmic dimensions. There are two reasons for this. In the first place, the coming messianic salvation is expected in the form of a new 'creative act' on God's part (Isa. 43.19). The first Exodus event showed God as Lord of the forces of nature – the Exodus *ruach* – and the End-time homecoming of the people will also go hand in hand with a change in nature: 'The mountains shall break forth into singing, and all the trees of the field shall clap their hands' (Isa. 55.12). Second, the messiah will not only bring God's justice to the nations. He will bring it to nature too. He would not be the Creator's messiah if he were not to bring the land 'the sabbath of the earth' (Lev. 26). These are not marginal poetical 'extras', or dramatic elaborations of the historical expectations of God. They have to do with the rights of the whole creation to the justice of its Creator, and to his messiah.

2. *The Rebirth of the Messianic People from the Spirit*

In Israel's early traditions, to talk about Yahweh's *ruach* meant talking about 'a unique, powerful divine efficacy, confined to a particular act'.[37] But later, and especially in the exilic and post-exilic writings, the efficacies of all God's works came to be ascribed to the Spirit, so that the historical bond linking these works and God's acts was seen in the uninterrupted operation of God's Spirit. It is only by remembering the continuity which the Spirit gives to history that the future operation of the Spirit can be trusted. Yahweh's *ruach* no longer dwells and rests merely in the temple. His dwelling place is the people and its history. In this way Yahweh's *ruach* became the expression for Yahweh's presence and Shekinah, outside the cult on Zion too. And this meant that after the fall of the temple, Israel was able to console herself with the accompanying presence in her history of her God. That is the reason why God's historical activity in and for Israel was then ascribed to Yahweh's *ruach*. Yahweh's *ruach* accompanied Moses – it divided the waters of the Reed Sea – it led the people through the wilderness: 'Like cattle that go down into the valley, the Spirit of the Lord gave them rest. So thou didst lead thy people, to make for thyself a glorious name' (Isa. 63.14; see the whole context, Isa. 63.7–19).

Ezekiel and Jeremiah emphasize *the corporate hope* for Israel's rebirth from God's Spirit, not so much the coming of a messianic representative for Israel. According to the tremendous and shattering vision in Ezekiel 37, the prophet is 'led in the Spirit' to the vast valley where the bones of Israel's dead are lying, as if after a murderous battle. He hears the Lord's promise:

> Behold, I will cause breath (*ruach*) to enter you, and you shall live again. And I will lay sinews upon you, and will cause flesh to come upon you, and cover you with skin, and put breath in you, and you shall live . . . Thus says the Lord God: Come from the four winds, O breath, and breathe upon these slain, that they may live . . . And the breath came into them, and they lived, and stood upon their feet, an exceeding great host . . . And you shall know that I am the Lord when I open your graves, and raise you from your graves, O my people. And I will put my Spirit within you, and you shall live, and I will place you in your own land; then you shall know that I am Lord . . . My dwelling place shall be with them; and I will be their God, and they shall be my people (Ezek. 37).[38]

Here, faced with the fields of the dead in Israel's history, the creative Spirit becomes the Spirit and power of the resurrection of the dead. The vision casts back to the original meaning of *ruach*, as the life-giving tempest, and it is from this that it takes its drama. It is not individual representatives who are going to be raised by the Spirit, but the whole people; and the whole people will itself be made a bearer of the Spirit. The last sentence makes this clear: when God puts his Spirit 'into' a people, his 'dwelling place' will be among them. To be filled with the Spirit is God's Shekinah. So in this way the people itself, in its historical and everyday life, is to become the 'temple' of God's Spirit, and the Shekinah of the Most High.

The consequence of this transference of temple theology to the people as a whole is that God 'arrives at his rest' and 'dwells' wherever his will is done and his Torah obeyed in spontaneous, matter-of-course obedience. This happens when God's Spirit itself fulfils the divine law by creating 'a new heart' in the people, as Ezekiel puts it, or by 'writing the law in their hearts', as Jeremiah says. 'A new heart I will give you, and a new spirit (*ruach*) I will put within you; and I will take out of your flesh the heart of stone and give you a heart of flesh. And I will put my spirit (*ruach*) within you, and will make you people who walk in my statutes and are careful to observe my ordinances' (Ezek. 36.26f.).

What is important here is the distinction suggested between the spirit of human beings, the Spirit of God, and the 'heart of flesh' which will be moved by God's Spirit. The divine power of life makes men and women 'flesh' in the true human sense – that is, sensuously alive – and through that very fact makes them ready to walk according to the commandments of life, and not according to the compulsions of death. The divine Spirit 'in us' means the Shekinah, whose living energy is experienced as acting against the hardenings of sin and the petrifications of death.

Jeremiah expects something similar from the new covenant: 'Behold, the days are coming, says the Lord, when I will make a new covenant with the house of Israel and the house of Judah . . . I will put my law within them, and I will write it upon their hearts; and I will be their God, and they shall be my people. And no longer shall each man teach his neighbour and each his brother, saying, "Know the Lord", for they shall all know me, from the least of them to the greatest, says the Lord' (Jer. 31.31, 33f.). Knowledge of God comes about in the Spirit of God, for 'in his light we see light' (Ps. 36.9). The law given in the heart means the spontaneous and matter-of-course obedience which no longer requires any stone tablets, or any Torah teachers. Mediated knowledge of God is replaced by unmediated knowledge, and the mediated will of God by God's self-evident will.

This presupposes a future in which God himself is manifested universally and without any mediations, and in which God's Spirit penetrates and quickens even the depths of the human heart. Joel 2.28 sees the gifts of the Spirit poured out on the whole people, so that the traditional privileges come to an end – the privileges of men compared with women, of lords compared with servants, of adults compared with children: 'I will pour out my spirit on all flesh; and your sons and your daughters shall prophesy, your old men shall dream dreams, and your young men shall see visions. Even upon the menservants and maidservants in those days, I will pour out my spirit.' In the final presence of God's Spirit, the whole people will become *a prophetic people*. According to the covenant with Noah (Gen. 9.8–11), the expression 'all flesh' extends beyond the human race to cover all the living. The outpouring of God's Spirit therefore leads to the rebirth of all life, and to the rebirth too of the community of all the living on earth.

The experience of God which is expected from the coming of the Spirit is

1. *universal* – no longer particular, but related to 'all flesh' in the whole breadth of creation;

2. *total* – no longer partial, effective in the human 'heart', in the depths of human existence;

3. *enduring* – no longer historically temporary, but conceived as the 'resting' or 'dwelling' of the Spirit;

4. *direct* – no longer mediated through revelation and tradition, but grounded on the contemplation of God and his glory.

This is God's eternal presence, to which the historical experiences of God point. And in this presence, both the remembrances and the expectations of the Spirit will be completed and gathered up.

III

Trinitarian Experience of the Spirit

In this chapter we shall be asking about the special structures of the
Christian experience of God, and we shall turn first of all to the
testimonies of the New Testament. These testimonies narrate and
proclaim the history of Jesus of Nazareth, God's messiah. They tell
the history of Christ, but they tell it as the history of the Spirit with
Christ; and they proclaim this history as Christ's history with the
Spirit. The synoptic gospels begin with *a Spirit christology*. Paul
and John have this as their premise; but they themselves stress *a
christological doctrine of the Spirit*.[1]

What is the relationship between the Christ of the Spirit and the
Spirit of Christ? This question takes up the old enquiry about the
relation between the Jesus of history and the Christ of faith. But it
already sees 'the historical Jesus' himself in theological terms, as
God's messianic child, the Spirit-imbued human being who comes
from the Spirit, is led by the Spirit, acts and ministers in the Spirit,
and through the Spirit surrenders himself to death on the cross. The
old 'quest for the historical Jesus' viewed the relationship between
Jesus and Christ in temporal terms, and talked about a chronological
transition from the historical Jesus of the past to the present Christ
of faith. But 'the new quest for the historical Jesus'[2] puts the time
question about the historical Jesus the other way round: is the Christ
of faith identical with the Jesus of history? Why, chronologically
speaking, was it only after the apostolic proclamation of Christ that
the story of Jesus came to be told in reminiscent narrative in the
gospels? When we turn the question upside down like this, the
historical Jesus no longer appears as the temporal precondition for
the Christ of the proclamation, or a preliminary form of the risen

Christ; he is now that Christ himself. The Christ proclaimed to the nations is Jesus, the messiah of Israel, who was filled with the divine Spirit. In this way a substantial relationship of mutual interpretation develops between *the Christ of the Spirit* and *the Spirit of Christ*. The proclaimed Christ does not displace the earthly Jesus, nor can the proclamation of Christ be reduced to the proclamation of Jesus.

Recognition of the substantially determined mutual relationship between the pneumatological christology of the synoptics and the christological pneumatology of Paul and John was largely ignored in the traditions of the Western church. And approaches to Spirit christology in the movements for Christian reform were actually resisted. The risen Christ alone was to be Lord of the church and the Christian empire. The Spirit of God had to be solely the Spirit of the Lord, and communicated only through the 'spiritual pastors' of the church and the anointed apostolic majesties of the holy *imperium*. Remembrances of the Christ of the Spirit, his Sermon on the Mount and his non-violent passion, had to be repressed; for these were 'dangerous remembrances'. And the simplest way of repressing them is to historicize this story of Jesus, assigning it to the period before his cross and resurrection, which means placing it firmly in the past 'before' the present of the church's kerygma.[3] But this means losing sight of the canonical meaning of the gospels, which rank equally with the apostolic writings. For in fact they are parallel to one another, and complement each other in their picture of Christ.

Ever since the Cappadocian Fathers, *the tradition of the Eastern church* has emphasized the reciprocity between pneumatological christology on the one hand, and christological pneumatology on the other.[4] In Protestant theology, Hendrik Berkhof worked out 'the double relationship between the Spirit and Christ' in his doctrine of the Holy Spirit (1964/1968), stressing the reciprocity of pneumatology and christology.[5] In the ecumenical reflections on the *filioque* controversy (published by L. Vischer in 1981 under the title *Spirit of God – Spirit of Christ*), this reciprocal efficacy of the Spirit and Christ, which springs from their mutual relationship, provides the christological and pneumatological basis for an expanded doctrine of the Trinity without the *filioque*.[6] We shall take up these ideas here, developing them further in the context of Trinitarian doctrine; for curiously enough, in Berkhof's outline, God the Father plays no part in the mutual relationship between the Spirit and Christ, Christ and the Spirit. Christ 'the recipient of the Spirit' becomes Christ 'the sender of the Spirit'. From this simple stance, the Spirit's 'turnover point' in Christ's death and resurrection (which is certainly difficult to interpret) is excluded altogether. But this is the point when the mutual relationship comes into being, and it is from this that the character of the relationship is formed. Christ's experience of the Spirit as it is narrated, and the proclaimed experience of Christ in the Spirit, do not simply follow one another in time. They are interlocked through the structure of the Trinity. Their relationship is not a consecutive relationship of logical consequence. It is a relationship of mutual interpretation.

In the first part of this chapter we shall give a brief summary of the Spirit christology found in the synoptics (especially Luke), and then go on to ask why the synoptic passion narratives are silent about the Spirit. Where is the Spirit in the death of Christ? How did 'the Spirit of God' become 'the Spirit of Christ'? In the second part we shall begin with Christ's rebirth from the Spirit, and shall describe believers' experience of the Spirit in their apprehension of Christ. Here we shall note particularly the trinitarian form of the sending of the Spirit through Christ from the Father, as John 14 describes it. In a third section, we shall offer a trinitarian exposition of the Spirit of God as Spirit of the Father and Spirit of the Son. Finally, in the fourth part, we shall discuss the relationship between the Spirit and the new creation, in the form of an eschatological pneumatology.

§1 THE CHRIST OF THE SPIRIT: THE SPIRITUALITY OF JESUS

Both chronologically and theologically, the operation of the divine Spirit is the precondition or premise for the history of Jesus of Nazareth.[7] Israel's experiences of the Spirit and her expectations of the Spirit are present in the ministry, preaching and fate of John the Baptist. John was already 'filled with the Holy Spirit' from his mother's womb. He grew 'strong in the Spirit' (Luke 1.15, 80). Consequently he was regarded by Jesus' disciples too as the Elijah who was to come at the End-time (Matt. 11.14). Jesus of Nazareth will have been one of John's disciples. He began his public ministry only after John had been forcibly silenced, and the wording of his message was the same as John's: 'Repent, for the kingdom of heaven is at hand' (Matt. 3.2; 4.17).

We must suppose that at his baptism by or before John in the Jordan, Jesus had his special experience of the Spirit, and that through this he perceived his own calling and mission. 'The Spirit descended upon him like a dove' (Mark 1.10). He hears a voice from God: 'Thou art my beloved Son; with thee I am well pleased' (Mark 1.11), and sees the heavens open. What is meant here is that this is the call to be the expected messiah of the End-time, on whom according to Isa. 61.1 the Spirit of God rests. It is in the special relationship to God in this Spirit that Jesus experiences himself as the messianic 'child', and experiences Israel's God as 'my beloved Father'. In the Spirit, Jesus prays 'Abba, dear Father'. In the Spirit he knows himself to be the beloved Son. So the Spirit is the real determining subject of this special relationship of Jesus' to God, and of God's to Jesus. And it is therefore the Spirit who also 'leads' Jesus into the mutual history between himself and God his Father, in which 'through obedience' (Heb. 5.8) he will 'learn' his role as the messianic Son. The phraseology about the 'descent' of the Spirit on Jesus, and its 'resting' on him, suggests that the Spirit should be interpreted as *God's Shekinah*. What is meant is the *self-restriction* and *self-humiliation* of the eternal Spirit, and his feeling identification with Jesus' person and the history of his life and suffering – just as, according to the rabbinic idea, God's Spirit has committed itself to the history of Israel's life and sufferings.

The indwelling of the Spirit brings the divine energies of life in Jesus to rapturous and overflowing fullness. John 3.34 describes this unique endowment with the Spirit as 'without measure'. It marks the beginning of the kingdom of God and the new creation of all things. The Spirit makes Jesus 'the kingdom of God in person', for *in the power of the Spirit* he drives out demons and heals the sick; in the power of the Spirit he receives sinners, and brings the kingdom of God to the poor. This energizing power of God is given him not for himself but for others: for the sick, the poor, sinners, the dying.

But in the synoptic gospels the account of Jesus' baptism and his endowment with the Spirit is followed by the story of the temptations. The Spirit 'drives' (Mark 1.12) and 'leads (Luke 4.1) Jesus into the desert. It is only after the temptations that he goes to Galilee 'in the power of the Spirit' (Luke 4.14). The temptations themselves are not levelled at his human weakness. They are aimed at his relationship to God: 'If you are the Son of God then . . .' Jesus' messianic kingship is put on trial, and in that trial the kingship is precisely defined. It is to be a messianic kingship without bread for the hungry masses, without the liberation of Jerusalem, and without any rule of violence.

And this already foreshadows the path of his passion, and makes its form and direction clear. If Jesus holds fast to his endowment with the Spirit, dispensing with the economic, political and religious methods of forcible rule, then all he can do is to suffer the forces that oppose him, and then he must die in weakness. But this is the way along which the Spirit 'leads' him, so this is also the way in which he is assured of his messiahship. It is as he follows the path that he comes to understand the messianic role that God's Spirit has assigned him.

But then what, conversely, does this way of suffering which Jesus takes mean for the divine Spirit itself? How does the Spirit experience Jesus' living and his dying? This question is seldom asked. But if we remember Israel's concept of the Shekinah, we can say that if the Spirit 'leads' Jesus, then the Spirit accompanies him as well. And if the Spirit accompanies him, then it is drawn into his sufferings, and becomes his *companion* in suffering. The path the Son takes in his passion is then at the same time the path taken by the Spirit, whose strength will be proved in Jesus' weakness. The Spirit is the transcendent side of Jesus' immanent way of suffering. So the '*condescendence*' of the Spirit leads to the progressive *kenosis* of the Spirit, together with Jesus. Although the Spirit fills Jesus with the divine, living energies through which the sick are healed, it does not turn him into a superman. It participates in his human suffering to the point of his death on the cross. According to Matt. 8.17, Jesus does not heal the sick through his supreme power. He heals them through his atoning representation.* 'He has borne our griefs and carried our sorrows' (Isa. 53.4).[8] Through the Shekinah, the Spirit binds itself to Jesus' fate, though without becoming identical with him. In this way *the Spirit of God* becomes definitively *the Spirit of Christ*, so that from that point onwards it can be called by and invoked in Christ's name.

But if the Spirit of God becomes the Spirit of Jesus Christ, then this Spirit is also the Spirit of the passion and the Spirit of the crucified one. Can we discover any indications in the New Testament for a *pneumatologia crucis* of this kind? 'The first complete early Christian sermon . . . that has come down to us' – in the Epistle to the Hebrews – stresses the operation of the Spirit in Jesus' passion and death.

---

* The German word *Stellvertretung* comprehends the whole range of nuances covered by the English semantic field 'representation – substitution' (with the related adjective 'vicarious'), and this should be borne in mind in the present text. The fundamental sense is always '*for*' – 'for us', 'for many' [Trans.].

Christ is presented as at once the high priest and the sacrifice.[9] Christ 'through the eternal Spirit offered himself without blemish to God' (Heb. 9.14). The value of the sacrifice does not depend solely on the one surrendered. It has to do with the mode of the surrender too. And in this happening Christ is determined through the eternal Spirit. The Spirit is not something he possesses. It is the power that makes him ready to surrender his life, and which itself sustains this surrender.[10] According to 7.16, it is 'the power of indestructible life' ($\zeta\omega\grave{\eta}\ \dot{\alpha}\varkappa\alpha\tau\alpha\lambda\acute{\upsilon}\tau o\varsigma$). Calvin thought that this is a way of saying that Christ did not suffer death outwardly or fortuitously, but experienced and affirmed it inwardly, '*a Spiritus virtute*' – through the power of the Spirit.[11] It is not the Romans who are the real controlling agents in Christ's passion and death, and not even death itself. It is Christ himself who is the truly active one, through the operation of the divine Spirit who acts in him. In 'the theology of surrender', Christ is made the determining subject of his suffering and death through the Spirit of God.

The Gospel of Mark tells the history of Jesus as the history of the Spirit with Jesus.[12] The Spirit lends his acts and his sufferings the divine power that is theirs. Peter's confession (8.29) and the charge 'to tell no one', the announcement of suffering and the call to the discipleship of the cross – all these things give a new definition to the notion of the messiah. This idea is now newly defined through Jesus' own experiences, which are expressed in sayings about the Son of man. The *fact* of Jesus' messiahship was derived from his endowment with the Spirit in baptism; but now its *content* is defined through the vista that stretches forward towards his death. What is known as 'the messianic secret' is unveiled in Jesus' sufferings and his dying.[13]

This affects Jesus' experience of the Spirit too, and his experiences of God in the Spirit. The prayer in Gethsemane (14.32–42) is the only prayer that is explicitly addressed to 'Abba, dear Father'. 'We know from Rom. 8.15 and Gal. 4.6 that in the early church the Spirit-impelled cry "'$A\beta\beta\grave{\alpha}\ \acute{o}\ \pi\alpha\tau\acute{\eta}\varrho$" was widespread, and moreover Paul does not merely assume that it was used in his own congregations (Gal. 4.6). He takes it for granted that this "'$A\beta\beta\acute{\alpha}$" cry was also used in a congregation which he had not founded himself, such as Rome (Rome. 8.15).'[14] In Gethsemane too Jesus utters this Abba prayer in the Spirit of God when he is face to face with his temptation and assailment. This means that Mark is giving a pneumatological interpretation to Jesus' passion – the passion which begins in Gethsemane with the experience of God's hiddenness, and ends with the experience of God-forsakenness on the cross. What begins with his baptism through the operation of the Spirit ends in his passion through the operation of the Spirit. The Spirit which 'leads' Jesus into the wilderness is beside him, sustaining him in his suffering from God. The parallel to the story of the temptations is brought out through Jesus' words to the sleeping disciples: 'Watch and pray that you may not enter into temptation' (14.38). The Spirit that is 'willing' evidently rests on Jesus. The disciples are ruled by the flesh that is 'weak'. The correspondences go even further. Whereas in Jesus' baptism God calls Jesus 'my beloved Son', in Gethsemane Jesus responds by addressing him as 'Abba, dear Father'. Both the call to life and the response in dying are given 'in the Spirit'. Jesus goes in the Spirit and through the Spirit to his death. And that means, in the awareness that he is the messianic son of God whom baptism with the Spirit has designated him to be. 'The self-emptying of the Spirit is accordingly the precondition for the self-humiliation of the Son. The Spirit of God is the spirit of kenotic self-surrender.'[15]

Jesus' passion, which begins with the unheard prayer to the Father in Gethsemane, ends with his cry of abandonment on the cross (Mark 15.34). What does Jesus' experience of God on the cross mean for the Spirit of God, if we assume that the divine Spirit went with him, and that it was in the Holy Spirit that he suffered and died? We started from the assumption that the history of Jesus is simultaneously the history of the Spirit, which descended on him, and rested on him. We may conclude from this that the story of the suffering of the messianic Son of God is the story of the suffering of God's Spirit too. But the Spirit does not suffer in the same way, for he is Jesus' strength in suffering, and is even the 'indestructable life' in whose power Jesus can give himself vicariously 'for many'. In Gethsemane the divine Spirit is present and frames the Son's response: 'Not my will, but thine, be done'. With this he reveals to Jesus the 'will' of God, which finds expression in the Father's silence in answer to the Son's plea. On Golgotha the Spirit suffers the suffering and death of the Son, without dying with him. So what the Spirit 'experiences' – though we must not overstress the metaphor – is surely that the dying Jesus 'breathes him out' and 'yields him up' (Mark 15.37; stronger, John 19.30). 'Of such a kind was Christ's death cry: as his senses left him and he went down to death, the Holy Spirit interceded for him, with inexpressible groanings, helping his weakness also.'[16]

Jesus' experience of God on the way from Gethsemane to Golgotha has to be understood as the experience of the hidden, absent, even rejecting Father. Paradoxically enough, Mark tells this passion story as the history of Jesus' growing certainty of his messiahship, to the point when he publicly acknowledges it before Pilate (15.2), an acknowledgment which then leads to his execution, and to the title 'king of the Jews' over the cross. This growing certainty of his messiahship is a clear sign of the presence of God's Spirit in the absence of God the Father which Jesus experienced. In the strength of the indwelling and sym-pathetic divine Spirit, Jesus endures the God-forsakenness vicariously, on behalf of the God-forsaken world; and by doing so he brings the world God's intimate nearness – that is, reconciliation with him. He himself brings into the God-forsaken world the Spirit of God, the Spirit who intercedes for us with sighs too deep for words, as Paul says in Romans 8.

When, with the Epistle to the Hebrews, we say that it was through 'the eternal Spirit' and through 'indestructible life', that Jesus *offered himself up* to suffer-God-forsakenness, then we are already looking beyond this death to Jesus' rebirth from this same divine, quickening power of the Spirit. Looked at pneumatologically, Christ's death and rebirth belong within a single movement. They are one event. They are not two different acts performed by God in Jesus. Jesus' passion and resurrection are described in pneumatological metaphors as the birth-pangs and birth-joys of the Spirit, and as the sowing and growth of a plant.[17] So the Spirit's suffering involvement in Jesus' passion allows his future beyond his death to be already discerned.

§2 THE SPIRIT OF CHRIST: THE SPIRITUALITY OF THE COMMUNITY OF HIS PEOPLE

The other side of Jesus' death is also presented as his experience of the Spirit – his raising through the Spirit and his living presence in the Spirit. Here we have to distinguish between Jesus' personal experience of the Spirit and the experience of Jesus in the Spirit that animates the community of his people.

Where his own person is concerned, the Spirit of God is not only the one who leads Jesus to his self-surrender to death on the cross. He is very much more the one who brings Jesus up out of death. This is especially emphasized in the early Christian testimonies. Paul, following an earlier text, understands his gospel to be the gospel of

God 'concerning his Son, who was descended from David according to the flesh and designated Son of God in power according to the Spirit of holiness by his resurrection from the dead' (Rom. 1.1–4). According to I Tim. 3.16, Christ was 'manifested in the flesh, justified through the Spirit'. I Peter 3.18 tells us that he was 'put to death in the flesh but made alive in the Spirit'. Ezekiel had already presented the Spirit's End-time efficacy as a creative act that raises the dead and makes them eternally alive (Ezek. 37); and the early Christian testimonies similarly discern that the raising of Christ from the dead is the first fruits of the newly creating End-time operation of the Spirit. If Christ has been 'raised from the dead' ahead of all others, as their representative and hastening ahead of them, then the activity of the Spirit in him, raising him and giving him life, must also be understood as an 'earnest', an advance payment and beginning of the End-time new creation of the world. Christ was raised through Yahweh's *ruach*, the divine energy of life, so that his raising and his presence as 'the living One' is the manifestation of God's Spirit, which will transform this transitory world into the new world of eternal life.

This discernment goes back to the appearances of the risen Jesus experienced by the women and the disciples, by Paul and by John, the author of the Apocalypse. They perceived the crucified Jesus in the radiance of the divine glory and power, *doxa* and *dynamis*, and in this exceptional perception they were evidently possessed by the Spirit of life. The Easter and the Pentecost appearances are very much closer to one another than the gap in time between the church's two festivals would suggest: in the seeing of the risen Christ, those who perceived him experienced the life-giving power of the Spirit; and conversely, it is this quickening power of the Spirit which allows Christ to be perceived, either through seeing or hearing. 'Behind the phrase about the raising "through the glory of the Father" in Rom. 6.4 is substantially speaking the raising of Christ through the divine pneuma.'[18]

It is in line with the Israelite view to say that God's eternal Spirit, like Wisdom, is the eternal 'radiance of his glory'. The metaphors for the divine Spirit always talk about *light* as well as power. There is nothing with which to compare Christ's Easter appearances, but we can surely conceive of them as visions of light, remembering here the story of Jesus' transfiguration on the mountain (Matt. 17.2): 'And he was transfigured before them, and his face shone like the sun, and his garments became white as light.' If God's Spirit is understood as eternal light, then it cannot be perceived directly. We can see this light only indirectly, from whatever it illuminates and from whatever it reflects it. This is the way Paul evidently senses 'the bright shining in our hearts' which comes from 'the knowledge of the glory of God in the face of Jesus Christ' (II Cor. 4.6), for he traces his own conversion back to the fact that God had revealed his Son 'in him' (Gal. 1.16).

The image of the *power* of the eternal Spirit is used even more frequently. Christ was 'crucified in (the) weakness (of God) but lives in the power of God' (II Cor. 13.4). Paul's identification of Christ and the Spirit in I Cor. 15.45 is unique. Christ, the new human being, 'became life-giving spirit'. What Paul means is evidently that the risen Christ lives from, and in, the eternal Spirit, and that the divine Spirit of life acts in and through him. Through this reciprocal perichoresis of mutual indwelling Christ becomes the 'life-giving Spirit' and the Spirit becomes 'the Spirit of Jesus Christ'. Because the eternal Spirit is *auctor resurrectionis Christi*, as Calvin rightly stresses,[19] it is from the Spirit that we expect the gift of eternal life, the raising of the dead, the rebirth of everything living, and the new creation of all things – the expectations summarily listed in the third article of most Christian creeds.

This brings us back once more to the God-event on the cross of Christ. We started from the postulate that the Spirit himself was involved in Jesus' suffering, because he rested on the Son and accompanied him into his passion. We have assumed a kenosis of the Spirit, which is to be seen in his Shekinah in the suffering, assailed and dying Jesus. But if we take a different starting point, looking only at the power of the Spirit, and not at this weakness too, then we are ascribing to the Spirit a merely external influence on the sacrifice which Christ brings the Father through his self-surrender. The Spirit 'directs towards the Father the sacrifice of the Son, bringing it into the divine reality of the Trinitarian communion', says the papal encyclical *Dominum et Vivificantem*.[20] The Spirit draws the Son out of the depths of this suffering, but he does not participate in the suffering itself. According to this image, however, the Spirit which descended on Jesus must have forsaken him before the passion, in order to bring 'the incense of the offering' to God the Father. But according to Paul's view, it is not Jesus who brings the Father the reconciling sacrifice: '*God* was *in* Christ reconciling the world to himself' (II Cor. 5.19). The papal view, like the mediaeval theology of the sacrifice of the Mass, derives from a different religion of atonement. If God himself was *in* Christ, then according to Pauline language (in which God always means the Father of Jesus Christ) the Father suffered *with* and *in* the Son; and he did so by virtue of his indwelling in the Son through the Holy Spirit, as we may interpretatively add. If the Spirit is God's empathy, this means that the eternal Spirit is also involved, in profoundest and identifying suffering. It is precisely his suffering with the Son to the point of death on the cross which makes the rebirth of Christ from the Spirit inwardly possible. The Spirit participates in the dying of the Son in order to give him new 'life from the dead'. Because he accompanies Christ to his end, he can make this end the new beginning.

In this way the eternal Spirit of God becomes 'the Spirit of Christ' (Rom. 8.9), 'the Spirit of the Son' (Gal. 4.6) and 'the Spirit of faith' (II Cor. 4.13), so that Christ becomes the determining subject of the Spirit: he sends the Spirit (John 16.7), he breathes the Spirit (John 20.22). The Spirit whom the disciples experience, and with them the community of believers, bears the impress of Christ. Through the Spirit they enter into Christ's saving and life-giving fellowship. In the experience of the life-giving Spirit they recognize Jesus as the Lord of God's rule.

It is important to stress both sides here. Christian faith is *response* to the word of the messianic gospel, and the *resonance* of that word in the hearts and lives of men and women. But in this very way, Christian faith is the experience of the quickening Spirit – experience of the beginning of the new creation of the world. Seen christologically, faith is a *response*, but seen eschatologically it is a *beginning*. If this faith is experienced 'in the Spirit', then here the Spirit itself is indirectly experienced. Directly, faith has Christ as its sole lodestone. Directly, hope has as sole lodestone the kingdom of God. The medium through which faith and hope come into being remains to some degree imperceptible, just as we cannot see the eyes we see with, or view the place where we are standing as long as we are standing there. 'It's dark at the foot of the lighthouse', says a German proverb. The Spirit as 'the broad place' in which the trust of the heart unfolds and the horizon of hope opens, is not concrete or objective. But it is for all that the hidden presupposition for the objectivity of Christ and the coming kingdom.

What is true of faith is true for the community of Christ's people too. On the one hand it is the community of women and men for whom Christ and Christ alone is the Lord, and 'the one Word of God', as the Barmen Theological Declaration of the Confessing Church declared in 1934, in its first thesis. But on the other hand it is the community of women and men who 'live and wish to live in expectation of his appearance', as the same declaration says in Thesis 3. In the concurrence of faith in Christ and hope for the parousia, this community grows in the sphere of the Holy Spirit into a charismatic community, where potentialities and capabilities are brought to life. The charismatically enlivened 'body of Christ' sees itself as a 'down payment' – as the advance pledge and beginning of the new creation of all things, so that in this way it is 'the temple of the Holy Spirit'.

Summing up, we can say that it is pneumatology that brings christology and eschatology together. There is no mediation between Christ and the kingdom of God except the present experience of the Spirit, for the Spirit is the Spirit of Christ and the living energy of the new creation of all things. In the present of the Spirit are both origin and consummation.

In 1964 Hendrik Berkhof talked about 'the twofold relationship between the Spirit and Christ'.[21] Talking about the Spirit christology of the synoptics, he says: 'According to their account, the Spirit takes divine precedence over Jesus, who appears as bearer of the Spirit.'[22] And talking about the Spirit of Christ, he says: 'Here Jesus is not so much the bearer of the Spirit as its sender.'[23] He says nothing further about the changeover point in Jesus' history, when from being the bearer of the Spirit he becomes its sender.

The encyclical *Dominum et Vivificantem* of 1986[24] goes somewhere deeper here and, with the farewell discourses in the Gospel of John, discovers the point of change in Jesus' death on the cross: 'If I do not go away, the Counsellor will not come to you; but if I go, I will send him to you' (John 16.7). 'Describing his "departure" as a condition for the "coming" of the Counsellor, Christ links the new beginning of God's salvific self-communication in the Holy Spirit with the mystery of the Redemption' (I, 13). The Holy Spirit comes at the cost of Christ's departure; the price of his coming is the cross, and he comes in the power of the Easter mystery. Christ, who on the cross as Son of man and Lamb of God *gave up his spirit*, goes to the apostles immediately after his resurrection in order to breath this power upon them. He shows them his hands and his side. 'It is in the power of this crucifixion that he says to them: "Receive the Holy

Spirit" ' (I, 24). 'The Holy Spirit as Love and Gift comes down, in a certain sense, into the very heart of the sacrifice which is offered on the cross . . . He consumes this sacrifice with the fire of the love which unites the Son with the Father in the Trinitarian communion.' The Holy Spirit 'is revealed and at the same time made present as the Love that works in the depths of the Paschal Mystery, as the source of the salvific power of the Cross of Christ, and as the gift of new and eternal life' (II, 41).

To define the changeover point from christology to pneumatology by way of the theology of the cross is an excellent deepening of pneumatology. It provides the genesis for a *pneumatologia crucis*. The encyclical is even able to talk about 'the pain of God' which now 'in Christ crucified acquires through the Holy Spirit its full human expression' (II, 41). Even if one is unable to share the sacrificial religion employed in the encyclical, one must pay tribute to an outstanding theological document.

If we read the farewell discourses in the Gospel of John more closely, however, we find that we can no longer talk about an 'automatic' turn from the Christ of the Spirit to the Spirit of Christ, from the bearer of the Spirit to its sender, or from the departure of Christ to the coming of the Spirit. The proceeding is rather a trinitarian one, and begins with something new initiated by *God the Father*. The Father's role receives insufficient attention in both Berkhof and the encyclical. Let us look at the texts. John 14.16 says: 'I will pray *the Father* and he will give you another Comforter.' John 14.26: 'The Comforter, the Holy Spirit, whom *the Father* will send in my name.' John 15.26: 'When the Comforter comes, whom I shall send to you *from the Father*, even the Spirit of truth, who proceeds from the Father.' According to these passages, the Spirit is with the Father. Christ 'prays' for his coming. He is sent by the Father in Jesus' name. He proceeds from the Father and is sent by Jesus. The origin of his existence is the Father, but the cause of his coming is the Son. Between Christ, the recipient of the Spirit, and Christ, the giver of the Spirit, stands the hearing of Christ's plea by the Father and the sending into time, through the Father and the Son, of the Spirit who in eternity proceeds from the Father. If these pointers in the Gospel of John provide us with an adequate description of the mystery of Christ's self-surrender on the cross and the sending of the Spirit, then it is not sufficient to talk merely about a reciprocal efficacy between Christ and the Spirit, the Spirit and Christ. Nor is it enough to talk only about a twofold relationship between the Spirit and Christ. What we are looking at here are the threefold relationships of the Son, the Father and the Spirit, and the reciprocal trinitarian efficacies in God, which are multiple in kind.[25]

§3 TRINITARIAN MUTUALITY BETWEEN GOD'S SPIRIT AND HIS SON

As we have seen, there are two contexts in which it is necessary to talk about the Holy Spirit. The first is Christ's history with God, and the second is our history with Christ. It is impossible to talk about Christ, his person and his efficacy, without at the same time talking about his experience of God and his experience of God's Spirit. Because he speaks and acts and goes his way out of his experience of the Spirit, the Spirit precedes the coming of Christ. It is one-sided to look solely at the sending of the Spirit through the risen Christ. But the trinitarian structure maintained in the Western church did precisely that.[26]

With the introduction of the *filioque* into the Nicaeno-Constantinopolitan creed, the Spirit was considered as subordinate to the Son from its very origin, the Son being put ahead of the Spirit. It is true that this trinitarian structure is clearly detectable in salvation history, but that means: only in the Christian community's experience of the Spirit, since the community is grounded on the sending of the Spirit by the exalted Lord. Through this trinitarian structure, *christological pneumatology* is laid down hard and fast, as the only form pneumatology can take. But if instead we note the experience of the Spirit out of which Christ himself comes and acts, and ask about the trinitarian structure which can be detected in that, we discover that the Spirit proceeds from the Father and determines the Son, rests on the Son and shines through him. The roles of Son and Spirit are then exchanged. The Son proceeds from the Father and has the impress of the Spirit. We might say that Christ comes *a patre spirituque*, from the Father and the Spirit – though in fact it is better to avoid any undifferentiating 'and' in the trinitarian structure altogether.[27]

This remodelling will only be possible, however, if we once again remove the *filioque* from the Western creed, leaving it that the Spirit proceeds from the Father alone. There is then no difficulty in conceiving the image of the Father who breathes out the Word in his eternal Spirit. The Father begets the Son in the power of the eternal

Spirit. The Father breathes out the eternal Spirit in the presence of the Son. The Son and the Spirit – if we keep the image of Word and Breath – proceed simultaneously from the Father. The one does not precede the other. We shall be talking about the Spirit if we talk about the eternal birth of the Son from the Father. We shall be talking about the Son if we think of the 'procession' of the Spirit from his Father. It then becomes possible to discern the reciprocal relationships between the Holy Spirit and Christ the Son, in all their complex interworkings. It is not a matter of two separate acts, when the Son proceeds from the Father, and the Spirit is breathed out by the Father. On the contrary, the eternal birth of the Son from the Father and the eternal issuing of the Spirit from the Father are, in spite of all the differences, so much one that the Son and the Spirit must be seen, not as parallel or successive to one another, but *in* one another. If the Spirit proceeds from the Father, then this 'procession' presupposes the Son, for the Father is Father only in his relation to the Son. If the Son is born of the Father, then the Spirit accompanies the birth of the Son and manifests itself through him.[28] But this is conceivable only if the Spirit does not merely rest on the Son, and does not manifest itself only in his eternal birth, but if the birth of the Son from the Father is already accompanied by the 'procession' of the Spirit from the Father. The Spirit is inconceivable without the Son, and the Son is inconceivable without the Spirit.

The intellectual difficulties here are due to the fact that in the doctrine of the Trinity two different metaphors have been intermingled:

1. The eternal birth of the Son from the Father, which corresponds to the Abba experience of God through Jesus;

2. The eternal utterance of the Word in the breath of the Spirit through God. Because the Son has been simultaneously understood as the Logos, the Father-Son concept and the Spirit-Word concept intermingle. Once we grasp this, the difficulties become soluble.

'The mutual relationship between pneumatology and christology must be viewed as a fundamental principle of Christian theology.'[29] But this ecumenical requirement can be met only if Christomonism is given up, and if enthusiastic pneumatomania is avoided, and if both christology and pneumatology are seen in the framework of a trinitarian structure that embraces both. This preserves theocentrism from either christocentrism or pneumatocentrism. It is only in this structure that christology and pneumatology can be mutually related in such a way that the historical interactions of Spirit and Christ, Christ and Spirit are comprehended.

In ordering these doctrinal tenets in theology, it is not a question of one schematic arrangement rather than another. The doctrine of the Trinity has *a doxological form*, since it expresses the experience of God in the apprehension of Christ and in the fellowship of the Spirit. This means that in this doctrine no definitions are permissible which simply pin something down, as a way of 'mastering' it.

Every kind of thinking and speaking, feeling and acting, suffering and hoping which is directed to the unfathomable, eternal God is *doxological* in character. For all these things are ways of expressing before God overpowering experiences and profound expectations. These are the threads in life which lead to the living reality of God himself. Trinitarian ways of speaking, singing and thinking grew up in this doxological context, and if they are not to lose sight of their divine Opposite, that context must be kept in mind. 'Concepts create idols. Only wonder understands', said Gregory of Nyssa.[30] And this wonder over God respects God's unfathomable mystery, however great the delight in knowing. Theological talk *about* God stems from doxological talk *to* God, and remains talk *before* God. This unique character is best preserved when theology expresses the experience of God *apophatically*. This does not mean any restriction of knowledge, or any impoverishment of thinking. On the contrary, it means that knowing is set free in 'the broad place' of God's Spirit 'who searches out even the depths of the Godhead'; and it means that thinking is immeasurably enriched.

§4 THE EXPECTATION OF THE SPIRIT IN HOPING AND LAMENTING

In Christianity as in Judaism, the experience of God's Spirit awakens new and hitherto unsuspected expectations about life. The experience of the Spirit is the reason for the eschatological longing for the completion of salvation, the redemption of the body and the new creation of all things. Impelled by the Spirit, Christians cry 'Maranatha, come, Lord Jesus!' (Rev. 22.20). It is the experience of the Spirit which makes Christians in every society restless and homeless, and on the search for the kingdom of God (Heb. 13.14), for it is this experience of God which makes them controvert and contravene a godless world of violence and death. The Spirit makes them rich in experience and rich in hope, but poor and lonely in a world gone wrong. The cry for the coming of the Spirit takes up out of the depths the cries of the dumb, and brings them before God. In praying for the coming of the Spirit, men and women open themselves for his coming. Let us work out two dimensions in the expectation of the Spirit.

1. The Positive Dimension

The more deeply the presence of the Spirit is experienced in the heart, and in fellowship with one another, the more certain and assured the hope for the Spirit's universal coming will be. It was Paul particularly who interpreted the presence of the Spirit eschatologically. The experience of the Spirit in the present is the beginning (ἀπαρχή) and advance pledge or foretaste (ἀρραβών) of the coming kingdom of glory (Rom. 8.23; II Cor. 1.22; 5.5; Eph. 1.14). In this the new creation of all things is already experienced – experienced now, for all, representatively and in anticipation. In the experience of the Spirit, the Spirit's charismatic energies will interpenetrate body and soul. These energies are not 'supernatural' gifts. They are 'the powers of the age to come' (Heb. 6.5). That is why experience of the Spirit is described as a rebirth to true life, a personal rebirth which anticipates the rebirth of the whole cosmos. Paul also describes the experience of the Spirit as 'the first fruits' of a coming harvest (Rom. 8.23).

These are the images of hope with which the present experience of the Spirit is described, as the experience of life's new beginning: it is the springtime of life, a new birth and a new start. If the present experience of the Spirit is understood as the presence here and now of the coming new creation of all things, then – conversely – the new creation of all things is conceived as the completion of that which is already experienced here and now. Then the 'life-giving' Spirit will wake the dead to eternal life and drive the violence of death out of the whole creation. He will make petrified conditions dance, so that everything can join in the joyful song of praise. In this sense he will 'spiritize' all created beings, and the spheres in which they live in heaven and on earth. We cannot take this to mean the *spiritualization* of creation; it can only mean its *vitalization*. This hope for the newly creating efficacy of the Spirit in everything that lives is not derived from any experience of deficiency in the present. It springs from the overflowing rapture of experience of the Spirit, and extravagant joy over the coming of God to his world. 'The more the patient detects the tokens of returning health, the more restless and expectant he will be. That is the paradoxical situation of the children of God in the world. The hope that sways them is due largely not to what they are lacking but to what they have already received.'[31]

2. The Negative Dimension

When freedom is close, the chains begin to hurt. If there were no such thing as freedom, or if every hope for liberation in us were dead, we should get used to our chains and, once having got used to them, should no longer feel them. 'Bend down so low, 'til down don't bother you no more', said the sad wisdom of the black slaves in the Southern states of America. Probably all of us, in our different ways, have got so much accustomed to the negations of life that we do not notice them any more. 'Happy in forgetting / the things that can't be helped', lied a popular German song during the Second World War. But if positive experiences let us suddenly perceive that things can be changed after all, and that we do not have to put up with life's denials, then we become restless, and begin to suffer, and to contradict, and to resist. Because of these experiences, what we thought was impossible – and what we were intended to think was impossible – begins to seem possible after all. The chains begin to hurt, for we already sense that we have the power to break them.

It is in the negation of the negative first of all that prisoners and people who have never been able to participate in life experience what is positive in freedom, and a full, true life. We do not yet know what real, true, free life looks like, but we do already know what repression is, and we know that repression should not exist. Anyone who starts from what is positive in his own present experiences of happiness, and extrapolates this into some future consummation, easily loses sight of reality and becomes a dreamer. What distinguishes Martin Luther King's 'I have a dream' from the daydreams cherished in the cosy religious corners of our churches is its determined negation. If we are realistic, we always experience what is positive first of all from the determined negation of what has been experienced as negative. The eschatological visions of the future in Jewish and Christian tradition are strong in their determined negation of the negative, and open in their development of the positive. This has to be so, for the future's sake. What is going to be? 'God will wipe away every tear from their eyes, and death shall be no more, neither shall there be mourning nor crying nor pain any more' (Rev. 21.4). About this positive condition, all we are told is: 'They shall be his people, and he himself, God with them, shall be their God . . . And he who sat upon the throne said, "Behold, I make all things new" ' (21.3, 5).

Because only positive experiences can show the negative that has been suffered to be clearly and obviously negative, what is positive can at present be described only through a determined negation of the negative. But the negation of the negative, for its part, presupposes the positive position that has been experienced. For nothing positive emerges of itself simply from the mere negation of the negative, since no positive conclusions can be deduced from negative premises.

The determined negation of the negative is the reason why present experiences of the Spirit are by no means expressed merely in exhuberant jubilation over the future of salvation that has already dawned. These experiences issue just as much, and simultaneously, out of the depths of the sighs over this unredeemed world. God's Spirit is experienced as impelling and consoling when it leads to prayer, sighs, lamentation and complaint before God: 'prayer always remains the voice of all those who apparently have no voice – and in this voice there always echoes that "loud cry" attributed to Christ by the Letter to the Hebrews (5.7).'[32] When people are reduced to silence, under humiliation and persecution, it is often only prayer that keeps their hope alive, so that they do not give themselves up. For praying, sighing, complaining, and crying out for God are not religious gifts or performances. They are the realistic expressions of the abyss into which people have fallen, or have put themselves, and which they discover in their own hearts. Wherever the cry from the depths is heard, the Spirit who 'helps us in our weakness' is present. When in our torment we ourselves fall dumb, the Spirit is there too, interceding for us 'with sighs too deep for words' (Rom. 8.26), We can even say that the cry for the advocacy of the Spirit is itself the Spirit's own cry. The sighs of fettered creation are taken up by the sighs of the Spirit who dwells in it, and are brought before God. The cry for God is itself divine. Inherent in human yearning for God is the power with which God draws human beings to himself. What the liturgy calls the 'invocation of the Holy Spirit', the *epiklesis*, is in the reality of this world identical with the cry *de profundis* which we find in Ps. 130.1: 'Out of the depths I cry to thee, O Lord.'

There is a cry from the depths at the beginning of every experience of God-given salvation: the cry of Israel's tormented people out of its slavery in Egypt (Ex. 3.7); Christ's death-cry on the Roman cross (Mark 15.34). And God hears the cry from the depths of desolation. He leads his people out of oppression into the land of liberty. He leads his Christ out of death into the eternal life of the new creation. So today the cries of the oppressed people and the dumb silence of the dying children in the Third World rise up to God. They are the sighs of the Spirit. So from the ruined nature of our earth the sighs of the created beings oppressed and exploited by human beings rise up to God. They are the sighs of the Spirit. Christianity's *epiklesis* of the Holy Spirit is related to these cries of the Spirit from the depths, and it must take them up; for it is the one same Spirit who interpenetrates the depths of all creation and the depths of the Godhead.

PART TWO

LIFE IN THE SPIRIT

In the next seven chapters we shall essentially be considering what early Protestant dogmatics called the *ordo salutis* – the order, or way, of salvation. Following 'Christ's threefold office' as prophet, priest and king, the grace of the Holy Spirit was presented in the subjective appropriation of the salvation objectively brought about by Christ. Under the heading *De gratia Spiritus Sancti applicatrice*, the following topics were treated, in an ingenious if not always felicitous sequence: faith, justification, calling, illumination, regeneration, mystical union, renewal and good works.[1] Of course these were not meant as stages in the growth of salvation; so the sequence was also presented in a different form. In Reformed dogmatics, everything began with election, which becomes efficacious in a person's calling. Election was followed by the justification and sanctification of this life, which issues in good works. Perfecting was expected in the glorification following the resurrection of the dead.[2]

More important than the sequence is the description of the work of the Holy Spirit. Because in Protestantism Christ's redemptive work was seen one-sidedly in his death on the cross, and only rarely also in his resurrection, his present lordship and his parousia still to come, this redemptive work could be objectivized: on the cross Christ *accomplished* salvation, but did not confer it. It was only in the appropriating work of the Holy Spirit that salvation was actually *conferred*, by way of word and sacrament. The objectification of christology made this subjectification of pneumatology necessary. Christology and pneumatology together then *added up* to soteriology. The objectification of Protestant theology positively cried out for the complement offered by Pietist or Enlightened subjectivism.[3]

But in chapter III we assumed that there is a *reciprocal relationship* between the Spirit and Christ, and by way of this reciprocal relationship we shall now try to get beyond the traditional Protestant pattern, which simply adds together Christ and the Spirit, the objectivity of salvation and its subjective appropriation.

Since in the volume on christology we defined the experiences of the Spirit christologically,[4] in the pneumatology we shall define the fellowship of Christ pneumatologically. What the christology presented as 'the discipleship of Jesus' must be seen in our present context as 'life in the Holy Spirit'. I shall not restrict the experiences of the Spirit to experiences of 'the Spirit of Christ', which is to say Christ's efficacy in and among us. I shall also include in the experiences of the Spirit experience of 'the Spirit of the Father', and that means taking in perceptions of the Spirit of creation in the *kairos* of history.

Finally, remembering the relations of the Spirit to the Son and the Father, we shall stress the Spirit's relational independence: the eternal Spirit is *the divine wellspring of life* – the source of life created, life preserved and life daily renewed, and finally the source of the eternal life of all created being. I have therefore developed an *ordo salutis* which is entirely aligned towards *the concept of life*; and I shall treat the liberation and the justification of life, life's regeneration and endowment, as well as its development, in the living space of the Spirit, so as finally to describe mystical experiences of our life in God and God's life in us.

Of course these are not stages in the experience of the Spirit. They are different aspects of the one single gift of the Holy Spirit, although in terms of time we can certainly discover these aspects successively.

IV

The Spirit of Life

§1 SPIRITUALITY OR VITALITY?

1. The word spirituality is derived from the French 'spiritualité', and
has only come into vogue in its present sense quite recently, in the
course of ecumenical exchange between the denominations.[1] What
does it mean, and to what misunderstandings can it lead? It means
more than 'religiousness', since that word is used rather for the
(religious) feeling (or need) of men and women for something 'higher'
than themselves. Nor does it merely mean 'devotionalism', or what
used to be described as 'piety', although spirituality includes what
those words denote, in the sense of the inward or subjective side of
religion. Literally, spirituality means life in God's Spirit, and a
living relationship with God's Spirit. Talk about Eastern or African
spirituality unfortunately blurs this precise sense of the word and
reduces it again to 'religiousness'. In a strictly Christian sense, the
word has to mean what Paul calls the new life ἐν πνεύματι. But
in saying this we already find ourselves involved in the complex
hermeneutics of linguistic history. For when we are talking about the
Spirit, what remains the same, and what do we lose in meaning, when
we cease to speak of Yahweh's *ruach*, and talk instead about the
πνεῦμα τοῦ θεοῦ, and then the *Spiritus Sanctus*, and the Holy
Spirit, thus arriving at what we today call 'spirituality'? We are at
least no longer at the source, as anyone who reads and loves the Old
Testament can immediately see. We have in fact moved from the
vitality of a creative life *out of* God to the *spirituality* of a not-of-
this-world life *in* God. What are the differences?

When we hear the word 'spirituality', we do not merely think about the history of the word. We also remember tangible figures and ways of living. The experience of nuns and monks who renounce 'life in the world' counts as spiritual. 'Spirituality' takes its colour from people who are in 'holy orders', or belong to 'the spiritual estate', celibates and men and women vowed to poverty, who for their 'way of perfection' feel bound to the evangelical counsels – that is, the Sermon on the Mount. Their special, inward experiences of God are often linked with asceticism, with the lesser and greater fasts, and with quiet times of meditation and contemplation. If these people and groups determine what we call 'spirituality', this means that a clear line divides spirituality from everyday life. The clergy are one thing, the laity another, men and women in the religious orders are set over against Christians living in the world, the evangelical virtues are contrasted with the civic virtues of society. People then like to contrast spiritual experiences with sensory ones. Whatever is spiritual and 'not of the flesh' is higher than what is bodily and sensuous. The one is inward, the other external, the one profound, the other superficial, the one reflective, the other thoughtless. *Soul-searching* takes the place of practical *conversion*. But that means that this kind of spirituality introduces an antithesis which splits life into two, and quenches its vitality.

Is this biblical? We find nothing of this kind in the Old Testament or Judaism. There, God's Spirit is the life-force of created beings, and the living space in which they can grow and develop their potentialities. God's blessing does not quench vitality. It enhances it. The nearness of God makes life once more worth loving, not something to be despised. We do not find anything comparable in the New Testament or Christianity's original messianism either. There God's Spirit is the life-force of the resurrection which, starting from Easter, is 'poured out on all flesh' in order to make it eternally alive. In the tempest of the divine Spirit of life, the final springtime of creation begins, and the men and women who already experience it here and now sense that life has come alive again and is worth loving. The sick, frail and mortal body becomes 'the temple of the Holy Spirit'. 'The body is meant for the Lord, and the Lord for the body', proclaimed Paul (I Cor. 6.13). 'Glorify God in your body', he demanded. It wasn't Paul who talked about 'God and the soul'. It was Augustine; and he did so in order to leave the body, nature and society behind him so that he could 'separate himself from this world'.

So what has happened? How did we move away from the *vitality* of a life lived out of God to the *spirituality* of a 'not of this world' life in God? Can we turn back again and rediscover the origin of the Spirit which makes us free to live?

Before we go into the various conflicts into which 'spirituality' and 'vitality' take us, we must clarify the meaning of the word *vitality* too. In Germany this term acquired a new meaning in the framework of the late bourgeois cultural revolution before the First World War. This revolution was characterized by 'the youth movement', *art nouveau* (the style known in Germany as *Jugendstil*), health stores, the rediscovery of 'the natural life', and the 'philosophies of life' that were in line with these things.[2] In the industrial world of bourgeois society, life was ordered according to that world's purposes and goals, and was judged according to utilitarian values. In these reform movements, life was considered good, right and beautiful simply for its own sake. 'To be here is glorious', said Rilke. What Bergson called the *élan vital* makes life inherently creative. Life that wants to live is innocent. 'The philosophy of life' always started from the struggle against the prevailing morality, which breaks the drive to live and spoils people's joy in living. The liberation of life from the iron grip of morality, and the intensification of life in 'the will to power', was the message of Nietzsche's *Zarathustra*. The moral instrumentalization of life was to be replaced by life's free intensification, by way of its creative expression.

This was the way theologians understood vitalism too. In his *Ethics*, Dietrich Bonhoeffer restored the category of 'the natural'. 'Natural life is life that is given form. What is natural is the Gestalt which indwells life itself and ministers to it.'[3] In order to define this category more closely, Bonhoeffer rejected both the mechanization which lends life a merely relative value, as the means to an end, and the vitalism which makes life an absolute end in itself. Instead he interpreted natural life as the equilibrium between life's rights and its duties, seeing life theologically both as a creaturely end in itself, and as a means to the end of the kingdom of God.

Paul Tillich, who was quite closely associated with this late bourgeois cultural revolution, linked vitality with what he called 'the courage to be'. In the language of biology, vitality means 'the mastery of being'.[4] But as a cultural and political movement, 'vitalism' is a will to power which holds all spiritual and moral values in contempt. Fascism and National Socialism justified their brutality with these very ideas. Tillich therefore tried to see true vitality as something that was neither an end in itself nor a means to an end, by letting 'the power of life' mean something similar to 'intentionality of living'. 'Vitality is the power to transcend oneself without losing oneself.'[5] This enabled him to make the following distinction: 'Vitalism as what divides the vital from the intentional inevitably re-introduces the barbaric as ideal of courage.'[6] On the other hand the intellectualization of the intentional leads to loss of vitality. Vitality vacant of meaning on the one hand and bloodless intellectualism on the other split human beings in two.

Here we shall interpret vitality as *love of life*. This love of life links human beings with all other living things, which are not merely alive but want to live. And yet it challenges human beings in their strange liberty towards life; for life which can be deliberately denied, has to be affirmed before it can be lived. Love for life says 'yes' to life in spite of its sicknesses, handicaps and infirmities, and opens the door to a 'life against death'.[7] Born out of love for life, this vitality is nothing other than true humanity, so it has nothing to do with the health idols of late bourgeois society, where 'vitality' is worshipped as 'the capacity for performance'. It is fear that the sense for true life may vanish that makes modern men and women reach out for products which promise to increase their vitality. Today, the living vigour which springs from a love for life has not only to be defended again the petrifications of life in the routines of technological society. It has to be safe-guarded against the pathogenic health cult of our modern meritocracies too.

§2 THE CONFLICT BETWEEN THE 'SPIRIT' AND THE 'FLESH'

In his anthropology Paul is an apocalyptist, and in his apocalyptic he is an anthropologist. He starts from the universal conflict between *the coming age* or aeon of life, righteousness and justice, and *the transitory age* or aeon of sin and death; but he presents this conflict in mainly anthropological terms as a struggle in the human being between 'the spirit' and 'the flesh'. If we follow Bultmann's existential interpretation of the two terms, we shall have to do so critically, remaining aware of the apocalyptic dimensions of this conflict in men and women. Bultmann rightly starts from the assumption that sin is rebellion against God, 'who as Creator is the origin of life and whose commandment is a "commandment unto life" '.[8] This means that the person who fails to find God loses the source of his own life, acts against the 'commandment unto life', and so instead of finding life, finds death instead. Anyone who turns away from the living God and relies on created things, deifies these things and himself, and in so doing destroys both himself and them. We might pursue this interpretation further and say that sin is trust in God that has become deranged, and a love of God that has miscarried. Trust is placed in what is non-divine instead of in God, and this turns what is not-God into an idol. Love is directed towards things that are not divine, overtaxing them and destroying their finite and transitory beauty. And in the process the lover is himself destroyed.

For Paul, flesh ($\sigma\acute{\alpha}\varrho\xi$) means a number of different things:

(*a*) It is *the sphere of the created world*. It is finite, frail and transitory. 'All flesh' can mean 'everyone' and also 'everything living', which wants to live and yet has to die. When Paul is thinking about the eternity of God, flesh is the world of created finitude in all its transience. Anyone who depends alone on what is flesh is left alone by God. He himself will pass away like the flesh to which he trusts. In this sense 'flesh' means the same as 'cosmos',[9] for a human being is part of this transitory world. What he experiences in himself he experiences in other living things too. Like all created earthly things, human beings are fleeting, subject to 'futility' (Ps. 90). 'Flesh' is both a cosmological and an anthropological term.

(*b*) It is also *the sphere of the transitory time of this world*. When Paul uses the phrase '$\dot{\varepsilon}\nu$ $\sigma\alpha\varrho\varkappa\acute{\iota}$', in the flesh, he is contrasting flesh with life '$\dot{\varepsilon}\nu$ $\pi\nu\varepsilon\acute{\upsilon}\mu\alpha\tau\iota$' – life in the Spirit – and is talking apocalyptically. Life in the flesh is false life, life that has missed its way, life that cannot live and leads to death. Life in the Spirit is the very opposite. It is true life, life springing up from its divine source, life that leads to resurrection. This gives particular emphasis to the sphere of the flesh as the sphere of sinning, and the sphere too of death because of sin.[10] It is not a question of an ontologically lower rung on the ladder of being, compared with the higher rung of the soul or spirit. What is meant is sin and death as a field of force into which the whole person has entered, body and soul, together with his whole social world. 'To set the mind on the flesh leads to death', says Paul in Rom. 8.6. We can turn this round, and say that whatever leads to death is 'fleshly'. Rom. 7.14 does not read, in the sense of (*a*): 'I am fleshly sold under sin', but 'I am fleshly, sold under sin', in the sense of (*b*).[11] Here 'flesh' is a total statement about human beings, and must not be restricted to their physical nature. The sin which misses the mark of life is not centred in sensuality, the drives, or so-called lower instincts. Its centre is the whole person, and especially that person's soul or heart, the centre of his consciousness, or of his will if he is possessed by the death instinct.

(c) 'Flesh' can also mean *the world-time of sin, injustice and death*. Paul also brings out this idea by using the phrase κατὰ σάρκα, according to the flesh. When this phrase qualifies a substantive, it can mean sphere (a) – the sphere of the natural and transitory (Israel κατὰ σάρκα, Christ κατὰ σάρκα, etc.). But when it qualifies a verb it has the sense of (b) and describes certain ways of acting and behaving as being sinful and erring.[12] Bultmann interprets this ambiguity anthropologically, taking it to mean that 'The sinful has its origin in "flesh" in the sense that the conduct or attitude that is directed by the "flesh", and takes "flesh" for its norm, is sinful.'[13] If we set aside his fear of mythology, we may put it as follows: in the coming of the Spirit of the resurrection of the dead and in the power of the new creation of all things, this world is revealed as a world of death which has failed to find God and itself. Transitory time and the mortality of all the living was hitherto held to be the 'natural' condition of created things, because there was no alternative; but this condition now emerges as sick. In the daybreak colours of their new creation, all things are revealed in their 'sickness unto death'. Once there is reason to hope for the world's redemption, that world ceases to be seen as natural and finite. It can now be perceived as an unredeemed world. Out of the general transience of things, unredeemed creation can be heard 'sighing and groaning' for its liberation. If redemption is as near as Jesus proclaimed the kingdom of God to be, then the chains to which living things had hitherto resigned themselves begin to hurt. But this means that it is the new life 'in the Spirit' and 'out of the Spirit' that manifests what 'flesh' really is.

When Paul sees 'flesh', 'sin' and 'death' as supra-personal forces which enslave people, destroy their world, and make the whole creation beyond the world of human beings 'groan', this is not a matter of unenlightened mythology. It is apocalyptic realism. The greater the hope, the more profound the exposure of misery. When in Romans 7 Paul talks about sin as if it is a personified power, he is not merely saying that the person enslaved by sin has surrendered to it his existence as determining subject.[14] He is also saying that sin rules – and rules universally – the time of this whole world. The conflict only begins when the new aeon dawns in the midst of this one, making the time of this world the old aeon that is passing away. For Paul and for all the early Christians, this has already happened with the resurrection of Christ from the dead, and with the outpouring of the life-force of the Spirit on believers. Ever since then, the light of the new day has been fighting against the darkness of the night that is drawing to its close (Rom. 13.12). In men and women this universal struggle takes the form of the conflict between the Spirit's drive for life and sin's death-drive. 'If the Spirit is thus detected to be *the feeling for life*, it emerges as the Spirit that contradicts the existence that is dead and threatening.'[15]

The conflict between 'spirit' and 'flesh' in human beings is simply the anthropological spearhead of the universal apocalyptic, which says that 'this world is passing away' because the new creation of everything has already begun with Christ's resurrection from the dead. This means that we shall be redeemed *with* the world, not *from* it. Christian experience of the Spirit does not cut us off from the world. The more we hope for the world, the deeper our solidarity with its sighing and suffering.

§3 THE GNOSTIC MISUNDERSTANDING OF THE APOCALYPTIC CONFLICT

In the degree to which Christianity cut itself off from its Hebrew roots and acquired Hellenistic and Roman form, it lost its eschatological hope and surrendered its apocalyptic alternative to 'this world' of violence and death. It merged into late antiquity's gnostic religion of redemption. From Justin onwards, most of the Fathers revered Plato as a 'Christian before Christ' and extolled his feeling for the divine transcendence and for the values of the spiritual world. God's eternity now took the place of God's future, heaven replaced the coming kingdom, the spirit that redeems the soul from the body supplanted the Spirit as 'the well of life', the immortality of the soul displaced the resurrection of the body, and the yearning for another world became a substitute for changing this one. As redemption was spiritualized, 'the realm of the flesh' was correspondingly reduced to the body and its earthly drives and needs. People ceased to hope for 'the redemption of the body' (Rom. 8.23) in 'the resurrection of the flesh' (the down-to-earth phrase used in the German version of the

Apostles' creed). They now hoped for the soul's final deliverance *from* the body, with what Marcion described as its 'toilsome' nourishment, its 'painful' reproduction system, and its 'miserable' death. It was now no longer the raising of life that was celebrated as the festival of redemption; it was death.

In the world of late antiquity, Christianity encountered the Platonic dualism of soul and body in the form of the gnostic contempt for the body, and its other-worldly longing for redemption. The soul, condemned to life-long incarceration in the body, yearns to be freed from this prison. It does not long for the prison to be changed into a home in which it likes to live. In this gnostic form, the Christian hope no longer gazes forward to a future when everything will be created anew. It looks upwards, to the soul's escape from the body and from this earth, into the heaven of blessed spirits.

All the Greek and Latin Fathers had to fight against this contemporary gnostic religiosity, and most of them succumbed to it, developing a Christian spirituality which went half-way to meet these religious requirements. Right down to our own time, the Platonic time-eternity dualism has pushed out the apocalyptic conflict between past and future, and put it out of commission. As a result, the dualism of body and soul has continually repressed and abolished the conflict between the death-drive and the drive for life. And this is so even today. But the consequence is that a spirituality more or less mildly hostile to the body, a spirituality non-sensuous, unwordly and non-political – a gnostic spirituality, in fact – replaces the original Jewish and Christian vitality of life reborn out of the creative God. 'The lusts of the flesh' are still identified with bodily needs, although it is obvious that the death-drives of this world are to be found in the covetousness and greed for power of the godless, self-deifying souls of modern men and women, rather than in their bodies, which are hardly capable of the great passions at all any more. The bodily life of human beings is still 'spiritually' disciplined and regemented, although the self-righteousness and self-conceit that triumph in this self-mastery and self-abasement are patent enough.

It is in Augustine that we find the theological and anthropological basis for Western spirituality. The concentration of his theology on 'God and the soul'[16] led to a devaluation of the body and nature, to a preference for inward, direct self-experience as a way to God, and to a neglect of sensuous experiences of sociality and nature. Knowledge of the self is a more certain affair than knowledge of the world. 'Close the gateways of thy senses and seek God deep within', wrote Gerhard Tersteegen.[17] Human beings are *related* to themselves, yet at the same time they are *withdrawn* from themselves. In their souls they find their *immanent transcendence*. 'Infinitely does man transcend man', said Pascal, in true Augustinian fashion.[18] Augustine calls this inner self 'the heart' or 'the soul'. 'Our hearts are restless till they find rest in Thee', he writes in his *Confessions*, for 'Thou hast made us for thyself'.[19]

This spiritual self-transcendence in the direction of the infinite God means that the innermost nature of the human being is desire, and nothing but desire. Men and women are by nature on the search for happiness, but nothing finite can satisfy their infinite yearning. So everything finite points to the unending craving of the human heart, which reaches out beyond itself to the infinite God.[20] Human beings are erotic beings, but their eros can never be satisfied in the world because their lodestone is the *summum bonum* as their *eidos*. If, now, this hunger of the human heart for God loses sight of God, then the *aversio a Deo* brings about a *conversio ad inferiora*: having turned away from God, the heart turns to something less. The soul that is on the search for God divinizes the finite beauty of transitory things, and through its immoderacy overtaxes and destroys them. If the seeking soul thinks that what is transitory is God, then it begins to be afraid that these transitory things will not live up to what it expects of them, and this fear in its turn evokes hate of the things and hate of the self – that is to say aggression.[21]

This enduring longing of the soul for God engenders the miscarried love for God which is called *concupiscentia*, and its consequences in the destructive lusts and the dreadly drives. Augustine saw these mainly in 'the lusts of the flesh', to which the soul becomes subject once it has lost God. That is the weakness of this theological anthropology. But he had the whole person in his sights too, and that is the strength of his psychology. The person who loses sight of God and puts something else in his heart instead of God becomes *homo incurvatus in se*, to use Luther's phrase – he becomes turned in on himself. A love for God that has miscarried makes people try despairingly to be themselves – or despairingly not to be themselves.[22]

Self-deification springs from *superbia, hybris*. People fall victim to what H. E. Richter called 'the God complex'.[23] They cannot let God be God. They have to make proud and unhappy gods out of themselves, because they are unable to accept their creatureliness, their frailty and their mortality.[24]

But self-destruction is also the outcome of the *tristitia* which is simply the reverse side of *superbia*. People no longer believe that they are capable of the things of which God thinks them capable. They do not make themselves greater than they are. They make themselves smaller and more unnoticeable. They do not want to fulfil themselves. They want to get rid of themselves. Self-overestimation and self-underestimation are generally very close to one another.

The love of God that has gone wrong manifests itself in both *hybris* and *tristesse*. The first tends to be a masculine form of unhappy love for God; the second is more often the feminine form of the same unhappiness.

Augustine's solution of the problem is his teaching about the redemption of the restless heart: 'Tota vita christiani boni sanctum desiderium est' – the whole life of the good Christian is holy desire.[25] If the soul directs its striving and searching wholly towards the God beyond, this leads to the deliverance of the human soul and the world surrounding it. Nothing earthly must impede the soul on its pilgrimage through this finite life to its eternal home in God. Nothing must suffice it. It must 'leave behind' everything and 'divest' itself of everything, and must endure its unrest in this world until the fulfilment of the world beyond. Then things will once again be what they truly are, and will no longer be overtaxed by the human soul's hunger for God. And then human beings will also be able to accept themselves with love and humour as finite and transitory creatures, without either *hybris* or *tristesse*.

The mediaeval mysticism that followed Augustine's anthropological theology drew on his psychology in delineating the soul's ways of meditation on the path to God. Bernard of Clairvaux saw before him a spiritual ladder leading up to God, on which the soul progressed from love of its neighbour to love of itself, and from self-love to the love of God.[26] Bonaventure drew up the *itinerarium mentis ad Deum*, the mind's journey to God. Teresa of Avila found the way into the 'castillo interior', the castle of the soul, by way of seven steps.[27] For our own time, Thomas Merton wrote a book about 'the seven storey mountain'.[28] Dorothee Sölle set out with Meister Eckhart on 'the inward road'.[29] These journeys into the interior mystery of the individual soul as a way of arriving at God have put a profound impress on Western spirituality. And in our present context two fundamental theological ideas are important here.

1. At its apex, the human soul attains to the divine essence. For at its apex, or innermost chamber, is hidden that for which God has created it: the *imago Dei*. This is the created mirror in which God perceives himself. It is also the mirror in which the soul can perceive God. 'Know thyself, for thou art my image, and thus wilt thou know me, whose image thou art, and wilt find me in thyself.'[30] Those who penetrate this seventh chamber of the soul see God as they are seen by him. This mutual knowing between God and the soul is also called the soul's 'mystical bridal' with God.

2. The desire of the soul in its search for God is only the reverse, human side of God's love in his search for men and women. The soul's self-transcendence reflects God's Spirit-immanence in the soul. People *seek* God because God *draws* people to him. These are the first experiences of God's Spirit in the human being. We should not search for God if God did not draw us to him. And God draws souls to himself in the way that perfect beauty draws the eros, or as a magnet attracts iron filings. Men and women feel what Tersteegen calls 'the gentle, inward tug of God's love' in their hunger for life and their search for happiness, which nothing on earth can satisfy and still.

> From the best bliss that earth imparts
>   We turn unfilled to thee again

wrote Bernard.[31]

Western mysticism of the soul takes its stamp from Augustine, and has in its turn put its own impress on the western psyche and western psychology. But this mysticism has also led to the repression of the body and to nature's subjection to the dominance of the human mind. It generated western individualism, for which the values of the human person take precedence over the values of human sociality. If in tracing the theological premises for western mysticism and spirituality we go back to their biblical roots – and that means their roots in Old Testament and Hebrew thinking too – what difference will this make to spirituality? How will it change?

§4 NEW VITALITY: LIFE AGAINST DEATH

(*a*) According to biblical ideas, it is not the soul of the individual person, detached from the body, which is *imago Dei*, God's image. *Imago Dei* are men and women in their wholeness, in their full, sexually specific community with one another, for 'male and female he created them' (Gen. 1.27). If we keep the image of the mirror, this then tells us that God is not perceived and known in the innermost chamber of the heart, or at the solitary apex of the human soul – the places where human beings perceive and know themselves. He is known in the true human community of women and men, parents and children. And if this is so, then the place for the experience of God is not the mystical experience of the self; it is *the social experience of the self* and *the personal experience of sociality*. The individual soul, detached from the body and isolated from the community, must first of all again become 'in-corporated' and socialized, before it can know God as God himself knows the soul. There is no mysticism of the soul without the mysticism of sociality. It is only the spirituality of the body and the spirituality of sociality or fellowship which realize, or 'embody', what the Fathers of the church again and again tried to assert, with all possible emphasis, in opposition to the Platonism of the cultured, and the gnosticism of the common people: the expectation of 'the resurrection of the body'. 'By nature man remains wholly human in soul and body, but by grace he becomes wholly God both in his soul and in his body', said Maximus Confessor; for – according to the Orthodox mysticism of Gregory Palamas – the light that shone on Tabor transfigured Jesus' body and his clothing as well as his soul, and was a visible anticipation of the 'transfigured body' of the risen Christ, to which our bodies are to be conformed (Phil. 3.21).

The spirituality corresponding to this fundamental concept cannot be directed to the suppression of the body, and the detachment of the soul from the body. It must point towards 'the transfiguration of the body'. But what does the transfiguration of the body mean in this life?

(*b*) The inward experience of God's Spirit as it draws the soul in its search for God cannot have God himself and his essential eternity as its goal. That would mean the dissolution of the finite soul in God's infinity. The Spirit of God is the Spirit of Christ, and is as such *the Spirit of the resurrection of the dead*. The Spirit of the Father and the Son is the divine quickening power of the new creation of all things, the power empowering the rebirth of everything that lives. The light in which the risen Christ appeared to the women and the disciples was not interpreted as what a German hymn calls the 'radiant dawn of eternity'. It was understood as the light shining on the first day of the new creation. The attractive power and inner force of the Spirit of the new creation of all things are not orientated towards 'the world beyond'. Their direction is the future. The Spirit does not draw the soul away from the body, nor does it make the soul hasten towards heaven, leaving this earth behind. It places the whole earthly and bodily person in the daybreak colours of the new earth. That is why Paul can also describe the raising of the dead as 'giving life to our mortal bodies' (Rom. 8.11). Anyone who experiences the Spirit of the new creation in fellowship with the risen Christ already experiences here and now something of the 'life given' to his mortal, sick and repressed body. If hope looks forward to the final spring-time of the whole creation, then in the Spirit the charismatic quickening of one's own body is already experienced even now. In the experience of the Spirit, the spring of life begins to flow in us again. We begin to flower and become fruitful. An undreamt-of love for life awakens in us, driving out the bacillus of resignation, and healing painful remembrances. We go to meet life expecting the rebirth of everything that lives, and with this expectation we experience our own rebirth, and the rebirth we share with everything else.

If according to the Christian hope 'the transfiguration of the body' consists of the raising from death to eternal life, then it is already experienced here and now in the Spirit of life, which interpenetrates body and soul and wakens all our vital powers. Eternal love transfigures the body. As 'love's body', the body comes alive, receiving and giving life.[32]

The spirituality which matches the idea of creation will therefore be directed towards *the liberation of the body* from the repressions imposed by the soul, and the suppressions of morality, and the humiliations caused by self-hate. That is to say, its direction will be the liberation of the body for its true health. If from this standpoint we look back self-critically at traditional ascetic practices, such as fasting and meditation, we shall find that many of them are not mortifications hostile to the body at all. They are rather ways of freeing and releasing the body from its exploitation through work, and its nervous tensions. In the Old Testament, this recovery of health of body belongs to the laws about the sabbath. We can see this from Isa. 58:

> This is a fasting that I choose:
> loose the bonds that you have wrongly imposed,
> undo the thongs of the yoke,
> let what you have oppressed go free
> and break every yoke,
> share your bread with the hungry . . .
> Then shall your light break forth like the dawn . . .
> and the glory of the Lord shall be your rear guard.
>
> (Isa. 58.6–8)

The weekly sabbath and the recurring sabbath years are the biblical foundations for the spirituality of the body and the spirituality of the earth, without which there can be no spirituality of the soul that gives health and life.[33] After six days of work, human beings and animals are meant to find rest, and are not to intervene in nature, so that everything can recover its strength, and so that nature may again be seen and acknowledged as God's creation. The pulse of life is found in the rhythms of the times and in the alternation between work and rest. Mind and soul must cease to be concentrated on will and reason, and must relax their tension. On this day of rest, the Spirit can again return to the body which it had made its instrument during the working days. According to the biblical understanding, the holy of holies of God's silent presence is not to be discovered in a separated space, either an outward space on earth, or the inward space of the soul. It is to be found in the sabbath rhythm of the times. When 'Queen Sabbath' enters Jewish and Christian homes, the Shekinah dwelling in God's people is reunited with the eternal God. 'Holy spaces', whether in the countryside or the innermost regions of the soul, are shut off by the *temenos*. But the 'sacred time' of the sabbath is meant for everything that lives, and is given to the bodies of all human beings just as much as to every soul.

What we find in Israel is not some special mysticism of the soul. It is *the sabbath mysticism* for everything living. The sabbath year recurring every seven years is meant for both the people and the earth. According to Ex. 23.10–11, in every seventh year Israel is commanded to leave the ground uncultivated 'so that the poor of your people may eat': 'Share your bread with the hungry.' Debts are to be remitted and slavery for debt is to be ended, so that God's justice may be restored among the people of the covenant. According to Lev. 25.1–7, God's earth is to remain uncultivated every seventh year as 'a sabbath of solemn rest for the land, a sabbath to the Lord', when the land can recover its strength. Here the reason is ecological, no longer merely social. If the weekly sabbath and the sabbath years are the form taken by Israel's spirituality, then we have to see the resting earth which celebrates the God of its sabbaths as *the spirituality of the earth*. The land breathes again, and comes to itself once more, and is respected in its dignity as God's creation. It is no longer weighed up and assessed according to its utility for human beings.

The constant disciplining and repression of the body which modern industrial society requires of its members, and the constant subjection and exploitation of the earth which that society pursues, make human beings numb and the earth infertile. Because the end will be the death of human beings and their replacement by machines, and because ecological death waits at the end of nature, these trends in modern society can be described with total accuracy as death-drives. In the rebellions of the body and the earth we can today see among created things signs of the will to live. In this world, with its modern 'sickness unto death', true spirituality will be the restoration of the love for life – that is to say, *vitality*. The full and unreserved 'yes' to life, and the full and unreserved love for the living are the first experiences of God's Spirit, which is not for nothing called *fons vitae*, 'the well of life'. If we wish to resist the cynical annihilation of what is alive in the world of human beings and nature, we must first of all resist in ourselves the tendency to grow accustomed to this annihilation. It is not merely mass death that is so frightful. It is even more the fact that people have gradually got used to it, and have become callous towards the suffering of the victims. The spirituality of life breaks through this inward numbness, the armour of our indifference, the barriers of our insensitivity to pain. It again breaks open 'the well of life' in us and among us, so that we can weep again and laugh again and love again.

The spirituality of life inevitably conflicts with the mysticism of death, which made the Fascist generals in Spain cry 'Viva la muerte!' The stronger the will for life, the fiercer the resistance of the death-drives. The more sensitive people are toward's life's happiness, the more they sense the pain of life's denials. Life in God's Spirit is *life against death*. It is not life against the body. It is life that brings the body's liberation and transfiguration. To say 'yes' to life means saying 'no' to war and its devastations. To say 'yes' to life means saying 'no' to poverty and its humiliations. There is no genuine affirmation of life in this world without the struggle against life's negations.

What do I love when I love God?

Augustine writes: (Confessions, X, 6, 8): 'But what do I love when I love you? Not the beauty of any body or the rhythm of time in its movement; not the radiance of light, so dear to our eyes; not the sweet melodies in the world of manifold sounds; not the perfume of flowers, ointments and spices; not manna and not honey; not the limbs so delightful to the body's embrace: it is none of these things that I love when I love my God. And yet when I love my God I do indeed love a light and a sound and a perfume and a food and an embrace – a light and sound and perfume and food and embrace in my inward self. There my soul is flooded with a radiance which no space can contain; there a music sounds which time never bears away; there I smell a perfume which no wind disperses; there I taste a food that no surfeit embitters; there is an embrace which no satiety severs. It is this that I love when I love my God.'

Answer: When I love God I love the beauty of bodies, the rhythm of movements, the shining of eyes, the embraces, the feelings, the scents, the sounds of all this protean creation. When I love you, my God, I want to embrace it all, for I love you with all my senses in the creations of your love. In all the things that encounter me, you are waiting for me.

For a long time I looked for you within myself, and crept into the shell of my soul, protecting myself with an armour of unapproachability. But you were outside – outside myself – and enticed me out of the narrowness of my heart into the broad place of love for life. So I came out of myself and found my soul in my senses, and my own self in others.

The experience of God deepens the experiences of life. It does not reduce them, for it awakens the unconditional Yes to life. The more I love God the more gladly I exist. The more immediately and wholly I exist, the more I sense the living God, the inexhaustible well of life, and life's eternity.

V

The Liberation for Life

§1 EXPERIENCE OF GOD AS EXPERIENCE OF LIBERATION: EXODUS AND RESURRECTION

According to the testimony of the Bible, people's first experience with God is the experience of an immense liberation – of being set free for life. The people whom the word of God calls forth and who are possessed by God's Spirit experience liberation in different sectors of their lives. Inwardly, their energies for living are freed from the obstructions of guilt and the melancholy of death. Outwardly, the compulsions of economic, political and cultural repression are broken. Inwardly life can be newly affirmed. Outwardly new free spaces for living open up.

For Israel, the experience of God and experiences of liberation are two aspects of the same thing. According to the first commandment (Ex. 20.2), God reveals himself to the people as 'the Lord' by leading them out of slavery into the promised land of liberty. Israel experienced God's 'lordship' as her liberation, and in the experience of her liberation had this unique experience of God. Through faith in Jesus the messiah, Christians have very much the same experience: 'Now the Lord is the Spirit, and where the Spirit of the Lord is, there is freedom' (II Cor. 3.17). In the Spirit, Christ is manifested as 'the Lord', and in the Spirit people experience what it is to be free. According to the experiences of Israel and according to the experiences of Christian faith, the experience of God and the experience of freedom are so deeply fused that they belong indissolubly together and become almost synonymous. It is true of both that 'He who loves liberty loves God', as Angelus Silesius said, and that whoever loves God loves liberty.[1]

To identify the Lord with liberation and his lordship with liberty is difficult for us today because of our own painful experiences. We are used to subordinating servants to the master, and to seeing the lordship of the one as the repression of the other. Moreover, to talk about God the Lord awakens patriarchal emotions in men and feelings of alienation in women. Neither feeling is acceptable, because neither is liberating. So it does not take us any further if we simply purify the terms 'lord' and 'lordship' from their misuse, and merely *define* them afresh.[2]

In order to say who 'God the Lord is', we have to *tell the stories* of what people have experienced, the experiences which made them call God 'Lord'. In the Old Testament it is the Exodus story. 'The God of Abraham, the God of Isaac and the God of Jacob' was not the God of the Pharaohs and the despots, the God who subjugates others. He was already the God who 'calls forth' and puts people on the free path of hope, so that they can see the fulfilment of his promises. He is not the idol of the slave-owners in Egypt or Babylon, who spread anxiety and terror.

Moses' experience of God on Mount Horeb (Ex. 3.1ff.) is the experience of the God who 'sees' the misery of his people and 'hears' their cries and who 'comes down' in order to lead them out of the land of slavery and fear into the liberty of the promised 'land flowing with milk and honey'. The mysterious name of this God is 'I will be who I will be' (Ex. 3.14), and his experienced presence brings the enslaved people deliverance into a free life. That is the reason he is called 'the Lord'. To say God is the Lord means: 'God is *the liberator*. So God's rule means the wide, *free space* he gives for the freedom of his people. God's power manifests itself in 'the strong arm' with which he delivers his people from slavery and saves them from their armed pursuers; so we can call it his *free power*. To believe in God means trusting his promise and his guidance, and experiencing one's own liberations. The people which emerged from the Exodus experience has therefore always acknowledged God's lordship and its own freedom in a single breath. At every Passover feast, Israel's succeeding generations have retrospectively experienced the way God leads his people out of slavery into freedom; and in this seminal experience of Israel's they have discovered that they themselves are the ones who have been liberated. To call God Lord, promises freedom, so in captivity people call on the Lord. Real experiences of liberation, inward and outward both, are interpreted as experiences of God, and are told as such.

According to the testimony of the New Testament too, the experiences of God which people have in the neighbourhood of Jesus and in fellowship with him are also experiences of freedom: deliverances from sicknesses and demonic possession, deliverances from social humiliation and insults, deliverances from the 'godless powers of this world'[3] and, as the Apostle Paul especially stresses, deliverances from the compulsions of sin and the power of death (Rom. 7 and 8). The God whom Jesus called 'Abba', and whom the church has therefore always called 'the Father of Jesus Christ', is not a God of tyrants and slave-owners. He has nothing whatsoever to do with Jupiter, the Roman father of the gods, although in the Roman empire after Constantine the Christian church attempted to fuse the two.[4] We can see who God 'the Father of Jesus Christ' is, solely from Jesus' experiences of God, and from people's experiences of the Spirit when they live in fellowship with Jesus: 'He who has seen me has seen the Father' (John 14.9). But the person who sees Jesus sees the one who was crucified in the name of the mighty gods of the *imperium Romanum*.

So who is this God of Jesus'? He is the healing power which Jesus brought to the poor and the sick, sinners and the dying. He is the God of the crucified Jesus, who was the victim of power. He is the liberating energy that raised Jesus from the dead and led him into eternal life. God is the one 'who raised Jesus from the dead': that is the New Testament's definition of God, according to one of the earliest Christian creeds (Rom. 10.9–10). The formulation noticeably parallels the phrase in the first commandment: God is the liberator – there from the power of one of history's tyrants, the Pharaoh, here from the tyrant over history, death; there he frees people for 'the land flowing with milk and honey', here for the new creation of all things for the eternal life in which death will be no more. There the experience of God is bound up with the Exodus experience, here with the experience of resurrection. In both cases, to believe God simply means getting up out of oppression and resignation, and laying hold of our freedom, and living. In every celebration of the Lord's supper Christ's people remember the way Christ took to death, and his raising from death; and in this future of Christ that is made present to them, they experience their own, immeasurable liberty: 'Where the Spirit of the Lord is, there is freedom' (II Cor. 3.17).

In both the Israelite and the Christian acknowledgment of God a singular distinction is made between 'God' and 'the Lord'. Israel knew 'the God of Abraham, the God of Isaac and the God of Jacob' from the traditions about the patriarchs. But 'Lord' as a name for God is evidently not connected with the patriarchs' experiences of God. It has to do with the Exodus event (Ex. 3.15). Ex. 6.2f. makes the same distinction: 'I am *the Lord.* I appeared to Abraham, to Isaac, and to Jacob as the almighty God, but by my name "Lord" I did not make myself known to them.'[5] The Christian creed we have already cited makes a corresponding distinction: 'If you confess with your lips that Jesus is *the Lord* and believe in your heart that *God* raised him from the dead, you will be saved.' This distinction says that in Jesus 'the Lord' is present – that is to say *the power of the Exodus,* and this is true of the Holy Spirit too when he is called 'the Lord' (II Cor. 3.17). But '*the God* of Abraham, Isaac and Jacob' is identified with 'the Father of Jesus Christ', and his almighty power is seen in the raising of Jesus from the dead. Of course the testimonies make it plain that it is the One God who is meant in every case, but a differentiation is nevertheless made, according to the different experiences of God.

The history of Christ and the history of the Spirit accordingly stand in continuity to Israel's *history with Yahweh,* 'the almighty God'; but 'the Father of Jesus Christ' is identified with *the God of the patriarchs.* For Israel, the Exodus history belongs in the wider framework of Abraham's history of promise, and this history of promise belongs in the wider framework of creation history. And in the New Testament the history of Christ and the Spirit belong similarly within the broader framework of the history of God the Father, to whom Christ is to 'hand over the kingdom' at the end of days, so that 'God may be all in all' (I Cor. 15.28); while this history of the Father's glorification belongs within the broader framework of the new creation of all things, for the kingdom of glory.

We have drawn attention to these inner distinctions in the experience of God which is called freedom, so that we may grasp the wider horizons and the free spaces of this event. For if we wish to comprehend the liberating experience of the Spirit, it is important for us to understand the Spirit as both 'the Spirit of Christ' and 'the Spirit of God'. 'No one can come to me unless the Father who sent me draws him', says the Johannine Christ (John 6.44; similarly 6.64). Faith then, according to this, comes into existence when God the Father and Jesus the Lord act together in the Spirit. How are we to interpret this?

The experience of freedom always springs from a coincidence of the liberating word and the proper time, the *kairos*. The divine word becomes the word that binds or looses when it is spoken as the right word at the right time in the right place. Then the word that comes from outside sets free the inner energies of faith, hope and love. We call these enfranchisements the *testimonium Spiritus Sancti internum*, the inward testimony of the Holy Spirit. The word effects in us what it promises. It goes 'through our hearts' (Acts 2.37) and we 'ponder it in our hearts' like Mary (Luke 2.19). The word 'happens'. But this is only one side of the event. The *kairos* of a historical situation, whether it be personal, social or political, opens up external potentialities too, just as it can of course also stifle potentialities.[6] As God's Spirit, the Spirit 'opens doors' which were shut before. That is, it throws open new chances and possibilities for the gospel. This is the Spirit of the One who created the world and guides its history by bearing and enduring its contradictions. Out of his hidden providence new possibilities develop where no one expected them. The person who waits for God is always ready for these surprises in personal, social and political life. For here Heraclitus's saying really does hold good: 'He who does not hope for what can never be hoped for, will never find it.'[7]

The 'Spirit of Christ' effects in us the raising of new energies through the word of the gospel. The 'Spirit of God' opens new possibilities round about us through the circumstances of history. If the workings of the Holy Spirit are seen only as the subjective operation of the objective word of God in the hearts of believers, they are being too narrowly defined. In the experienced reality of our lives the two work together and show themselves to be one – the Spirit of Christ and the Spirit of God, the word and the *kairos*, inward powers and outward possibilities.

To experience God is to experience freedom. Does this Jewish and Christian testimony meet the longings of men and women? Our natural attitude to freedom is usually ambivalent, for freedom in a world that isn't free is a perilous happiness. Of course men and women want to be free of their burdens and inward pressures, but many of them are afraid of the inevitable cost. Of course many people would generally speaking like to be independent, but some are afraid of the responsibility for their own lives which they would then have to assume. Many people are on the search for their own freedom, and discover that they are on the run *from* freedom at the same time.[8] We seek opportunities for free development, and yet we are simultaneously on the look-out for some sheltering security. We are not just people hungry for freedom. We are underlings looking for authority too. For us Germans at least, the trend to conformity is as strong as the feeling for freedom. Many people gladly take flight into a kindergarten mentality, quite content to be secure and safely provided for, and to make over their freedom to 'Big Brother' and 'Mother Church'. Protests against their authority and retreats behind their sheltering cloak are often not very far removed from one another. To lead a free, self-reliant and responsible life, with independent judgment and independent conviction, is a laborious happiness, and often enough a perilous one. This freedom can make people solitary, and when it comes down to rock bottom can even cost them their lives.

But it is not only freedom that has its risks. A life without freedom has them too. And there the risks are especially apt to take the form of resignation, and the renunciation of a life of one's own. People cease to be alive before they have ever lived. They make themselves small, and as unnoticeable as possible. From my own experience of a long period as a prisoner of war, from 1945–48, I can say that life without freedom has two special perils. We experience an outward hostility against which we can no longer defend ourselves, so we creep into our shells and protect ourselves against the hostile world outside through indifference and callousness. But by doing so we are blocking our own vital energies. Our self-esteem diminishes. We cease to believe that we are capable of anything. Moreover we come to terms with the barbed wire and the life of captivity. We fade unobtrusively into the background so as not to run into trouble. But this means becoming inwardly submissive. This submission then becomes dependence, and dependence makes us irresolute. Our lack of initiative develops into general apathy. We stop living. We just let ourselves be pushed around. When everything has then become a matter of indifference, we cease to be aware of the barbed wire. In both dangers, the danger of self-contempt and the danger of conformity, we lose our lives and give ourselves up for lost. But at moments when our will to live is kindled once more, and experiences which we call experiences of God awaken in us the hope for life, we begin to rebel against the apathy within us and the barbed wire round about us. We rub ourselves raw. We begin to suffer consciously, and to cry out. We become free. The sighs and cries of prisoners are always the first signs of life they show, and are anything but signs of death.

So we are faced with the alternative of being free and living dangerously, or renouncing a life of our own and being in bondage. And there can be no doubt about the decision to which we are challenged by the Bible's testimonies to experiences of God. The person who loves life loves liberty, and the person who loves liberty says 'yes' to his own life, in spite of all outward intimidations and all inward fears. True security is to be found, not in the renunciation of freedom but only in freedom's own foundation.

§2 THE MODERN ALTERNATIVE: GOD OR FREEDOM?

To identify God with freedom rouses protest from two opposite quarters in the countries of the Western world today. The conservatives are afraid of 'too much' freedom. They think it destroys the authority of the state, dissolves family ties, is a breach of the moral law, and drives people out of the church, so that what begins in the name of freedom always ends up in anarchy and chaos. This, at least, is what they are afraid of. Instead they maintain the authoritarian principle. Modern atheists, on the other hand, wish to keep 'God' out of freedom altogether. Either there is a God, they say, and then human beings are not free; or human beings are and should be free, and then there must not be a God. 'If there were no God everything would be permissible', postulated Dostoievsky anxiously. 'But everything is permissible, and human beings are entirely free, so there is no God': that was Jean Paul Sartre's reply.[9] Ernst Bloch carried this argument for atheism further still: 'Where the great lord of the world reigns, there is no room for liberty, not even for the liberty of the children of God.'[10] In his view, 'Liberty, equality and fraternity' is a vision that can be upheld only without God and contrary to the earthly authorities who reign 'by the grace of God'.[11]

Let us look first at the revolutionary principle of liberty and the conservative principle of authority as these have developed in modern European times, ever since the French Revolution, and then go on to see how these false alternatives have been got over in today's liberation theology.

1. The Revolutionary Principle of Freedom

The revolutionary principle of freedom became the ideological basis of the bourgeois world from the time of the American and French revolution onwards.[12] The old European clerical and feudal society was destroyed, and the egalitarian meritocracy took its place. Performance, not birth, decided a person's value and status. Popular sovereignty replaced the sovereignty of princes 'by divine right' or 'the grace of God'. Absolute monarchies gave way to the democratic constitutional state. Countries dominated by a single religion now became religiously neutral and in principle secular, church property being secularized in the process. Political democratization went hand in hand with industrialization in economics. The urbanization of the population created 'the secular city'.[13] As work-force and as consumers, everyone everywhere is in principle treated equally. Nationality, race, sex, religion, and all the other things that determine a person's identity recede behind these egalitarian categories, are privatized and restricted to personal life. The fundamental notions of liberty and equality are universal, and have been universal in their influence: once the bourgeoisie had built up a new class of property-owners, the proletariat took these ideas over. When the European countries proceeded to colonize the other nations, the oppressed peoples took up the same concepts, and fought for liberation in their name. The freeing of the slaves and the abolition of slavery dominated the first half of the nineteenth century. Since the middle of that century, the liberation of women from the disabilities imposed by a patriarchal civilization has been on the agenda. The revolution of freedom began with the French Revolution, and that revolution ushered in the revolutionary age in the history of humanity. Because freedom is indivisible and illimitable, the vision of freedom continually evokes ever new movements for liberation.

In the early European liberation movements, belief in God and the will to be free were connected. In his three postulates of 'practical reason' Kant listed 'God, freedom and immortality' in a single sequence, and makes them mutually justifying: without God no freedom, without freedom no God.[14] Hegel saw the meaning of world history in the realization of liberty, and interpreted the coming kingdom of God as 'the kingdom of freedom'.[15] 'The revolutionary wish to bring about liberty is the pivot of all progressive education, and the beginning of modern history', declared Friedrich Schlegel. Where belief in God went together with the messianic hope for the coming kingdom, the link with the political will to be free was forged automatically. Mazzini talked about 'the free church in a free state', Hegel about 'the religion of freedom' for 'the kingdom of freedom'. But where belief in God was tied to notions about authority and law, this alliance with freedom was never forged. It was especially difficult to link belief in God with the will to be free in the clerical churches, where the upper clergy were in league with feudalism. In these countries, especially in France and Italy, the movement for political freedom had to take anti-clerical and laicized form. That is why Catholic France saw the rise of the laicized atheism whose famous motto was 'ni Dieu – ni maître'. 'Neither God nor state', cried the anarchists in Orthodox and autocratic Russia too. Where the church and belief in God are on the side of the forces of repression, atheism is the only possible religious foundation for the will to be free. The struggle against religion and the people who represent it is then at the top of the agenda in the fight for freedom, for 'criticism of religion is the premise for all criticism'.[16]

Ever since, the visible symbol of the will of oppressed people to be free has not been 'the praying hands' of the churchly devout, which we see in Dürer's picture; it has been the clenched fists raised on the streets. Prometheus, who stole fire from the gods, became the revolution's saint, and drove out the figure of Christ. Now the alternative is 'God *or* freedom'. The argument is a simple one: if I believe in God I surrender my liberty and put myself under his protection. And this means that I will also acknowledge as God-given authorities the other powers-that-be, which look after me in family, state and church. But if I want to be free, I have to break all these fetters and cut loose from these securities, and take over my own life, and assume responsibility for myself. The only authority complete liberty recognizes is itself, because to acknowledge other authorities is always a matter of personal decision, and one must answer for it accordingly.

On the other hand, reaction against the age of revolutions generated the authoritarian principle: God – king – country. This became the slogan of the conservative counter-revolution. Here the phenomena of the modern world are not interpreted as messianic signs of the hope for freedom. They are viewed as apocalyptic tokens of the threatening end. The conservative option developed out of the Holy Alliance, with which Czar Nicholas I hoped to save Europe and Christendom. It was imposed on the German states by Prussia, in a counter move to the bourgeois revolution of 1848. The German Lutheran theologians Julius Friedrich Stahl and August Vilmar presented the religion of the state church as the only saving power that could heal 'the sickness of revolution' among the nations.[17] They depicted the revolution of freedom with the apocalyptic symbol of 'the beast from the abyss' and called it the Antichrist's rebellion straight from hell. In the struggle against the Antichrist and these forces of his, the state church was to be a bulwark for the state itself, and was supposed to act as a precursor of the returning Christ. On the Catholic side too similar apocalyptic pictures of history were painted, depicting the approach of the final struggle between the Red Dragon and the Mother of God with the Saviour Child. Abraham Kuyper, the Calvinist theologian and president of the Netherlands, set up 'Reformation against revolution', believing that popular sovereignty, liberalism, socialism and secularism heralded the approach of the chaos of the End-time, and extolling the Christian church as the one divine ordering dispensation which could sustain the state and provide the foundation for morality.[18]

The more vociferous the atheistic slogans in the liberation movements, the more vigorously the mainstream Christian churches promoted the conservative option. The development of democracy in politics, the growth of liberalism or socialism in economics, and the striving for equal rights in cultural life therefore always came up against the opposition of clergy, theologians and the churches. There is hardly a single movement of this kind which was not forced to make its way against ecclesiastical resistance.

Of course the revolutionary principle of freedom and the authoritarian principle have often enough split churches too, and have led to internal conflicts. We can see this even today in the relationship between the mainstream churches and the peace movement in Europe and the United States. We see it too in the relationship of the hierarchy to the *iglesia popular* in Latin America, where – in the name of that authoritarian trio 'God, family and country' – military dictatorships are religiously supported in opposition to the people and their strivings to be free.[19]

But are the intertwining threads of Christian history meant to be wrenched apart like this? Must belief in God go together with authority, while freedom is made over to atheism? If these are turned into opposing positions, faith in God is corrupted, because it loses its biblical and messianic foundation; and so is human freedom, because it loses its most vital driving power. Christians can only get over this false alternative 'God or freedom' if they become radicals and remember the experiences of their own roots – the God of the resurrection, and the Spirit of freedom. Why are the traditions about Israel's Exodus and Christ's resurrection not at the very centre of the Christian churches? Why do the pictures and religious imaginings of the divine majesty resemble earthly potentates rather than the crucified and risen Liberator? Surely these ideas about God's majesty are drawn from the Christian rulers of Byzantium, rather than from the radiance that streams from the face of Jesus Christ?

2. *Latin American Liberation Theology*

The liberation theology of Latin America is the first convincing outline to combine belief in God with the will to be free, as the biblical traditions enjoin.[20] Because of this, it has of course become involved in conflict with the conservative option we have already described, and has to make its way in opposition to the idols and values of that alliance between religion and conservative politics.[21] It can also to some extent find itself at variance with the religious feeling of the poverty-stricken, intimidated people themselves, who cling to the rituals of religious security and the cults of consolation, rather than to the prophetic visions of their own liberty.

The starting point of this theology is not theory but praxis – the praxis of the poor, who have to suffer most from violence and injustice because they cannot defend themselves, and who are crying out for liberation. An alien praxis determines the people's historical situation, and only a new praxis of their own can lead them to freedom. In this situation – the historical situation in which the people now are – Christian theology recognizes its own *kairos*. It thinks about historical praxis in the light of the biblical traditions of freedom, so that it can arrive at a new praxis of its own. In the movement of history it searches for 'the things that move us in the direction of the future'. 'To reflect, making the historical praxis of liberation the starting point of our reflection, means reflecting in the light of the future we believe in and hope for, and keeping our gaze fixed on an act which will give new form to the present.'[22] Like 'the theology of hope', liberation theology does not merely want to interpret the world differently. It wants to change it, since it sees the world, not in the transcendent light of religion, but in the eschatological light of the coming kingdom of God. This means that liberation theology is a contextual hermeneutics of the gospel, and is related to the *kairos*. And for this two theological conceptions are important: first, the historical experience of God, and then the perspectivist mediation of liberation and redemption.

Compared with metaphysical, transcendental or personalist theologies, liberation theology begins with history, as the space of God's revelation and the place where human beings encounter God.[23] In this way it links up with the biblical traditions about Israel's history and the history of Christ, but in doing so it also avails itself of the paradigm of the modern world, which ever since the political and industrial revolutions of the eighteenth and nineteenth centuries has ceased to see the world in relation to the 'cosmos', replacing this by the future orientation of history. The modern understanding of reality as 'history' is an ethical and political interpretation of the history made by human beings. The historical experience of God therefore coincides with the ethical experience of our neighbour; for there can be no historical knowledge of God without the praxis of justice.[24] People experience God in, with and beneath the historical experiences of liberation for the people, the righteousness that creates justice for the poor, and the raising up of those who have been humiliated.

Of course we can put a critical question at this point, asking whether religious experiences are being used here as a way of hallowing the people's struggles for liberation, or whether the protests against oppression and the energies that work for liberation are really primarily derived from experiences of God? For we might then say that in the first case the functionalization of religion actually makes religion superfluous (since liberation can be achieved even without it, and can be fought for and won by other people too); while in the second case the same religious experience apparently turns some people into freedom fighters and others into their adversaries. But in the reality we actually experience, this alternative is forced and illusory. People in the base communities read the stories they find in the Bible, and recognize their own historical situation, and experience together the Spirit who liberates them. Or people become aware of their historical situation and begin to understand the stories they find in the Bible because in them they recognize themselves. We can proceed from text to context, or from context to text. In the practical hermeneutics of real life, the two go hand in hand, and reinforce one another.[25] Anyone who turns this into an alternative is trying to destroy what belongs together.

Experience of God in real history, like every historical experience, is bound up with memories and expectations. The biblical remembrance of Israel's Exodus, and of Christ's suffering and death, are – if we take them seriously – revolutionary remembrances. They have a liberating effect on the enslaved and are therefore dangerous for their masters. Because the Bible has continually had so revolutionary an influence, it has often enough been kept from the people by church and king, or has been expounded only under supervision. The Bible movement and the base communities in the Catholic church are an important source of liberation theology in Latin America. If the historical experience of God is to be aligned towards liberation, then these remembrances are not the recollections of dream-days belonging to the past. They are practical remembrances of hope. 'The Lord' whose liberating acts are experienced in history aligns his historical acts towards 'the Day of the Lord'. Historical experience of God is joined through an inward necessity to expectations of the future. So from the very outset, liberation theology linked the historical concept of God with the eschatological concept of the kingdom of God. The God of history is on the way to his kingdom. Believing God means hoping for his kingdom.

If this is so, the dynamic of the future becomes constitutive for experience of God in the present. The kingdom of God ahead of us that is going to change the world becomes more important than the religious heaven above us. Its prophecy overcomes religious fatalism, and calls to life the freedom that strides beyond the present into the future. If the God of history cannot be thought without the eschatological kingdom of God, then historical experiences of God are anticipations of the kingdom, just as the kingdom will be the consummation of historical experiences of God.

The unified perspective stretching towards liberation *and* redemption is the logical consequence of this unified historical perspective that stretches towards God and the kingdom of God. Liberation theology does not accept two different histories, a world history and a salvation history, for salvation history has to do with the salvation of this whole created world. Consequently nature and grace belong together.[26] Redemption embraces every human being and the whole human being; and we must add that it embraces humanity and the earth, for the Redeemer is the Creator of all things. To look at Christ is to see that redemption takes in all the dimensions of being and brings the whole of existence to its perfecting. So it follows that 'There is only *one* history, which has Christ as its goal'.[27] If this is true, then the economic, political and cultural liberations of men and women from exploitation, repression and alienation belong just as much to the work of redemption as the forgiveness of sins and hope for eternal life. 'Anyone who fights against a situation of misery and exploitation, and builds a just society, participates . . . in the movement of redemption, which is certainly as yet only on the way to its fulfilment.'[28] The eschatological redemption from death to eternal life is experienced here and now in historical liberations from the powers of death, and in our raising to our own true life.

In the historical perspective that stretches forward to eschatological redemption there are no fixed frontiers between this world and the next. In praxis, the experiences of liberation here and the hope for redemption there belong together. Of course we cannot transform all these expectations into experiences, but we can have the new experiences that match these expectations. So we can only regret Rome's lack of understanding, expressed by Pope John Paul II in a sermon preached in Nicaragua in 1983, in which he said that the priests of his church must not participate in the people's struggle for liberation, or in the building of a free Nicaragua, since their function was 'to prepare the people for eternal life'.[29] This alternative puts asunder what is joined in God's Spirit. Just because I believe in 'the resurrection of the dead and the life of the world to come' I must already resist the forces of death and annihilation here and now, and must love life here on earth so much that I try with everything I have to free it from exploitation, oppression and alienation. And the opposite is equally true: because I love life, and stand up for its justice, and fight for its freedom wherever it is threatened, I hope that one day death will be swallowed up in the victory of life, and that then 'there will be no mourning nor crying nor pain any more' (Rev. 21.4f.).

Anyone who sees this world and the next in the Christian hope as an Either-Or is robbing that hope of both the courage to live and consolation in dying. The reproaches which the Roman Congregation for the Doctrine of the Faith levelled against Latin American liberation theology in 'Libertatis nuntius' (1984) are groundless, for liberation theology does not 'reduce' redemption to political liberation, or 'instrumentalize' the gospel through a political option. What it does do is to forge a new bond between historical liberation and eschatological redemption, so that salvation is understood as finitely healing and holistic, and is no longer cut short, reduced to the religious sphere, and pushed off into the next world.[30]

More important than this unwarranted polemic on the part of the hierarchy, however, would seem to be the longing of ordinary people for consolation *here*, not merely hereafter, and for security without leading strings. Oppressed people can never be freed if they themselves are dominated by the nursery-school mentality of people who have never come of age. This means that it is important to ask: Is there consolation in liberation? Is there peace in action? And is there safekeeping in the midst of danger? The story of the Exodus answers by pointing to the presence of the liberating God that travels with his wandering people, in the cloud by day and the pillar of fire by night. That is to say, God does not merely deliver people from slavery. He remains present among the people, as the foundation of their freedom. In the limited opportunities for developing one's own freedom, to trust in the sustaining foundation of freedom that accompanies us means believing. People who win freedom can also trust themselves to that freedom. The Jewish and Christian 'sacraments' and rituals are related to the 'signs and wonders' accompanying the Exodus, and give us a foretaste of the promised land and eternal life.

Liberation theology aims to 'make us free for freedom' (Gal. 5.1). So for its further development it will take its bearings from the biblical events: the *Exodus* leads to the *covenant*. This means that liberation theology will turn into federal theology simply of its own accord, and the liberating politics of the people in which liberation theology is embedded will turn into democratic politics.[31] It is only in a covenant of free men and women that liberation, once experienced, can be preserved, and it is only in such a covenant that the dangers of new oppression can be averted. The Exodus has been the driving power of revolutions for political freedom from the English Puritans down to the oppressed of Latin America; and in the same way the covenant has motivated the political democracies from the time of the Swiss Confederation, by way of the Scottish clans and the peasant associations, down to the constitutional states of modern times.[32] For the Huguenot monarchomachists, God's covenant with the people provided the basis for the political doctrine of popular sovereignty in the covenant or 'contract' between people and rulers, and thus laid the foundation for the people's right to resist tyrants.[33] Liberation theologies which do not develop into democratic federal theologies of this kind are failing to achieve free life, and can easily become the ideology of élitist groups and their didactic dictatorships. While the Exodus is the historical foundation for liberty, the covenant is the practical form of life in freedom.

§3 SPIRIT THAT LIBERATES FOR LIFE

Taking the three dimensions of Christian experience of God's Spirit, we shall now try to explore what true liberty of life means. Here it is not merely a question of the subjective factors of faith, hope and love. It is a matter of defining the freedom that ministers to life.

1. *Liberating Faith: Freedom as Subjectivity*

Faith is often thought of merely as formal assent to the doctrine of the church, or as participation in the church's faith – indeed sometimes even as 'blind obedience' to God's commandments. But *liberating faith* is a faith that takes us personally captive. The truth that makes me free is the truth to which I myself assent because I myself understand it, not because tradition and custom compel me. Personal faith is the beginning of a freedom that renews the whole of life and 'overcomes the world', as the Gospel of John says (John 16.33). This faith is an experience which never again leaves the people who have once really been possessed by it. It means being freed from anxiety for trust, being born again to a living hope, loving life without reserve. 'For freedom Christ has set us free', writes Paul in Gal. 5.1: 'Stand fast therefore, and do not submit again to a yoke of slavery.' In political history, nations have often enough been 'freed' from one slavery by another. But in faith we experience *liberation for freedom*. What are we to understand by this freedom?

The Greeks interpreted freedom as the harmonious ordering of the individual into the *polis*, and of the *polis* into the divine cosmos; for the cosmos is shot through by divine *nomos* and *logos*. To live in harmony with the divine is true liberty. We meet this notion again in

Karl Marx, when he defines freedom as 'insight into necessity' – by which he means the historical necessity of the given situation.[34]

In the modern world, however, people understand freedom very differently. They consider freedom to be the individual's independent right of disposal over his own life and his own property; and they see collective freedom as the sovereign disposal of political bodies, people or nations over their own affairs.[35] Here freedom is viewed as an individual's (or a nation's) 'right to self-determination'. Here freedom means rule over oneself.

But for the Christian faith, true freedom is found neither in insight into a cosmic necessity or a necessity of world history, nor in the autonomous right of disposal over oneself and one's property. It means being possessed by the divine energy of life, and participation in that energy. Through trust in the God of the Exodus and the resurrection, the believer experiences and partakes of this liberating power of God which raises to new life. 'All things are possible with God', so 'All things are possible to him who believes' (Mark 9.23). God manifests his creative energies in these confronting historical events, and the people touched by them are interpenetrated by these energies.[36]

Through faith, the hitherto unexplored creative powers of God are thrown open in men and women. So faith means becoming creative with God, and in his Spirit. Faith leads to a creative life which is life-giving through love, in places where death rules and people resign themselves, and surrender to it. Faith awakens trust in the still unrealized possibilities in human beings – in oneself and in other people. So faith means crossing the frontiers of the reality which is existent now, and has been determined by the past, and seeking the potentialities for life which have not yet come into being. 'All things are possible to him who believes'; and this being so, believers become what Musil calls 'possibility people'.[37] Paul goes even further when, talking about believers who live from the powers of the risen Christ, he says: 'All things are yours; and you are Christ's; and Christ is God's' (I Cor. 3.22f.).

The Reformers rediscovered this freedom in faith in the liberating gospel. According to Luther's treatise 'On the Freedom of a Christian' (1521), faith makes people 'the free lords of all things, and subject to no one'; but love makes them at the same time 'the ministering servants of all things and (freely) subject to everyone'.[38] For justifying faith liberates men and women from the compulsion to evil, from the law of works, and from the violence of death, setting them free for unhindered and unmediated eternal fellowship with God. Believers become 'God's children' and in community with Christ have direct access to the Father. In prayer they become 'God's friends', and God listens to what they say. Finally, in the Spirit and in love they become so much one with God that God remains in them and they remain in God. According to the Protestant understanding, freedom in faith is a relational term. It means the relation between human beings and God. In his relationship to human beings God reveals himself as the justifying, accepting and liberating God; and in their relationship to God sinners become righteous, the lost are accepted, and the enslaved freed.

In the revival movements of the seventeenth and eighteenth centuries, the personal dimension of this freedom in faith was discovered and stressed: an essential element of freedom *in* faith is freedom *of* faith, that is, the liberty to make a personal decision of faith, and the right to this decision. This means that the relational concept of freedom in the relationship to God is complemented by the subjective concept of freedom of decision in the human being's own personal relationship. The newly perceived subjectivity of the person now put its impress on the human side of the relationship to God. Insistence on a personal decision of faith, the personal experience of conversion, and the inner testimony of the Holy Spirit which 'warms the heart', has been the mark of modern Protestant denominations – Quakers, Baptists, Methodists, and others. Rightly understood, this is not a reversion to a righteousness of works. It is the necessary pneumatological complement to the Christocentricism of the Reformers. The freedom in faith created by the gospel is always personal freedom in God's Spirit at the same time. No church and no state can prescribe this personal experience of faith, or take it away from anyone. 'Subjectivity is truth', declared Kierkegaard, the Protestant philosopher.

For all its weaknesses, this Protestant subjectivity introduced into the legal thinking of our civilization the dignity of the individual person, as well as individual human rights.[39] Without the right to freedom of faith, there is no right to freedom of religion and conscience either. Freedom of faith and personal responsibility for one's own life entered the modern world through Protestantism. Without this 'religion of freedom' there is no such thing as 'a free society'.

And yet the discovery of subjectivity is not enough to take the soundings of freedom in God's Spirit adequately; for subjective freedom involves social freedom too, and subjective powers also require the objective scope of the possible. Otherwise there is no subjective development.

2. *Liberating Love: Freedom as Sociality*

(*a*) We know the first definition of freedom from political history. There freedom is defined as *domination*. Because the whole of history down to our own day can be seen as an on-going struggle for power, the only person who is called free is the victor in this struggle. The losers are subjugated, and are therefore said 'not to be free'. The history of the word freedom shows that it derives from a slave-owning society. In a society of that kind, only the master is free. The slaves, women and children he rules over, are not free at all. Paul uses this language too when he is talking about the conflicts which have been ended in the Christian congregations: the conflicts between Jews and Gentiles, freemen and slaves, men and women (Gal. 3.28). But the person who interprets freedom as lordship over other people can be free only at the expense of someone else. His freedom means oppression for the rest. His wealth makes other people poor. His power crushes the weak. So for the masters, freedom always involves 'security problems'.

Anyone who interprets freedom as domination is really only aware of himself and his own possessions. He is not aware of other people as persons at all. Even when we say: a person is free if he can do and leave undone what he likes, we are interpreting freedom as mastery – as a person's mastery over himself. Even when we say: a person is free if he is not determined by any inward and external compulsions, we are interpreting freedom as mastery: everyone is supposed to be his own king, his own master, his own slave-owner. The very words 'lord-ship' and 'master-y' show the degree to which this interpretation of freedom is drawn from a male society.

The middle-class liberalism which succeeded feudalism in Western Europe nevertheless continued to cling to the feudal lord as model. Everyone who has a human visage has the same rights to liberty, say the liberals. This universal individual liberty comes up against its limits only when it infringes the liberty of other people. The person who claims freedom for himself must respect the same freedom for other people. But this means that even for middle-class liberalism, freedom means domination. Everyone sees everyone else as a competitor in the struggle for power and possessions. Everyone is for everyone else merely the restriction of his own liberty. Everyone is free in himself, but no one takes an active interest in anyone else. Carried to its logical conclusion, this is a society of free and equal but solitary individuals. No one disposes over anyone else, everyone disposes over himself. Freedom has then certainly become general. Everyone has a right to freedom. But is this freedom in the true sense at all?

(b) We know the other definition from social history. This defines freedom as *sociality*. Then freedom is a qualification of the relationships in which, and from which, the people concerned live. This is the concept of *communicative freedom*. The truth of subjective freedom is mutual love. It is only in love that human freedom enters its free world. I am free and feel free when I am respected and accepted by other people, and when I for my part respect and accept other people too. I become truly free if I open my life for other people and share it with them, and if other people open their lives for me, and share them with me. Then the other person is no longer the limitation of my freedom, but its extension. Life is communion in communication. We give one another life, and come alive from one another. In mutual participation in life, individuals become free beyond the borders of their individuality. That is *the social side of freedom*.[40] We call it love, or solidarity. In it we see isolated individuals coming together. In it we see the coming together of things that have been forcibly separated.

Divide et impera – divide and rule: that is the weary old method of domination. As long as freedom means domination, everything has to be divided, isolated, singled out and differentiated, so that it can be ruled. But if freedom means *sociality*, then we find all the things that have been separated coming together again. The estrangement of person from person, the separation of human society from nature, the cleavage between soul and body, and finally religious fear are all at an end. We discover what liberation is when we are again one with each other, one with nature, and one with God. Freedom as community is therefore a counter-movement to the history of class conflict and the struggle for power, in which freedom could only be interpreted as domination.

The history of our language shows that sociality is the other root of the word 'freedom'. The person who is free is friendly, well-disposed, open, pleasant and loving.[41] We still find this interpretation in a German word for hospitable, *gastfrei* (literally 'guest free'). The person who is *gastfrei* does not dominate any of his guests, nor is he ever without guests. He is capable of fellowship with strangers. He lets them share his life, and is interested in theirs.

Freedom as domination destroys life. As domination, freedom is not freedom in its true sense. The truth of human freedom is to be found in the love that longs for life. This leads to unhindered, open community in solidarity. Only this freedom – freedom as community, or sociality – is able to heal the wounds which freedom as domination has inflicted and still inflicts.

3. *Liberating Hope: Freedom as Future*

The definition of freedom to which Christian faith brings us goes even beyond freedom as sociality. We said that the faith of Christians is essentially the hope of resurrection. In the light of this hope, freedom is *the creative passion for the possible*. It is not like lordship, directed only towards existing things. Nor is it like love, directed only towards community with existing people. It is directed towards the future, the future of the coming God. For God's future is the limitless kingdom of creative possibilities, whereas the past is the limited kingdom of reality. Creative passion is always directed towards the project of a future of this kind. We long to implement new, unguessed-at possibilities. That is why we press forward with the passion that transmutes reason into fertile imagination. We dream the messianic daydream about the new life, the whole, healed life, the life that is at last entirely living. We explore the possibilities of the future in order to implement this vision of life. This future dimension of freedom has long been overlooked, because the freedom of the Christian faith was not understood as participation in God's creative acts, and because Christianity was dominated by religious reverence rather than by messianic hope. But in fact freedom in faith is the creativity in the forecourt of the possible which breaks down frontiers.[42]

Up to now we have seen freedom either as domination, in the relationship between subject and object, or as sociality, in the relationships between equal determining subjects. Now we discover freedom in the relationship of determining subjects to the project they share. Without this dimension freedom has not been fully understood. In the relationship to a shared project, freedom is a creative movement. Anyone who transcends the present in the direction of the future in thought, word and act is free. Freedom has to be understood as the free space for creative freedom.

To what is freedom's hope directed? 'How much more', Paul often says, when he is no longer thinking about 'freedom from . . .' but is talking about 'freedom for . . .'. How much greater is the future than the past! How much greater is God's grace than the sins of men and women! How much more is freedom in its own world than mere liberation from slavery! It is true that in the history we experience, it is easier to name the negative thing *from* which we want to be freed than the positive thing *for* which we hope to be free. But it is hope for the greater future which leads us to ever new experiences in history. That is the surplus of hope in life, and the added value of the future in history.

§4 THE EXPERIENCE OF FREEDOM AS EXPERIENCE OF GOD: THE LORD IS THE SPIRIT

1. 'The Lord is the Spirit' (II Cor. 3.17). If the power in which people experience their inward and outward liberation is called God's 'Spirit', then this power is given a transcendent foundation in its immanence. By that I mean that its creative foundation is inexhaustible, and that the liberty experienced has its permanent existence in that foundation. 'The Spirit' is the name given to the experienced presence of God. If this 'Spirit' is then called 'Lord', that gives it the Israelite name for God according to the first commandment. What Israel in its liberation from Egypt experienced as God's revelation of himself as Lord, is experienced by believers in their fellowship with Christ. In it they experience freedom in the Spirit. The general context of II Cor. 3, in which 'the glory of God in the face of Christ' is contrasted with the veil over the face of Moses, points to the Israelite name for God. In 'the Christ', the liberating God of Israel is efficacious for Jews *and* Gentiles. The messianic time is beginning, and will bring with it the Exodus for all the oppressed and lost of this earth. Israel's history with Yahweh will become universal. 'The Lord' is 'the Spirit which will be poured out on all flesh'. In the Spirit people experience God as 'the Lord', and that simply means that they experience their liberation for life.

2. 'Where the Spirit of the Lord is, there is freedom' (II Cor. 3.17).

With this turn of phrase, Paul relates experience of the Spirit and the experience of liberty to Christ.[43] Here it is not the Spirit itself who is 'the Lord'. It is the Spirit of Christ. This corresponds to the way the Old Testament talks about Yahweh's *ruach*. Wherever Christ is called the *kyrios*, he is being given the Israelite name for God, and that means that the history of Christ is being set in the framework of the history of Yahweh, and presented as the messianic expansion and deepening of that history. The phrase about 'the Spirit of the Lord' presupposes that the risen Christ himself has become 'the life-giving Spirit' and acts as such (I Cor. 15.45). Life-giving Spirit is the mode of existence of the risen One, and the efficacy which proceeds from him.

So the experience of freedom encompasses a double experience of God: the Lord is the Spirit, and the Spirit is the Spirit of the Lord. Liberation reveals that there is a reciprocal operation between God's Spirit and his Christ.[44] Out of their co-operative activity comes the freedom which has its foundation, its existence, and its never-to-be-exhausted future in God's presence. In practical terms this means that *discipleship of Jesus* and *the liberating Spirit* act together,[45] in order to lead people into true freedom. Pentecostal and charismatic experiences of the Spirit become spiritualistically insubstantial and illusory without the personal and political discipleship of Jesus. Personal and political discipleship of Jesus becomes legalistic and arid without the spirituality which 'drinks from its own wells', to quote Gutiérrez.

3. Freedom is present where Christ is experienced in the Spirit. What from the side of the intervening, apprehending God is called 'lordship' is called freedom on the side of the people who are apprehended or possessed by that lordship; and this freedom has nothing to do with slavery, either outward or inward. That is why this 'lordship' is better described as 'the free power' and 'the free space' or 'free place' of human freedom. Through it and in it people are raised above earth and heaven, life and death, present and future, to God himself, and participate in his creative freedom (cf. I Cor. 3.22 with Rom. 8.38f.). Anyone who experiences God and a 'deification' (*theosis*) of this kind, is freed from all the godless ties of this world, and is nobody's slave. He lives in the free space of God's creative possibilities, and partakes of them. But for that very reason he also participates in the complex web of relationships through which the Creator loves everything he has created, and preserves its

life. Freedom is not merely sovereignty. It is communication too, life in the communicative relationships out of which life begins and in which life comes alive. Without love, freedom becomes the arbitrary liberty that kills, because it is isolating. But life in communicative freedom would stagnate in the spider's web of its relationships if it did not as *creative expectation* bring forth projects for the future and thrust beyond reality into the realm of the possible. These three dimensions of freedom are explored through faith, through love, and through hope. In them we correspond in our relationships to the liberating, the social, the coming God.

VI

The Justification of Life

It is one of the unique features of human life that it can be denied, and so has to be affirmed if it is to live.[1] Denied and rejected life is death. Accepted and affirmed life is happiness. Other people can be denied life. Then they lose their rights. Their very right to existence is disputed. People are outlawed and stripped of their rights and privileges. They are exposed to premature death. These people without rights are what F. Fanon calls 'the accursed of this earth'. But we can deny ourselves life too. Then we become unjust and violent towards people who are weaker than ourselves, and take away the life they have. But in fact we are then taking our own lives as well, in the suicidal sense. Unjust people like this are the 'accursors' of life and the destroyers of this earth.

How can life return to this world of injustice, in which some people are deprived of justice, and others have become unjust? This happens when God's justice restores their rights to the people who have none, and makes the unjust just, and makes both righteous. Only justice creates peace. It is only on the foundation of justice that our life together can prosper. We cry out for God's justice in our want of justice and in our injustice, and we experience God's Spirit when the people who are unjustly treated and the people who act unjustly are set right, each in their own way. It is 'the Spirit of truth' who convinces the world of its sins (John 16.7f.), puts the unjust world to rights, and turns believers, from being the slaves and victims of sin, into free servants of the divine justice and righteousness which leads to eternal life in this world and the next (Rom. 6.13ff., 22). The Spirit of Christ is called 'the advocate' (John 14.16ff.). He is the accuser of the guilty, the defender of the accused, and the merciful judge, all in one.

In the first part of this chapter we shall look at some problems about the traditional Protestant doctrine of justification, seen from a pneumatological point of view, so that in the second part we can go on to present the justification of the people who are deprived of justice, on the basis of Christ's solidarity with them. Here we shall take up the recent insights of liberation theology. In a third section we shall focus the traditional doctrine of justification on the justification of the unjust through Christ's atonement. And in the fourth part of the chapter we shall discuss the surmounting of unjust structures in economics and politics, which would mean that the victims could rise up out of what is called 'structural sin' and the perpetrators could be converted from that structural sin, for a just, shared community with one another.

§1 THE JUSTIFICATION OF SINNERS: GENERAL OR SPECIFIC?

The Reformation doctrine of justification is based on Paul's teaching,[2] and Paul's presupposition is the universality of sin: 'For there is no distinction; since all have sinned and fall short of the glory they should have with God' (Rom. 3.22ff.). Here 'all' means Jews and Gentiles, as Paul explains in Romans 2 and 3. 'Glory' means the divine *doxa*, which was originally associated with the nature of human beings as God's image. Like Paul, the Reformers were convinced that through original sin (*peccatum originale*) 'the godless nature and unrighteousness of human beings' have come upon the world, and have provoked God's wrath. That is to say, they have wounded his love for the humanity he has created. The saving and justifying gospel is therefore directed with equal universality to all sinners, and calls them all to faith, for 'they are justified by grace as a gift through the redemption which is in Christ Jesus'. He is a God for everyone, and 'will justify the Jews on the ground of their faith, and the Gentiles through their faith' (Rom. 3.30).

The Pauline teaching about the justifying righteousness of God has the *de facto* universality of sin as its premise, and the intended universality of salvation from sin as its objective. 'For one man's trespass led to condemnation for all men, so one man's act of righteousness leads to acquittal and life for all men' (Rom. 5.18). The doctrine has its christological foundation in an atonement christology which sees both Christ's death and his resurrection as vicarious, on behalf of all men and women, since Christ 'was put to death for our trespasses and raised for our justification' (Rom. 4.25).[3]

The universal concept of sin is so widespread in Protestantism that it is hard to discover the alternative. Yet that alternative is obvious enough if we look at the synoptic gospels. They talk about 'sinners', quite specifically and in a social context. There are the 'sinners and tax collectors' who do not keep God's law and live an unrighteous life. There are the outcasts, the poor and the homeless, who cannot keep God's law and are therefore outside the law, and without any rights. The parables in the synoptics show that the situations into which Jesus enters are always situations in which there is human conflict – between the healthy and the sick, the rich and the poor, men and women, Pharisees and tax collectors, the good and the wicked, the evil-doers and their victims.[4] In these conflicts, the one group is always dependent on the other. It is the rich who make the poor poor; it is the healthy who handicap the handicapped; it is the good people who impose the stigma of being 'sinners' on the weak. It is generally 'possessions' to which 'the Haves' cling, and from which they exclude 'the Have-nots'.[5] Possessions can mean money, health or strength. It can mean justice, or being good. It can even be masculinity. But it is always a question of power. Whenever these life's gifts are grabbed and monopolized by a few, the merciless distribution struggle begins: the struggle for the opportunity to work – for possessions – for chances in life. And in these conflicts we ourselves are always 'the good', and the others are always on the side of 'wickedness'. Then only either-or, friend-enemy relationships exist. These are the very devil, and the end of them is death: the death inflicted on other people.

Of course there are also situations in which people are both victims and perpetrators – whether they change from being victims to being perpetrators, or whether as perpetrators they become the victims of other people. And there are onlookers too, and people who try to keep out of it all. Victims can also be latent perpetrators, and are not necessarily saints just because they are victims. But complex though human behaviour is, there is an acting and a suffering in every act of violence and in every injustice, whether this is between person and person or in individuals themselves. So the differentiation we are making here between perpetrators and victims is a justifiable one.

The real history of human sin begins with Cain's fratricide (Gen. 4) and with the spread of wickedness on earth through 'violence' (Gen 6). The eating of the forbidden fruit in the Garden of Eden (Gen. 3) belongs to the world of myth, which offers a metaphysical interpretation of the physical history of the world. The myth about paradise and the Fall never played as fundamental a role in Judaism as it did in Christianity. Judaism never deduced from it any doctrine of original sin. So it is important for Christians not merely to look at the mythical story, but to see the real history of injustice and violence as sin too, so as to find from God's Spirit the energy to act justly, and the strength for peace.

The weakness about the universal concept of sin underlying the Pauline and Protestant doctrine of justification is that collective guilt of this kind makes people blind to specific, practical guilt. Indeed it can actually be used as an excuse for specific, practical guilt. The universality of sin leads to a universal night in which everything is equally black, and even to use weapons of mass extermination is no longer anything special. Some of the declarations made by Christian churches show how the Christian doctrine of sin can be misused to justify sin, and as a way of adjusting to the compulsions of a so-called 'fallen world'.

Some of the people involved also hide their individual guilt in collective guilt, maintaining that 'We are all more or less guilty, and supported the totalitarian regime.' Other people are glad enough to lose themselves in obscure and cloudy speculations about allegedly 'tragic combinations of circumstances' to which we all succumbed – to a greater or lesser degree, of course. These attempts to exonerate oneself personally through collective accusations founder in the face of the people who resisted, and did not become guilty, and were imprisoned or murdered as a result. These people force us to confess personally where we failed, and when, and to find out why. Anyone who remains general and abstract at this point accuses himself by excusing himself.

Protestant pessimism about sin is also defended in these connections as 'Christian realism' (Reinhold Niebuhr's phrase). But it is theologically untenable. On the contrary, the consequence of justifying faith is optimism – optimism about grace, since 'Where sin abounds, grace abounds much more' (Rom. 5.20).

On the other hand, the doctrine about the universality of sin can also lead people to perceive a solidarity which knows no limits because it is limitless. 'All are guilty towards everything and for everything', says Dostoievsky, and the special criminals are merely the 'unfortunate' among us, with whom we have to sympathize, because each and all of us are capable of the same crimes at any time. Then we stop accusing 'the others', and assume responsibility for them.[6]

The doctrine about sin's universality is really a metaphysical view of sin. Just as all human beings have to die, they are all also subject to the sinfulness that leads to death. *Sub specie aeternitatis* sin, like death, is the universal fate of human beings. But particularly if sin is brought into such close proximity to physical death as this (on the grounds that death is 'the wages of sin'), what is sinful loses its concrete character, and sin becomes a component in a general feeling about life *coram Deo*. And the lordship of sin then sets off the general vicious circle of law, guilt and death which Paul describes in Romans 7. In this vicious circle, every human life is bound to appear as a life that in God's sight has gone astray and foundered. 'Who will deliver me from this body of sin?' and 'Who will deliver me from this body of death?'

It is this generality that prevents many people from finding either the Catholic doctrine of grace or the Protestant doctrine of justification convincing. These doctrines seem to them vague and abstract. So why should they confess that they are in need of redemption, and accuse themselves of being 'sinners'? If people no longer ask the question about the divine righteousness, justifying faith loses its foundation and is left in the air.

What is this question about righteousness, and what does it mean? For Luther, in the sixteenth century, it meant the fear of judgment and the pangs of conscience: 'O when wilt thou at last be good, and do enough to get a gracious God?' For Kierkegaard, in the nineteenth century, it meant the inward loss of identity: 'The principle of Protestantism has a particular premise: a human being who sits in mortal dread, in fear and trembling and greatly beset.' For the Jewish Christian Paul, in the first century, it was the impossibility of keeping the Torah: 'I do not the good I want, but the evil I do not want is what I do' (Rom. 7.19). Is there any point today in looking round for general phenomena to 'convince the world of sin' and persuade men and women that in God's sight they are sinful? Or is it better to be specific and practical, and to ask about the victims of sin, and its perpetrators?

If belief in the universality of deliverance through Christ is the presupposition for an awareness of sin, then functionally, the doctrine of sin belongs strictly within the therapeutical circle which embraces knowledge of Christ, knowledge of our own misery, *and* the new life in faith. Outside this therapeutical circle, and in isolation from it, the doctrine of sin does nothing but harm. But this therapeutical circle of faith revolves round the justice and righteousness of God which justifies and sets things to rights, and which has become manifest in Christ. It is therefore related to the practical and specific personal and social conflicts of people who have never received justice, and people who are themselves unjust.[7]

The interpretations of sin and the forgiveness of sins which we find in Paul and the synoptics must not be turned into opposite fronts. Nor must we put what is general over against what is concrete, or play off the metaphysical interpretation of justification against the political interpretation. These different aspects can also be seen as mutual substantiations and reciprocal enforcements: because God has mercy on all sinners generally, he quite specifically brings justice to people who have been deprived of it, and leads the unjust to repentance. If there is a divine liberation from the universal power of sin through the energy of the creative Spirit which works for righteousness, this legitimates the liberations from economic injustice, political oppression, cultural alienation and personal discouragement.[8] If there is an eternal life which will drive out death from the whole of God's creation, then everything is justified which already ministers to life and resists death here and now.

The Protestant doctrine about the justification of sinners, and today's theology about the liberation of the oppressed, do not have to be antitheses. They can correct and enrich one another mutually. The full and complete Protestant doctrine of justification is a liberation theology: it is about the liberation of people deprived of justice, *and* about the liberation of the unjust, so that they may all be freed for a just society. The one-sided limitation to the perpetrators, and the forgiveness of their active sins, has made Protestantism blind to the sufferings of the victims, and to God's saving 'option for the poor'.[9] Protestantism has underrated the importance of 'structural sin' by looking too exclusively at individuals. But this is a one-sided approach.

§2 THE RIGHTEOUSNESS AND JUSTICE OF GOD WHICH CREATES JUSTICE FOR VICTIMS

It is surprising that Protestant theology has not noticed the analogy between God's 'justifying' righteousness and his righteousness that 'creates justice'.[10] This is probably because so sharp a separation has been made between the Old and New Testaments; for just as in Paul *the justification of the sinner* becomes the revelation of God's righteousness in the world, so in the Old Testament *the establishing of justice* for people deprived of it is the quintessence of the divine mercy, and hence of the divine righteousness. Nor is the righteousness which establishes justice retributive justice, requiting good with good, and evil with evil (*iustitia distributiva*). It is a creative righteousness (*iustitia iustificans*).

The one who 'executes justice for the oppressed' (Ps. 146.7; Ps. 103.6) is the God who 'executes justice for the fatherless and the widow' (Deut. 10.18; Ps. 82.3; Isa. 1.17). The messiah is expected to 'judge the poor with righteousness, and decide with equity for the wretched in the land' (Isa. 11.4). Because God lets his Spirit rest on his messiah, the messiah 'will bring forth justice to the nations' (Isa. 42.1), and when 'the Spirit is poured out from on high . . . then justice will dwell in the wilderness and righteousness abide in the fruitful field, and the fruit of righteousness will be peace' (Isa. 32.15ff.).

This means in the first place that the God who in his almighty power created heaven and earth is on the side of the people who have to suffer violence because they cannot defend themselves. Their rights are his divine concern. It also means that God places the weak and vulnerable under his divine protection. The person who hurts them hurts him. 'All these things my hand has made . . . says the Lord. But this is the man on whom I will look, he that is wretched and of a broken spirit' (Isa. 66.2). When we say that God is on the side of his most vulnerable creatures, we can call this his 'preferential option for the poor',[11] if we add that God's empathy – his *feeling with* the least of those he has created – is involved in this option, so that their experience is his experience too. According to Matthew 25, the Son of man-Judge of the world identifies with the least of his brothers and sisters to such an extent that whatever happens to them happens to him. God himself is the justice of the unjustly treated, just as he is the power of the powerless. For God himself is the victim of the violent. God himself suffers the wrong they do. And God will judge according to what he has experienced in the poor and in all vulnerable creatures. God, that is to say, creates justice for the people who have been deprived of it, and for those without any rights, and he does so through his *solidarity* with them.

This impression becomes stronger still if we then look at the figure of the Suffering Servant in Isaiah 53. For to say 'he has borne our sicknesses and taken upon himself our pains' (53.4) means that *in* the sick and tormented the messiah himself is sick and tormented. He himself bears the world's suffering. He himself is the victim of violence. This profound solidarity 'with us' explains why we can say that he suffered vicariously 'for us': 'The chastisement that made us whole was upon him, and through his wounds we are healed' (Isa. 53.5). For as the one who carries the suffering of the world, he also endures the sins of the world that cause the suffering. Through this 'carrying' and enduring of sins, he brings about atonement for the victims of violence, and brings the perpetrators of violence to repentance, so that they too are put right, and become just.

The image of the Suffering Servant of God in Isaiah 53 put a profound impress on the stories about Christ's passion, and became the foundation for Christian christologies. With the help of this image we first of all discover along Jesus' way to his death on the cross a *solidarity christology*: the messianic Son of God unreservedly takes on himself the conditions of our vulnerable and mortal existence, and becomes a human being like us. He takes the way of non-violent suffering. He carries and endures – suffers and suffers under – injustice and violence, betrayal and denial, forsakenness by God and human beings, and dies on a Roman cross. These 'sufferings of Christ' are also the sufferings of the poor and vulnerable, the people (*ochlos*) and all the weaker creatures. People who suffer violence discover what happens to them in what happened to Jesus. They can find themselves in him, and find him beside them.[12] The suffering, tormented and murdered Christ is on the side of the victims, not the agents. He himself becomes a victim among other victims. The forsaken Christ is the most beset of all the people who are beset, and who despair of God. He is the divine martyr among the millions of unknown martyrs in the suffering histories of Israel, humanity and nature. In this sense 'the sufferings of Christ' are not just Jesus' sufferings; they are the sufferings of the poor and weak, which Jesus shares in his own body and his own soul, in solidarity with them

(Heb. 2.16–18; 11.26; 13.13). Because of this, 'the sufferings of Christ' are open for the sufferers still to come, both the men and women who suffer with Christ (Col. 1.24) and those with whom Christ will suffer – open for the sufferings of the martyrs for his name and kingdom, and for the coming apocalyptic sufferings which will fall upon all vulnerable creatures.

In his early period, Luther maintained this solidarity christology in the form of a *conformitas* christology: Christ is the first-born among many brothers and sisters.[13] He is for them the exemplary human being, and the prototype to whom they will be 'conformed' through their experiences of life and suffering (Rom. 8.29). As our brother, Christ experienced and suffered our distress, so that in our distress we can experience his brotherhood. Christ, the brother, is the Christ with us – tormented among the tormented, suffering injustice among the victims of violence, forsaken among all the other forsaken people. But the brother in our distress also makes us his brothers and sisters in *his* distress. 'Only the suffering God can help', wrote Dietrich Bonhoeffer in his Gestapo cell.[14] And it is true that a God who cannot suffer, and suffer with us, could not even understand us. That is why Christians then 'stand by God in his suffering', as Bonhoeffer says in one of his poems.[15] Unlike the notion of 'Christ the Lord', the idea about 'Christ the brother' brings out the deep community and mutuality in this fellowship with Christ.

Does the suffering which Christ suffers in solidarity with the victims in humanity's history of violence have any significance for the victims themselves? If he were only one victim more, his suffering would have no special meaning or importance. But if God himself is *in* Christ (II Cor. 5.19), then through his passion Christ brings into the passion history of this world the eternal fellowship of God, and the divine justice and righteousness that creates life; and he identifies God with the victims of violence. But the reverse is then also true; for this means the identification of the victims with God, so that they are put under God's protection and with him are given the rights of which they have been deprived by human beings. Not least, in this way these 'accursed of the earth' have a determining part in the divine judgment of the world: 'As you did it to one of the least of these my brethren, you did it to me.'

§3 THE JUSTIFYING RIGHTEOUSNESS AND JUSTICE OF GOD FOR THE PERPETRATORS

Violence committed by people against other people, and by human beings against weaker creatures, is sin, and a crime against life. Violence always has two sides: on the one side is the person who commits the act, and on the other is his victim. On the one side the master sets himself up as superior, on the other the slave is humiliated. On the one side the exploiter wins, on the other the exploited person loses.

An act of violence destroys life on both sides, but in different ways – on the one hand through the evil committed, on the other through the suffering. The person who commits the act becomes inhumane and unjust, the victim is dehumanized and deprived of his or her rights. Because violence has these two sides, the road to freedom and justice has to begin with both: the liberation of the oppressed from the suffering of oppression requires the liberation of the oppressor from the injustice of oppression. Otherwise there is no liberation and no justice that can create peace. For the goal can only be an open community, free of fear, between people, and between human beings and other creatures, a community from which acts of violence have disappeared and into which justice and righteousness have entered. In many situations it is self-evident that the oppressed have to be freed, and that rights have to be created for those who have none – at least it is self-evident for the victims of violence. But the liberation of the people who commit violence from the wrong they do is not at all self-evident as a general rule – at least not for the perpetrators themselves, who profit from the wrong they have committed. They do not see the suffering which they have caused their victims. They are blinded. They justify the wrong they have done with a score of reasons. They are self-righteous, because in their heart of hearts they know that they are acting unjustly, and are themselves unjust, and because they know too that they can never again make undone the wrong that has once been committed. How can unjust people become just?

Wrong has been done. No better future can ever 'make good' the suffering of the past. But how can one *live* with a guilty past? According to the ancient notions of justice shared by all peoples, what is required is *atonement*, or *expiation*, so that the justice that has been infringed is restored. And this atonement has to take place in three different dimensions: first for the victim – then for the person who has committed the wrong – and finally for the community in which victims and perpetrators live together. Guilt without the experience of atonement leads to the repression of guilt, to the compounding of injustice, and to the compulsion to repeat the injust act. Unless his guilt is forgiven the guilty person cannot live. But there is no forgiveness of guilt without atonement, just as there can be no reconciliation without the restoration of justice. But what is atonement? Who can atone? These questions are of vital importance for the perpetrators, and for the people who have to live in the long shadows they cast.

Let us feel our way towards an answer, cautiously so as not to go wrong. When Germans make this attempt they remember 'Auschwitz'. When we ask about atonement we are asking about a power which frees the perpetrators and those who come after them from self-hate, and makes them capable of life in righteousness and justice.[16]

Guilt, whether it be individual or collective, weighs heavily on the guilty person and destroys his self-esteem. The result is self-justification or self-destruction. And the consequence of both is the scapegoat syndrome. One looks round for 'the people responsible' on whom one can off-load one's own failure because 'it's all their fault'. Since no one can *live* with guilt over injustice and violence, because it is unendurable, and since it cannot be got rid of through repression, or by pushing it off on to someone or something else, the person concerned 'has forfeited the right to live', as people used to say. Even if the person is never punished, he never finds the strength to affirm a life that has personally been so negated.[17]

Is atonement humanly possible? In the religion of many peoples there is an idea that the gods are roused to wrath by human wrong and violence. Sacrifices have to be offered in order to reconcile them. Behind this is the notion about the universal harmony of the world, which is disturbed by human wrong-doing, and can only be healed through the appropriate sacrifices. That is why evil has to be requited with evil. This has nothing to do with retribution. It is part of the restoration of order in the world.

According to Israel's rituals and theology, God's love for his people is injured by injustice among the people and by their breach of the covenant.[18] Violence against members of God's covenant, or against God's image in other people, or against God's creatures, is always an injury to God himself too. God's anger is injured love. This divine anger is experienced in the hiding of God's face, and in the person's own God-forsakenness, as well as in the atrophy of the divine life-force in the person himself. But if God's wrath is nothing other than his injured love, then God must bear the pain of his love and put up with the hurts. God suffers injustice and violence as an injury to his love because, and in so far as, he holds fast to his love for the unjust and the person who commits violence. So his love must overcome his anger by 'reconciling itself' to the pain it has been caused. This is what happens when God 'carries' or 'bears' the sins of his people. This divine 'carrying' of the sins which for human beings are unendurable can be expressed in different ways:

1. In the cultic ritual of the *atoning* or *expiatory* sacrifice which God himself institutes as a way of reconciling his people with himself. The people's sins are ritually transferred to 'the scapegoat' and it 'takes them away' into the desert.

2. In the prophetic vision of *God's Suffering Servant*, who 'carries' the sins of the people in his vicarious suffering.

3. In the theological understanding of *the divine compassion* out of which sinners are made righteous.

In each case it is God himself who atones for the sins of his people. God gives himself as ransom for Israel. There is no liberation from sin without atonement, but the only one who can atone is someone who is not himself a sinner. Atonement is not humanly possible. It is possible only for God. God atones by transmuting human guilt into divine suffering, through the 'carrying' of human sin.[19] The God who himself endures the God-forsakenness of the sinner is *the atoning God*. So it is right to pray 'Thou that *bearest* (not 'takest away') the sins of the world, *have mercy* upon us'. The divine compassion presupposes that human sin is carried and endured. Through the divine compassion, a life that has gone astray and been forfeited is born again out of its death from sin to a new life in righteousness. As long as the world exists, God does not merely carry the world's history of suffering. He carries humanity's history of injustice too. He endures it as victim among the other victims.

A human being is responsible for what he does, so no one can take his place. Everyone is alone with his guilt. Only God can take our place and carry us, together with our guilt. Modern insight into the dignity and personhood of human beings makes the old notions about propitiation and satisfaction, expiatory offerings and ransom obsolete. I can no doubt pay my debts but I shall not be able to dissociate myself from myself, as debtor. Guilt and sin affect human beings in what they are, not in what they have. Even if we have burdened ourselves with sins, we nevertheless confess 'God be merciful to me *a sinner*' (Luke 18.13). The sins I 'have' can be forgiven. The sinner I am has to be accepted and born again. So let us try to transfer atonement theology from its objectifying, legalistic concepts into human and personal terms.

As Christians see it, a drama is played out in the violent arrest, torture and crucifixion of Jesus by the Romans which is totally different from the one which these external human, or inhuman, circumstances suggest. In the suffering and death of the Son, atonement is given for the sins of human beings, and God's reconciliation of the world is consummated. The first Jewish Christian congregations already interpreted Christ's death as a divine atoning sacrifice, and in their faith in the justifying gospel they experienced the great liberation from the power of sin and the compulsion to sin. Because of the vicarious, atoning death of Christ, Christians had broken with this world of injustice, violence and death, and pledged themselves to the ministry of life (Rom. 6.12–14, 19–23). In the symbol of baptism, they knew that they had been born again with Christ to eternal life.

In what sense can we interpret Christ's death on the cross as atonement? It can only be understood as atonement for the sins of the world if in Christ we see God. That is why in these connections Paul always stresses Christ's divine Sonship.[20] But this means that Christ's sufferings are God's sufferings, and that his death is the death endured by God vicariously for all sinners who have fallen victim to death. So it is wrong to assume that through his vicarious suffering Christ appeased God's wrath over the sins of human beings, or that God sadistically crucified his own Son, or allowed him to be crucified. The crucified Christ has nothing to do with a God of retribution, or a divine judge presiding over a criminal court. Notions of this kind are in cross contradiction to 'the Father of Jesus Christ'. 'The cross is atonement *because* God is the Father';[21] for the atoning Christ is the revelation of the compassionate God. Atonement whose purpose is the reconciliation of the hostile, sinful world, is the suffering form taken by God's love for this world. The love of God wounded by human injustice and violence becomes the love of God which endures pain; God's 'wrath' becomes his compassion.

What did Christ suffer on the cross that can be described as atonement? Not the pains of body and mind, for he shares these with the many crucified and murdered people in world history. What he suffered is his special *divine* pain: the unheard prayer in Gethsemane, and the God-forsakenness he experienced on the cross. By suffering forsakenness by God – the God whose nearness he had so incomparably experienced that he knew himself to be the messianic child, God's Son – he experiences the pain of the divine love for sinners and takes it on himself. Christ's suffering on the cross is human sin transmuted into the atoning suffering of God. That is why this experience of Christ's on the cross – his experience of being forsaken by God – cannot be qualified or played down in any way at all. It is *the experience of hell*, as the young Luther so emphatically stressed in his theology of the cross.[22] Paul interpreted the God-forsakenness of Christ on the cross in the same way: 'For our sake he made him to be sin who knew no sin' (II Cor. 5, 21). Christ 'became a curse for us' (Gal. 3.13). On the cross hangs the Son of God, forsaken, cursed and damned. He hangs there 'for us', so that we might have peace: through his wounds we are healed.

There is more in this than Christ's *solidarity* with 'the accursed of the earth'. In this is the divine atonement for sin, for injustice and violence on earth. This divine atonement reveals *God's pain*. But God's pain reveals *God's faithfulness* to those he has created, and his indestructible love, which endures a world in opposition to him, and overcomes it. God reconciles this world-in-contradiction by enduring the contradiction, not by contradicting that contradiction – not, that is to say, through judgment. He moulds and alchemizes the pain of his love into atonement for the sinner.[23] In this way God becomes *the God of sinners*. He does not desire their death, and so that they can turn back he turns to them; so that they may live, he endures their death.

If we understand sin and atonement personally and relationally in this way, we are dissociating ourselves from the inadequate images of sacrificial theology: ransom, expiatory sacrifice, satisfaction, and so forth. It is not our objectified sins – sins in the plural – that have to be made good through objective propitiatory acts. It is we ourselves, as sinners, in our contradiction to life, who have to be justified and given back to life again. This happens through God's atoning love. For Christ's intervening love for us reveals nothing less than God's own intervening love.[24] The suffering and dying of Christ 'for us' gives us the assurance that 'God is for us', as Paul says in the hymn of faith's assurance, Romans 8.31–39: 'If God is for us, who can be against us . . . God is here . . . Christ is here . . . nothing can separate us from the love of God which is in Christ Jesus, our Lord.'

The mystery of God's atoning intervention for the world is unfolded once we grasp that the event on the cross is an event in God, and interpret it in trinitarian terms. A concept of God applied to the cross from outside, whether it be the *Deus impassibilis* or the God of retribution, makes it impossible to recognize in Christ the love of God which is 'for us'. But the power of the divine atoning intervention is the power of *the eternal love* with which the Father, the Son and the Holy Spirit are there 'for' one another in eternity. For the love with which the Father loved the world – loved it so greatly that through his Son, and the Son's suffering and death, he took on himself the atonement for the world's sins – is the very same love which the triune God *is* in eternity. To say 'God so *loved* the world that he gave his only begotten Son . . .' (John 3.16) presupposes: 'God *is* love' (I John 4.16). It is just that the eternal love is turned towards different objects. In the Trinity the divine Persons, in their mutual differences of being, are there for one another, and correspond to one another. On the cross of Christ this love is there for the others, for the sinners – the recalcitrant – enemies. The reciprocal self-surrender to one another within the Trinity is manifested in Christ's self-surrender in a world which is in contradiction to God; and this self-giving draws all those who believe in him into the eternal life of the divine love.

So how does atonement reach the people who commit injustice and violence? It reaches them out of the compassion of the Father, through the vicariously suffered God-forsakenness of the Son, and in the exonerating power of the Holy Spirit. It is a single movement of love, welling up out of the Father's pain, manifested in the Son's sufferings, and experienced in the Spirit of life. In this way God becomes *the God of the godless*. His righteousness and justice justifies the unrighteous and the unjust.

According to the traditions of the Western church, the atonement that frees us from sin has its foundation solely in *Christ's death*, not in his resurrection. His resurrection has always been understood simply as a divine legitimation, or as God's identification with Christ. But as we have already said, this is not in line with Paul's christology, according to which Christ died for us, 'indeed much more' ($\mu\tilde{\alpha}\lambda\lambda o\nu$ $\delta\acute{\epsilon}$), has been raised (Rom. 8.34). He 'intercedes for us' not merely as the one who died for us, but much more even, as the one risen and exalted (to the right hand of God). Even in our own lives it is not enough merely to atone for past guilt so as to be able to live with the past, important though that is. Something new has to be created, so that 'the old has passed away' (II Cor. 5.17) and we do not have to think about it any more. That is what is meant by 'the resurrection of Christ from the dead': it is the beginning of the new creation of the world. And that means 'And God will wipe away every tear from their eyes, and death shall be no more . . .' The beginning of the new creation of all things in righteousness and justice begins with the dead. That is why this new beginning can be called 'the raising of the dead', as Ezekiel 37 already sees in its anticipatory vision on the fields of the dead of Israel's history.

Is this God's answer to the dead of 'Auschwitz', whose remembrance weighs so heavy on our souls? The Orthodox church has proclaimed forgiveness at Easter, and celebrates it as the great feast of reconciliation:

> The day of resurrection,
> Let us be light on this feast.
> Let us embrace one another.
> Let us speak to those who hate us.
> For the resurrection's sake we will forgive one another
>   everything,
> And so let us cry together: Christ is risen from the dead.
> He is risen indeed.'[25]

§4 THE RECTIFYING RIGHTEOUSNESS AND JUSTICE OF GOD FOR STRUCTURES

In the world of injustice there are not merely victims on the one hand and perpetrators on the other. Between the two there are also political conditions and economic structures which actually turn some people into victims and others into perpetrators.[26] Sin is not just what one person does and another person suffers. There are also what Willem Visser't Hooft – talking about the apartheid laws of the racist Boer state – called heretical structures. And there are 'structural sins' too, of the kind we find in the dictatorships, with their surveillance systems. A world-wide economic order has grown up which makes the poor poorer and the rich richer, and which can therefore be seen as the 'power of sin' in a supra-personal form, because there is no real escape from it, either as victim or as beneficiary.[27] I have called unjust systems like this 'vicious circles',[28] because unless their very beginnings are resisted they develop a kind of potential of their own, through which the whole system inexorably impels itself towards its own death. First of all the weaker and most vulnerable creatures die, and then the stronger ones too. First of all the children of the poor die, and later the rich will die as well. 'First of all the forests die, and afterwards human beings.'

There are trends and laws in the major project 'modern society' which are going to end in ecological death for humanity and most other living things, through a progressive destruction of the environment, both the atmosphere and the earth.[29] The facts are plain: the deserts are spreading, the forests are shrinking, the greenhouse effect is on the increase, the ozone hole is getting bigger and bigger.[30] We human beings are both the perpetrators and the victims of these vicious circles and their deadly spirals. The strong and rich can for a time shuffle off the costs on to the weak and the poor, but in the end they are going to become victims themselves. The phenomena are familiar and sufficiently obvious. What we are dealing with here are the concepts of structural sin and the righteousness and justice of God which creates peace.

1. *Structures are made by people.* Permanent violence creates a violent society. Unhindered exploitation creates dependent colonies. And unthinking, predatory exploitation of raw materials and the earth creates the ecological crisis. Sin as the violent *act* of human beings creates a *disposition* towards violence. People get used to the fact that this is 'just the way things are'. The first sin is committed out of free choice, the second out of habit and the third out of an inward compulsion. The sinner is then no longer free. It is like drug addiction. The result is what Augustine accurately described as *non posse non peccare* – I am unable not to sin. But this is not merely so in the personal sector. On the social and structural levels too syndromes develop which in their turn govern and coerce human beings. The products of evil get out of hand. They begin to enslave men and women and to destroy them. Structural sin is sin that has taken on an independence of its own. Now sin is no longer a human act. It is a quasi-objective compulsive force dominating human beings. It is sin in the form of idolatry and legalized injustice. Anyone who exists in these structures becomes sin's accomplice, even if he

wants only what is good. How much good was done personally in Germany under the system of Nazi dictatorship! And yet it all contributed to evil – to the prolongation of the war and the annihilation of the nations.

2. Structures are made by people. But this is only half the truth. *People are determined by structures too.* That is the other half. Men and women are not merely the producers of the conditions in which they live. They are also the products of these conditions. But curiously enough this is not true of all structures. Unjust and evil structures compel people to do evil, because the men and women who will not conform to them are threatened with torture and death. But just structures and beneficial conditions do not automatically make people good. In this case it depends much more on the people themselves whether they use their freedom to promote what is right and just. That is the difference between dictatorships and democracies too. There can be a dictatorship of evil, but there cannot be a dictatorship of the good. The many, many causes of human unhappiness can be reduced – many of them can perhaps even be eliminated – but we cannot make people happy, because there is not – and fortunately never can be – any such thing as one and the same happiness for everyone. Whereas there can very well be one and the same unhappiness for everyone.[31]

3. The world needs to be a parable of the kingdom of God and its righteousness, and it is capable of being this parable: that is the way Karl Barth described the relationship between politics and the kingdom of God.[32] The political world is not the kingdom of God but it can correspond to, or controvert, the divine righteousness and justice. If we call institutionalized injustice 'structural sin', we are then experiencing the righteousness of God as running counter to 'the pattern of this world'. The debt crisis of the Third World today is not a matter of indifference for the kingdom of God. God's justice dwells among the victims of this crisis and cries out that the people deprived of their rights should be given those rights. Christ is among the least of his brothers and sisters, in solidarity with them. The righteousness and justice of God puts the people who cause this crisis, and the people who profit from it, in the wrong, and through the atoning sufferings of Christ frees them for the faith that converts.

The person who perceives that his righteousness is to be found in Christ's sufferings and death begins to die to this unjust world. He is 'as if dead' to the requirements and rewards of the oppressive system. He or she no longer recognizes the laws of structural violence. People who have found their righteousness in the Christ crucified 'for us' break with the world of injustice. They are righteous in Christ, no longer because of their race, class, sex or possessions. According to the standards of racism, the way Christ's disciples then behave is 'a disgrace to their race'. And according to the standards of capitalism they are 'betraying their class'. They put themselves on the side of the victims, and break with the perpetrators. To do this, means often enough that they become 'strangers to their own people'. For the sake of solidarity with the victims they relinquish their loyalty towards their own class and their own country. And they then quickly find themselves in a social no-man's land. One can also thereby manoeuvre oneself into a position where one stands aloof from society altogether, and loses all chances of influence. Unrealistic radicalism is often merely an adolescent rejection of life. *One* practical step towards more justice is more important than the purity of noble conviction. But of course in trying to find our way through these things, personal integrity is the most important inner criterion for where to resist and where to adapt.

4. What does God's righteousness and justice mean in the context of structural sins? Jews and Christians will start from their experiences of God in trying to say what righteousness is. As we have seen in this chapter, God's righteousness and justice is experienced as a creative righteousness that brings about justice and justifies. God is just because he creates justice for the people who are deprived of it, and puts the unjust on a just path. He creates justice for the people who suffer violence, and he saves through his righteousness. Through this justice and righteousness God brings about the shared peace which also means true life: *shalom*.

Finally, let us relate this biblical experience of God's righteousness to the concepts of justice in the legal thinking of our civilization.

(*a*) An early concept of European legal thinking defines justice as *iustitia distributiva: suum cuique* – to each his own. This brilliant formula combines equality before the law for everyone with the real differences between people: to each according to his and her abilities, to each according to his or her needs (Marx's version) or, as the Hutterian Brethren say: 'Everyone gives what he can – everyone gets what he needs'. But this concept of justice is largely *objectively* conceived, and has to do with work and performance and commodities: everyone has a claim to life, food, work and liberty because these are human rights.

(*b*) The *personal* concept of justice goes beyond this objective concept, and it is this that establishes human sociality. It consists of the mutual recognition and acceptance of other people. Mutual recognition of human dignity, and mutual acceptance, create a humane and just community. This is in line with Christian experience: 'Accept one another, as Christ has also accepted you, for the glory of God' (Rom. 15.7). This personal concept of justice is also the basis of the modern federalist ideas we find in democratic society, such as covenant and constitution.[33]

(*c*) The highest form of justice, however, is *the justice of compassion*, which creates justice for people deprived of it. This is the justice of 'the God of widows and the fatherless'. In this world of human injustice and human violence, the divine justice assumes the structure of the 'preferential option for the poor', as the liberation theologians in Latin America put it. This does not mean 'tempering justice with mercy'. It means that people receive the rights of which they have been deprived, and that the unjust are converted to justice. This divine justice is not something outside the human rule of law. It is itself the creative source of justice for every rule of law which leads to lasting peace. Like the recognition of the human dignity of other people, to establish and protect the rights of the poor, weak and sick is the foundation for every lasting, humane legal system.

§5 THE SPIRIT AS JUDGE

We have talked about establishing rights for people deprived of them, and about the justifying of the unjust, and the rectifying of their relations and circumstances. So who, then, is the Holy Spirit?

(*a*) *In negative terms*, he is the Spirit of righteousness and justice who can be sensed in *the pain of people without rights* over their deprivations. Without a feeling for justice this pain would not exist. Without the pain there would not be the struggle for the justice of which they have been robbed.

In negative terms, he is the Spirit of righteousness and justice who speaks in *the guilty conscience* of the people who commit violence. The 'guilty conscience' does not necessarily mean a conscious sense of guilt. It can also provoke inner uncertainty, fear of one's own self and aggression towards oneself and other people. 'The godless know no peace.' That is to say, the people who commit violence have lost their inner identity and try to compensate by inhumane acts of this kind.

In negative terms, this divine justice is shown in world history by *the instability of unjust conditions*, which have to be kept on an even keel by more and more violence, more and more police, more and more military control. Peace is a fruit of justice. This is true of social peace in a society too, and it is no less true of peace between nations. All that grows on the foundation of injustice is organized peacelessness. So unjust systems have feet of clay. They have no lasting development. The hidden presence in world history of the divine justice in God's Spirit 'destabilizes', so to speak, human systems of injustice, and sees to it that they cannot last.

(*b*) *In positive terms*, the Spirit of God is *the presence of Christ* among and in the victims of violence: Christ is their brother – they are his family and the community of his people, whether they know it or not. The Spirit is Christ's solidarity with them.

In positive terms, the Spirit of God is *the atoning power* of Christ's substitution among and in the perpetrators. Christ is 'the God of sinners'. The Spirit is Christ's atoning power for them and in them.

In positive terms, the fellowship of the Holy Spirit is *the divine love* which holds in life even self-destructive human communities in order to heal them. So the fellowship of the Holy Spirit is also the antitype of the human communities which are built up on injustice and violence, for the fellowship of the Holy Spirit gives to each his or her own. In the fellowship of the Holy Spirit, people accept one another mutually, and reciprocally recognize each other's dignity and rights. In the fellowship of the Holy Spirit compassion is alive. In that fellowship human socialities are as good as the fortunes of their weakest members.

(*c*) The Holy Spirit is the righteousness and justice of God which creates justice, justifies and rectifies. In the Spirit, lasting community with God, with other people and with nature become possible. That is why we can in this sense also call the Holy Spirit *the justification of life*. In the Spirit life again becomes worth loving. In the Spirit, human beings again become capable of loving life. In the Spirit life's intricate interactions again become fruitful. The rectifying Holy Spirit is God's 'yes' in justice to the life of each and all of us, and the life of each with all of us.

VII

The Rebirth to Life

The Reformation's central concept was what Article IV of the Augsburg Confession formulates as *the justification* of the sinner through God's grace for Christ's sake through faith alone. The central concept of pietism and the revivalist movements of modern times is *the rebirth* of lost men and women, to become children of God through the Holy Spirit. In Reformation theology, *regeneratio* and *renovatio* were really discussed only in the context of the doctrine of justification. But nineteenth-century experiential theology, following Schleiermacher's teaching about faith, took as its great theme the rebirth to believing life and the religious and moral renewal of the individual, in addition to – or even in detachment from – the doctrine of justification. In Germany, this can be said especially of the Erlangen school of F. H. R. Frank and J. C. K. von Hofmann.

In the New Testament, the message about God's justifying righteousness is without any doubt at the centre of Pauline theology, whereas it is only rarely that we come across the term regeneration and its related semantic field.[1] The *fact* described by the words 'regeneration' or 'rebirth' is certainly always implicit in baptismal theology, since from Christianity's very beginnings women and men who arrived at faith were baptized. But how are the ideas and terms 'justification' and 'regeneration' related? Do the two really mean the same thing? Are they saying the same thing in different ways? Do they mean two different aspects of the one, single salvation? Are they complementary terms for two different experiences on the path of salvation? In this chapter we shall be asking about the experiences of the Spirit which have to be described as 'rebirth' or 'regeneration'. And we shall enquire about the human experience of the self in this experience of the Spirit, and about the divine experience of the Spirit in this human experience of the self.

§1 BIBLICAL INTERPRETATIONS

The word παλιγγενεσία derives from oriental cosmology, which was introduced into the ancient world by the Pythagoreans. It means the rebirth of worldly time. The aeons or eras of world time take a cyclic course. Their return is based on the periodical 'rebirth' of the world. So the festival of the New Year celebrates the rebirth of the year, and every Sunday celebrates the rebirth of the week. Applied to human beings, 'rebirth' is part of the doctrine of reincarnation.

In Jewish apocalyptic, however, this concept was refashioned eschatologically. There it meant the unique and final 'rebirth' for the eternal kingdom of the creation which had become old, transient and mortal. In this context the prefix 're-' changes its meaning to 'new', for this can in fact no more be a 'rebirth' to the old life than it is a restoration of the old world. The expressions 'reborn' or 'born again' which are frequently used in America do not make the point, for what is in fact meant is not *re*generation but the beginning of a new life. 'Incipit vita nova' – a new life begins, as the conversation with Nicodemus in John 3.3–5 shows. What Daniel and the apocalyptists who followed him expected of the coming of the Son of man and his enduring righteousness and justice was just such a universal new birth of the world (Daniel 7). We meet this cosmic, apocalyptic interpretation of 'rebirth' in Matt. 19.28: 'In the rebirth (παλιγγενεσία; RSV: 'new world'), when the Son of man shall sit on his glorious throne, you who have followed me will also sit on twelve thrones, judging the twelve tribes of Israel.' The Son of man who suffers here will there be exalted; the Son of man who is judged here will there himself be the judge, the Son of man put to death here will there live eternally. His followers will be drawn into his humiliation here and his exaltation there.

Neither the Reformation nor the Pietistic and revivalist theologians took this cosmic, apocalyptic character of 'rebirth' into account, however.[2] They always viewed regeneration from the very outset as something that happens in human beings themselves. They saw rebirth only as an inward personal experience in the soul, not as an expectation for the whole suffering and dying world. Even today there are lexicon articles about 'regeneration' which do not cite Matt. 19.28.[3]

The classic passage Titus 3.5–7 explains regeneration as 'renewal', using it to describe the baptismal experience of faith: 'He saved us . . . in virtue of his own mercy, by the washing of regeneration and renewal in the Holy Spirit, which he poured out upon us richly, through Jesus Christ our Saviour, so that we might be justified by his grace and become heirs in hope of eternal life.' What has happened? A person believes. He or she is baptized in the congregation. Their personal experience belongs from the outset within the experience of sociality, for baptism is a happening to, and for, the individual, but in the congregation. 'Regeneration' as 'renewal' comes about through the Holy Spirit. The Spirit comes through Christ out of the compassion of the Father. The Spirit is 'poured out'. The metaphor says that the divine 'wellspring of life' in a human being begins to flow (John 4.14). Through this experience of the Spirit, who comes upon us from the Father through the Son, we become 'justified through grace' and, in hope, 'heirs of eternal life'. I Peter 1.3 follows the same progression of ideas, but stresses that 'through the resurrection of Jesus Christ from the dead' we have been 'born anew to a living hope'.

If we put these two assertions together systematically, we find that the eternal foundation of regeneration is the mercy of God, the Father of Jesus Christ. His compassion is his love, which creates and gives birth. The historical foundation for regeneration is Christ, or to be more exact: the resurrection of Christ from the dead. Whereas for the reconciliation of the godless and the forgiveness of sins we are pointed to the significance for salvation of Christ's death on the cross,[4] here the saving significance of Christ's resurrection is perceived in the rebirth to a living hope. The theology of regeneration is Easter theology.

The medium of regeneration is the Holy Spirit, which is 'richly' poured out. Because the Spirit is mediated through Christ, it must at this point be called 'the Spirit of Christ'. Because it proceeds from Christ's resurrection from the dead, it has to be understood as the quickening power of the resurrection (Rom. 8.11). The operation of the Spirit as we experience it is therefore a double one: it is the justification of the godless out of grace, and their rebirth to a living hope through their installation in their right to inherit God's future. The justification of the godless is the initial operation of the outpouring of the Spirit on all transient and mortal flesh. According to Titus 3.5–7, regeneration is grounded on the experience of the Spirit, and is primary, including the justification of the godless and their installation in their right to inherit eternal life. According to I Peter 1.3, rebirth comes from Christ's resurrection, and points the hope of men and women towards eternal life.

In these texts the interpretation of regeneration or rebirth as new creation is christologically based, pneumatologically accomplished and eschatologically orientated. The experience of the Spirit makes Christ – the *risen* Christ – present, and with him makes the eschatological future present too. Precisely because of this, experience of the Spirit is the experience of the presence of eternity. What is born from God is divine. So regeneration means emerging from this mortal and transient life into life that is immortal and eternal. In the moment of 'rebirth', eternity touches time. The believer's personal experience – the experience of being born anew and of being given the gift of true life – will have to keep these dimensions present.

§2 THE DISCUSSION IN SYSTEMATIC THEOLOGY

We shall now look at some of the theses which have been explored in the discussion between supporters of Pietism and proponents of Reformation theology.

1. Regeneration Complements Justification

The justification of the sinner through grace alone for Christ's sake was largely objectified in sixteenth- and seventeenth-century Lutheran orthodoxy, being put forward as represented only through the church's institutions of word and sacrament. And this meant that the hunger for some subjective complement was bound to arise. The Christ of the doctrine of justification is the Christ who died 'for us'; but what has happened to the risen Christ, and the Christ who lives 'in us'? If Christ intercedes 'for us' as our representative, are we too not then 'in him' as 'the new creatures' whose lives are hidden 'in him'? Where, according to the church's experience of Christ, is the personal experience of the Spirit? Melanchthon made justification terminology legalistic through and through. It became a terminology of accusation and pardon *in foro Dei*. But then what becomes of the effectively justifying righteousness of God in believers? This was the

question with which Andreas Osiander already challenged Melanchthon's forensic doctrine of justification. So for these reasons it is quite
understandable that at the time when cultural subjectivism was
beginning in Europe, the revival movements should have chosen the
term 'rebirth': justification is conferred on me; but I experience my
rebirth as manifestly and unmistakably my own – as uniquely so as
my birth. Justification puts me in a new relationship to God, but
regeneration or rebirth changes my inner substance, provides a new
nucleus for my existence, puts a new self in me, and renews me
myself, with my attitude to life and my conduct. Justification says
what God does for human beings; regeneration says what then
happens within them.[5]

The ideas echoing in the words regeneration or rebirth have to do
with the future of a new life. They are not about coming to terms
with the past, like 'the forgiveness of sins' and 'the justification of
the godless'. They awaken ideas about the growth of life, springtime
in the world of nature, and the greening of all the trees and plants,
which Hildegard of Bingen called the *viriditas* of the Holy Spirit.[6]
They do not remind us of final judgment and the day of wrath, like
the Reformation spirituality of guilt and grace.

But can we say that the experience of regeneration through the
Spirit means a complementary 'second grace' following justifying
faith, an experience which true believers have to have, if they are to
count as Christians who have been 'born again'? According to our
texts this is not possible. For it is not only justifying faith that springs
from the pentecostal experience of the Spirit. This is already true of
justification through grace (Titus 3.5–7). There is no justification
without the Spirit. Justifying faith is itself the experience that the love
of God has been poured out into our hearts 'through the Holy Spirit'
(Rom. 5.5).

If this is correct, then we have to put a critical question to
Reformation theology, asking whether it formulated its doctrine
of justification in such a way that the doctrine presupposes this
experience of the Spirit, or is at least open for it. Ernst Cremer certainly
bravely maintained the thesis that 'justification is regeneration',[7] and
also found evidence for his postulate in the Lutheran confessional
documents. But he did not modify Melanchthon's doctrine of justification in respect of regeneration. How could this be done?

2. Justification is Regeneration

If this thesis is correct, the lopsidedness we find in the viewpoint and emphases of Reformation theology has to be rectified and supplemented. The salvific meaning of Christ's death for men and women is undoubtedly, according to Paul and Luther, the forgiveness of injustice and the justification of those who know no justice. But if Christ 'was raised again for our justification' (Rom. 4.25), then the saving significance of his *resurrection* must be given its due weight too. The forgiveness of sins is a backward-looking act. The forward-looking act of justification is the new creation of life, the awakening of love, and the rebirth to a living hope.[8]

Even at the Reformation, a one-sided theology of the cross reduced the justification of a man or woman to the forgiveness of his or her sins. But if the justification of the unjust puts the unjust on the path of a just life, then between the forgiveness of sins and new life in the righteousness of God is the acceptance of the human being as a child of God; for it is only as God's children that men and women become heirs of God's kingdom. But as Paul stresses, the experience of being the child of God is the experience of the Spirit which lets believers cry like Jesus himself: 'Abba, dear Father' (Rom. 8.8, 15; Gal. 4.5, 6). 'For all who are led by the Spirit of God are children of God' (Rom. 8.14). For Paul, to be God's child through justification points forward eschatologically towards the coming divine righteousness, which will be the foundation for the new creation of all things (Gal. 5.5). So in order to present the regeneration of men and women as their justification, the Reformation's doctrine of justification has to be expanded:

1. It must show the saving significance of Christ's death *and resurrection*.

2. It must from the outset be presented pneumatologically as *experience of the Spirit*.

3. It must be *eschatologically orientated*. Because the doctrine of justification still has to be recast in this sense, pietistic and revivalist teachings about regeneration are still important challenges to Reformation theology.

3. The Regeneration of Men and Women Took Place on Golgotha

By shifting the problem from anthropology to christology in this way, Karl Barth tried to solve it once and for all.[9] At this point he followed Hermann Friedrich Kohlbrügge, the precursor whom he initially venerated but later criticized. Kohlbrügge had answered the question about the date of his conversion by saying: 'I was converted on Golgotha.'[10] 'In His death there took place the regeneration and conversion of man. They took place in Jesus Christ as the One Crucified because it is finally and supremely in his cross that He acted as the Lord and King of all men, that He maintained and exercised his sovereignty, that He proved His likeness to the God who is so unassuming in the world but so revolutionary in relation to it, and that he inaugurated His kingdom as a historical actuality.'[11] But if the regeneration and conversion of every individual has already been brought about in Christ's vicarious death for all human beings, then the work of the Holy Spirit can only be to bring men and women to the knowledge and recognition of this fact, which took place without them on their behalf. Because the salvation of the world has been brought about in Christ and is therefore already existent, the work of the Holy Spirit can only be *recognition* of this salvation. Even the reconciliation of the world with God in the form of *sanctification* has for Barth already taken place in Christ *de jure*, even though it will certainly *de facto*, like justification, be discerned, acknowledged and confessed by the people wakened to faith as *their* justification and *their* sanctification. Those who in faith perceive salvation in Christ consequently perceive something which is for the benefit of all human beings: 'What has happened to him [i.e., the believer] *de facto* has happened to all men *de jure*.'[12]

If we compare this statement with the biblical texts interpreted, it becomes noticeable that for Barth the eschatological rebirth of the whole creation has already taken place in the universal, vicarious Christ event – whereas for the New Testament this rebirth is the object of eschatological hope. As Barth sees it, moreover, it is on Golgotha that the rebirth of the whole world and all human beings has taken place, whereas in I Peter the rebirth 'to a living hope' is based on the resurrection of Christ from the dead. Barth sees the work of the Holy Spirit pre-eminently in the perception and recognition of that which has already, objectively and *de jure*, been accomplished in Christ for all human beings, whereas regeneration surely means the personal beginning of a new life in hope for God's future. Knowledge of Christ certainly leads to fellowship with Christ; but life in the Spirit is not absorbed by, or completely congruent with, the mere knowledge and acknowledgment of Christ. Just because it is a resonance of Christ, it is the overture to a new future. Through a one-sided theology of the cross, real futurist eschatology is lost, and then pneumatology is not given its proper status. Of course the whole universe is present and represented in Christ's universal representation, as what he represents. But that is only the basis for its rebirth, not as yet the goal.

4. *Those Who Have Been Born Again Live From What Comes to Meet Them*

With this consistently eschatological thesis, Otto Weber tried to free the doctrine of regeneration from its individualistic confines. He takes up its original cosmic, apocalyptic significance and in that light defines the hope for which men and women are born again from the Spirit. It is the kingdom of God which those who are 'born anew' from the Spirit are going to see (John 3.3–5). 'Dogmatic tradition has almost entirely failed to take proper account of the eschatological character of *regeneratio*.'[13] But what are people born again *for*? 'Is the human being the goal of all things? The New Testament throws open a different horizon: regeneration or renewal comes about in the new creation (II Cor. 5.17; Gal. 6.15), in the emergence of the new salvific event which comes to meet human beings and the appearance of the new salvific reality.' If one starts consistently and exclusively from this eschatological perspective, it must be said that 'The regenerate person is not as such already existent' and that regeneration 'belongs to the reality present to us only as something to be expected. The regenerate person is ahead of himself, as it were; he lives from what is coming to meet him, not from what already exists in him.'[14]

Although Otto Weber otherwise counts as Barth's faithful pupil and selfless interpreter, his eschatological postulate about regeneration is diametrically opposed to Barth's christological thesis. Now, Weber would of course have been the last to deny the christological foundation of the eschatological perspective, and the vista it opens towards the new creation of the world. But for all that, by shifting the problem of regeneration into eschatology his postulate is as

radical as Barth's christological solution of the problem. Both really
evade the question about the *experience* of the Holy Spirit. For Barth
this experience is to be found wholly in knowledge of Christ –
for Weber wholly in expectation of the future. But can we treat
expectation and experience as antitheses – on the one hand the reality
expected, on the other reality as it already exists? Surely we always
have experiences with our expectations too?

The 'rebirth to a living hope' contains a surplus of hope which
only the eternal life of the new, future world can fulfil. It is important
to understand this eschatological immeasurability in the experience
of the Spirit. It is the reason why rebirth from the Spirit in this
life never becomes an experience that is finished and done with,
something we could look back to and rely on. Here the new life in
the Spirit is never any more than a beginning, if we compare it with
the new creation in which hope is to be fulfilled (Rev. 21). But this
means that what is existent does not, for all that, remain what it is.
It is fundamentally changed. With a 'living hope' men and women
do not merely experience love and pain, life and death in a different
way. They have other experiences too – experiences in the discipleship
of Christ. Weber's antithesis between existing and expected reality
applies only to the question about where a person puts his trust: does
he rely on the things of this transitory world, or on the powers of the
world to come? Once this question has been clarified, the regenerate
person will find himself in experiences of life and the world which
he can also narrate. Expectations hurry ahead. Experiences follow.
They follow like *a divine trail* laid in the life of the individual, the
community and creation. Every exodus is accompanied by trials and
perils, but also by 'signs and wonders', which are perceived by the
men and women who are travelling the same road.

5. *Regeneration Makes Christ's Resurrection Present and is the Opening of Eternal Life*

This thesis gives pneumatology a justification of its own between the
christology which is its premise and the eschatology towards which
it is aligned. Because in Christ's resurrection 'from the dead' the
annihilation of death through the prevenient mercy of God the Father
has already come about in advance, we can also see in the resurrection
the beginning of the rebirth of the whole creation, and can call it
'the rebirth of Christ'. Believers are possessed by the Spirit of the

resurrection, and through it are born again to a well-founded hope for eternal life. A coherent process issues from the rebirth of Christ from death through the Spirit, by way of the rebirth of mortal human beings through the Spirit, to the universal rebirth of the cosmos through the Spirit. In this process God the Father acts through the Spirit on Christ, and through Christ on the Spirit. The operations of his acts are the operations of the Spirit and are present in the Spirit. In the event in which believers are born again to become children of God and heirs of his kingdom, the efficacies of Christ and the efficacies of the Spirit interpenetrate. If we call this event *justification*, we are describing it as the operation of Christ. If we call it *regeneration*, we are describing the operation of the Spirit. We need both viewpoints if we are to understand the event completely. If the discipleship of Jesus has also to be understood as life in the Spirit, then being-in-Christ and life-from-the-Spirit mean the same thing, but seen from different sides.

The presence of eternity which people perceive in the rebirth of life is something we shall try to describe in the following section.

§3 PERSONAL EXPERIENCE IN REGENERATION: INCIPIT VITA NOVA

It would be presumptuous to describe the ways in which people experience the rebirth to life. They are as multifarious and protean as human life itself. Nor can we make particular inward experiences a yardstick for regeneration, as a way of testing the state of faith of other people. Yet theology must not be prevented from describing the experiences of the Spirit out of fear of singular experiences and pietistic introspection. In the New Testament, at least, believers and apostles talk extensively about their experiences.[15]

The first experience we have to mention is the experience of rapturous *joy*. When the Spirit of the resurrection is experienced, a person breathes freely, and gets up, and lives with head held high, and walks upright, possessed by the indescribable joy that finds expression in the Easter hymns.[16] When life is reborn out of violence and guilt, wrongs committed and hurts endured, and finally out of the shadow of death, this means a tremendous *affirmation of life*. Pain and disappointments have made our spirits what Paul Gerhardt calls 'Trauergeister' – sad or grieving spirits. Now they wake up again. We begin to love life once more with the love of God which we experience in his Spirit. If we replace the word 'Spirit' by the biblical word *ruach*, God's life-giving energy, we immediately understand the personal experiences that are bound up with the experience of this energy.

Peace is another experience of the Spirit in our restless hearts: peace with God in Christ, because the love of God has been poured out in our hearts through the Holy Spirit (Rom. 5.1, 5). 'Heart' means more than the cognitive faculty of our understanding. It means all the deep levels of our inner life. The energy of God's love penetrates us through and through, creating peace not only for our souls but physically too. Here we again have to follow the Old Testament, and interpret peace as *shalom*. For then it presupposes justice, and comprehends both salvation *and* well-being – in short, *happiness* of both body and soul.

We do not need to go into the many other experiences of God's Spirit. If we list them, as Paul does in Gal. 5.22, they all seem to be purely positive and somewhat illusory. By listing them in this way we cut them loose from the antipoles and antinomies of reality. But this is wrong, for life in the Spirit is always discipleship of Jesus, and discipleship leads to conflict with the powers and the powerful of 'this world', and to the bearing of the cross. Separation from the powers and compulsions of 'this world' necessarily conduces to solidarity with the victims of these powers and compulsions, and to intervention on their behalf. The indescribable joy over the Easter rebirth of life therefore shows itself in resistance to this world of death and in the determined refusal to accustom ourselves inwardly to death.

Peace with God the Creator inevitably and inescapably means not making peace with the systematic destruction of creation by this society of ours. For the person who experiences the peace of God 'in the heart' begins to hope for peace on earth, and therefore begins to resist peacelessness, armaments and war in the world of human beings, and exploitation and devastation in the world of nature. People who experience the justification of those without rights under Christ's cross begin to hope for the new creation of justice for everyone and everything, so they begin to resist the wrong that is done to the weak. In *faith* we experience the peace of God, in *hope* we look ahead to a peaceful world, and in *resistance* to violence we confess God's peace. In faith we receive the consolation of the Spirit in suffering, but in hope we look to the future of a new creation in which there will be no more mourning and no more pain and no more crying; and in the struggle against the unnecessary suffering of other creatures, we witness to life. The people who believe God acquire hope for this earth and everything living in it, and do not despair. They see through the horizon of apocalyptic terrors, as it were, into God's new world, and act in accordance with that world now, even today, in the midst of this world's terrors.

We call these experiences of peace with God and Easter joy in the rebirth to life, *experiences of the Holy Spirit*. What do we mean by that? We are saying that these experiences are of unfathomable depth, because in them God himself is present in us, so that in the immanence of our hearts we discover a transcendent depth. If this Spirit of God is 'the Spirit of the resurrection', then we are possessed by a hope which sees unlimited potentialities ahead, because it looks towards God's future. The heart expands. The goals of hope in our own lives, and what we ourselves expect of life, fuse with God's promises for a new creation of all things. This gives our own finite and limited life an infinite meaning. The transcendent depths of the divine Spirit and the eschatological breadth of the Spirit of the resurrection mean that we cannot talk about our 'rebirth' or 'regeneration' as if it were a once-and-for-all experience, something finished and done with that is now behind us. We are still involved in the experience of renewal, and the becoming-new travels with us.

In mediaeval times people thought that for particular sins one could perform acts of penance once and for all, and then everything would be all right. But at the beginning of his Ninety-Five Theses Luther affirmed that the Christian life is an unceasing 'daily act of repentance'. Renewal in the Holy Spirit (Titus 3.5) means a process which begins in this life but is completed only in the life that is eternal. Luther has two sayings about this: 'To go forward on God's ways means continually beginning afresh' and: 'Not to go forward on God's ways means going backwards.'

Of course there is a growth in faith and a growth too in the new life of the Spirit to which people are born again. It is also very important to be clear about the various stages of life, with their individual characters and crises, so that faith can go on growing as the person grows, and does not stop short at the stage of one's confirmation classes, as it does for many grown-up people.[17] But our biographies develop out of interactions with other people and are always part of social and political events too. The images of 'growth', 'development' and 'progression' are taken from the world of nature, and seldom fit human history, that 'hotchpotch of error and violence', as Goethe termed it. In the trials and defeats of real history, it may well be the supreme stage of life in the Spirit to sigh: 'Lord I believe, help my unbelief.'

For Christians living in a minority situation or under persecution another question was more important: can the experience of the Holy Spirit in the rebirth to new life and to a living hope ever be lost or not? The answer of the Reformed theologians who remembered the experiences of the Huguenots and the Dutch and other persecuted Christians was the doctrine of *perseverantia sanctorum usque ad finem* – the perseverance of the saints to the end.[18] Because rebirth in the Spirit comes from the mercy of God, it is held fast in the faithfulness of God and never forsakes believers. Some theologians thought that faith as an act of decision becomes in time faith as a permanent state of soul, and that this *habitus*, or disposition, could then never be lost, provided that it was strongly enough developed.[19] Others thought of the seed of the Spirit, out of which faith grows in the heart, and which is still there even when every feeling of belief and all the certainties of faith have been lost.

The Reformed theologians did not think as psychologically as this. Their train of thought was theological: 1. God the Father is faithful; he cannot deny himself (II Tim. 2.13). He never lets go of the person he has chosen. 2. God the Son prayed for those who are his 'that your faith might not fail' (Luke 22.32). 3. As advance payment and beginning of eternal life, the Holy Spirit remains with the people who are his to the end (*usque ad finem*). The Holy Spirit 'seals' God's children for the day of redemption. These three statements are not analytical judgments about the steadfastness of believers. They are synthetic judgments about the faithfulness of the triune God, and his unshakable reliability. That is not a reason for self-assurance, but it is a reason for trust: even if we are lost to ourselves, we are never lost to the faithful God. Even if we give ourselves up, God never gives us up.

Corresponding doctrines of perseverance can be found in the other Christian traditions too, but they are always ecclesiologically aligned, not anthropologically, and apply to the institution, not the people. The Augsburg Confession, for example, says in the opening sentence of Article VII: 'Item docent, quod una sancta ecclesia perpetuo mansura sit' ('. . . that one holy Christian church will be and remain forever'). And the reason given for this endurance is 'that even the gates of Hell shall not prevail against it'.[19a] But how can the holy church have the assurance of *perseverantia usque ad finem* if the holy sinners who constitute the church are not permitted this assurance? Are only the institutions to survive, not the people? Does God's Spirit rest on the institution but not in the hearts of believers? Assurance of faith is the assurance of God's faithfulness, and therefore the assurance of remaining in that divine faithfulness whatever happens. This certainty of preservation, of 'being kept', is part of the experience of the Holy Spirit, as it is also the experience of God.

§4 THE EXPERIENCE OF GOD IN REGENERATION: THE SPIRIT AS THE MOTHER OF LIFE

If the new life is experienced and lived *in* the Spirit, then the Spirit is not itself the object of experience; it is the medium and space for experience. It is therefore not objective, and we cannot talk *about* the Spirit. We can only talk *out of* the Spirit. God's Spirit is then closer to our inner being than we ourselves. The Spirit is our standpoint, which we cannot confront unless we move away from it. The Spirit is the broad place in which we have experiences. We know so little about the Holy Spirit because he is too close, not because he is so far away from us. The heart of the lived moment always remains dark, and yet we live in it. If we think about it, it is either too soon or too late. The same is true about life *in* the Spirit and *out of* the Spirit. We perceive Christ and we expect the kingdom of God, but the Spirit *in* which we perceive and expect is something we cannot perceive, because he is directly in us and we in him. Yet theological reflection can arrive at the Spirit from the operations experienced, and can develop ideas about him. If these experiences are thought of as re*birth* or as being *born* again, this suggests a singular image for the Holy Spirit, an image which was quite familiar in the early centuries of Christianity, especially in Syria, but which came to be lost in the patriarchal Roman empire: *the image of the mother*. If believers are 'born' again from the Holy Spirit, then the Spirit is 'the mother' of God's children and can in this sense also be termed a 'feminine' Spirit. If the Holy Spirit is 'the Comforter' (Paraclete), it comforts 'as a mother comforts'. In this sense it is the motherly comforter of believers. Linguistically this again brings out the characteristics of the Hebrew expression 'Yahweh's *ruach*'.

The earliest testimonies are probably to be found in the Gospel of Thomas: 'He who will not love his Father and his Mother as I do, cannot be my disciple. For my mother gave me life.'[20] In Jerome we find a quotation from a Hebrew gospel: 'When the Lord came up out of the water, the whole wellspring of the Holy Spirit came down and rested on him, and said to him: "My Son, in all the prophets I awaited thy coming, so that I might rest in thee. For thou art my rest, thou my first-born Son, who reigneth in eternity." '[21] The Hebrew gospel has passed down the following saying: 'Then my mother, the Holy Spirit, seized me by the hair and bore me away to the great Mount Tabor.'[22] In the Christian-Gnostic 'Hymn of the Pearl' (in the apocryphal Acts of Thomas), the Trinity consists of God the Father, the Holy Spirit as Mother, and the Son. In the Syrian version of the poem we find the prayers: 'Come merciful Mother' and 'Come, giver of life'. The Holy Spirit is also addressed as 'Mother of all created being'.[23] In the Greek translations of these Gnostic texts, 'Mother' is then often already replaced by 'Holy Spirit'.

Right down to Irenaeus, there was a struggle in the mainstream church against the Gnostic-Christian congregations, and this opposition also extended to feminine images for God, especially in the Roman empire.[24] But among the Syrian Fathers this language held its ground. Aphraates is an early witness. In order to justify his problematical ascetic and celibate way of life, he said: 'Why does a man forsake father and mother when he takes a wife? This is the explanation: as long as a man has no wife, he loves and reverences God his Father and the Holy Spirit his Mother, and has no other love. But when the man has taken a wife, he leaves this Father and Mother of his, and his heart is fettered by this world.'[25] The typically semitic, motherly form of the Holy Spirit can also be found in his view of the Paraclete.

The famous Fifty Homilies of Makarios the mystic come from the sphere of Syrian Christianity, and they inspired and influenced both the Orthodox churches and the churches of the West. The real author was in fact the theologian Symeon of Mesopotamia, who was a Messalian, not the desert father Makarios.[26] These homilies talk about 'the motherly ministry of the Holy Spirit', using two arguments. 1. The promised Comforter (the Paraclete) will 'comfort you as a mother comforts' (here John 14.26 is put together with Isa. 66.13); and 2. Only the person who has been 'born anew' can see the kingdom of God. Men and women are 'born anew' from the Spirit. They are 'children of the Spirit' and the Spirit is their 'Mother'. These homilies were translated into German in the seventeenth century by Gottfried Arnold, and were widely read in the early years of Pietism. John Wesley was fascinated by 'Macarios the Egyptian',[27] and August Hermann Francke gave extensive treatment to 'the motherly ministry of the Holy Spirit' in his treatise on nature and grace.[28] For Count Zinzendorf, this perception was a kind of revelation, and in 1741, when the Moravian Brethren founded their community in Bethlehem, Pennsylvania, he officially proclaimed 'the motherly office of the Holy Spirit'. In 1744 this finding was elevated to the rank of community doctrine.[29]

By doing this, Zinzendorf made the divine Trinity, conceived according to the pattern of a family, the prototype for the community of brothers and sisters on earth: 'since the Father of our LOrd JEsus Christ is our true *Father*, and the Spirit of JEsus Christ is our true *Mother*; because the Son of the living GOd . . . is our true *Brother*.' 'The Father must love us and can do no other, the Son, our brother, must love souls as His own soul, and must love the body as His own body, because we are flesh of His flesh, bone of His bone, and He can do no other.'[30] The biblical grounds Zinzendorf puts forward are the reasons given by Makarios. The idea of the family as a way of depicting the Trinity has Gnostic-Christian origins, as we can still see today from Ethiopian icons. What Zinzendorf contributes was inspired by the era of 'sensibility' – the cultivation of the feelings – which was now beginning. What is motherly about the operations of the Spirit can be sensed in its tenderness and sympathy: '. . . they are driven forward by a certain tender Impulse, through Delight in the matter, through a blessed Attraction which souls feel for this and that thing, through a *Sympathy* which they also discover in themselves, and yet the awareness of the Saviour and his Image is the *concept*.'[31] Paul Gerhardt describes the leadings of the Spirit in much the same way as a guiding 'with motherly hand' ('Mit Mutterhänden leitet er die Seinen ständig hin und her . . .').

The metaphor of re*birth* or new *birth* makes it seem natural to talk about an engendering Deity. Here God is experienced, not as the liberating Lord but as 'the well of life'. Giving birth, nourishing, protecting and consoling, love's empathy and sympathy: these are then the expressions which suggest themselves as a way of describing the relations of the Spirit to her children. They express mutual intimacy, not sovereign and aweful distance.

In trinitarian theology, the image of the divine family raises the Spirit to the same rank as the Father, and puts the Spirit before the Son. Unless, like Ludwig Feuerbach, we wish to cast the image aside altogether as a pure projection of a family idyll, it does offer interesting corrective possibilities, if we compare it with the other pictures of the Trinity – Irenaeus's image of the One God with two hands, for example.

But more important than these speculative possibilities is the new definition of what it means for human beings to be the image of God. If the Trinity is a community, then what corresponds to it is the true human community of men and women. A certain de-patriarchaliz-ation of the picture of God results in a de-patriarchalization and de-hierarchalization of the church too.

Of course by calling God the Holy Spirit 'Mother' we are merely putting parallel to the 'Father' another power as primal source. Psychologically speaking, inward liberation from the mother is as much a part of human development as emancipation from the Father. Like Israel's prophets, Christianity actually replaced the patriarchal and matriarchal powers of origin by *the messianism of the Child*, as the bearer of hope and the beginning of the future.[32] 'Unless you become like children, you will never enter the kingdom of heaven' (Matt. 18.3). But this is not brought out by the patriarchal or matriarchal images of God.

VIII

The Sanctification of Life

Every life that is born wants to grow. When someone is born we talk about their birthday. Life begins, the senses awaken. The child opens its eyes and sees the light. It begins to breath, and feels the air. It cries, and hears the sounds. It lies beside its mother and feels the warmth of her skin.

The life we say has been 'born again' or 'born anew' from God's eternal Spirit also wants to grow, and to arrive at its proper form, configuration or Gestalt. Our senses are born again too.[1] The enlightened eyes of the understanding wake to the awareness of God, to knowledge of the glory of God in the face of Christ. In the dictates of life the liberated will explores its new energies. The beating heart experiences God's love, is warmed by it into love for life, and comes alive from its source. The experience of God's Spirit is like breathing the air: 'God is continually breathing, as it were, upon the soul, and the soul is breathing unto God.'[2] God's Spirit is life's vibrating, vitalizing field of energy: we are in God, and God is in us. Our stirrings towards life are experienced by God, and we experience God's living energies. In the open air of the eternal Spirit, the new life unfurls. In the confidence of faith we plumb the depths of the Spirit, in love we explore its breadth, and in hope its open horizons. God's Spirit is our space for living.

If the primal experience of the Spirit is called rebirth, this metaphor itself implies 'growth' in faith, in knowledge and in wisdom. But we must not interpret this growth in faith individualistically and linearly. We experience life in the interplay between what is inward and what is outward. Our biography is woven into our social history, and into the political history of our era; and it is only in relatively peaceful times that the naturalistic expression 'growth' is an appropriate way of describing history at all. In times of major catastrophes, inflations and revolutions, continuous growth is impossible for most people. The daily struggle to survive makes their own experience a different one.

We talk about 'growth in faith' in three different ways:

1. We talk about the stages in the growth of faith which correspond to a person's age.[3] Life led 'in the Spirit' in its own turn influences the way the Spirit is experienced at different periods in a person's life. A child's faith, adolescent faith, the faith of parents and working people and, finally, the faith of old age all take different forms. It is dreadful if faith does not grow with people, and if they go on cherishing childish beliefs and notions about faith after they are grown up. It is the mutual influence between beliefs and the experience of life which essentially speaking constitutes the *vita christiana*.

2. But it was not this that was really meant by 'growing in faith', and the striving for a continually deeper sanctification of life. Does 'the spiritual life' have its own laws and its own special developments, parallel to people's different ages and experiences of life?

For Paul, the new 'life in the Spirit' is eschatologically aligned: 'The Spirit brackets the present with the future, lets us wait for the future in the present, and in the present promises the future. In Pauline language it is the 'pledge' or advance payment, which guarantees that what is still to come will really follow.'[4] The Spirit is the great Mover in the direction of the future in which 'God will be all in all'. The protean gifts of the Spirit are 'the powers of the age to come' (Heb. 6.5).

When the metaphor of rebirth declares that the people concerned are 'like newly born children', it is implying that they will grow and mature into 'adults in faith'. In this sense there is tested and tried and mature faith, and there are progressions in the knowledge of God, in the liberation of the will, and in the assurance of the heart. Of course these progressions are experienced as beginnings and fragments, approaches and anticipations. And often enough we never get beyond *oboedientia inchoata* of this kind.[5] But every beginning reaches forward to completion. If not, it is not a beginning. Where do we have to look for this completion? What we have here called rebirth and growth in faith cannot be directed towards fulfilment in this world, before we die, in the sense of a 'sinless perfection'; for regeneration here is the new birth for eternal life, and will be completed only in the resurrection of the dead. Consequently the knowledge of God here is fragmentary and 'in part', and will be perfected only in the seeing face to face (I Cor. 13). What is experienced here in the Spirit as God's love is only the beginning of what will be experienced then as God's glory. Sanctification is the beginning of glorification; glorification is the consummation of sanctification.

3. We have to think of growth in faith qualitatively, not quantitatively. Life grows by expressing itself. Its expression emerges from the depths of the unconscious which the consciousness does not illuminate; and it both shapes the consciousness and is shaped by it. In expressing itself, life is intensified, structured and developed. There is expression through words. There is expression through actions. There is expression through bodily attitudes, the play of features, and the gestures of the hands. The creative power of life is to be found in its expression. Life in God's Spirit is also 'minted form, which takes shape as it lives', as Goethe said.[6]

In the first part of this chapter we shall look at two traditional concepts of sanctification and shall transpose them into our own time and the problems of our own lives, for the *vita christiana* is always related – and must always be related – to its time and context, whether affirmatively or critically. We shall then explore the development of 'life in the Spirit' in the energies and possibilities which God's Spirit gives us. Because life in the Spirit is nothing other than the discipleship of Jesus, we must clarify the real conflicts between life's sanctification and the ways it is being destroyed today. Finally, we shall ask again: if these are the experiences of God's Spirit in our lives, who is the Spirit?

§1 JUSTIFICATION AND SANCTIFICATION IN LUTHER AND WESLEY

Luther saw justification and sanctification as interrelated and interlocked. People always require justification because they are sinners: And people always require the sanctification of the justified life.[7] So justification cannot mark a particular moment in someone's life at which sanctification begins. Justification takes place in the verticle before God *sub specie aeternitatis*. Sanctification is accomplished in the horizontal that is aligned towards God *sub specie temporis futurae*. To use the basic terms of the doctrine of justification: the believer is 1. *simul iustus et peccator* (at once righteous and a sinner); 2. *peccator in re et iustus in spe* (a sinner in fact, righteous in hope); and 3. *partim peccator – partim iustus* (partly a sinner, partly righteous).[8] The second of these theses is the line connecting the enduring justification of the sinner with the commencing sanctification of the justified life, for *in re* means the life of sin which is passing away, and *in spe* means the life of righteousness, which is already beginning to take shape in the Spirit. If these two aeons overlap in believers, they experience in themselves the retrogression of sin and the progression of righteousness (Rom. 13.12). The decay of sin and the coming of righteousness can also be interpreted as *mortificatio sui* and as *vivificatio in Spiritu*, according to the concepts of the mediaeval doctrine of penance, which Luther and Calvin employ. Because for Luther the forgiveness of sins and – as its foundation – the theology of the cross was at the centre of the justification of life, in his teaching about sanctification we find a strong emphasis on *mortificatio sui* and daily penance, and very little development of the *vivificatio in Spiritu* and daily resurrection.[9] The Reformers' description of the *vita christiana* bears the marks of its time, mediaeval ecclesiastical society, and the legalistic ideas of conversion that accorded with Roman canon law. They presuppose infant baptism and therefore do not define any temporal beginning for life in faith.

With John Wesley we enter the eighteenth-century world of rising industrialization, with its notions about discipline at the machines in the factories, and its proletariat.[10] For Wesley, sin is a sickness that requires healing rather than a breach of law requiring atonement. He therefore interprets the justification of the sinner with the concepts of regeneration or rebirth rather than with those of judgment, just as the Anglican theology of his time – turning away from the legalistic theology of Rome – also cast back to the doctrine of physical redemption held by the early Greek Fathers. Wesley was therefore less interested than Luther in the permanent justification of the sinner, and more interested than Luther in the process of the sinner's religious and moral renewal. If sanctification is really the healing of spiritual life in men and women, then it must also be possible to detect the stages of returning health. Like a sick person, the sinner can also contribute to the process of recovering his spiritual health. Of course everything is always dependent on God's grace, but this grace also lays hold of the sinful will and liberates it, awakening new energies in it.

Wesley was able to discern five stages in the sanctification of life: 1. A preliminary divine grace awakens the natural conscience and strengthens the will. 2. God's convincing grace effects a repentance that hastens ahead of justification. 3. God's grace is experienced objectively as justification and subjectively as regeneration. 4. It necessarily leads – or perhaps better: it leads as a matter of course – to a gradual sanctification of life until 5. Believers are wholly interpenetrated by the Holy Spirit and arrive at the state of Christian perfection, the *theosis*. This would be 'perfect love'. The expression 'sinless perfection' is often used in books and essays about Wesley, but he himself rejected the term. He no doubt saw the fifth stage as the final goal, rather than as an achievable experience, so as to view sanctification as an active waiting for complete salvation. After all, there is no recuperation process without the goal of complete health.[11]

Compared with Luther, Wesley saw sanctification – sanctification in our experience of life – as the inevitable consequence of justification. He saw divine grace, as it could be understood by men and women, as 'convincing grace', to which faith can assent by virtue of discernment. In this he followed Melanchthon, who thought didactically. But what gave his message its compelling power was the discovery of the subjectivity of the believer. 'Inward feeling' was for him the most convincing proof. For Wesley himself, the experience of faith was something he could actually date. It was an experience in which he 'felt his heart strangely warmed', not merely assent to a correct doctrine, valid universally and at all times. But he did not make experiences of this kind normative for true believers. Nor did he, like Luther, see the sanctification of life in the faithful performance of duties in the station to which a person has been called; he saw it taking place in a deliberate, voluntary, organized, personal and social life of faith. He organized believers into regular classes and disciplined groups. He discovered the discipline of personal conduct in almost every sector, from commerce to hygiene. 'Holiness is happiness' and 'cleanliness is next to godliness', as Wesley's mother liked to say. Holiness means harmony with God, happiness a person's harmony with himself.

Most of Wesley's rules of conduct[12] have since proved to be sound and beneficial. The industrial proletariat that was coming into being was made up of isolated people who had been forced to leave their villages and familiar neighbourhoods in order to find work in the factories. Wesley gave them a home in the congregations which they joined voluntarily, and in the discipline of a Christian life, in which they found a direction, and stability in their unstable situation. This gave them back the self-confidence of which their work deprived them.

Yet the Christian discipline to which they submitted themselves and their bodies also corresponded precisely to the discipline of their work in the factories. If people have to work according to the mechanical time of the clock (which Lewis Mumford calls 'the key machine of the industrial age'), they get used to eating, sleeping, praying, holding services, and so forth, according to the mechanical time of the clock too. These people are not merely subjected to discipline in their work. They submit themselves to religious and moral discipline as well, and rule their bodies through self-control. Self-control leads to self-command and to self-possession in the literal sense: the self is something one 'has' and calls one's own. This puts people at their own disposal at all times. That is what C.B. Macpherson calls the possessive individualism of the modern world. It reduces the body to a machine or instrument, and puts it at the person's disposal.

What did this mean for the bodies of men, and of women? Methodical behaviour at work and Methodist conduct in faith corresponded to one another. In this respect Methodism became the religion of the rising industrial societies.[13] But its 'this-worldly' asceticism also linked it critically with the instrumentalist reason of industrial society. It was Methodist Christians who founded trade unions among the workers. The Tolpuddle Martyrs (1834) and the Chartist movement (1839–1848) were symptoms of the social unrest which gave rise to the Labour movement. Wesley himself was a social reformer, not a politician, but the leaders of the early Labour party (founded in 1900) were largely Methodist. Some historians even maintain that Methodism anticipated the ideas of the French Revolution in England.[14] The following verse from one of Charles Wesley's hymns sounds revolutionary enough to remind us even of today's liberation theology:

The rich and great in every age
Conspire to persecute their God.

Our Saviour, by the rich unknown,
Is worshipped by the poor alone.

The historic conversation between John Wesley and Count Zinzendorf in
London documents the difference between the Methodist and Lutheran
doctrines of sanctification. The conversation also marks the final severance
of the Methodist movement from the Moravian brethren.

On 3 September 1741, shortly before Zinzendorf's departure from
England for Pennsylvania, he met Wesley for a discussion. But this did not
bring about the desired reconciliation. The conversation took place in Gray's
Inn Walks, and Wesley recorded 'the most material part' of it in Latin in his
journal, while Zinzendorf authorized its publication, so to speak, in the
Büdingischen Sammlung. The English translation was made later by Henry
Moore.[14a]

Z.   Cur religionem tuam mutasti? (Why have you changed your religion?)
W.   Nescio me Religionem meam mutasse. Cur id sentis? Quis hoc tibi
     retulit? (I do not know that I have changed my religion. Why do you
     think so? Who has reported this to you?)
Z.   Plane tu. Id ex epistola tua ad nos video. Ibi, Religione, quam apud nos
     professus es, relicta, novam profiteris. (Plainly, yourself. I see it from
     your epistle to us. There, having departed from the religion which you
     professed among us, you have held out a new one.)
W.   Quis sic? Non intelligo. (How so? I do not understand you.)
Z.   Imo istic dicis, vere Christianos non esse miseros peccatores. Falsissi-
     mum. Optimi hominum ad mortem usque miserabilissimi sunt pecc-
     atores. Siquid aliud dicunt, vel penitus impostores sunt, vel diabolice
     seducti. Nostros fratres meliora docentes impugnasti. Et pacem volenti-
     bus, eam denegasti. (Nay, you say there, that Christians are not
     miserable sinners. This is most false. The best of men are most miserable
     sinners, even unto death. If any speak otherwise, they are either manifest
     impostors, or diabolically seduced. Our brethren who taught better
     things, you have opposed; and when they desired peace, you have
     refused it.)
W.   Nondum intelligo quid velis. (I do not yet understand what you aim
     at.)
Z.   Ego, cum ex Georgia ad me scripsisti, te dilexi plurimum. T[u]um corde
     simplicem te agnovi. Iterum scripsisti. Agnovi corde simplicem, sed
     turbatis ideis. Ad nos venisti. Ideae tuae tum magis turbatae erant et
     confusae. In Angliam rediisti. Aliquandiu post, audivi fratres nostros
     tecum pugnare. Spangenbergium misi ad pacem inter vos conciliandam.
     Scripsit mihi, 'Fratres tibi iniuriam intulisse'. Rescripsi, ne pergerent,
     sed et veniam a te peterent. Spangenberg scripsit iterum, 'Eos petiisse;

sed te, gloriari de iis, pacem nolle'. Iam adveniens, idem audio. (When you wrote to me from Georgia, I loved you very much. I perceived that you were simple in heart, but troubled in your ideas. You came to us. Your ideas were then still more troubled and confused. You returned to England. A little after, I heard that our brethren were contending with you. I sent Spangenberg to make peace between you. He wrote to me, that the Brethren had injured you. I wrote again, that they should not pursue the strife, but desire forgiveness of you. Spangenberg wrote again, that they had desired this, but that you, glorying over them, had refused peace. Now that I am come, I hear the same thing.)

W.   Res in eo cardine minime vertitur. Fratres tui (verum hoc) me male tractarunt. Postea veniam petierunt. Respondi, Id supervacaneum; me nunquam iis succensuisse; sed vereri, (1) ne falsa docerunt; (2) ne prave viverent. Ista unica est, et fuit, inter nos quaestio. (The matter does not at all turn on this point. Your Brethren, it is true, did not use me well. Afterward they desired forgiveness. I answered – that was superfluous, that I had never been offended with them; but I feared, (1) lest they should teach falsely; (2) lest they should live wickedly. This is, and was, the only question between us.)

Z.   Apertius loquaris. (Speak more fully [on that question].)

W.   Veritus sum, ne falsa docerent, (1) de sine fidei nostrae in hac vita, scil[icet,] Christiana perfectione; (2) de mediis gratiae, sic ab Ecclesia nostra dictis. (I feared lest they should teach falsely; (1) Concerning the end of our faith in this life, to wit, Christian Perfection. (2) Concerning the means of grace, so termed by our church.)

Z.   Nullam inhaerentem perfectionem in hac vita agnosco. Est hic error errorum. Eum per totum orbem igne et gladio persequor, conculco, ad internecionem do. Christus est sola perfectio nostra. Qui perfectionem inhaerentem sequitur, Christum denegat. (I acknowledge no inherent perfection in this life. This is the error of errors. I pursue it through the world with fire and sword. I trample upon it: I devote it to utter destruction. Whoever follows inherent perfection, denies Christ.)

W.   Ego vero credo, spiritum Christi operari perfectionem in vere Christianis. (But, I believe, that the spirit of Christ works this perfection in true Christians.)

Z.   Nullimode. Omnis nostra perfectio est in Christo. Omnis Christiana perfectio est, fides in sanguine Christi. Est tota Christiana perfectio, imputata, non inhaerens. Perfecti summus in Christo, in nobismet nunquam perfecti. (By no means. All our perfection is in Christ. All Christian Perfection is, Faith in the blood of Christ. Our whole Christian Perfection is imputed, not inherent. We are perfect in Christ: In ourselves we are never perfect.)

W.   Pugnamus, opinor, de verbis. Nonne omnis vere credens sanctus est? (I think we strive about words. Is not every true believer holy?)

Z.   Maxime. Sed sanctus in Christo, non in se. (Highly so. But he is holy in Christ, not in himself.)

W.   Sed, nonne sancte vivit? (But does he not live holy?)

Z.   Imo, sancte in omnibus vivit. (Yes, he lives holy in all things.)

W.   Nonne, et cor sanctum habet? (And has he not a holy heart?)

Z.   Certissime. (Most certainly.)

W.   Nonne, ex consequenti, sanctus es *in se*? (And is he not consequently holy *in himself*?)

Z.   Non, non. In Christo tantum. Non sanctus *in se*. Nullam omnino habet sanctitatem *in se*. (No, no. In Christ only. He is not holy in himself: He hath no holiness at all in himself.)

W.   Nonne habet in corde suo *amorem Dei* et proximi, quin et totam imaginem Dei? (Hath he not the *love of God*, and his neighbour, in his heart? Yea, and the whole image of God?)

Z.   Habet. Sed haec sunt sanctitas legalis, non evangelica. Sanctitas evangelica est fides. (He hath. But these constitute legal holiness, not evangelical. Evangelical holiness is Faith.)

W.   Omnino lis est de verbis. Concedis, credentis cor totum esse sanctum et vitam totam: Eum amare Deum toto corde, eique servire totis viribus. Nihil ultra peto. Nil aliud volo per perfectio vel sanctitas Christiana. (The dispute is altogether about words. You grant that a believer is altogether holy in heart and life: That he loves God with all his heart, and serves him with all his powers. I desire nothing more. I mean nothing else [by the term] PERFECTION, OR CHRISTIAN HOLINESS.)

Z.   Sed haec non es sanctitas eius. Non magis sanctus est, si magis amat, neque minus sanctus, si minus amat. (But this is not his holiness. He is not more holy if he loves more, or less holy, if he loves less.)

W.   Quid? Nonne credens, dum crescit in amore, crescit pariter in sanctitate? (What! Does not every believer, while he increases in love, increase equally in holiness?)

Z.   Nequaquam. Eo momento quo iustificatur, sanctificatur penitus. Exin, neque magis sanctus est, neque minus sanctus, ad mortem usque. (Not at all. In the moment he is justified, he is sanctified wholly. From that time he is not more nor less holy, even unto death.)

W.   Nonne igitur pater in Christo sanctior est infante recens nato? (Is not therefore a father in Christ holier than a new-born babe?)

Z.   Non. Sanctificatio totalis ac iustificatio in eodem sunt instanti; et neutra recipit magis aut minus. (No. Our whole justification, and sanctification, are in the same instant, and he receives neither more nor less.)

W.   Nonne vero credens crescit in dies amore Dei? Num perfectus est

amore, simulac iustificatur? (Does not a true believer increase in love
to God daily? Is he *perfected in love* when he is justified?)

Z.   Est. Non unquam crescit in amore Dei. Totaliter amat eo momento,
sicut totaliter sanctificatur. (He is. He never can increase in the love of
God. He loves altogether in that moment, as he is sanctified wholly.)

W.   Quid itaque vult Apostolus Paulus, per, Renovamur de die in diem?
(What therefore does the Apostle Paul mean by, 'We are renewed day
by day?')

Z.   Dicam. Plumbum si in aurum mutetur, est aurum primo die, et secundo,
et tertio. Et sic renovatur de die in diem. Sed nunquam est magis aurum,
quam primo die. (I will tell you. Lead, if it should be changed into gold,
is gold the first day, and the second day, and the third: And so it is
renewed day by day; but it is never more gold than in the first day.)

W.   Putavi, crescendum esse in gratia! (I thought that we should grow in
grace!)

Z.   Certe. Sed non in sanctitate. Simulac justificatur quis, Pater, Filius, et
Spiritus Sanctus habitant in ipsius corde. Et cor eius eo momento aeque
purum est ac unquam erit. Infans in Christo tam purus corde est quam
pater in Christo. Nulla est discrepantia. (Certainly; but not in holiness.
Whenever anyone is justified, the Father, the Son, and the Holy Spirit,
dwell in his heart; and from that moment his heart is as pure as it ever
will be. A babe in Christ is as pure in heart as a father in Christ. There
is no difference.)

W.   Nonne iustificati erant apostoli ante Christi mortem? (Were not the
apostles justified before the death of Christ?)

Z.   Erant. (They were.)

W.   Nonne vero sanctiores erant post diem Pentecostes, quam ante Christi
mortem? (But were they no more holy after the day of Pentecost, than
before Christ's death?)

Z.   Neutiquam. (By no means.)

W.   Nonne eo die impleti sunt Spiritu Sancto? (Were they not on that day
filled with the Holy Ghost?)

Z.   Erant. Sed istud donum Spiritus, sanctitatem ipsorum non respexit.
Fuit donum miraculorum tantum. (They were. But that gift of the Spirit
did not respect their holiness. It was a gift of miracles only.)

W.   Fortasse te non capio. Nonne nos ipsos abnegantes, magis magisque
mundo morimur, ac Deo vivimus? (Perhaps I do not comprehend your
meaning. Do we not while we deny ourselves, die more and more to
the world and live to God?)

Z.   Abnegationem omnem respuimus, conculcamus. Facimus credentes
omne quod volumus et nihil ultra. Mortificationem omnem ridemus.
Nulla purifactio praecedit perfectum amorem. (We reject all self-denial.
We trample upon it. We do, as believers, whatsoever we will, and

nothing more. We laugh at all mortification. No purification precedes perfect love.)

W.   Quae dixisti, Deo adiuvante, perpendam. (What you have said I will thoroughly weigh, God being my helper.)

The *vita christiana* is always related to its time and context. If the Christian life sees itself as a witness to Christ and God's Spirit, then it cannot be a religious reflection of the given ethics of a particular society; nor can it be related to these ethics in a merely negative sense either. As a witness to salvation, the Christian testimony must be related to the sicknesses of the given society *in a healing way*. How else can we talk about 'the Saviour'? It can be shown that the Reformation's testimony to freedom of faith acted therapeutically on the public sicknesses of mediaeval ecclesiastical society. It can be shown that the Methodist testimony to personal sanctification acted therapeutically on the sicknesses of the rising industrial society in England. Today we are at the end of industrial society and in the transition to a post-industrial society. The ethic of industrial society is: 'produce more – consume more'. But today the cost incurred by this maxim is greater than the profit. The faith in progress it implies is crumbling away in the face of the progressive destruction of the environment. People feel dehumanized when they are seen only as producers, consumers and commuters, and if their behaviour is rationalized along these lines. They are losing the subjectivity which was set free when industrial society began. Neurotic derangements and what we call the diseases of civilization are on the increase. The upwardly mobile classes in industrial and consumer society are becoming infertile – physically so, as well as psychologically. What form is the *vita christiana* going to assume in this transitional phase? For what sicknesses of our time will the Christian life prove to be healing?

§2 SANCTIFICATION TODAY

1. 'Sanctification today' means first of all rediscovering *the sanctity of life* and *the divine mystery of creation*, and defending them from life's manipulation, the secularization of nature, and the destruction of the world through human violence. Life comes from God and belongs to God, so it has to be sanctified through the people who believe God. The earth is not 'unclaimed property' and nature is not 'ownerless'. It is God's beloved creation. So it must be encountered

with reverence and drawn into the love for God. Today sanctification means integrating ourselves once more into the web of life from which modern society has isolated men and women, and is separating them more and more.

2. If life has to be sanctified because it is itself holy, then the first conclusion to be drawn is the ethic which Albert Schweitzer rightly called *'reverence for life'*.[15] Reverence links a religious attitude towards life with a moral respect for it – one's own life and the life of other creatures. In order to appreciate the ecological dimension fully, we should do well to strengthen the religious side of creation spirituality, extending the double commandment of love to creation too: love this earth as yourself, and yourself as this earth! You shall love God and this earth and all your fellow creatures with all your heart, and with all your soul, and with all your might! Anyone who loves 'the living God' loves the life of all living things. Reverence for life always begins with respect for weaker life, vulnerable life. In the world of human beings this means the poor, the sick, and the defenceless. The same is true for the world of nature. The weaker plant and animal species are the first creatures to be threatened by extinction. Reverence for life must apply to them first of all, since they require protection.

Today sanctification means defending God's creation against human aggression,[16] exploitation and destruction. This has a personal dimension: what am I doing about my consumerism and my refuse? Am I part of the throw-away society or am I resisting it in creation's name? It has a social dimension too: how can Christians, in joint discussion and shared worship, arrive at a reverent life-style? And there is also a political dimension: what laws for protecting the environment and other creatures do we speak out for?

3. The ethic of reverence for life requires *the renunciation of violence* towards life. The early Methodists refrained from drinking and smoking and keeping slaves; and Christians living in countries bristling with armaments, and in societies destructive of nature, are similarly committed to non-violent service for life, if they wish to sanctify life. Freedom from violence means conscientious objection and the preparedness to live without armaments. But it also means minimizing the technological use of violence towards nature, turning from hard to soft technology, and reducing the expenditure of energy, since the expenditure of energy is always an indicator of violence towards nature. Not least, living without violence means letting one's

own life grow, and ending the violent regimentation of one's own body by the intellect.

In one sense this runs counter to Wesley's Methodist discipline, but it does not contradict his intention, which was to heal soul and body. If modern men and women are to be healed, the segregated intellect has to be integrated into receptive and perceptive reason, and reason has to be woven into the fabric of the feelings, and consciousness has to be assimilated into the experiences of the body. The long struggle against one's own body, to win self-mastery, has meant that whole sectors of life have been split off, especially in men, and this has led to continual self-mistrust. Reverence for one's own life and life from the Spirit of life lead beyond moral self-control, and throw open a new spontaneity of faith. *Ama et fac quod vis*, said Augustine: love, and do what you like. This means a new spontaneity of life beyond reflection, not a regression into a childish lack of conscience, as Kierkegaard showed. It is a self-confidence self-forgetfully embedded in confidence in God. In this sanctification of one's own life, *being* is sanctified, not acts. The *person* begins to shine, though not of his own accord, and without being aware of it.

4. I would also call 'sanctification today' the search for *the harmonies and accords* of life. 'The individual and his property' was the prototype of modern society. People were trained to become the determining subjects of understanding and will, and nature was atomized.[17] Abolishing these deadly segregations means coming alive once more. We can make this clear to ourselves if we see life as intersecting circles: the soul in the body, the person in the community, the community in the sequence of generations, the generations of human beings in the shared house of the earth.[18] If we perceive human life as existing in these interrelated sectors, we begin to live less ruthlessly and more sensitively. Then life *at the expense* of others is no longer possible. Life *together with* others is enjoined on us.

But the more we perceive the warp and weft of life, the more we sense the vulnerability and frailty of our own lives, and that also means their mortality. It was this *condition humaine* which people wanted to conquer with the help of the gigantic project 'modern society'. The genetic restructuring of the human being is moving into the realm of the medically possible. But human beings will then no longer be the same. 'Sanctification today' does not merely include a healthful life. It also means accepting human life's natural frailty and mortality. To resist the death-drive does not mean suppressing death.

On the contrary, it means accepting it, and making it a part of life. In the love that is 'strong as death' the death-drive is extinguished.

§3 THE SANCTIFYING GOD

Having seen what Luther and Wesley understood by sanctification, and having thought about the way we see it today, let us now return to the foundation of sanctification. This foundation is found in the sanctity or holiness of God himself. God alone is essentially holy. He is 'the Holy One of Israel' (Isa. 43.3). The word holy is applied to God in the context of the power and terror that proceed from him (Ex. 15.11). He is holy and 'jealous' (Josh. 24.19), holy and 'true' (Rev. 3.7), holy and 'just' (Ps. 145.17). His holiness is always a pointer to his uniqueness: God only and only God is holy.

The word 'sanctification' is then used for a divine act through which God chooses something for himself and makes it his own, thus letting it participate in his nature. In this way the Creator 'sanctifies' the sabbath and makes it the feast of creation. In this way he sanctifies the chosen people of Israel, making them his people. In this way he sanctifies the temple, the holy city, the holy land, and finally everything he loves, because he has created it. What belongs to God is holy, like God himself. It follows from this that sanctification is an act of God in us and for us, like justification and calling. The people whom God justifies he also sanctifies (Rom. 8.30). We unsanctified, sinful men and women are pronounced holy, and made holy, by God out of grace for Christ's sake. 'The communion of saints' in the Apostles' Creed is not an assembly of people who are saints in the moral sense. It is simply the community of pardoned sinners, reconciled enemies, believers. The person who finds grace in God's sight is also in God's sight good, just and holy. Sanctification as an act of God in a human being signifies a relationship and an affiliation,[19] not a state in itself. What God loves is holy, whatever it may be in itself.[20]

This theological concept of sanctification then leads to the anthropological one. Sanctification as gift leads to sanctification as charge. For whatever God declares to be holy ought to be kept holy by human beings: the sabbath, the people, created beings. God's community with us is the foundation and motive for our community with God. Reformation theology drew the first aspect into the concept of justification, so that 'sanctification' on the basis of justification always meant only the new conduct of life. That led to the moral misunderstanding of sanctification. But if we sanctify what God has already sanctified, this misunderstanding is excluded.

In the response of their lives to the life-giving word of God, believers are not merely the passive objects of divine sanctification. They are also the new determining subjects of the Gestalt or configuration of their own lives. As determining subjects of their own lives in the covenant with God, they take the beginning of life in rebirth, or regeneration, seriously, using the enlightened eyes of their understanding, the liberated powers of their will, and the assurance of their hearts. They lead a 'special' life, because instead of living according to the ethics of their own society, they increasingly already live according to the law of God's kingdom, Jesus' Sermon on the Mount. Sanctification is *the discipleship of Jesus* and means coming to life in God's Spirit. In this new life one can develop distinctive features too. An inward holiness can grow. But it doesn't develop from the habit of good deeds. It springs from the goodness of the person who is loved by God and already sanctified. We can also term the sanctification of life by believers the life corresponding to God. This then makes the goal clear: it is the restoration of *the image of God* in human beings from the human side. Harmony with God, the source of life, goes hand in hand with harmony with all the living, who live from this source; and it therefore goes together also with reverence for life itself, wherever we encounter it.

§4 THE HOLY LIFE

What does the English word 'holy' and the German word 'heilig' mean? The etymology tells us that 'whole'/'hale', 'heal' and 'holy' is a semantic group that belongs together,[21] meaning roughly speaking: entire, healthy, unhurt, complete, and 'belonging especially' to someone. To heal then means making something whole that has been divided, making a sick person healthy. 'Heiligen' in German ('hallow' or 'sanctify') primarily means 'own', 'to appropriate or consecrate', 'to show to be one's own'. What belongs to a deity is consecrated to it and thus 'sanctified' to it. Since holy and whole belong so closely together, what is holy is that which has become whole again, and is unscathed and healthy. If we go back to these linguistic roots, we can then describe 'holistic thinking' as 'healing thinking', because it takes account of the wholeness of what has been separated, and tries to restore that wholeness. There is no essential difference here from Old Testament thinking, if we note the phraseology of 'being someone's own' and consecrating appropriation.[22] Certainly only God and God alone is 'the holy One of Israel'. But his people and his land are his own, and his whole creation is his (Ps. 24.1). Consequently the earth is holy as God is holy, and everything that lives on earth must be loved with the same reverence as God himself. It is not as the Wholly Other that God and God alone is holy. He is holy as the one whose Spirit fills the world and is the life of all the living.

If whatever God has made and loves is holy, then life is holy in itself, and to live life with love and joy means sanctifying it. We do not first sanctify it through what we make of our lives. We already sanctify it through our very existence. 'I am glad that you are you, that you are there', says love; for love looks at the person, not the works. So to sanctify life does not mean manipulating it religiously and morally. It means being freed and justified, loved and affirmed, and more and more alive. Life in God's Spirit is a life entrusted to the guidance and drive of the Spirit, a life that lets the Spirit come.

Let us look at the biblical images. The Bible turns readily to images of *the tree and its fruits*: 'The fruit of the Spirit is love, joy, peace, patience, kindness, goodness, faithfulness, gentleness . . .' These fruits are directed against 'the works of the flesh': 'strife, jealousy, anger, dissension, party spirit, hate, murder . . .' (Gal. 5.22, 19). If this image is correct, then the works of the flesh are 'made' but the fruit of the Spirit 'grows'. We cannot make it, but we can let it grow in us.

The Spirit itself is *'the well of life'* (John 4.14; Ps. 36.9), and the well brims over and the water of life flows wherever the eternal Spirit indwells. This gives us the other picture: the Spirit of life is poured out and flows. The fruits ripen on the trees and the water streams from its fountainhead.

The third image talks about *light and shining*. With these metaphors we leave behind the world of the solitary individual and what he does, and enter the spheres of life's living relationships. The images are taken from nature. Where the spring rises from its source and flows, life can blossom. Where the sun shines, things become bright. Where nature becomes fertile, there is life. If we transfer this to experiences of God, it tells us that separations from God and the mutual isolations of men and women are abolished where God's presence is experienced in the Spirit, and the divine energy interpenetrates body and soul once more, and makes them fruitful.

All three images – the fruit, the source and the light – leave the difference between Creator and creature behind, and show the torrent of energies flowing from God to human beings. These three metaphors for God are aptly described by the neo-Platonic term 'emanation'. God is not merely a determining subject, over against the world. He is also the wellspring from which all life comes; he is the tree that brings forth fruit; he is the light whose rays give light and warmth to everything. Through the Holy Spirit, God's eternal life brims over, as it were, and its overflowing powers and energies fill the earth. Life which is experienced in this overflowing Spirit is divine life, life in eternal community with God, holy life.

It is obvious that no one can 'make' this life, either through asceticism or through discipline. But one can *let it be* and let it come. The fruit of the Spirit ripens by itself. It ripens in us, and we ripen in it. The source of life wells up and flows of itself. 'When he breathes upon us with his power, he works divine life in us, so that we now no longer let ourselves be driven by ourselves, but are ruled by his guidance and his impelling potency: so all that is good in us is a fruit of his grace.'[23]

But we can clear away the hindrances. The light shines of itself, but we can open ourselves for it and let it shine. Of course there is a conscious sanctification of life through the energies of the liberated will. But there is also an unconscious sanctification of life through *being*. And there is a sanctification of the unconscious life in the Spirit. Life's expression comes from depths which the consciousness does not illuminate. In all the different dimensions, it is not a case of sanctifying a life that is unsanctified. It is a matter of sanctifying life that is itself holy. It means learning to see life and love it as God sees and loves it: as good, just and lovely.

§5 THE HOLY SPIRIT AS THE POWER OF LIFE AND THE SPACE FOR LIVING

Out of the experience of the life sanctified by God, the life perceived as holy, and one's own sanctification of this life loved by God, we again ask about the Spirit.

1. It takes its name 'Holy Spirit' from this experience of the sanctification of life by God and for God. Earlier, people differen-

tiated in talking about this experience. In the natural experience of life, they said, we feel the *spiritus vivificans*, in the supernatural experience of faith the *spiritus sanctificans*.[24] The justice of this distinction between creation and redemption is not in dispute. But if we are to prevent a gnostic disparagement of creation from creeping in, we must perceive the *spiritus vivificans in* the *spiritus sanctificans*, and sense the unfathomable intensification of life and the will to live, through the experience of the closeness of the living God. 'Eternal life quickens.'[25] In 'life in the Spirit' one even notices physically something of the 'life given to our mortal bodies'. We sense the exhilaration of existence and the élan of life in the Spirit. Spirituality is in a holistic sense new vitality. It is not a religious and moral restriction of life and its enfeebling reduction. It is a new delight in living in the joy of God.

Today life itself and actual survival are called in question. Death is threatening life on earth, not just here and there but universally. So 'the passion for life'[26] must be awakened and the numbing spell of apathy must be broken. Before the earth dies its nuclear and ecological death, men and women will die the death of apathy in their hearts and souls. The powers to resist are paralysed if the passion for life is lacking. People who today want to live and want their children to live must consciously *desire* life. They must learn to love it with such passion that they are not prepared to adapt to the forces of destruction, and to let the trend to death take its course unchecked. The 'Holy' Spirit is the Spirit who sanctifies life, and he sanctifies it with the Creator's passion for the life of what he has created, and with the Creator's wrath against all the forces that want to destroy it. At the edge of the abyss, the integrity of creation and rebirth to life become so intermingled that it is as the life-giving Spirit that the sanctifying Spirit is experienced.

2. When the heart expands and we can stretch our limbs, and feel the new vitality everywhere, then life unfolds in us. But it needs a living space in which it can develop. Life in the Spirit is a life in the 'broad place where there is no cramping' (Job 36.16). So in the new life we experience the Spirit as a 'broad place' – as the free space for our freedom, as the living space for our lives, as the horizon inviting us to discover life. 'The broad place' is the most hidden and most silent presence of God's Spirit in us and round about us. But how else could 'life in the Spirit' be understood, if the Spirit were not the space 'in' which this life can grow and unfurl? We explore the depths

of this space through the trust of the heart. We search out the length of this space through extravagant hope. We discover the breadth of this space through the torrents of love which we receive and give. God's Spirit encompasses us from all sides and wherever we are (Ps. 139). Christ's Spirit is our immanent power to live – God's Spirit is our transcendent space for living.

IX

The Charismatic Powers of Life

Life is always specific, never general. Life is everywhere different, never the same. It is female or male, young or old, handicapped or non-handicapped, Jewish or Gentile, white or black, and so forth.

Life is everywhere endowed. There is no such thing as unendowed life. There is only the social undervaluation of certain gifts, and the preference given to others.

What does God's Spirit have to do with this variety of life in all its specific forms? Aren't we all equal in God's sight – sinners and righteous, dying and reborn, the anything-but-saintly and the saints? Whatever we may say in general about ourselves and other people *sub specie aeternitatis*, 'the Spirit of life' is only there as the Spirit of this and that particular life. The experience of God's Spirit is as specific as the living beings who experience him, and as varied as the living beings who experience him are varied.

Paul makes this clear from the simple event of *calling*: 'Everyone as the Lord has assigned to him, everyone as the Lord has called him' (I Cor. 7.17). Call and endowment, *klesis* and *charisma*, belong together, and are interchangeable terms. This means that every Christian is a charismatic, even if many people never live out their gifts. The gifts which the one or the other person brings or receives are at the service of their calling; for God who calls, takes people at the point *where* he reaches them and *as they are*. He accepts people quite specifically, as man or woman, Jew or Gentile, poor or rich, and so on, and puts their whole life at the service of his coming kingdom, which renews the world. So if we ask about the charismata of the Holy Spirit, we mustn't look for the things we don't have. We must first of all discern *who* we are, *what* we are and *how* we are, at the point where we feel the touch of God on our lives. What is given to all believers in common and equally, is the gift of the Holy Spirit: 'The charisma of God is eternal life in Christ Jesus our Lord' (Rom. 6.23; Eph. 5.18ff.). What is given to each person individually and uniquely is different and full of diversity: to each his or her own! The theologically interesting and teasing question is the query about the multiplicity in the unity, and the unity in the diversity. How do the many-coloured gifts of the Spirit fit in with the One Spirit? How does the one *charis* become the many *charismata*? The practical question is: how is unity in diversity, and diversity in unity actually implemented in the community of believers?

We shall first of all direct our attention to the Pauline doctrine of the charismata, though looking at it pre-eminently in its bearing on the personal endowment of life. We shall then ask about the endowments and disablements of life in the Spirit, and shall formulate the unity in the diversity in the fellowship of the Spirit and in our common work for the kingdom of God. After that, in the light of charismatic experiences, we shall ask: who is the Holy Spirit, and how can we describe the Spirit's vitalizing and fascinating power?

§1 THE CHARISMATIC VITALITY OF THE NEW LIFE

We have to distinguish between the Pauline and the Lucan doctrine of the charismata. Of the two, the Pauline doctrine is the more stringently reflected theologically, and it is also the more praxis-orientated. So we shall look at that first.[1] It is generally treated under the heading 'ministry and community'. But that is misleading, for in the charismatic community everyone has his or her 'ministry'. So we shall focus on the vitality of the new life in the Spirit, taking I Cor. 7 and I Cor. 12 together.

In I Cor. 7 Paul talks about the one *calling* and the many people who are called. All are called to the peace of God, but everyone should remain in the particular calling to which he has been called (I Cor. 7.20). He is to walk and live as a Christian as the Lord has called him. In talking about 'calling', Paul is thinking about being a Jew and being a Gentile, being a man and being a woman, being a master and being a slave. But when he is talking about the social difference, he adds: 'If you can gain your freedom, avail yourself of the opportunity.' But if not, the slave should feel that he is 'a freedman of the Lord' and a freeman should see himself as 'a slave of Christ'

(vv. 21f.) When a person is called, whatever he is and brings with him becomes a charisma through his calling, since it is accepted by the Spirit and put at the service of the kingdom of God. So a Christian Jew should remain a Jew, and live according to the Torah. A Christian Gentile brings his Gentile existence into the community. Being a woman is a charisma and must not be surrendered in favour of patriarchal and male ways of thinking and behaving. And in social conflicts too, being a Christian begins at the point where the man or woman is reached.

Why does Paul see what a person is, or brings with him or her, as a charisma, although this is surely a matter of natural gifts and everyday circumstances? According to Ernst Käsemann, what he wants to say is that the lordship of Christ thrusts deeply into the secularity of the world. It is not merely special religious phenomena which become a 'charismatic experience' for the believer. It is the whole of bodily and social existence.[2] Paul went even further, and made charisma the foundation for his whole parenesis: whatever we do, we do it 'in the Lord'. Sin is only whatever is not done out of faith, and wrong is only whatever cuts across love of our neighbour. 'Life in the Spirit' is the presence and the influence of the Spirit in life as it is lived. No sector is excluded. Everything which believers do and leave undone is at the service of the discipleship of Jesus, and is therefore a charisma of Christ's Spirit.

This then pegs out the dimension of the charisma as well: it is whatever is 'in the Lord', as Paul likes to say. Whatever can be put at the service of Christ's liberating lordship is a charisma, a gift that then becomes a charge: 'Now everything can become for me charisma. It would be not only foolish but a slight to the honour of Christ, who wills to fill all things, if I were to attempt to take the realms of the natural, the sexual, the private, the social out of his sphere of power.'[3] That is why Paul says: 'I know and am persuaded in the Lord Jesus that nothing is unclean in itself' (Rom. 14.14). So the whole of life and death is gathered into the promise of charismatic existence. Every Christian is a charismatic in his or her own particular way. It is not only a few chosen or especially endowed people who have the right to the name. The *whole* of life, and *every* life in faith is charismatic, for the Spirit is 'poured out upon all flesh' to quicken it. Individual powers and energies become charismatic in the *relationships* which give form to the shared life-process. It is often in these living relationships that people discover these powers for the first time, and become aware of them. 'The doctrine of charisma is for him [Paul] the concrete expression of the doctrine of the new obedience, just because it is at the same time the doctrine of the *justificatio impii*. God gives life to the dead and, through the invasion of grace, sets up his kingdom where before demons and demonic energies held sway.'[4] As Paul describes them in Romans 12, these are the gifts and the tasks given to believers for their 'reasonable service' in the everyday world. We may call them the *everyday charismata of the lived life*.

If this makes it clear that through calling in faith every individual potentiality and power is charismatically quickened and put at the service of the liberating kingdom of God, we can then go a step further and ask about the *special* charismata which are newly created by the Holy Spirit, and are therefore experienced for the first time in the discipleship of Jesus. For Paul these are especially the gifts and tasks connected with the building up of the community of Christ's people, which witnesses to the coming kingdom. For him, the community – the congregation – is the place where the Spirit is revealed. If we sum up these charismata, we find the *kerygmatic charismata* of the female and male apostles, prophets, teachers, evangelists and exhorters, but also phenomena such as inspiration, ecstasy, speaking with tongues, and other ways of expressing faith. In addition there are the *diaconal*, or charitable, *charismata* of the deacons, the people who nurse the sick, the people who give alms, and the widows; but again there are special gifts too, such as the healing of sick bodies, exorcism, the healing of memories, and other kinds of help. Finally there are the *kybernetic charismata* of 'the first' in faith, the 'presidents', shepherds and bishops; but there are also particular phenomena in the context of peace-making and building up community.

These tasks and functions emerge only when the community of Christ's people come into being, so they have to be seen as special gifts and tasks given by the Spirit. I would not call them 'supernatural', over against the 'natural' charismata mentioned earlier; for practically speaking, what believers do is to put their natural gifts at the service of the congregation. But in the service of the congregation they make out of their gifts something different from what they were in other contexts. The transitions are as fluid here as real life itself, for the gifts put at the service of the congregation, and the gifts practised in family, profession and society, must not be separated.

They are not subject to different laws. Being a Christian is indivisible. The yardstick is the same everywhere: the discipleship of Jesus.

According to Paul's teaching about the charismata, the rule for the community of Christ's people has to be *unity only in diversity*, not unity in uniformity. It is only the diversity which makes a living and viable unity possible, for if it is merely a case of 'birds of a feather flock together', the people who are no different from each other will become a matter of indifference to one another, and each will make the other superfluous. The acceptance of other people in their difference and their particularity is constitutive for the community of Christ. Only the free wealth of individually different charismata ministers to life and its liberation. Every restriction and uniformity in ideas, words and works benumbs the community and bores other people. It is only unity in diversity that makes the Christian community an 'inviting church' and a healing community in this uniform society of ours. Life is plural, and the new creation of life especially so. The person who cannot endure this is choosing death, and petrifies here and now in the monotonous standardization of what is diverse.

Paul was living in the enthusiastic springtime of a young Christianity. The first congregations evidently experienced an 'overflowing abundance' of spiritual gifts. That is why Paul emphasizes the *unity*: 'There are varieties of gifts, but there is *one Spirit*' (I Cor. 12.4). Today we have to stress the very opposite: there is one Spirit but there are *many gifts*. There is one God, who creates everything, but there are as many powers and energies as there are created beings. Love should unite the different gifts, says Paul; but freedom must release these different gifts, is what we have to say today.

But here we have to put a critical question to Paul. Do the charismata have to be judged exclusively according to their usefulness in building up the Christian community and our life together? 'To each is given the manifestation of the Spirit for the common good' (I Cor. 12.7). Don't the charismata have a value in themselves, quite apart from their utility for the community? And don't charismatic experiences also have a value for the people concerned, even apart from 'the common good'? Bearing these questions in mind, and unprejudiced by the 'for' and 'against' of today's 'charismatic movement', let us approach two special phenomena: speaking with tongues and healing.

§2 SPEAKING WITH TONGUES

It is a historically indisputable phenomenon that the birth of the Christian congregations was accompanied by 'speaking with tongues'. This is already reported in the Acts of the Apostles, chapter 2, in its account of the first Pentecost.[5] It can also hardly be disputed that the Christian revival movements have been accompanied by the same phenomenon. Finally, there is no doubt at all that today the pentecostal and charismatic congregations are growing everywhere, not only in the countries of the young churches but in the older Christian countries too. I have no personal experience of this phenomenon, so I can neither explain nor dispute it. I can only describe it from the outside, from its effect on the people concerned. It would seem to me to be an inward possession by the Spirit which is so strong that it can no longer find adequate expression in comprehensible language, so that it utters itself in glossolalia – just as intense pain is expressed by unrestrained weeping, or extreme joy by jumping and dancing. 'With praise and adoration a charismatic community responds to what God has revealed in word and act. New love and words, spontaneous prayers, speaking with tongues, prophecies and testimonies springing spontaneously from the immediate situation, as well as an expressive body language in the form of raised hands, clapping, kneeling, throwing oneself on the ground before God, and dancing: all these have become typical characteristics of gatherings in the context of charismatic renewal.'[6]

It is certainly true that our regular, mainline church services display a wealth of ideas and reflections in their sermons, but are poverty-stricken in their forms of expression, and offer no opportunity at all for spontaneity. They are disciplined and disciplinary assemblies for talking and listening. But does the body of Christ really consist simply of one big mouth and a lot of little ears? So it is liberating for us Europeans to share the charismatic worship of black people in Africa and the United States, and to see and learn a body language which is different from our European 'sitting-still-with-folded-hands'. I would interpret 'speaking with tongues' as the beginning, when the tongues of the dumb are loosened, and they express what they themselves experience and feel. Perhaps we can see an analogy in scream therapy, although speaking with tongues goes beyond any purely human possibility. It is at all events a new way of expressing the experience of faith, and it is a *personal* way. Paul also advises the congregation to 'strive for' (RSV: 'earnestly desire') charismata (I Cor. 14.1), but most of all 'that you may prophesy'. By this he means personal, comprehensible witness in preaching and pastoral care. In his view, therefore, speaking with tongues can be interpreted in the Holy Spirit, and he believes it is God-given.

Prophetic speech is a special charisma, for in a particular personal or public kairos it discovers the appropriate, binding and liberating word, and says specifically and at the right time what sin is, and what grace. This appropriate word cannot be deduced from any doctrine, nor can it be psychologically figured out from the situation. But one can develop sensibility for the congruity of the appropriate word and the proper time, and can become open for it, so that it can happen.

The fact that the congregations who listen to sermons with us are hardly enabled to give any personal testimony also paralyses personal Christian life, and the development of personal conviction. Many people are quite satisfied to belong to the church, to go to church occasionally, and to agree by and large with the church's doctrine, even if they do not know much about it, and it does not mean very much to them. The awakening of personally experienced and personally expressed faith is the 'charismatic experience' today. Before the mainline churches and the bishops and other leaders 'quench' the Spirit of the 'charismatic movement', we should all make room for the Spirit, not only in church services, but in our bodies too, since those bodies are, after all, supposed to be 'a temple of the Holy Spirit' (I Cor. 6.19).

But we have to put a critical question to the 'charismatic movement': what about the *neglect* of charismata? Where are the charismata of the 'charismatics' in the everyday world, in the peace movement, in the movements for liberation, in the ecology movement? If charismata are not given us so that we can flee from this world into a world of religious dreams, but if they are intended to witness to the liberating lordship of Christ in this world's conflicts, then the charismatic movement must not become a non-political religion, let alone a de-politicized one.

§3 THE AWAKENING OF CHARISMATIC EXPERIENCE

Many people can do more than they think they can. Why? We are afraid of attempting things because we are afraid of failing. 'If you don't try, you can't fail' we tell ourselves. But people who withdraw into themselves and creep into their shells out of fear of defeat, or because they are anxious about the way other people will react, or because they are afraid of losing some personal relationship, will never get to know their own potentialities. They are not living in all the opportunities life is offering them. But to do this is never to learn one's own limitations either. It is only when we try to get beyond our limitations that we learn what they are, and accept them.

There are people who think everything is impossible from the outset. 'It's pointless', they say. 'Nothing will come of it in any case', and 'I can't'. In this way they save themselves a lot of conflicts, but they experience very little about true life either. And they learn least of all about themselves. To themselves they remain anonymous.

But there are also people who believe in the possible. That is the way believers are described in the synoptic gospels: 'All things are possible with God.' The people who trust to that then sense that 'All things are possible to him who believes.' Of course this faith in the possible brings them some defeats, but they also experience the strength to get up again after their setbacks. The person who believes becomes a person full of possibilities. People like this do not restrict themselves to the social roles laid down for them, and do not allow themselves to be tied to these roles. They believe they are capable of more. And they do not tie other people down to their own preconceived ideas. They do not imprison others in what they are at present. They see them together with their future, and keep their potentialities open for them. 'Love frees us from every image', said Max Frisch. Love does not pin people down. It sets them free. If love gives trust, the other person can grasp his own potentialities for good. Our charismatic potentialities are awakened by trust: trust in God, trust in ourselves and trust in our neighbour. And in this free space of trust we can then trust ourselves to do something too.

If this trust in ourselves is to be strengthened, self-love is required as well.[7] 'Love your neighbour as yourself', we are told in the biblical command for humanity. It does not say: love your neighbour instead of yourself, though this is the way Kierkegaard interpreted it. Love of our neighbour presupposes love of ourselves. We cannot love other people if we do not love ourselves. But we cannot love ourselves if we do not want to be ourselves, but want to be someone else. 'Self'-less love in the literal sense is no love at all, for it has no subject. Self-love is the strength to love our neighbour. Self-love is the foundation for a free life.

We can make the counter-check: how can a man who despises himself love his neighbour? How can a woman who cannot endure herself bear other people? How can someone who does not trust himself trust other people? Won't someone who hates himself, and has never accepted himself, hate other people too? Self-hate is the torment of hell. For self-love in the true sense has nothing whatsoever to do with selfishness. Selfishness springs from the fear of not getting enough. The people who are afraid of that are simply the people who have lost themselves and cannot find themselves again. Selfishness leads to the struggle of everybody against everybody. Selfishness is not self-love. Selfish self-seeking is merely the reverse side of self-hate. But self-seeking and self-hate are only two sides of the same thing: the search for the lost self, and the inability to love oneself.

If in faith we have the charismatic experience that God loves us without conditions and without reserve, how should we hate what God loves so much? God loves us as we really are, not as we want to be – or do not want to be. To love ourselves means accepting ourselves as God has accepted us, in spite of all our unacceptability, as Paul Tillich said. The person who still goes on despising himself after that is despising what God loves. Self-trust on the foundation of trust in God, self-love on the basis of God's love, are the powers and energies which our charismatic experiences awaken in us. In loving our neighbour and trusting our neighbour we mutually confer on one another the experience of our potentialities for good.

The essential impediment to the charismatic experience of our potentialities for living is to be found in our passive sins, not our active ones; for the hindrance is not our despairing attempt to be ourselves, but our despairing attempt not to be ourselves, so that out of fear of life and fear of death we fall short of what our own lives could be. The charismata of the Spirit are present wherever faith in God drives out these fears of life, and whenever the hope of resurrection overcomes the fear of death. According to the testimonies of the first Christians, it was the Easter jubilation over Christ's resurrection that released the stream of charismata in the congregations. The pentecostal movement begins at Easter.

§4 THE HEALING OF THE SICK

Together with the proclamation of the gospel, the healing of the sick is Jesus' most important testimony to the dawning kingdom of God.

According to Matt. 10.8 it is also a charge given to Jesus' disciples, so it is an essential part of the church's apostolate. The experiences of healing in physical and mental illnesses therefore also belong to the charismatic experience of life. In the context of faith, healings are signs of the new creation and the rebirth of life. If, in the light of Easter, God's Spirit is experienced as the Spirit of the resurrection of the dead, then the healings experienced should be understood as foretokens of that resurrection and of eternal life. Just as eternal life quickens those who believe, so the eternal salvation heals those who trust it; for like heal and holy (see the previous chapter, § 4), healing and salvation (*heilen* and *Heil* in German) are related.[8]

The first thing that people discovered in Jesus, according to the synoptic gospels, was the healing power of the divine Spirit. That is why people who come into contact with him are revealed not as 'sinners' (as they are in Paul), but as 'the sick'. Out of the corners into which they had been forced, out of the wildernesses to which they had been banished, out of the shadows into which they had crept, the sick and possessed emerge, and try to be near him. In the neighbourhood of Jesus men and women reveal themselves, not as people who fulfil the Greek ideal of the healthy mind in the healthy body, but as sick, suffering and in need of help.[9] In the vicinity of Jesus, people do not show themselves from their sunny side but from the sides that are dark and shadowed.

Why do the sick come forward and show themselves when they are near him? They evidently discovered that his life possessed a healing power that was infectious: 'At evening, at sundown, they brought to him all who were sick or possessed with demons. And the whole city was gathered together about the doors. And he healed many who were sick with various diseases, and cast out many demons' (Mark 1.32ff.). 'Demons' are destructive powers conceived in personal terms. They are characterized by their pleasure in tormenting. When the Messiah comes, says the old Jewish hope, these tormenting spirits will disappear from the earth, and people will recover their health and will be able to live reasonable lives again.[10]

Miraculous healings were common enough in the ancient world. We find them today too. But in the case of Jesus they belong within the context of his proclamation of the kingdom of God: when God assumes power over his creation, the demons retreat. When the living God comes and indwells his creation, every creature will be filled with his eternal vitality. Jesus does not bring the kingdom of God only in words that waken faith; he also brings it in the form of healings which restore health. God's Spirit is a living energy that interpenetrates the bodies of men and women and drives out the germs of death. Jesus' miraculous healings are what Christoph Blumhardt called 'miracles of the kingdom'. In the dawn of the new creation of all things, they are really not 'miracles' at all. They are completely natural and just what we have to expect. It is only if this eschatological hope is lost that these 'wonders' appear to be miracles in an unchanged world. But in the framework of hope for the kingdom of God, Jesus' healings are reminders of hope. They justify expectations brought to the Spirit of Jesus now, in the present.

Serious illnesses are foreshadowings of death, and in the same way the healings are to be understood as foretokens of the resurrection. In every grave illness 'we fight for our lives'. In every healing we feel that 'we have been restored to life' and as if we were 'new born'. In the context of sickness, the kingdom of God means healing. In the context of death, the kingdom means resurrection.

But Jesus did not heal all the sick. In his home town Nazareth 'he could do not a single mighty work' (Mark 6.5). When could he heal, and when could he not? What were the conditions? In the case of a sick boy it was the unbelieving faith of the father that made healing possible: 'Lord I believe, help my unbelief!' (Mark 9.23f.). The woman 'with an issue of blood' (Mark 5.25ff.) 'procured' her healing herself. It was only afterwards that Jesus noticed that 'power had gone forth from him'. 'Your *faith* has made you well', he says to her. As a Jew, he rejects the Gentile woman who seeks help for her daughter, but when she makes it clear to him that the kingdom of God does not stop short at the frontiers of Israel, he says to her 'Be it done to you *as you desire*' (Matt. 15.21ff.).

Healing, that is to say, comes about in the *interaction* between Jesus and *expectation*, a person's faith and his will. That means that these healings are contingent. They are not 'contrived', or brought about. They happen when and where God wills it. There are no methods for healings of this kind, for they are not repeatable, and repeatability is the premise for every method. Prayers are offered for the healing of the sick person. Hands are laid on him so that the desired healing may come about. If the sicknesses are psychosomatic, confession and the forgiveness of guilt help to heal the oppressed soul and body.[11] But there are also ways of working with the body so that the mind and soul can be healed. Tormenting and oppressive memories can also be healed if the tense body is relaxed.[12] Whenever sicknesses are sicknesses of the whole person, the whole person has to be healed. Whenever sicknesses belong in the context of disrupted human relationships, the relationships in which, and from which, the person lives have to be healed too. So there is also healing through caring commitment, through trust and through new sociality. Modern medicine treats the body, and has objectified and material-ized healing to such an extent that for us healing means only 'health', and health means no more than the restoration of the functions of particular organs. It is only psychosomatic and holistic medicine which again gives us a generally comprehensible way of access to the experiences of faith healing, and takes from them the odour of peculiarity.

How does Jesus heal? What constitutes the healing power of his Spirit? We find an answer in Matt. 8.17: '. . . and he healed all who were sick. This was to fulfil what was spoken by the prophet Isaiah, "He took our infirmities and bore our diseases".' Jesus' healing power is not to be found in his supreme power over sickness and disease. His power to heal is *the power of his suffering*. He heals by 'carrying' our sicknesses. 'Through his wounds we are healed' (Isa. 53.5). His passion and his self-surrender on Golgotha are the secret of his healings of the sick.

But how can the wounded find healing in his wounds? Healing consists of the restoration of disrupted community, and the sharing and communication of life. Jesus heals the sick by restoring their fellowship with God. He restores to the sick their community with God through his solidarity with them, and his vicarious intervention for them. In Christ God has become human, and has assumed limited and mortal humanity and made it part of his eternal divinity. He assumed it so that he might heal it. In the passion of Jesus Christ God has assumed sick, weak, helpless and disabled human life and made it part of his own eternal life. God heals the sicknesses and the griefs by making the sicknesses and the griefs *his* suffering and *his* grief. In the image of the crucified God the sick and dying can see themselves, because in them the crucified God recognizes himself. Through his passion Jesus brings God into the God-forsakenness of the sick and into the desolation of dying. The crucified God embraces every sick life and makes it his life, so that he can communicate his own eternal life. And for that reason the crucified One is both the source of healing and consolation in suffering.

§5 THE CHARISMA OF THE HANDICAPPED LIFE

Accounts of the charismatic movement often sound like American success stories. But 'the religion of success' makes no religious sense in the pains, the failures and the disablements of life. 'The theology of the cross' does not fit this 'officially optimistic society' or its civil religion.

But Paul discovered 'the power of God' not merely in the strong places of his life, but in his weakness too: 'My strength is made perfect in weakness' (II Cor. 12.9). That is why he also boasts of his weakness, the ill-treatment, the necessities, the persecutions and fears which he has endured. These 'sufferings of Christ' which he has personally experienced are for him the proof of his apostolate and are therefore charismata: 'For even if we are weak in him, we shall live with him by the power of God' (II Cor. 13.4). 'The Spirit of the resurrection' is there at the places where we experience the shadow of the cross.[13]

So Paul expects that the congregations will include the strong and the weak, wise people and foolish ones, the handicapped and the non-handicapped. No one is useless and of no value. Nobody can be dispensed with. So the weak, the foolish and the people with disabilities also have their special charisma in the community of Christ's people. Why? *All* will be made like in form to the crucified Christ, because the crucified Christ has assumed not only true humanity but the whole misery of men and women too, so that he can heal it. Every human life is life assumed by God in Christ, and in him already partakes here and now in God's eternal life.

'What is not assumed will not be healed' says one of the principles of patristic christology. But this means that whatever has been assumed by the Son of God who became human and was crucified, is then already whole, good and beautiful in God's sight. Today it is important to recognize this in the people we call 'handicapped', so that we can overcome this public, and also highly personal, conflict between the non-handicapped and people with disabilities in the community of Christ's people.[14] The handicapped are not handicapped merely by the lives of the strong and effective. They are often robbed of their independence by solicitude and protective care. If this is to change, we have to recognize that *every handicap is an endowment too*. The strength of Christ is also powerful in the disablement. Those of us who are not handicapped generally stare only at what another person lacks, or has lost, and see 'disabled persons'. But if we forget our own scale of values, we detect the dignity and worth of a handicapped life and notice its importance for our life together. Anyone who has experienced disabled persons in his own family knows how important they are for the family as a whole, and has perhaps discovered what God is saying and doing through the charisma of these handicapped people. If whatever a person is and brings with him becomes a charisma through his calling, this has to be true of his disablement too. If through the calling the splendour of God's love falls on a life, it begins to shine. There are handicapped, sick and disfigured people whose faces shine in just this way.

Finally, according to Paul the body of Christ needs weak and handicapped members as well as strong ones, and God gives the weak and handicapped members the most 'honour and glory' (I Cor. 12.24). Why? Surely because the body of Christ is the body of the one exalted and *humiliated*, the risen and the *crucified* Christ. The astonishing 'powers' of the Spirit manifest God's *power to raise*. In the pains, slights and disablements, and in 'the sufferings of the Spirit', God's *suffering power* is revealed. So there is no good diaconal, or charitable, service given by the non-handicapped to the handicapped unless they have previously perceived and accepted the diaconal ministry of the handicapped to the non-handicapped. Congregations without any disabled members are disabled and disabling congregations. The congregation which is charismatic in the Christian sense is always *a diaconal congregation*, since charisma also means *diakonia*. The great charitable works of the churches are necessary, but what we need is to bring to life the diaconal congregation of handicapped and non-handicapped people: a congregation which looks after its own handicapped and sick members as far as possible.

§6 EVERYONE ACCORDING TO HIS ABILITIES, EVERYONE ACCORDING TO HIS NEEDS

The charismatic community is *a unity in diversity* and *a diversity in unity*. Everyone as the Lord has called them, everyone as the Lord has given them. This is basically the formula for equal justice for all: in Ulpian's maxim, *suum cuique*. This brilliant formula links equality before the law for everyone with the real differences between people: what is hers – what is his. Everyone according to his abilities – everyone according to his needs. That is the law of the truly humane society (Acts 4.32–35). According to Paul, the power that unites such differing people and their multifarious gifts is *love*, by virtue of which believers are there for one another, so that together they may be the body of Christ. He can also call this love *the presence of Christ*, in which one person should serve the other (Eph. 5.21ff.). At this point it would be better to talk about 'the fellowship of the Holy Spirit', in which the people who are so variously endowed come together. There are many gifts – but there is one Spirit. And this unity of the Spirit is the fellowship joining the variously called and endowed believers. This relativizes every other guarantee of unity: it is not the one doctrine, not the one pope, and not the one faith which creates the unity in the diversity, and in the multiplicity of gifts; it is *the fellowship of the Spirit*. If this fellowship of the Spirit in the multiplicity of the Spirit's gifts did not exist, then none of the other guarantees of the church's unity would have any force.[15]

The power of unity is *love*. The power of diversity is *freedom*. The fellowship of the Spirit is the free space in which the manifold and many-faceted gifts of the Spirit can be awakened and grow. Where the church of the Spirit is concerned, Mao's slogan is particularly apt: 'Let a hundred flowers blossom.' As the fellowship of the Holy Spirit, the church is the last who should sacriligiously cast a blight on the buds, as the apocalyptic sniffers-out of heresy and the timid condemners of 'error' do. To be a woman is a charisma in faith, to be a man is a charisma in faith. To everyone their own, and all hand in hand for the kingdom of God![16] For the kingdom of God is nothing other than *the new creation of all things* and the rebirth of everything living. It is as brilliantly variegated as the creation which we know now. The kingdom of God is not an impoverishment of creation. It is creation in a still greater wealth. The kingdom of God does not destroy this creation, as Marcion maintained, thereupon being quite rightly excluded from the Christian congregation in Rome. On the contrary, the kingdom of God is the eschatological springtime of the whole creation. So charismatic experience is the experience that this life, which has become old, has lost its way and is so heavy-laden with wrongs, begins to flower again and becomes young once more.

In time we become old, but eternity makes us young. The new creation of all things gives back the possibilities that were spoilt and neglected: 'They who wait for the Lord shall renew their strength, they shall mount up with wings like eagles, they shall run and not be weary, they shall walk and not faint' (Isa. 40.31.).

§7 THE HOLY SPIRIT AS SOURCE OF ENERGY AND FIELD OF FORCE

In the light of the charismatic experience of life let us ask, finally: who or what is the Holy Spirit according to these experiences?

In the charismatic experience, God's Spirit is felt as a *vitalizing energy*. In the nearness of God we are happy, and life begins to vibrate. We experience ourselves in the vibrancies of the divine field of force. That is why charisma is also described as *dynamis* or *energeia*. From earliest times, the charismatic experience of the Holy Spirit has been pictured as a flowing, an outpouring and a shining. If we take these experiences as starting point, we can say that the Holy Spirit appears as the well of life – the origin of the torrent of energy – the source of the light that gives the shining splendour. The expressions used here point to the doctrine of emanation.

What does that mean for a Spirit which is 'poured out upon all flesh'? The gifts of the Spirit are then not creations of the Spirit, for the Spirit himself is poured out in the gifts. So we cannot distinguish here between created and uncreated energies. The water of life which flows from the wellspring of life has the same quality as the spring itself. The relation between the one Spirit and the many gifts of the Spirit, and the relation of the one light to its many reflections, is not the detached relation of the creator to what he has created. It is much more intimate than that. Through the Spirit who is 'poured out' on all flesh, all flesh becomes spiritual. In the love of God which is 'poured out' in our hearts through the Holy Spirit, God himself is 'in us' and we ourselves are 'in God'. In the experience of the Spirit, God is primal, all-embracing presence, not a detached counterpart. In the charismatic experience of the Spirit, we experience the reciprocal perichoresis of God and ourselves. That is a much more intimate communion than the community between Creator and creature. It is the communion of reciprocal indwelling. In the Holy Spirit the eternal God participates in our transitory life, and we participate in the eternal life of God. This reciprocal community is an immense, outflowing source of energy.

We have called the energies of the Spirit which we charismatically experience, *vitalizing energies*, because they bring us to life. Since human life always becomes living only through love, we can, with great caution, call this divine energy an eroticizing energy.[17] By eros we mean the force which holds the world together and keeps it alive, anthropologically and cosmologically: the power of attraction which unites, and the individual weight which simultaneously distinguishes. The rhythm of attraction and distance, affection and respect is the power of eros. So 'in the Spirit' we experience both the community and the diversity of the Spirit: unity in the diversity, and diversity in the community. We experience at one and the same time our socialization and our individuation. 'In the Spirit' we come to know the *love* that binds us and the *freedom* which makes us our own individual, separate selves.

Finally, when men and women lay hold of their existence charismatically, the Holy Spirit makes that existence *shine*. In pictures, earlier generations liked to depict this shining power of being in the form of a halo. What they were trying to say was that the life that is charismatically possessed and sanctified again becomes the image of God, and is illuminated by the divine glory (*kabod, doxa*) which it reflects. After he had encountered God, Moses was forced to veil his face because the people found the reflection of the divine glory unendurable (Ex. 18). Paul discovered 'the glory of God in the face of Christ' (II Cor. 4.6), and in the same passage describes the experience of the Spirit as being 'a bright shining in our hearts'. Today we should talk about the 'aura' or 'charm' of which the person concerned is unaware.[18] We also talk about the 'atmosphere' in a group, which can be 'poisoned' or 'good'. There is a 'climate of trust' and 'a climate of mistrust'. Every life radiates its own atmosphere. This atmosphere results from the things that concern us, and with which we concern ourselves, but it has to do above all with the things we most of all fear and most of all love. Other people are either unnerved and oppressed by this unconscious ambience, or stimulated and quickened by it. Life can radiate ambition and fear, or peace and tranquillity; and in the same way it can radiate experiences of God.

This divine radiance of existence is something of which we are unaware, and this has to be so; for 'the person who looks at himself does not shine. But the person who does not look at himself will be filled with light', says the book of Chinese Wisdom *Tao-te-Ching* in its twenty-second chapter.

X

Theology of Mystical Experience

Mystical theology aims at being a wisdom drawn from experience, not a doctrinal wisdom.[1] It is not the theology itself that is mystical. It is mystical only because it tries to put mystical experience into words. By 'mystical' we do not mean here special supernatural experiences. We mean the intensity of the experience of God in faith, so that in this sense we are talking about the deep dimension of every experience of faith. Mystical experiences cannot be conveyed through doctrinal tenets. So the theology of mystical experience always talks only about the way, the journey, the crossing-over to that unutterable experience of God which no one can tell or communicate. As far as its doctrinal content is concerned, the theology of the mystics down to the present day does not seem particularly impressive. In terms of the history of thought, it is easy enough to recognize the Augustinian, Neoplatonic and gnostic ideas, and to trace them back to their historical roots. But this way of looking at things does not put us on the same road as the mystical theologians themselves. So it is more appropriate to ask about the experiences they were trying to express with the help of these particular images and ideas. If we want to share their experiences, the best thing is to accompany them on the same journey.

The mystical *sapientia experimentalis* is always ethical and mystical at the same time. It is both a teaching about virtue and a search for experience, for only 'the pure in heart shall see God'. This does not mean dividing life superficially into one sector called praxis and another called knowledge. For the mystics ever since Augustine, life itself has been *the drama of love* – unhappy love, despairing love, liberated love, seeking love, and the love for God that has achieved the bliss which it sought for. All the mystics start from a single assumption: that men and women are erotic beings, driven by hungry hearts which can find fulfilment only in God. For the infinite God arouses in men and women who are his image an infinite passion which destroys everything that is finite and earthly unless it finds rest in his infinity. That is why the only measure of mystical love is the immeasurable.[2]

What the early and the modern mystics describe is really the history of the liberation of human passion from the melancholy forms of satisfaction which have so wretchedly miscarried. What they describe is in fact the love affair between human beings and God. That only sounds sentimental if we forget that disappointed love is the most terrible thing a man or woman can suffer. From it come the powers of destruction, the delight in torment and the furies of annihilation. The mystics have described their paths to the liberation of passion in different ways. I am not going to attempt here to analyse the different 'heavenly journeys of the soul' historically, or to reduce them systematically to a common denominator. But I should like to describe a journey of this kind which leads to mystical experience – an experience not of the world beyond but of this one, the experience not of a spiritual life but of vital life in the midst of the world in which we live.

§1 ACTION AND MEDITATION

Ever since 'practice' was elevated into the criterion for truth, meditation has been judged as remote from reality, because it is speculative. Truth must 'always be concrete', Berthold Brecht tells us; so meditation now counts as 'abstract', a flight from reality and action. In societies which force their members to active life, and reward only performance and success, meditation is considered useless and superfluous. That is understandable enough. What is not understandable is when meditation exercises are recommended to nervy activists and harrassed managers as a useful kind of counterbalancing sport, or when yoga techniques are sold as a way of increasing performance. Pragmatic and utilitarian marketing means the permanent destruction of the very nature of meditation. It does not let people find rest, and even if they do find rest they do not find themselves in the process.

Meditation is in fact an ancient method of arriving at knowledge which has been pushed aside by our modern activism. Meditation is a mode of perception which we continually practise in everyday life without noticing it particularly, and without surrendering ourselves to it. We see that a tree is beautiful – but we still drive past it at fifty miles an hour. We become aware of ourselves – and hurry off to work, forgetting ourselves altogether. We have no time to become aware of things, or of ourselves.

When we try to get to know something by the methods of modern science, we know in order to achieve mastery: 'knowledge is power', proclaimed Francis Bacon. We take possession of our object and no longer respect it for what it is. We become just what René Descartes promised, 'maîtres et possesseurs de la nature' – the masters and possessors of nature. And nature becomes mute. Modern reason has been made operational. It 'knows only that which it brings forth according to its own design', as Kant said. Nothing else? No, almost nothing else. Reason has become a productive organ which is hardly still capable of perceiving things. But meditation is pre-eminently a way of sensory perception, of receiving, of absorbing and participating.

We can make this difference clear to ourselves if we think of it in the following way. It is by no means true that we comprehend the world solely through 'the little grey cells' of our brain. We always understand it with our senses too. What senses do we use in order to acquire knowledge and understanding?

The Greek philosophers, the Fathers of the church and the monastic Fathers comprehended things *'with their eyes'*. They 'theorized' in the literal sense of the word (θεορεῖν = to look at). We really arrive at understanding when we go on looking at a flower or a sunset or a manifestation of God until *this* flower is *the* flower *per se*, and *this* sunset is *the* sunset, and *this* manifestation of God is wholly God and nothing but God *himself*. Then the observer himself becomes part of the flower, or part of the sunset, or part of God. For through his perception he participates in his object or counterpart, and is transported into it. The act of perception transforms the perceiver, not what is perceived. Perception confers communion. We know in order to participate, not in order to dominate. That is why we can only know to the extent in which we are capable of loving what we see, and in love are able to let it be wholly itself. Knowledge, as the Hebrew word (*yāda*) tells us, is an act of love, not an act of domination. When someone has understood, he says: 'I see it. I love you. I behold God.' The result is pure 'theory', and pure good-pleasure.

Today we generally understand things quite differently, for we perceive *with our hands*. Of course the sense of touch is the primal sense of the skin. By feeling, we develop feelings. By touching, we ourselves are touched. Through touch we become aware of other people and ourselves. Through touch every child explores the world, and itself in the world. But in the modern world self-awareness has been banished from awareness of the world. Objectively assured knowledge is acquired only by excluding all subjective factors. We want to 'grasp' everything. We acquire knowledge by means of our grasping, possessive and colonizing hands. Once we have 'grasped' something, we have it under control and possess it. Once we possess something, we can do what we like with it. So we know in order to 'master' our object. If someone thinks he understands something, he says: 'Yes, I grasp that. I've got it. I can cope with it.' The result is *pure domination*.

If we compare these two ways of knowing, it is easy to see that modern men and women need at least a balance between the *vita activa* and the *vita contemplativa*, the active and the contemplative life, if they are not to atrophy spiritually.[3] The pragmatic way of grasping things has very obvious limits, and beyond these limits the destruction of life begins. This does not only apply to our dealings with other people. It is true of our dealings with the natural environment too.

But the meditative way of understanding seems to be even more important when it is applied to our dealings with our own selves. People take flight into relationships, into social action and into political praxis, because they cannot endure what they themselves are. They have 'fallen out' with themselves. So they cannot stand being alone. To be alone is torture. Silence is unendurable. Solitude is felt to be 'social death'. Every disappointment becomes a torment which has to be avoided at all costs.

But the people who throw themselves into practical life because they cannot come to terms with themselves simply become a burden for other people. Social praxis and political involvement are not a remedy for the weakness of our own personalities. Men and women who want to act on behalf of other people without having deepened their own understanding of themselves, without having built up their own capacity for sensitive loving, and without having found freedom towards themselves, will find nothing in themselves that they can give to anyone else. Even presupposing good will and the lack of evil intentions, all they will be able to pass on is the infection of their own egoism, the aggression generated by their own anxieties, and the prejudices of their own ideology. Anyone who wants to fill up his own hollowness by helping other people will simply spread the same hollowness. Why? Because people are far less influenced by what another person says and does than the activist would like to believe. They are much more influenced by what the other *is*, and his *way* of speaking and behaving. Only the person who has found his own self can give himself. What else can he give? It is only the person who knows that he is accepted who can accept others without dominating them. The person who has become free in himself can liberate others and share their suffering.

It is a remarkable fact that when the misery of people with under-developed personalities is described, it is always the key words of mysticism that are used. But what are virtues for the mystics are torments for modern men and women: alienation, loneliness, silence, solitude, interior emptiness, stripping bare, poverty, not-knowing, and so forth. We only have to think of Ingmar Bergman's films to see how here mysticism is turned upside down. Modern men and women flee from what the monks sought for, as a way of finding God. Earlier, mystics withdrew into the solitariness of the desert in order to fight with demons and to experience Christ's victory. It seems to me that today we need men and women who enter into the innner wilderness of the soul, and wander through the abysses of the self, in order to fight with demons there, and to experience Christ's victory – or simply so as to make an inner space for living possible, and to open the way out for other people through the experience of their own souls. And in our present context that means wresting a positive meaning out of the loneliness, the silence, the interior emptiness, the suffering, the poverty and 'the knowledge-that-knows-nothing'. The mystics expressed this meaning by way of a paradox. It meant learning to live in the presence of the God who is absent, or in the hiddenness of the God who is present, and enduring what John of the Cross called 'the dark night of the soul'. Can it still mean that today?

§2 MEDITATION AND CONTEMPLATION

There are many definitions of meditation and contemplation, and many distinctions have been made between the two.[4] For my own practical purposes I would interpret *meditation* as the loving, suffering and participating knowledge of something; and *contemplation* as the reflective awareness of one's own self in this meditation. In meditation, people submerge themselves in the object of their meditation. They are wholly absorbed in it and 'forget themselves'. The object is submerged in them. In contemplation, they recollect themselves once more. They become conscious of the changes in themselves. They come back to themselves, after they had gone out of themselves and forgotten themselves. In meditation we become aware of the object. In the contemplation that is bound up with it we become aware of our awareness. Of course there is no meditation without contemplation, and no contemplation without meditation. But if we want to understand the two, it is useful to make this distinction.

As far as the Christian faith is concerned, this has certain consequences.

(*a*) Christian meditation is not transcendental meditation. It is meditation on an object. It is at its innermost heart *meditatio passionis et mortis Christi* – the stations of the cross, meditation on the passion, Good Friday mysticism.[5] Here the history of Christ is perceived as an open, inclusive history 'for us'. His giving of himself to death 'for us' makes that manifest. That is why this history is accessible to the knowledge mediated through meditation – the participatory knowledge, that is, which transforms the knower. The observer is drawn into the history of Christ. He does not apply the history to himself; he applies himself to Christ's history. He then discovers himself again in that history, finding himself accepted, reconciled and liberated for God's kingdom. He participates in the history that is Christ's.

(*b*) When the people who are meditating on the inclusive history of Christ are recalled to themselves, they discover that what they know of the history of Christ is determined by that history itself. By finding the 'Christ for us', Christ is 'in them' and they are 'in Christ'. They come to know the history of the Christ crucified for them in the presence of the Spirit of the Christ who is risen in them. Just by knowing nothing except Christ crucified (I Cor. 2.2), they can say with Paul, 'It is no longer I who live, but Christ who lives in me' (Gal. 2.20). According to Paul, in faith 'the fellowship of Christ's sufferings' and 'the power of his resurrection' are experienced simultaneously; and so the self-forgetting knowledge of the story of the cross of Christ *extra nos*, and the self-knowing perception of the risen Christ *in nobis*, belong together as a single whole. The meditative knowledge of Christ *for us* and the contemplative perception of Christ *in us* condition one another mutually.

If we ignore 'the mysticism of the apostle Paul' and are aware merely of the 'Christ for us' in word and sacrament, we easily become orthodox in the sense of an institutionalized spirituality. But if we depart from word and sacrament, and with them leave on one side the open history of 'Christ for us', in order to give ourselves up solely to the mysticism focussed on Christ, we lose sight of Christ by losing sight of his history, and then we lose ourselves in nothingness. In seventeenth-century Protestantism, the dispute between orthodoxy and pietism was fought out with this pernicious alternative between the 'Christ for us' and the 'Christ within us'.[6] We can avoid the alternative between salvation as an objective truth and salvation as a subjective conviction if we discover the open, inclusive history of Christ, and find the history of our own lives together with this history. For our own history with Christ's history is the history of the Holy Spirit. Without the contemplative awareness of the Holy Spirit's activity 'in us', the history of Christ 'for us' will not come alive.

We called contemplation the perception of our perception of Christ's history. But because the perception of an objective perception is not itself objective, particular caution is called for. It is an indirect knowing of knowing, and an indirect awareness of the self that is given along with the awareness of the object as such. As long as knowing is viewed as an activity on the part of the knower, this knowing of knowing is an awareness of subjectivity. But this cannot be sustained, since the awareness of it again presupposes subjectivity, and so on. It is a different matter if knowing can be viewed as the activity of the counterpart which lays itself open to the act of knowing, or makes itself known ('*gives* itself to be known', says the equivalent German verb). Then knowing is a suffering of impressions and is based on the knower's receptivity. The knowing of the knowing that is constituted in *this* way leads to awareness of our own objectivity. That can be sustained. The changes which the impressions perceived make in the knower can be consciously realized through contemplation.

What happens to the knower through his or her knowledge of the history of Christ? What does the Holy Spirit effect in the fellowship of Christ? The traditional answer is: the restoration of the image of

God in the human being, the institution of God's friendship as gift to the believer, and ultimately likeness to God in the glory of God. The person becomes Christ's image, and in being Christ's image becomes the image of God.[7] So knowledge of Christ leads at the same time to what the mystics called 'the birth of God in the soul'.

It is only possible to stress this subjective side of faith in Christ as emphatically as mysticism does if contemplation is prepared to explore this renewal, liberation and perfecting of the believer's soul in God. As far as the activity of the knower is concerned, everything is directed towards the object of his cognition. But as far as his receptivity is concerned, everything – even the object of his cognition – is aligned towards him himself. So the open history of Christ 'for us' is continued in his history 'with us' and 'in us', and in our history 'with him' and 'in him'. The subjective goal of this history is the restoration of the believer as God's image. This is what contemplation thinks about. This is the process of which it makes itself aware. Here, to be the image of God is understood as what men and women are destined for, and are capable of: to look upon God. This destiny is fulfilled in the beatific vision.

The experience of 'the mystical moment' is an anticipation of the eschatological, immediate and direct seeing of God 'face to face'. But can there be any such thing as a 'moment' of direct experience of God like this? 'The man who looks on God must die', says the Old Testament. So the indirect knowledge of God in his word and through his image on earth is not simply a hindrance; it is also a protection for men and women. And so the knowledge of Christ's divinity through his humanity is not merely a veiling of God, but is also a sparing of human beings. God's hiddenness in his revelation is not only a torment. It is also a grace. God's absence in his presence is not merely an estrangement. It is a liberation too. And yet the passion of the seeker for God thrusts forward beyond the mediations into what is direct and unmediated.

§3 CONTEMPLATION AND MYSTICISM

Here we shall consider mysticism in the narrower sense of the *unio mystica*: the moment of fulfilment, the ecstasy of union, the submerging of the soul in 'the infinite ocean of the Godhead', 'the birth of God in the soul', or however the mystics paraphrase it. This ecstatic moment is dark, unknowable and inexpressible. Because it can only be experienced with the whole soul or not at all, no one can be present to observe it, or be directly sensible of it. In moments such as these the experience of God becomes so intensive that there is no more remembrance and no more expectation. God is pure present.

But in order through the silence to describe the 'mystic stillness' (*silentium mysticum*) in the unveiled presence of God, we are bound to speak. We are bound to speak in order that speech may be abolished and caught up into silence.

The mediations through which the soul arrived at communion with God have to be abolished, or absorbed into what is beyond them, so that the soul does not linger at them, but uses them for what they are: the rungs of a ladder, the handrails on a path, the halts on a journey. All the mystics have talked about these abolitions of mediations, for the human being's love for God is enticed and drawn by God's love for human beings. Just as God descended to men and women in his love, so human love ascends to God on the paths struck out by God himself in creation, incarnation and the sending of the Spirit.

This can happen quite simply, so that from the gifts of grace for which it prays and for which it gives thanks, faith finds and grasps *the gracious hand* of God from which these gifts come. And from this gracious hand of God it moves to *the open heart* of God. So in the end it loves God no longer for his gracious gifts, and no longer for his gracious hand – not even any longer for the loving indulgence of his commitment. It loves him simply *for his own sake*. On this ladder, love is withdrawn from the objects of love in creation and is turned towards God himself. It is withdrawn too from the image of God and directed to God in his primal, archetypal being. It is not out of a gnostic contempt for the world that the mystics face human beings with the alternative: God or the world; it is in the interests of undivided love. In order to free creation and human beings themselves from their infinite and hence destructive love for God, they demand 'the work of grief', which means a stripping-bare, estrangement, poverty, the abandonment of everything, and finally spiritual surrender. The human being's love for God is withdrawn from the world and the self. This means the end of the service of idols which idolatrous love pursues with the world and the self. The strain put on the world and the self is now ended through the love for God. Creation and the self become free for what they are, and God is enjoyed for his own sake: in Augustine's phrase, *fruitio Dei*.

Meister Eckhart described this abolition of the mediations of God with particular logical stringency in his sermon 'On Detachment'. The love which has been drawn away from creation by God (who is love's true fulfilment) is directed first of all towards the Creator. But God continues to withdraw from the Creator of all things, guiding it towards God himself. It then leaves the Trinity behind and enters the womb of the divine nature. It finally leaves the 'God for us' and turns wholly towards *God in himself*, in order to enter into God's separation from the world and, through its own detachment, to correspond to God's detachment. Eckhart heightens this detachment to its utmost conclusion: 'When God created the heaven and the earth, he might not have made anything at all, for all it affected his detachment . . . When the Son in the Godhead desired to become man, and became so, and suffered martyrdom, God's immovable detachment was as little touched as if he had never been made man.' Eckhart describes the mystery paradoxically and apophatically: 'Detachment stands upon a pure nothingness' and if the soul in its detachment comes to resemble the detachment of God, 'then it is ignorant with knowing and loveless with loving and dark with light'.[8]

In his sermon 'Qui audit me', he reduces love-stripped-bare to the well-known formula: 'Let God go, for God's sake.' The love of God reaches perfection when it lets even God go for God's sake.[9] We can call this 'mystical atheism'. But it is an atheism for God's sake.

In his sermon 'Beati pauperes spiritu' Eckhart expressed this abolition of all the mediations in the progress of the soul's journey home to God: 'A man should be so empty of all things and all works, both inwardly and outwardly, that he can be a place of his own where God can work.' And then he goes further, to abolish even this 'place': 'So then we should say that the man must be too poor to have or be a place for God to work in. Where the man still has a place in himself, then he still preserves distinction.' It is only 'when the man is thus empty of God and all his works that God, so be he desire to work in the soul, is himself the place in which he desires to work . . . so God works his own work and the man thus suffers God to be in himself.'[10] The breaking of the shell, so as to reach the kernel; the abolition of the mediations, so as to arrive at the goal; the step by step withdrawal of created things, revelations and divine condescensions, so that God may be loved for himself; and then the abolition of God for God's sake – these are the ultimate possibilities of the mystical journey which are expressible at all.

Let us sum up the different steps. *Action* led us to *meditation*. Meditation on the history of Christ *for* us led us to *contemplation* of the presence of his Spirit *in* us, and to the restoration of ourselves as God's image. As Eckhart makes plain, the road from contemplation to *the mystical moment* leads to the abolition of man's likeness to God for God's sake, and ultimately to the abolition of God for God's sake. Then the soul is at home, then love has found bliss, then passion ends in infinite enjoyment, then the ineffable deification begins which the patristic church called *theosis*.

§4 MYSTICISM AND MARTYRDOM

The mystical way is always described as the soul's journey into loneliness, into silence and detachment, into the casting off, stripping bare and abandonment of all earthly and physical things, into the inner self-emptying and letting go of all spiritual things, and finally into 'the dark night of the soul'.[11] If we ask about the actual experience of this journey and its *Sitz im Leben* – its real-life situation – the answer we get is not religious at all; it is political. We meet not the monk but the martyr. 'Blessed are those who are persecuted for righteousness' sake, for theirs is the kingdom of heaven' (Matt. 5.10).

In prison the person who is persecuted for righteousness' sake is stripped of everything he loves. He is cut off from all his human relationships. Celibacy is forced on him. Under torture his nakedness is laid bare and he is subjected to physical torments. He loses his name and becomes a number. His spiritual identity is destroyed by drugs. In the soundless isolation cell he falls into the dark night of the soul. If he is liquidated he disappears, and dies 'outside the camp' with Christ and is 'buried with him in his death'. The way of mystical experience is in fact the discipleship of Christ in resistance against the inhuman forces of death which are anti-God.

The place of mystical experience is in very truth the cell – the prison cell. 'The witness to the truth' is despised, scoffed at, persecuted, dishonoured and rejected. In his own fate he experiences the fate of Christ. His destiny conforms to Christ's destiny. This is what the mystics called *conformitas crucis*, the conformity of the cross. That is why he also experiences the presence of the risen Christ in the fellowship of Christ's sufferings, and the deeper the fellowship in suffering, the more assured of his fellowship the witness will be. Eckhart's reminder that suffering is the shortest way to the birth of

God in the soul applies to the very real and practical sufferings of 'the witness to the truth'. God in the cell, God in the interrogation, God in the torture, God in the body's agony, God in the darkness that has descended on the soul – that is the political mysticism of the martyrs. It is not going too far to say that today prison is a very special place for the Christian experience of God. In prison, Christ is experienced in the Spirit. In prison the soul finds the *unio mystica*. That is what 'the cloud of witnesses' in Korea, South Africa, Latin America, Turkey, Northern Ireland and the former socialist countries tells us.

Church history too points back from the mystical devotion of the cloister to the experience of the martyrs in their prison cells.[12] The spiritual discipleship of Christ in the soul tries to correspond to bodily and political discipleship. The mysticism of the stations of the cross is an echo of the very real paths of suffering taken by the martyrs. It is true that on the way from martyrdom to mysticism, communion with Christ is raised to another level; discipleship becomes imitation, the sufferings of humiliation become the virtue of humility, external persecution becomes inner assailment, and murder becomes 'spiritual death'. And yet the mysticism that is centred on Christ keeps alive the recollection of Christ's sufferings and the remembrance of the martyrs. This also means a firmly held hope for the future of Christ in history. If we understand the spiritual dying-with-Christ in this sense, then mysticism does not mean estrangement from action; it is a preparation for public discipleship. If we understand 'the dark night of the soul' as a Golgotha experience, that dark night points beyond itself to the death of the witnesses themselves. Mediaeval and baroque mysticism had as its goal the purification of the soul for God, but ever since John of the Cross, the idea of participation in Christ's passion has increasingly gained ground. In Theresa of Lisieux it was a mystical *compassio Christi* that was physically suffered. Her experience of dying in the absence of God links the mysticism centred on Christ with everyday life.

Mysticism and discipleship belong together and are of vital import- ance for the church which calls itself by the name of Christ. The apostles were also martyrs, and the church was called to life out of their message and their suffering.[13] Paul's catalogues of tribulations (I Cor. 4; II Cor. 11 and 12) are not told as personal stories about Paul himself. They have a power that testifies to the gospel.[14] They are an expression of the apostolic mediation between Christ's passion and the End-time sufferings of the world. For Paul's eschatology is *theologia crucis* because his theology of the cross is the profoundest expression of hope for Christ's coming.

The sufferings of the apostles are not simply sufferings *for* Christ, in the sense that a soldier dies for his country. They are sufferings *with* Christ, in which the End-time sufferings of the world are accepted by the people who are his, and are overcome through the power of his resurrection. Suffering leads Christ's witness deeper and deeper into community with Christ. Because his suffering brings this about, he is giving expression to the eschatological hope for the whole creation in its fears and anxieties. The person who accepts his *own* suffering and does not try to repress it or push it away, shows the power of hope. So Erik Peterson was right when he wrote: 'The apostolic church, which is founded on the apostles who became martyrs, is always at the same time the suffering church, the church of the martyrs.' As an established religion and in its civil form, Christianity has become estranged from this truth.[15] But passion mysticism must not be allowed to become a substitute. It must be the reverberation of martyrdom and the preparation of a church which lives with its martyrs.

It is useful to prepare for the prison cell in the monastic cell. It is useful to learn to be alone and to be silent, before we are condemned to these things. It is liberating to sink into the wounds of the risen Christ in meditation, so as to experience our own torments as his fate. It is redemptive to find God in the depths of our own souls before we are cut off from the outside world. The person who has died in Christ before he dies, though he die, yet shall he live.

Finally, like the special paths of the mystics and the martyrs, everyday life in the world also has its secret mysticism and its silent martyrdom. The soul does not merely die with Christ and become 'cruciform' by way of spiritual exercises; nor does it do so only in public martyrdom. It already takes the form of the cross in the daily pains of life and in the sufferings of love. The history of the suffering and forsaken Christ is so open that the sufferings and anxieties of every loving man or woman find a place there and are accepted and assumed. If they find a place there and are assumed, it is not in order to give them permanence, but in order to transform and heal them. Suffering with Christ includes even the uncomprehending pain of a child and the inconsolable suffering of helpless parents. It includes the disappointments and public oppressions of the weak and unimportant. It embraces even the apocalyptic sufferings that have not yet been experienced. Because it has taken in the whole divine judgment, there is nothing that is alien to it, and nothing, either, which would have to alienate a person from Christ. And for that reason the experience of the risen 'Christ in us' is to be found not merely in the heights of spiritual contemplation, and not only for the first time in the depths of death, but already in the little experiences of suffering that is sustained and transformed. Anyone who loves dies many deaths. The life that is lived with Christ consoles us in the life we go on living and gives us hope for the resurrection of love. It strengthens the power of the weak and unimportant to resist, when they are disheartened by the strong. It gives creative energy when no possibilities seem open any more. The mystics and martyrs are exceptional; but there is also a *meditatio crucis in passione mundi* which many people practise without realizing it.

There is the simple experience of resurrection wherever there are experiences of love. We are in God and God is in us whenever we are wholly there, undividedly present. The mysticism of everyday life is probably the most profound mysticism of all; the acceptance of the lowliness of one's own life is the true humility, and simple existence is life in God. For in what Ernst Bloch called 'the darkness of the lived moment' the beginning and the end are both present. In that moment time touches eternity. The mystical moment is the divine mystery of the simple life. To find it is so easy, and therefore so difficult. The key to this mystery is childlikeness, wonder, or – in the words of an earlier piety – simplicity.

§5 THE VISION OF THE WORLD IN GOD

Mysticism has continually been reproached with contempt for the world and hatred of the body. And it is easy enough to point to the ideas drawn from Neoplatonic idealism and gnostic dualism in the writings of the mystical theologians. So it is all the more surprising to find in many of them a panentheistic vision of the world in God, and God in the world: 'Everything is one, and one is everything in God', says the *Theologia Deutsch*, and for the Nicaraguan poet monk Ernesto Cardenal the whole of nature is nothing other than 'God's palpable, materialized love', 'the reflection of his beauty', and 'full of love letters to us'.[16] Of course the mystical theologians accept the Old Testament doctrine of creation as it continued to be maintained by the theology of the church. But for their own vision of *the world out of God* they prefer expressions such as 'pouring' and 'flowing', 'source' and 'fountain', 'the sun' and 'the shining'. We may think of Mechthild of Magdeburg's 'flowing light', for example. And for their vision of *the world in God*, they use the words 'homecoming', 'entering in', 'sinking into' and 'dissolving'. In terms of the history of ideas, this is the Neoplatonic language of the emanation of all things from the All-One, and their remanation into the All-One.

Theologically, however, what we have here is the language of pneumatology. Here, in a different way from the world of 'creation' and God's 'works' in history, the Holy Spirit is 'poured out' on all flesh (Joel 2.28ff.; Acts 2.16ff.), and into our hearts (Rom. 5.5). Out of the Spirit we are 'born' again (John 3.3). The light of the Spirit makes the world shine. The gifts of the Spirit are not created gifts; they spring from their source, the Holy Spirit. They are divine energies. The life-giving Spirit 'fills' creation with eternal life by 'descending' on all things and 'indwelling' them. A different divine presence is revealed in the experience of the Holy Spirit from the presence revealed in creation-in-the-beginning. First of all men and women in their physical nature (I Cor. 6.13–20), and then the new heavens and the new earth (Rev. 21), will become the 'temple' which God himself indwells. That is the eternal sabbath: God's rest, and rest in God. That is why the history of the Spirit points towards that consummation which Paul describes in the panentheistic-sounding formula: 'that God may be all in all' (I Cor. 15.28).

This history of the Spirit who will be poured out on all flesh, and this new world which will be transfigured in God, is what the mystical theologians mean by their doctrine of redemption, with its neo-Platonic overtones. 'He who possesses God thus', said Meister Eckhart, 'that is to say in his very being, that man takes God in his divinity, and to that man God shines in all things; for all things taste to him of God, and God's image is visible to him out of all things.'[17] This implies a new, specifically Christian vision of reality, which is moulded by the experience of the indwelling in God's Spirit.

Let us come back once more to the foundation and justification for the panentheistic vision of the world in God.

In the cross of Christ God took evil, sin and rejection on himself, and in the sacrifice of his infinite love transformed it into goodness, grace and election. Evil, sin, suffering and damnation are 'in God':

'Thou who bearest the sins of the world . . .' – thou who bearest the suffering of the world . . . It was suffered by him, has been gathered up in him, in him is transformed 'for our sake'. His suffering is what Paul of the Cross called 'the wonder of wonders of the divine love'. From this nothing can be excluded. So everything that lives, lives from the almighty power of his suffering love, and out of the inexhaustibility of his self-giving love (I Cor. 13.7).[18] There is no longer any Nothingness to threaten creation. For in God the Nothingness is annihilated and 'immortal being' has been manifested. So because of God's cross, creation already lives from God, and will be transformed in God.

Without the cross of Christ this vision of 'the world in God' would be pure illusion. The suffering of one, single child would prove it to be so. Without perception of the suffering of God's inexhaustible love, no pantheism and no panentheism can endure in this world of death. They would very soon end up in pan-nihilism.

It is only knowledge of the crucified God which gives this vision of the world in God its foundation and endurance. In the lordship of the crucified Jesus the living and the dead arrive at eternal fellowship. In the cross of the risen Christ the sins and suffering of the whole world sink away. That is why under the cross the vision comes into being of God in all things – all things in God. If we believe that God is present in the God-forsakenness of the crucified Christ, we see him everywhere, just as after we have experienced what death is like, we live life more intensively than ever before, because every moment is unique.

This vision of the world in God is alive in the experiences of persecuted men and women and the martyrs, who sense God's presence in their imprisonment. It lives among the mystics, who find God's presence in the dark night of the soul. It shines in the devotion of the simple life, where God is present in the darkness of the lived moment: 'In him we live and move and have our being' (Acts 17.28), since 'from him and through him and to him are all things' (Rom. 11.36).

PART THREE

THE FELLOWSHIP AND PERSON OF THE SPIRIT

XI

The Fellowship of the Spirit

§1 EXPERIENCE OF THE SPIRIT – EXPERIENCE OF FELLOWSHIP

1. *The Trinitarian Concept of Fellowship*

'The fellowship of the Holy Spirit be with you all', runs an ancient Christian benedictory formulary (II Cor. 13.13). Why is the special gift of the Spirit seen to be its fellowship (*koinonia*), whereas grace is ascribed to Christ, and love to the Father? In his 'fellowship' the Spirit evidently gives himself. He himself enters into the fellowship with believers, and draws them into *his* fellowship. His inner being is evidently capable of fellowship – of community – of sociality. Does this mean that the Spirit draws human beings into the community he shares with the Father and the Son? Is he present *as* community, and is he experienced *in* the community of believers with one another? For an understanding of the Spirit himself, and also for the theological understanding of community or fellowship in general, it is of decisive importance whether we start from a trinitarian or from a unitarian concept of the fellowship of the Spirit.

If we look at the word fellowship itself, we can say that fellowship does not take by force and possess. It liberates, and draws others into the relationships that are essentially its own. Fellowship means opening ourselves for one another, giving one another a share in ourselves. It creates respect for one another. Fellowship lives in reciprocal participation and from mutual recognition. Fellowship comes into being when people who are different have something in common, and when what is in common is shared by different people. There are fellowships of shared objective concerns – interest groups,

working and study groups. There are fellowships of mutual relationship – fellowships constituted by a shared life. Of course this is merely
a theoretical, stylized distinction, like the distinction between a
society and a community.[1] In every true fellowship, objective and
personal relationships are linked. But the emphases can vary.

Fellowship or community can exist not merely between people
who are alike or similar, but also between those who are not alike
and are quite dissimilar. In the two cases the mutuality of the
relationships is not on the same level. The phrase about human
'fellowship with God' is the formula for a community of those who
are unlike and dissimilar. If it is true that 'like draws to like', as
Aristotle said, then human beings cannot have 'fellowship with God'
in the literal sense. So the New Testament phrase about 'the fellowship
of the Holy Spirit' is all the more astonishing. It means both the
fellowship with itself which the Holy Spirit throws open, and the
fellowship which human beings have with the Holy Spirit. The
subjective genitive – 'the Holy Spirit's fellowship' – will be the primal
meaning. The objective genitive – fellowship with the Spirit – will be
the secondary one. Fellowship is never merely unilaterally determined. It is always reciprocally defined too. The partners must have
something in common, and must be able to share mutually in each
other. Otherwise it is meaningless to talk about their 'fellowship'. In
'the fellowship of the Holy Spirit', God the Spirit evidently enters
into a relationship of reciprocity and mutuality with the people
concerned and – in line with this – allows these people to exert an
influence on him, just as he exerts an influence on them.

If it is characteristic of the divine Spirit not merely to communicate
this or that particular thing, but actually to enter into fellowship with
believing men and women – if indeed he himself becomes their
fellowship – then 'fellowship' cannot merely be a 'gift' of the Spirit.
It must be the eternal, essential nature of the Spirit himself. Whereas
Christ, the Son of God, is called the source of grace, and God the
Father is called the source of love, 'fellowship' is designated as the
nature of the Spirit himself. The Spirit does not merely bring about
fellowship with himself. He himself issues from his fellowship with
the Father and the Son, and the fellowship into which he enters with
believers corresponds to his fellowship with the Father and the Son,
and is therefore a *trinitarian fellowship*. In the unity of the Father,
the Son and the Holy Spirit, the triune God himself is an open,
inviting fellowship in which the whole creation finds room: 'That

they also may be *in us*', prays the Johannine Christ (John 17.21). The fellowship of the Holy Spirit 'with you all' (II Cor. 13.13) corresponds to his fellowship with the Father and the Son. It is not merely an external bond joining human nature with the divine essence. It issues from the essential inward community of the triune God, in all the richness of its relationships; and it throws this community open for human beings in such a way that it gathers into itself these men and women and all other created things, so that they find eternal life. It follows from this that 'the fellowship of the Holy Spirit' has to be understood in trinitarian terms as a *community of persons*, and not in a unitarian sense as a *community of essence*.

On the other hand, the link between the Holy Spirit and community brings the experience of the Spirit into the community experienced by human beings and God's other creatures. The experience of sociality is the experience of life, for all life consists in the reciprocal exchange of foodstuffs and energy, and in mutual participation. There is no life without its specific social relationships. Isolated life without relation – that is, life that is literally individual and indivisible – is a contradiction in itself. It is incapable of living, and dies. Total lack of relationship is total death. So 'the fellowship of the Holy Spirit' is simply another way of describing 'the life-giving Spirit'. In fellowship with himself and through his creative energies, God the Spirit creates the network of social relationships in which life comes into being, blossoms and becomes fruitful. In this sense 'the fellowship of the Holy Spirit' is the activity of the Spirit that confers fellowship or community. Life comes into being out of community, and wherever communities spring up which make life possible and further it, the divine Spirit is efficacious. Wherever community of life comes into being, there is also community with God's life-giving Spirit. *The creation of community* is evidently the goal of God's life-giving Spirit in the world of nature and human beings.[2] All created beings exist in other beings, not out of themselves, and they are therefore dependent on one another. They are there together, and are alive for one another, and exist in one another. *Bios* – life – is always symbiosis, and symbiosis – conviviality in the literal sense – is the clearly detectable goal whenever more complex, open systems are built up in the world of the living. The richer and more complex the communicative relationships between human beings and living things become, the more vitally and abundantly life unfolds.

The trinitarian concept of community envisages *diversity in unity* from the very outset. To create community does not merely mean uniting what is different. It differentiates the One as well. The unfolding differentiation of the potentialities given and opened up through a common reality in no way contradicts this movement towards community, for differentiation is one of the essential elements in community. It is only standardization which reduces community to the lowest common denominator. True community is different. It opens up individual potentialities in the greatest given diversity.

The fellowship of the Holy Spirit is experienced by those who know it as both *the love* that binds and *the freedom* which allows everything to arrive at itself, in its own unique nature. Love confers that which is held in common, freedom opens up the scope of what is individual and singular. Both aspects must be noted when we are talking about the fellowship of the life-giving Spirit. Without freedom, love crushes the diversity of what is individual; without love, freedom destroys what is shared and binds us together. Community which serves life can therefore only be understood as integrating, and as creating unity in diversity, while at the same time differentiating and making diversity in unity possible. The unity of this unity and this diversity is to be found in *the rhythm of the times* of life. We call this *the trinitarian fellowship* of the Spirit.

God is experienced not merely individually, in the encounter of the individual, solitary soul with itself. He is experienced socially too, in the encounter with others. According to what we have said, the experience of the self is not unimportant for the experience of God, but it does not have any special pre-eminence, compared with experience of our neighbour. Social experience stands in the same correlation to experience of God as experience of the self. It was one-sided and had fateful consequences when, from Augustine onwards, the West related the knowledge of God solely to knowledge of the self (as Protestant theology also continued to do).[3] The person who knows God, knows himself. The person who knows himself, knows God. This applies to one's neighbour equally: 'You shall love God and your neighbour as yourself.' In experiencing the affection of others we experience God. In being loved we sense the nearness of God, in hate we feel God's remoteness. In love we are seized by the creative energies of the divine Spirit, in hate we are consumed by the poisons of death. That is God the Spirit: Hölderlin's deity who is sociality (his *gemeinschaftliche Gottheit*), the one whom J. V. Taylor calls the Go-Between God, Feuerbach's 'divine unity of I and Thou'. For God created human beings: 'male and female he created them' (Gen. 1.27). From one another, with one another, and in one another human beings discover that mirror of the Godhead which is called *imago Dei*, and which is in actual truth *imago Trinitatis*.

Experience of God in the experience of sociality, and experience of God in the experience of the self must not be turned into opposites, as if they were alternatives. In fact they are two sides of the same experience of life, in which we experience others and ourselves. Anyone who makes a severance here, or assigns different values to the two aspects, is 'quenching' the life-giving Spirit and damaging the wealth of life which the Spirit confers.

Not least, through the fellowship of the Spirit, the experience of God will reach out beyond experience of the self and the experience of sociality, and become experience of nature too; for the Spirit is the Creator, and new Creator, of all things. That is why bodily experiences, sensuous experiences and experiences of our fellow creatures in nature enjoy the same rank in experience of God as experience of the self, or the social experience of love. These experiences of nature are inseparably bound up with experiences of the self and the experience of sociality, and are a constitutive element in these experiences. Anyone who disparages this community of creation compared with a community of soul is quenching God's creative Spirit and denying him the fellowship which he seeks with all created being, so as to redeem them. Anyone who disparages the 'it' in favour of the I-Thou relationship – and we find this in the early personalism of Martin Buber and Ferdinand Ebner – is overlooking the essentially material nature of the salvation that heals and saves. The trinitarian fellowship of the Holy Spirit is the full community of the Creator, Reconciler and Redeemer with all created being, in the network of all their relationships.

2. The Unitarian Concept of Fellowship

Entering into dialogue with theological tradition, let us look at the pneumatology we find in Friedrich Schleiermacher's book on *The Christian Faith*, because what he says about the Holy Spirit as 'the common Spirit' sounds so similar to the ideas about the fellowship of the Spirit developed here, and is yet so very different. It is the difference between a *trinitarian* and a *unitarian* way of grasping the Holy Spirit and the community between human beings.

Schleiermacher took over the expression 'common spirit' from Count Zinzendorf's Moravian Brethren, as well as from secular usage, and understood it to mean 'exactly what we mean in any earthly system of government, namely, the common bent found in all who constitute together a moral personality, to seek the advancement of this whole; and this is at the same time the characteristic love found in each for every other'.[4] In the church, the life lived with Christ and the indwelling of the Holy Spirit coincide, so that 'all living in the state of sanctification' are conscious of the Holy Spirit as 'the common Spirit of the new corporate life founded by Christ'.[5] The Spirit is the 'inward impulse' which leads the regenerate and those living in the state of sanctification 'to become more and more one in their common co-operative activity and reciprocal influence'.[6] The special 'common Spirit' of the Christian church and the general 'love of man' are the same Spirit, for this is on the one hand love for those who have already become citizens of the kingdom of God, and on the other love for those who have still to be incorporated in that kingdom.[7] As far as the divinity of the Holy Spirit is concerned, Schleiermacher proceeds from three doctrinal tenets:

1. 'The Holy Spirit is the union of the Divine Essence with human nature in the form of the common Spirit animating the life in common of believers' (§ 123).

He does not consider that the Holy Spirit is one Person in the divine essence, but thinks that the Spirit is only 'the union' of the divine essence with human nature. The form of this union between the divine and the human is the 'common Spirit animating the life in common of believers', a power or entity already given beforehand to the individual believer. The 'common Spirit' precedes the Spirit of the individual.

2. 'Every regenerate person partakes of the Holy Spirit, so that there is no living fellowship with Christ, without an indwelling of the Holy Spirit and *vice versa*' (§ 124).

With this tenet Schleiermacher identifies the Holy Spirit with 'the Spirit of Christ', and no longer distinguishes between the Spirit of the Son and the Spirit of the Father. What is under consideration is solely the 'living fellowship with Christ' the Redeemer, who perfects creation, not also the 'living fellowship' with creation and its Creator, and the integrity and redemption of non-human creation.

> 3. 'The Christian Church, animated by the Holy Spirit, is in its purity and integrity the perfect image of the Redeemer, and each regenerate individual is an indispensible constituent of this fellowship' (§ 125).

Here Schleiermacher once more takes up the content of his first proposition: The divine-human union in the church, which constitutes its fellowship, corresponds to the union of the divine essence with human nature in Christ, which constitutes his Person.[8] He calls this correspondence 'image', and presupposes that Christ is its archetype. But to say this is to be in danger of obscuring the difference between the *unio essentialis* and the *unio gratiosa* – that is, the incarnation of the Logos and the inhabitation of the Spirit – and of seeing Christ as merely the first example of Spirit-imbued Christianity. Schleiermacher then goes on to develop his curious *doctrine of the two natures of the Holy Spirit* in such a way that he sees the divine essence in the 'union' as that which is permanent, and the human nature of the 'union' as that which is mutable (§§ 126 and 127). Because he does not see the Holy Spirit in his trinitarian fellowship with the Father and the Son, he is compelled to start from the one, undifferentiated divine essence, and has to think of the 'union' as a *unio simplex*.

The inevitable result of this is a *unitarian concept of community*, which threatens to abolish the differences between the persons. Schleiermacher himself makes this clear in his analysis of Sabellius: 'That the Holy Spirit was efficacious only in believers was also admitted by the theologian's opponents; but Sabellius could not think of the Spirit in the individual as such. To do so would have meant that he had to think of the Spirit pluralistically, and since the Godhead was the same in all members of the Trinity, every individual would have been a Christ. So he could only think the Spirit in believers and the church as a whole, the One in the one.'[9] If the divine Spirit is not a Person, but merely the bond uniting divine and human nature, then the 'common Spirit' which takes its impress from this union can still be termed a 'moral person', but in this community the individuals are not given the impress of independent persons.

Are all the different believers merely 'modes of appearance' of the one common Spirit of the church? Does the Holy Spirit animate only the common life, but not the individual life of believers equally? Who then determines what has to count as the 'common Spirit' in the church? Does this not rob individual believers of their personhood and reduce them to mere 'constituents of the fellowship'? Why was Schleiermacher unable to think the fellowship of the Holy Spirit as a diversity? The unitarian concept of the Spirit leads to a unitarian concept of fellowship, and to a one-sided stress on the love that binds, over against the freedom that differentiates.

Joseph Ratzinger has developed the notion that in the church people surrender their old 'isolated ego subjectivity' and find themselves in a new, higher 'unity of determining subjects';[10] but this idea too stresses only the union of divided humanity 'in Christ', not the diversity of the different charismata 'in the Holy Spirit'. The over-extension of the head-body image for the church leads to a graduated hierarchy: God – Christ – the body of Christ. It is self-evident that this is a way of legitimating the hierarchical constitution of the church. In as much as Christ is considered to be a 'determining subject', the community of Christ can be christologically called a 'unity of determining subjects'. But in the abundance of the Spirit and its many gifts, it is a community in which everyone contributes what is his or hers: it is a non-hierarchical fellowship of equals in the Holy Spirit. To call it 'a unity of determining subjects' is too weak a definition of this fellowship in the Spirit, and the inadequate definition hinders the development of the fellowship's charismatic wealth. The true unity of the church is an image of the perichoretic unity of the Trinity, so it can neither be a collective consciousness which represses the individuality of the persons, nor an individual consciousness which neglects what is in common. In the church's true unity, the persons express the community by expressing themselves, and – conversely – the community gives expression to the persons by giving expression to itself. In this complementarity there is no priority.

The modalistic trend in Schleiermacher's doctrine of fellowship and the Spirit can be explained historically in the light of his criticism of the bourgeois industrial society which was then springing up; for this society dissipates the 'natural' community of men and women and individualizes them, so that they may always be available and disposable, as workers and consumers without any ties.[11] Over against this Schleiermacher saw 'the common Spirit' of the Christian congregation as a healing counter-image: sociable grace in an unsociable world. By giving the 'common Spirit' priority over the individual Spirit, and by putting the church before believers, Schleiermacher abolished the genetic simultaneity of socialization and personalization. But the experience of sociality and the experience of the self are merely two sides of one and the same experience of life, and they come into being together and simultaneously. It is impossible to talk about priority here. The unitarian concept of community is not a panacea for the individualism of the modern world. It is merely its opposite. It is only the trinitarian concept of community which leads to a balanced and harmonious relationship between person and community.

Finally, Schleiermacher lacks access to the world of nature and to the bodily character of experiences of the self, sociality and God. The romantic reverence for the cosmos which we find in his early *Addresses on Religion to its Cultured Despisers* (1799) was replaced by the anthropocentricism of his *Christian Faith*, where he writes: 'It is clear that in a system of doctrine the world cannot come under discussion at all except as it is related to man' (§ 71, 1).

3. Fellowship as Process

But in considering the fellowship of the Holy Spirit we must not confine our attention to human persons and communities. We must also keep in mind the communities found in nature. This is not the least important element in a full understanding of the fellowship of the Spirit, for all human communities are embedded in the ecosystems of the natural communities, and live from the exchange of energy with them. 'Community' is not merely the particular character of the redeeming Spirit of Christ, as Schleiermacher thought. It is already the essential nature of the creative Spirit of God the Father too. All creatures are aligned towards community and are created in the form of communities. To form community is the life principle of created beings. Creation is not made up of individual elementary particles. These are merely the end-product of the divisions which human beings introduce into nature. Creation itself lives in the complexity of ever-richer communal relationships. That is why it is appropriate to talk about *the community of creation*, and to recognize the operation of the life-giving Spirit of God in the trend to relationship in created things.[12] Even what mechanistic theory describes as the

'gradational build-up' of matter and life shows that the goal of evolution is 'community':
- elementary particle
- atom
- molecule
- macro-molecular cell
- multi-cellular organism
- living organism
- organism populations
- living thing
- animal
- transitional field from animal to human being
- human beings
- human populations
- community of humanity
- . . .

Parts come together to produce new communities – that is, new complex unities with new communication structures and their own organizational principles.[13] The whole is always more than the sum of the parts that have come together to form it. As the unities become more complex, the capacity for communication grows, and with the capacity for communication, the capacity for transformation increases too. The range of anticipation widens and fans out. The process brings with it an ever-greater wealth in the forms of individuality that are minted. Ever richer forms of social relationship develop, and a continual expansion of the scope for free behaviour. 'No two eggs are alike.'

Uniformity and the surrender of individuality in favour of an overriding unity are not the goal of life. They are the beginning of petrification and death. It is an impoverishment if the person is dissolved in an oceanic, cosmic feeling of symbiosis. It is not an enrichment of life. We can think of the development of community in life as an evolutionary principle in the sense that systems of life develop which are ever richer in relationship, ever more capable of communication, ever more open for their possibilities – that is to say, freer. To create community does not mean establishing uniformity. It means a richer variety of examples and species, for with every new reality the scope of what is possible increases. Another reason why to create community does not mean uniformity is that, as ever more complex life systems develop and fan out, the communicative relationships grow, and the warp and weft of the diverse life systems densifies into whole new organisms. The more the organization of information and the exchange of energy becomes possible, the richer life will become in the diversity of living beings and their relationships. In this process – the process in which life in community evolves – the living things that die are only those which cut themselves off, isolate themselves and are then no longer capable of any transformation and adaptation to changed environmental conditions. Living things that isolate themselves lose their flexibility and become calcified – that is, they die.

The dynamic of the life process is always greater than the diversity of the forms of life and the living relationships which the process creates. Life is fathomless, and is more than any individual expression of life. It is these creative living energies which we call *the divine Spirit*, because it transcends all the beings it creates, and even its own created energies. We call it *the cosmic Spirit*, because it is the life in everything that lives. Chinese calls it *chi*, Greek *eros*, Hebrew *ruach*. But for all that, we must not say that 'though God is not the Creator, he is no doubt the Spirit of the universe'.[14] It would rather be true to say that *because* God is the Creator, his creative Spirit is the dynamic of the universe and the power that creates community in the widening, differentiating network of the living.

The transcendence and immanence of the divine Spirit are not mutually contradictory. They are two complementary aspects of its dynamic. The pantheistic interpretation is just as one-sided as the transcendentalist one. Nor does process philosophy's bi-polar interpretation of the life process comprehend the dynamic moment lying between the divine Spirit's transcendence and its immanence. The orthodox theological distinction between the Spirit's 'uncreated' and 'created' energies does not take account of its *creative* energies. We understand the dynamic better when we begin to think triadically, so as to mediate between the world beyond and this world by way of *the forward movement* of process. Because the forward direction allows us to perceive the *time* element – the irretrievability of every event, the irreversibility of future and past, and the partial indeterminancy of that sphere of possibility which we call future[15] – we can then grasp the temporal rhythms of life, which vibrate between transcendence and immanence, and fan out the network of life's relationships into the spheres of the possible. Just as *symmetry* is the matrix of systems of matter,[16] so *rhythm* is the pulse of the living thing. This is true not only of individuals. It applies also to the ecosystems in and with which individuals live. The rhythm creates those accords and harmonies between the living things and their worlds which are necessary if they are to live.

Rhythm is dynamic that has been given form. To talk about an unformed *élan vital*, as Bergson does, or about a dumb 'life drive', means that one has not yet fully comprehended the livingness of life. In the rhythmic harmony between the living thing with its worlds, the continua of space and time are interlaced in such a way that we can talk about spaces of time and vibrating times of space. In the rhythmic interplay of communications, continually richer communities of life come into being. The diverse develops out of what is single, and these diversities enter into new community with one another.

The evolution process is not a linear progression. It would be better to compare it with a tree, whose branches fan out in the air in which it lives, or a forest which spreads out into its environment. The goal is neither unity nor difference, but the differentiated community which liberates the individual members belonging to it.

4. The Spirit of Life and the Consciousness

There is an old saying the origins of which are lost in obscurity:

> God sleeps in the stone,
> He dreams in the flower,
> He awakes in the beast,
> In human beings
> He arrives at consciousness.

And this is also the way Max Scheler described 'the position of the human being in the cosmos': 'Is it not as if there were a ladder on which some primordial being, in building the world, continually turns back on himself, so that on ever higher steps and in ever higher dimensions, he pauses and reflects, in order finally in the human being to possess and understand himself fully?'[17]

Both these reflections distinguish between the Spirit of life and the consciousness. Whereas the creative and life-giving Spirit moulds all material structures and all systems of life, the human consciousness is the Spirit that reflects and is reflected. The creative and life-giving Spirit therefore arrives at consciousness of itself in the human consciousness. If consciousness is reflected Spirit, then wide realms of the Spirit are already given beforehand to this reflection, and remain unconscious. But through reflection, the human consciousness can expand into these sectors and comprehend them.

Consciousness of the Spirit in the human being should not be understood as an act of human domination over life. It should rather be seen as the beginning of a new organization of the Spirit of life. It is true that consciousness distinguishes human beings from other life, but at the same time it links them with these other living things which they consciously experience. If the life-creating Spirit arrives at consciousness of itself in the human consciousness, then consciousness does not isolate human beings from the world in which they live. It leads that world into new forms of community.[18]

We have said that the life-creating Spirit is the Spirit of community. Through this Spirit, the consciousness and the body are linked together in the human configuration or Gestalt. Through this Spirit, human cultural systems are linked with the natural ecosystems of the earth. In its consciousness, these diverse forms of living in community, with all their many strata, can be related to one another. The important thing is only to re-shape the self-isolating consciousness which rules over itself and nature, into consciousness of the Spirit which creates life and community. It is then possible to expand the individual consciousness into social consciousness, human consciousness into ecological consciousness, and earthly consciousness into cosmic consciousness. The human consciousness will then itself become a new, relatively holistic organizational form of life. It then ministers to life, and intensifies it, and is not 'the adversary' of vitality, as Nietzsche and Ludwig Klages believed.

§2 CHRISTIANITY IN THE FELLOWSHIP OF THE SPIRIT

In this section we shall be asking about the fellowship experienced by Christians in the church and the world.[19] Here we are not merely concerned with the church, which in community with Christ becomes the place of the coming of the Holy Spirit. We have also to ask about Christian experiences of the natural communities in home and family, work and civic life. We have to consider Christian experiences of community in the voluntary groups of concerned people who are brought together by world problems and developments – peace, environmental and third-world groups, and other initiatives. And we need to think about the Christian experience of community in the self-help groups which are born out of some common difficulty or extremity. In addition we shall ask about the community shared by the church with the society in which it lives, on the various social levels on which it is present. Where does the congregation stand in its village or district, the regional church in its region, the national church in the nation? What do ecumenical conferences and assemblies have to do with the parts of the world in which they meet, with this one but divided world, and with the earth which we share but have destroyed?

1. Spirit and Word

We talk about the church *in* the fellowship of God's Spirit, and by doing so we are presupposing that this fellowship between people which is the work of the Spirit reaches beyond the church; it fills the church, but takes us beyond its frontiers. According to the messianic hopes of the Bible, the Holy Spirit is to be 'poured out upon all flesh'. When Christ's church invokes the Holy Spirit and pleads the presence of the Spirit, it is seeing itself as the beginning in history of this eschatological event, and it is placing itself in the cosmic context of this restoration of all things. Earlier, we stressed the church's relation to Christ. Now we are emphasizing its relation to the Spirit. The two relationships are complementary and mutually intensifying. Irenaeus was right when he expanded an ancient formula dialectically: 'Ubi Ecclesia, ibi et Spiritus Sanctus, et ubi Spiritus Dei, illic Ecclesia et omnis gratia: Spiritus autem Veritas' ['Where the church is, there is the Holy Spirit too, and where God's Spirit is, there is the church and all grace; for the Spirit is truth'].[20] At the very point when the church appeals exclusively to Christ, it experiences itself in the wider eschatological and cosmic dimensions of the coming of the Holy Spirit. It has no monopoly in the operation of the Holy Spirit. The Holy Spirit is not tied to the church. The Spirit is not concerned about the church as such. He is concerned with the church, as he is with Israel, for the sake of the kingdom of God, the rebirth of life and the new creation of all things.

The relation of the church to the Holy Spirit is the relation of *epiklesis*, continual invocation of the Spirit, and unconditional opening for the experiences of the Spirit who confers fellowship and makes life truly living. The church above all, which listens to the word of Christ and confesses Christ, exists wholly in its receptivity for the Spirit's coming, for the influence of its energies and the radiance of its light. That makes Christianity alive to the operation of the Holy Spirit *extra muros ecclesiae* – outside the church as well – and prepared to accept the life-furthering communities which people outside the church expect and experience. This does not mean that the church is giving itself up. It is simply opening itself for the wider operation of the Spirit in the world.

We experience the relationship between the Christian church and the natural and voluntary communities by way of a whole number of mutual influences: the church gets new ideas from outside, people outside derive impulses from the church. To describe the relationship in a one-sided way as 'prototype and example'[21] or 'model',[22] puts an undue strain on the Christian church, makes it incapable of learning, and sets up clerical claims to domination in society. It is not the person who points to himself who is the example; it is the person whom God makes an example, whether he or she knows it or not. There is certainly a line drawn between Christians and non-Christians through baptism and membership of the church, but as far as the natural and voluntary communities are concerned, there is in fact no inside and outside. There is only the complex web of life's relationships.

The special thing about the community of Christians is not so much its character as a social model (*exemplum*) as the redeeming experiences of the fellowship of Christ found there, and the liberating experiences of the Holy Spirit – in short, the assurance of the fellowship of God (*sacramentum*). These impulses have their effect on the natural and voluntary communities in which Christians live. Congregational and church structures – at least in the older Christian countries – seldom belong here.

As far as experience of the Spirit is concerned, we have to overcome the one-sided emphases which have been introduced into Christianity through the denominational divisions of the churches. We mean here the difference between the Protestant definition of the church of Christ as *creatura verba* and the Orthodox idea of the church as *invocation and coming of the Holy Spirit*.[23] These two perspectives must complement one another, for where the Word is, there the Spirit is too – otherwise the Word is not the Word of God; and where the Spirit is, the Spirit shines from the Word and illumines the understanding of faith – otherwise it is not God's Spirit.

The Word of the gospel makes Christ present: 'He who hears you, hears me.' It thrusts through the times of history and makes its way to us because it carries with it the promise of his presence. The Word remains with us from one generation to another, because it heralds and anticipates the future of Christ in the universal light of the new creation. The gospel is remembered promise. Through faith it creates a community of trust, a community between people who are equal and free, and who wait in the presence of the crucified Christ for his redeeming future. In this respect the church is called to life through the Word of the gospel, and its heart beats wherever Christ is given an utterance.

The Spirit which fills the church is 'the Spirit of Christ'. But why did Christ come, and why did he die? The purpose of his coming and the fruit of his death is nothing other than 'the outpouring of the Holy Spirit' – which means its outpouring *on all flesh*'. 'The Word took bodily form so that we might receive the Holy Spirit', said Athanasius: 'God became the bearer of a body so that human beings might be bearers of the Spirit.'[24] According to the promises of the Paraclete in the Gospel of John, the goal of Christ's work was always seen to be the coming of the Holy Spirit. In some pentecostal movements – for example in Montanus and Phrygian prophecy, and in Joachim of Fiore and the Joachimite movements – the work of Christ and the coming of the Spirit were viewed as a temporal sequence in salvation history, so that the 'era of the Spirit' followed and superseded the 'era of Christ'. But that is a misunderstanding of the eternal and the temporal inter-relationships of Word and Spirit.[25] The Logos is brought forth by the Father in the breath of his Spirit. Christ comes from the Father through the Spirit, as the synoptic gospels say. The Spirit is brought forth in eternity by the Father of the Son, and rests on the Son, out of whom he shines. That is why it is the Father and the Son who send the Holy Spirit,[26] and why it is from the Son and the Father that the Spirit comes upon all flesh. The church proceeds from this interaction between the Son and the Spirit, the Spirit and the Word. Once we perceive this reciprocity in their relationships and their operation, the verbalism of Protestant fundamentalism, with its forgetfulness of the Spirit, becomes just as inadmissible as the spiritualism of the Pentecostalist movements we have mentioned, with its forgetfulness of the Word.

In the interaction between Spirit and Word, two things should be noted especially:

1. The Spirit of Christ radiates from the Word of God that *has become flesh*: 'The Word became flesh and dwelt among us, and we beheld his glory . . .' (John 1.14). It is the earthly life, the bodily death, and the 'glorified bodiliness' of the raised Christ (Phil. 3.21) from which the Spirit shines, transfiguring the earthly world and 'all flesh' through his radiance. The verbal presence of Christ in the proclaimed Word is important, because it names the Name, but the figure or Gestalt of Christ and his taking this form upon himself among men and women goes beyond that. To understand the Word of the gospel is no more than the beginning. The transfiguration of bodiliness is the goal. Faith as understanding is the beginning; the lived Gestalt of faith is the purposed end. In the resurrection of Christ we understand the goal for which the world was created,[27] and in the experience of the bodiliness and sociality created by God we come to see why Christ has risen.

2. In the inter-relation between Christ and the Spirit there are emphases and movements. One movement is that from the One to the many – from the 'first-born' to the many sisters and brothers who experience the Spirit of adoption because they are made like in form to Christ (Rom. 8.29); and from the 'first-born of creation' to all creatures in heaven and on earth who experience in him their reconciliation and restoration (Col. 1.15ff.). The unity in this diversity is to be found in the common origin (I Cor. 12.4–6) and in the community which these many, in all their diversity, together constitute. The unity comes from the one Christ and moves towards the fellowship of the Spirit. It is therefore a creative unity, in which every created being is intended to arrive at itself and to develop its own unique character, being through that very fact related to other created beings. The creative Spirit loves originals, not imitations. Unfree uniformity is as inadmissible in the church as pluralism without relation.

The interactions between Christ and the Spirit must be understood as forces of historical movement and should be seen in the light of their goal. Irenaeus calls Word and Spirit 'the two hands of the Father' through which the world's salvation is created. 'The splendour of the Trinity shines forth progressively.'[28] There is an objective for these interactions, and so there are also rhythms in the movement, rhythms which call forth Word and Spirit. The objective of *Christ's* history is in this respect the coming and 'outpouring of the Spirit upon all flesh', that is to say the quickening of all mortal beings through their fellowship with God's eternal life, their transfiguration in God's eternal light, and their interpenetration with God's all-embracing love. The goal of this history of *the Spirit* is the eschatological restoration of all things and their new creation for eternal glory. The triune God creates and evolves a community of all his creatures with himself and with one another, a community which corresponds to him. The community which is his eternal nature is therefore both the origin of creation and its goal.

For the people who experience themselves in the presence of the Spirit, two movements follow which are rhythmically related to one another: 1. The *gathering* of Christians in the church. 2. The mission or *sending out* of the church to Christians in the world. Here we understand by the church the 'gathered congregation'[29] who come together for the sake of Word and sacrament; and by 'Christians in the world' we mean the church as it is dispersed in families, vocations, work and friendships.[30] The meaning and scope of the church is not exhausted when people become 'churchgoers'. Nor does it exist merely in worship on Sunday mornings. It is present among Christians in their worldly contexts – in families, socially and politically. It is present, not as the church but as 'Christians' – not through the clergy but through the Christians who are wrongly termed 'laity'. The men and women priests and pastors who have been authorized and commissioned are responsible for the worshipping and congregational assemblies; but in questions which have to do with Christianity in the world, 'the laity', are the responsible ones, and they are the experts who are authorized and commissioned. The mediaeval distinction between clergy and laity, which is still found in the Catholic church, has deprived the laity of their responsibility, and robbed them of their own charisma. The clericalization of Christianity has led to the emigration from the church of 'Christians in the world'. Modern attempts at being a 'church for others' and a 'church for the world' proceed from a churchified Christianity, and are attempts to breach the gulf which it itself has created between church and world.

Instead of the hierarchical division into clergy and laity, and in place of the separatist confinement of Christianity to the church, as a kind of ghetto, we shall talk about the two movements in the life of Christianity: its gathering in the congregation, and its mission or sending by way of its vocations in society. Gathering and sending are related to one another like breathing in and breathing out. The important thing is therefore to view life in the everyday world as just as important as the gathering of the congregation in the feast of worship. The life-giving presence of the Holy Spirit is experienced just as intensively in the homes to which people return when they leave church as it is in the church, if in these homes the Spirit is invoked and expected. People would be forgetting their individual and special callings and endowments if they were to identify their Christian existence with their membership of the church. The gathering of Christians for worship and congregational meetings ministers to Christian existence in all the different relations of life. The gathering serves the sending, and the sending leads into the full life and the living fellowship of the Spirit. The sending acquires its concrete form from the needs and distress of the world, which is threatened by injustice, violence, nuclear and ecological annihilation. It acquires its hope from the horizon of the future, the horizon of the kingdom of God.

Luther's transference of the religious concept of vocation (*vocatio*) to earthly and worldy work had a truly reformative importance.[31] It brings the call to faith and the charismatic endowment of life into this world, so that the world is pervaded by the energies of the divine Spirit and the powers of the new world, and so that the germs of life may be planted in the places where death threatens. At this point Luther wanted to avoid talking about the church, and chose instead the phrase 'gemein Christenheit' – ordinary Christians. He saw Christians working, suffering and experiencing the full life of the Spirit in their worldly vocations, not merely in the churches.

If Christianity in the world is to be aware of what it is, we must give up the pastoral church for taking care of people and call to life a Christian '*community church*'. Non-voluntary membership of the church is going to recede, because the factors that kept it going have already ceased to be effective in the older Christian countries, and no longer cut any ice. Personal and voluntary commitment is going to come to the fore. This means that natural communities and personal relationships will become more important too. The community of the church will be related to these other communities. More and more Christians are going to think it important to take over their own lives, act on their own responsibility, and shape life themselves in God's Spirit. Christianity in the world is not just there to say Amen to church meetings and events; it is there for something more and something different.[32]

With this development into the freely chosen *participatory congregation* and a life of one's own lived in God's Spirit, the over-taxed clergy, whose function has been distorted, will also be relieved of some of their load. Clergy too, men and women both, are first of all Christians like other people and, like the rest, have a right to their own life-style and their own personal conviction, before they take on the charges and services which are connected with their ministry. They are members of the congregation first of all, and must be accepted as such by the congregation, so that they can carry out the tasks assigned to them in the Spirit of Christ. The church of Christ is a community of free and equal men and women who exist with one another and for one another in the charismatic diversity of their gifts and life-styles. Both privileges and the withholding of responsibility are sicknesses in the body of Christ.

2. *The Community of the Generations*

Modern ecclesiologies often assume that the church consists of a collection of single, believing individuals. But that is not the case. It is an assembly of parents and children, sisters and brothers, that is to say, people with their families and social ties. The church is made up out of bodily people, and life's natural relationships are part of bodily life. But what is the relationship between the experience of sociality in the congregation and the natural social relationships from which, and in which, men and women live?

In pre-industrial village society, the Christian congregation was made up of families and households, not single individuals. The houses in which the different generations lived together were literally 'house churches'. Here grandparents and parents had their special gifts and duties in passing on faith to the coming generations and to other people living in the same house. Christian homes were the base communities of which the Christian congregation in village or town districts consisted. Luther's Small Catechism was written for Christian parents and their 'house churches'. Even the more exacting Heidelberg Catechism counted in Reformed congregations as the basis for the dialogue of faith between the generations in private homes.

It was only modern industrial society which dissolved these natural communities and turned people into isolated individuals. It made them free, mobile and flexible, at the cost of loosening the family ties binding the different generations. It strengthened the free, horizontal social ties between friends, comrades and colleagues. It made freedom of movement for individuals possible, in brotherliness and sisterliness. But at the same time it divided the generations so widely from one another that the 'generation contract', which is important for the survival of humanity, is threatening to break down.

The Christian church has also set aside the rights of children and parents through the community of 'brothers' and 'sisters'.[33] But many personal and marital problems go back to generation conflicts which have been suppressed – father-son complexes, for example, and unresolved mother-fixations. In the Christian congregations too, the accepted life-style is often given its impress by an older generation, which does not give the new experiences of younger generations a chance. So it is all the more important for the experience of Christian sociality in the congregation to be related to the experiences of sociality in families or – to put it more broadly – between the generations. Wherever different generations live together, they can only build a community which furthers life by going hand in hand with one another.[34] This presupposes that one is conscious of one's own age, and sees the limitations of the forms of faith and living that correspond to it. It requires one generation to withdraw, in order to give scope to the coming generations, in which they can live their own life.

In the relations between the generations, the task of the Christian congregations is to build up mutual trust. This is only possible if the different age-groups see their community together as *a community in time*, a community extending over the different periods of life, so that they can come to understand from the others who they themselves were, and who they are going to be, and so that they can see the possibilities they lived with, and the possibilities that are going to offer themselves in the future, It is certainly valuable for youth groups, young adults' groups, women's and men's groups to meet together, but when 'like draws to like' this is not yet the Christian community. That begins only with the recognition of people who are different, and with participation in other life. In the large families of earlier times, when four generations lived together under one roof, people were bound to come to terms with this conflict. In the small two-generation families of today, one must deliberately seek it. When modern society is threatened by the barbarism of 'disinterest', this destroys the community between the generations in families first of all.

The Christian community has its genesis in the community God shares with human beings, and grows out of the community which human beings have with one another in this community with God. It springs from the inexhaustible *trust* which God confers, and which makes people continually trust*worthy* – a divine trust which, because it is inexhaustible, can continually be experienced afresh.[35] God's Word is the word of promise, and awakens the faith in which we trust ourselves to him. In bread and wine, he gives himself into our hands, and trust himself to us. The eucharistic communion at the Lord's Table, with the forgiveness of guilt and the giving to one another of bread and cup, is the source of different kinds of trust: trust in God and ourselves, trust in our neighbour and the future, and trust in creation. The people who participate in this communion become for one another capable of community and prepared for trust.

> As antitype or antithesis we need only think of the catastrophe of Chernobyl. Quite apart from the appalling extent of the damage, this resulted in a shattering loss of trust in the state, in technology, and not least in contaminated nature. Where life is so disappointed, trust disappears, and when trust disappears one can no longer live.

People's relationship to God depends on their trust in him, and Christian fellowship is a matter of trust too. That makes it vulnerable. The community of mutual trust must not be blind. It comes into being with its eyes open, and knowingly. Christian faith in God is not blind and blissful confidence. It has gone through a perception of the way life can be destroyed. And similarly, the sustaining trust in our neighbours is only born when we know and accept ourselves and them with our own, and their own, weaknesses and burdens.

Whenever people live together there are conflicts. A community of trust cannot aim to be a community free of conflict. It would then merely become a community afraid of conflict. A conflict suffered and endured 'prevents stagnation, rouses interest, awakens curiosity'.[36] It strengthens the personality, even if it is painful. Suppressed conflicts spread mistrust, conflicts that are endured and suffered through to the end make us mutually trustworthy and capable of mutual trust.

Trust is the art of living not only in what we have in common, but in our differences as well – not merely with people like ourselves but with others too. If in the Christian community common trust springs from the love of Christ, and if it is the fellowship of the Spirit which brings together people who are different, that fellowship will become the source which strengthens our capacity for community in the natural relationships of life. Of course there are limits. Not every community is good, and not every separation is bad: if community stifles people, then separation is better, for without the free development of the people concerned, there is no true community. Not every trust is good, not every mistrust is bad: if trust is misused, caution is better, because trust between people can only be lasting if it is mutual; so trust is aligned towards response.

3. Community between Women and Men

Human beings have been created to be the image of God *as man and woman*. The community of the sexes corresponds to the community of generations. This too was already given to the Christian church beforehand by way of creation and history – and given, moreover, in its always specific psycho-social form. What fellowship do women and men arrive at in fellowship with Christ and in their experience of the Spirit who desires to give life to all flesh? How do women and men experience one another in the community of Christ's people, and in the fellowship of the life-engendering Mother Spirit? This is not merely a matter of church politics, and it is not solely an ethical question either. It is a question of faith, which means that it is a challenging question about the experience of the Spirit in the community of Christ. According to the promise in Joel 2.28–30 'It shall come to pass in the last days, says the Lord, that I will pour out my spirit on all flesh; and your sons and your daughters shall prophesy . . .' (cf. Acts 2.17ff.). The eschatological hope for experience of the Spirit is shared by women and men equally. Men and women will 'prophesy' and proclaim the gospel. According to the prophecy in Joel 2, through the shared experience of the Spirit the privileges of men compared with women, of the old compared with the young, and of masters compared with 'men-servants and maidservants' will be abolished. In the kingdom of the Spirit, everyone will experience his and her own endowment and all will experience the new fellowship together.

The 'new community of women and men' which is being sought in many churches today is a question of experience of the Spirit. This is disregarded by theologians who transfer the conditions of a hierarchically organized church to marriage in particular, and to the position of women in relation to men in general. Their monotheism knows only monarchy: one God – one Christ – one pope – one bishop – one church; and the man is accordingly the monarch in marriage (*pater familias*), with a God-given leadership role, and the woman is destined to serve, in subordination to him. This is to think in Roman terms, not Christian ones. It has meant that ever since Constantine, women have been excluded from the priestly ministry, although baptism has made them just as much bearers of the Spirit as baptized men.

Protestant theologians who proceed from a Christocentric concept of the church arrive at the same judgment: just as God is 'the head' of Christ, so Christ is 'the head' of the church, and the man has accordingly to be the 'head' of the woman (I Cor. 11). They transfer the relationship between Christ and the church to the relationship between men and women, as if the man represented Christ and the woman the church. This Christocentric interpretation also leads logically to the exclusion of women from the ministry or 'spiritual office', although through baptism women have received the Spirit just as much as men, and are destined to 'prophesy', and are therefore in faith already 'spiritual'.

Neither the hierarchical nor the Christocentric ecclesiologies cherish any further expectation of an experienceable outpouring of the Spirit, and they repress the early Christian experience of Pentecost. Both the hierarchical and the Christocentric notions of the church are clerical, because they transfer conditions in the church to family and social relationships between men and women in secular society, and are ready to make the 'anti-Christian spirit of the age' responsible for the protests which consequently arise.

If, on the other hand, we start from the early Christian experience of Pentecost, we have to develop a pneumatological concept of the church: there is one Spirit and many gifts. Everyone concerned, whether man or woman, is endowed and committed through his or her calling, wherever he or she is, and whatever he or she is. To be a woman is a charisma, to be a man is a charisma, and the different charismata operate together for the rebirth of life. Because the Spirit is poured out 'on *all* flesh', merely ecclesiastical flesh cannot be meant. Cultural experiences and movements too are shot through by the Spirit. Whatever accords with the fulfilment of the Joel promise in church and culture is the operation of the Spirit. Whatever contradicts it is spiritless and deadly. When, in the nineteenth- and twentieth-century, feminist movement women have risen up against the patriarchy and have broken the silence forced on them and 'prophesied', this is spirit from God's Spirit, which 'comes upon all flesh' so that it may live.

The pneumatological concept of the church discerns that church and culture are interwoven in the interplay of the 'spiritual' – which means life-giving – impulses conferred on 'all flesh'. In this case the eschatological experience of the Spirit takes in both Christianity and the feminist movement, and brings them into a mutually fruitful relationship. Feminist theology mediates between the two in as much as a powerful trend in it uncovers the often suppressed traditions in Christian history which have to do with the liberation of women, and works for the psycho-social liberation of women in church and society. Christianity learns from the feminist movement that the patriarchal disparagement and suppression of women's charismata are sins against the Spirit. The feminist movement can learn from Christianity, and from other movements, that it is not merely a question of the human rights of women; it is a matter of the rebirth of *all* the living. And through both Christianity and the feminist movement, men will be liberated from the dominating role which isolates them from life and alienates them from themselves, freed for their true humanity, their own charismata, and for a community with women on all levels in society and the church, a community which will further life.

4. Action Groups

Voluntary groups can have a difficult time in finding a place in some of the churches. We shall look here at the groups which are socially involved and politically active: peace groups, environmental groups, third-world groups.[37] Many of them have grown up in the last ten years in the wake of the 'conciliar process' for 'justice, peace and the integrity of creation'. Others come from the political peace movement, and from 'green' initiatives – Greenpeace and others.

These groups are seldom identical with traditional circles in the Christian congregations. They are born out of the pressure of the external needs they recognize, because the people concerned feel they have to do something, even if the prospects of success are slight.

Many of these groups include both Christians and non-Christians. They are bound together by their common awareness of the problem which concerns them, and through common action. They are often groups of like-minded people, which require total commitment, as sit-ins, and conscientious objection, non-violent resistance and the acceptance of prison sentences show. What brings them together with the Christian congregations is something which many of them clearly recognize: the closeness between consistent Christian faith and political good sense, between the Sermon on the Mount and peace politics, between reverence for life and the integrity of nature, between justice and policies affecting the third world. But underlying the practical commitment is also longing for a meaningful life. And what meaning is there if humanity dies in a nuclear war, if the earth becomes a desert in an ecological catastrophe, if people in the third world founder and perish, and we do nothing about it?

These groups expect the Christian church to interpret the Christian faith in its motivating and orientating relevance for the present situation in the world. They do not expect to be brought into the Christian faith itself, apart from these concerns. This often leads to tensions with the traditional congregations, which are afraid that their faith is being 'politicized' and who can discover little that is Christian in the political 'prayers for peace'. This difference in likeness is quite natural, for the congregation that gathers round Word and sacrament is not a group of like-minded people, and it is not an action group either. But conversely, the committed groups do not have to prove their identity with the church if they want to use the free spaces which the church provides.

The community that links the two sides is to be found in experience of the life-creating Spirit which descends 'on all flesh' and brings all those who love life into conflict with the destructive forces of death. Here the groups make the churches sensitive to the perils of the present, and make many Christians feel uneasy, so that they cease to accept poverty and misery as a matter of course. And the churches for their part can give these groups protection, and make their concerns more general, so that the groups do not turn into sects.

There are apparently two ways of access to the community of Christ. On the one hand through faith in Christ, mediated through Word, sacrament and fellowship; on the other hand through shared work for the kingdom of God, for the sake of which the church of

Christ is there – work in groups for political action and social self-help, and in diaconal, or charitable, concerns.

The horizon spanning everything is therefore *the kingdom of God*. The church sees itself as the people who gather together in the approach of the coming kingdom. What the groups who work for justice, peace and the integrity of creation are doing is 'Kingdom of God work'. That at least was the name given in nineteenth-century Germany to the social and charitable works of the day which were sustained by voluntary groups and associations. Christian congregations which are led beyond their own frontiers through the experience of the Spirit, will recognize and respect the groups in the light of this wider horizon.

5. Self-Help Groups

The self-help groups are close to the Christian congregation and remote from it in much the same way: these may be groups for the handicapped, for the HIV infected, or for cancer sufferers; they may be Alcohol Anonymous groups; but they may also be groups for the bereaved, the divorced, single parents, and so forth.[38] What brings people together here, in their search for counsel and solidarity, is not jointly recognized dangers for the world. It is some personally suffered distress. Common to many of them is the fact that they have dropped out of the accepted social norm, and the security of the social structure, and have lost their previous social status; and that the special distress in which they find themselves is intensified by social prejudice – and Christian prejudice too. These people feel that in their plight they have come down in the world and are vilified as social lepers. Other people encounter them with uncertainty and anxiety, if they do not avoid them altogether. This is true not only for individuals but usually for the whole group. In the case of Aids, homosexuality, drug addiction and alcoholism, fear of infection or temptation also produces the leper syndrome. In the case of bereavement, divorce and loneliness, it is the loss of status with which the society of the competent, the successful and the self-complacent react to these troubles. In its blind 'pursuit of happiness', society is quite prepared for a mass of 'failures' who 'haven't made it' and have to drop out of the race. They are pushed aside or kicked to the bottom of the ladder.

The churches' counselling centres and the special Christian self-help groups which brought these people together, quickly realized that these were not welfare cases. These are social conflicts in which both sides require 'counselling' – the people with disabilities and the people without, the infected and the people who out of fear of infection drive the infected into 'social death', the homosexuals and the people who want to ostracize them, the bereaved and the people who because they are afraid of death want to have nothing to do with them, the divorced and the people who break off relations with them. It also quickly became clear that the pitying, solicitous tone of pastoral letters and church newspapers and magazines actually promotes the isolation and disparagement which they were supposed to overcome. The counselling centres have therefore first of all to appeal for confidence, and have to break down existing prejudices in church and society before they can do anything; for mistrust is a part of the distress which afflicts people in these situations.

The path from counselling to the self-help group is certainly the first step. It is only the self-help group that can give what Luther in the Smalcald Articles described as real pastoral care: the mutual consolation of the brethren (*mutua consolatio fratrum*). The advice of people who are not affected remains secondary. In conversation with others who are similarly placed, one can talk about one's own situation without reserve and without palliation, because the other people in the group are experiencing the same thing. There is no need to pretend any more. But it is even more important for people to give each other the courage to break out of the internalized system of received social standards which makes them condemn themselves, punish themselves, or sink into self-pity. For many people this is particularly difficult because of the moral prejudices with which they are met, and their own corresponding self-accusations; for these people would after all really like to be once more respected members of the society which has shut them out. A particularly serious case is the victim mentality, in which a person pities him or herself, and seeks sympathy for the hurts of narcissistic self-love. When that happens, the self-help group can help no longer. On the other hand, once people's sense of their own value has been strengthened, it is important for them to leave the group.

At least equally important are self-help groups for close friends and relatives who are not themselves affected, for this helps to get rid of the prejudice syndromes, fear, disgust and the urge to escape. These are pathogenic psychological symptoms which in their effects are no less destructive of life than HIV infection itself. We recognize these symptoms in ourselves when we begin to perceive 'the others' in their difference, and when, through our interest in them, they cease to be unknown country.

The Christian church is Christian when it creates free spaces for the self-help groups on both sides, and when it brings the two together for discussion, so that people learn to live together with 'the others'. A valuable example are groups composed of people with disabilities and people without, who build up new life together where previously there was 'social death'.

The *closeness* of the self-help groups to the Christian community is to be found in Jesus himself, in the way he encountered the 'lepers', in the trust with which the humiliated and insulted approached him, and in the healings which came about in his vicinity. The *remoteness* of self-help groups from the Christian congregations is caused by the moral notions of church tradition, with which society's religion has always operated. So the challenging question which the self-help groups put to the church is this: how near is the Christian church to Jesus himself, or how far from him? The more a Christian congregation is pervaded by the Spirit of Jesus, the closer it will be to the people in the self-help groups, and the further it will distance itself from the moral notions dominating the religion of the society in which it lives. The stories about Jesus in the gospels make it clear that the community of Christ reaches beyond the circle of believers, and that the poor, the sick and people who have been thrust out of society – the people named in Matthew 25 – belong to it constitutively and essentially, not merely by the way and as welfare cases. But where Christ is, there the life-giving Spirit is too. That is why the fellowship of the Spirit must be sought at the place where distressed people seek and experience the nearness of Jesus.

6. Social Forms of the Church

Finally let us cast a glance at the different social forms of the church. We must be able to distinguish, so as not to put too much of a strain on one another, and so as to act together in our differences.

(a) At the base of society we find what are called *natural communities* and *voluntary groups*. The voluntary groups come together through some jointly recognized or jointly experienced need. Jointly recognized need leads to joint action. People involve themselves personally and endure the pain of conflict. They develop their own form of Christian spirituality, which links mysticism and politics. Dietrich Bonhoeffer described it as 'resistance and surrender'. In Taizé it is called 'contemplation and struggle'. The liberation spirituality of Latin America is characterized by its own interpretation of the Bible and by fellowship with the oppressed. Peace groups can join together in regional and international networks, building up a new ecumenism from below. These are groups of like-minded people and people with similar problems. That is why they are often at odds with traditional congregations and come into conflict with the leaders of their churches.

(b) The genesis of *the local congregation* is the proclamation of the gospel and the celebration of the sacraments, but it is fed most of all by the tradition of Christian families. The congregation gathers together for worship. People come who think differently about justice, peace and the integrity of creation – or who do not think about them at all. For they do not come to church in order to meet people who have similar views about political and social questions. That is why the local congregation will not always as a whole become a congregation specially committed to peace, or a third-world group. The different groups which are expressions of Christian discipleship would put an undue strain on the local congregation if they expected of it anything of this kind. This is even more true for the leaders of the mainline churches, who have to take social harmony and acceptable political conduct into account, and who aim to serve not only the groups but the others too.

For the same reason, however, church leaders must not take too much on themselves either, by issuing statements on the questions to which the groups already give Christian answers. The many pastoral letters and memoranda generally take no account of the particular situation in which they themselves are born, and the interests of the people who write and approve them. Consequently they sound abstract.

The local congregation will come closer to the natural communities and the voluntary groups the more it ceases to be merely a congregation for worship and turns into a fellowship of shared life, a 'diaconal congregation'; for then the various members of the congregation will see their social, economic and political conflicts in their local context, and will talk about them, so that they can help one another and find joint answers. Important though the service of worship is, for this side of congregational life the general *church meeting* is even more important, for there local assignments can be discussed and the groups can be heard.

(c) *The regional and national churches* are neither local congregations nor are they groups. Their contexts are the regions, the nations, and the supra-national political groupings. It is important for Christianity not to stick fast in narrow local contexts, and for it to be present in the contemporary processes which are moving towards community in Europe, America, Asia and Africa. Only churches which have strong ecumenical contacts, or are already members of supra-national ecumenical communities, have anything to contribute to the new political integration processes. Among us, the churches are particularly important where relations between political communities and the third world are concerned. For the churches are already present in the countries of the third world as 'non-governmental organizations', and for many Christians, moreover, Christian community with people far off has become more important than national loyalty shared with people close at hand.

Today's political amalgamations between the nations in any given region can only be federalist. The centralist state no longer functions, because it suppresses individual initiative and paralyses liberty. Centralist churches therefore have nothing to offer the new process towards political community. Their hierarchical structures paralyse the liberty of individuals and produce a passive welfare mentality. They are not compatible with democracy. The new political federations are therefore a challenge to Christianity, requiring it to develop new ecclesiastical structures based on community, and to distance itself from its traditional feudalist Byzantine, Roman and Protestant forms. Ecumenical experiments in 'conciliar process', 'covenants' and horizontal 'networks' offer chances for further development here.

(d) Because of the military, ecological and social dangers in the world, the nations are entering an *age of world-wide humanity* inasmuch as they are realizing that the dangers threatening them all can be contained only by joint efforts. It is time for the traditional churches too to enter their ecumenical age, leaving their denominational conflicts behind them. A help here is perception of 'the fellowship of the Holy Spirit' which crosses frontiers and denominational borders, and a new orientation towards the kingdom of God and the new creation of all things. Hitherto the kingdom of God has generally been viewed as orientated towards the church. The important thing today is to orientate the church towards the kingdom of God. Only then can the churches take the step which today is the most important step of all: to see themselves not merely as a church of human beings but as a *church of the cosmos*, and to perceive that the social and ecological crises in the world are crises in their own life too.

§3 THE THEOLOGY OF SOCIAL EXPERIENCE OF GOD

Patristic and mediaeval traditions always integrated earthly into heavenly love, and neighbourly love into the love of God; for God alone is the highest good and must be desired for his own sake. Modern European humanism reversed this direction, and reduced love of God to love of our neighbour, and love of our neighbour to sensual love: 'Person with person – the unity of I and Thou is God', declared Ludwig Feuerbach.[39] We shall look for a third way, so as to discover God's love *in* the love between human beings, and the love between human beings *in* God's love. We shall take up again the idea of the transcendence immanent in all happening. For both the middle ages and modern times, love is a virtue, that is to say, it is an activity. But we shall start from the passive as well as the active experience of love: being loved and loving. We shall carry over the Christian concept of love – the liberating and redeeming concept – into the different levels of social relationships, so as to arrive at the corresponding ideas of community and personality, friendship and sensual love. Finally, we shall look at some bodily ways of expressing the social experience of God.

1. *Neighbourly Love and Self-Love in the Love of God*

Love is a desire. It is not Being in itself that is desirable, but only Being that is good. God is both the highest Being and the highest Good (*summum bonum*). So for human beings God is the most desirable of all. Because desire presupposes a desirous subject, the love of God is in the highest degree related to the self. What has no relation to the self and its bliss cannot be loved. According to the idea of most mediaeval theologians, 'the ladder of love' led from love of our neighbour to love of the self, and from self-love to the love of God.

This 'physical conception' of love assumes that there is a hidden but indestructible identity between self-love and the love of God.[40] This identity is to be found in the *imago Dei* which dwells in the depths of every soul. The inner yearning for God is that which corresponds to God in the soul. If through his grace God pours the supernatural virtue of *caritas* into a person's heart, that person's natural yearning for God will be properly guided and fulfilled in the friendship with God which God confers. That person says 'yes' to God, to all his creatures and all his commandments. His will will be one with God's. So in the person who is thus inspired and blessed, the love for God extends as far as God's own love. Everything which God loves, will also become an object of human love for God, simply because God loves it. Everything is loved for God, and for God's sake: 'The summit of the love of God is to love one's own self exclusively for God's sake.' Our neighbour too – even our enemy – belongs as object to God himself in the movement of our love for God. Neighbour, sinner and enemy will be loved because they are the image of God, and so that they may be led to God and belong to God. The archetype which provides the orientation for this 'physical conception' of love can be clearly detected: the hierarchy of creation descends from the *summum bonum* to the *imago Dei*, and then to the *vestigia Dei* (the traces of God), in order to draw the desirous love of human beings up from the lower to the highest Good.

Parallel to this, from Pseudo-Dionysius onwards an 'ecstatic conception' of love developed.[41] According to this concept too, true love is directed towards God, because knowledge of God brings salvation. But love wrenches human beings out of their condition, and even out of themselves. It is something suffered rather than done. For this, the Fathers of the church preferred the word *eros* to the biblical word *agape*. Love is perfected to the degree in which it carries human beings out of their own selves. Not self-love but selflessness, not desire but surrender lead to the love of God. Mystical and Franciscan spirituality were pervaded by this idea. But to disregard one's own self of course also means disengaging oneself from other creatures too; so the person who loves God perfectly is the person who is totally forgetful of himself and indifferent towards the world. He loves his neighbour with the wish that the neighbour too may love God just as self-forgetfully. The neighbour himself is not loved.

It is surprising how little the mediaeval 'theology of love' takes as starting point God's love, and the human experience of being loved.[42]

'Let us love him, because he first loved us' (I John 4.19). Does the active love of human beings not first of all acquire its power, its attraction and the space in which it moves from the experience of being loved? It is clear from the New Testament, and especially the Johannine writings, that God's love for men and women precedes their love for God, and is its foundation and motive power. 'In this the love of God was made manifest among us, that God sent his only Son into the world so that we might live through him' (I John 4.9). We live through him because through him we are reconciled with God. If we are reconciled, we shall love one another as we are loved, and shall treat one another accordingly. Because of the incarnation of God's love in the sending and self-surrender of Christ, the love of God is realized *in* love of our neighbour, and realized in such a way that the neighbour is loved for himself, and not as means to a higher end. 'If we love one another, God abides in us and his love is perfected in us . . . He who does not love his brother whom he has seen, how can he love God whom he has not seen?' (I John 4.12, 20).

Compared with this *christological conception* of the love of God in love of our neighbour, the two mediaeval conceptions of God's love smack of docetism, because they threaten to do away with the incarnation, and seem to consider the responsive love for God on the part of human beings as more important than the love of God which gives life. The Christian experience of God is a sensuous experience of God: '. . . that which we have seen with our eyes, which we have looked upon and touched with our hands: the word of life . . .' (I John 1.1). It springs from the bodily immanence of transcendence, and debars us from dissolving the immanence in the transcendence, and even from disparaging the immanence compared with the transcendence. For Christian experience, the spirituality of the love of God is to be found *in* the vitality of true human love. Here the Christian experience of God's love preserves the Israelite and Jewish heritage: 'Love your neighbour as yourself' for 'I am the Lord'.

To illustrate this, Martin Buber tells the following story:

We are told that once upon a time a man filled with a passion for God left the realm of created things and entered into the great emptiness. He wandered about there until he found himself before the gate to the Mystery. He knocked. Someone within called out: 'What do you want?' 'I have proclaimed thy praise to the ears of mortal men and women', said the man, 'but they were deaf to it.

So now I come to thee, so that thou thyself mayest hear me and answer.' 'Turn back', called a voice from within, 'there is no one to listen to you here. I have sunk my hearing in the deafness of mortal men and women.'[43]

2. *Ego-mania and Self-Dispersion in Society*

The social relations of persons and the personal relations of social groups can be threatened from two sides: on the one hand through the ego-mania of the self-separated, self-mastering individual, and on the other through the self-dispersion in the social network of relationships of the person whose self is insufficiently developed.

Ideally, sociality and personhood come into being together and condition one another mutually. The person is not there ahead of the community, not is the community there in advance of the person. Persons come into being in relationships, and relationships proceed from persons. The modern concept of person is *the social concept*: 'person' no longer means the all-sufficing, self-sufficient, universal and reflective figure portrayed in the formative ideal of German classicism from Goethe to Karl Marx.[44] And the modern idea of community is the idea of *a community of persons*, not the concept of trans-personal collective unities, from which the persons are alienated. Persons find protection for their freedom in community, and the community finds its creativity in the persons that constitute it. Paradoxically, it is entirely in the spirit of liberalism when the Communist Manifesto of 1848 writes: 'The bourgeois society of old, with its classes and class antagonisms, is replaced by an association in which the free development of every individual is the condition for the free development of all.' But it must also be established that in their community persons are joined in their concern for the common good.[45]

However, this only applies in the ideal case, which never exists. Modern industrial society does everything to individualize people through the pressure of competition, and to set one person against the other. In a competitive society there is never 'enough for everyone'. The competitive struggle is fuelled by shortage of opportunities. The army of unemployed acts as pressure on the people who have jobs. The person who wants to climb the ladder must often enough sacrifice his relations with neighbours, friends and family, for what is required of climbers is not merely creativity and flexibility, but mobility and

continual availability as well. On the other hand, industrial society
has hitherto developed as a centralistic society. The great industrial
and administrative centres have created the metropolises, and have
impoverished and emptied the peripheries. The great trek from the
country into the mass cities is continuing, although it is incompatible
with both social and ecological requirements. The idea of centralism
is the child of absolutism; it does not derive from the industrial world
itself.

If we look for an alternative to the individualism and the centralism
of modern societies, the obvious course would seem to be to recon-
struct these societies from below, starting from the local communities
which people can survey, keep track of and live with, and where they
can develop as persons. Centralism, with its increasing rigidity, its
total controls and its deadening bureaucracies, can be replaced
by federalism, which gives back their own liberty to the local
communities, regions and nations.[46] In the age of modern communications, decentralization is not a technical problem. Society will
become more humane and more creative in a federation of independent communities. Military states based on power need strong central
controls; democratic states based on commerce need decentralized
federal structures.

The *covenant* or constitution of free citizens is the mature, practical
form of mutual trust, and the foundation for democracy. It is equally
threatened by centralistic socialism and by the extreme inequalities
produced by capitalism. The covenant guarantees both personal
liberties and social justice. It is aligned towards consensus, not
subjugation. It requires personal initiative and personal responsibility, as well as consideration for others and the recognition of their
own individual character. In politics, the covenant formulates the
rights and duties of a participatory democracy, and in economic life
it defines the rights and duties involved in co-determination by way
of trade unions. It therefore prevents the sense of impotence felt by
the modern, solitary individual. It debars people from shifting
responsibility on to others, and by so doing it hinders them from
becoming alienated from themselves. It dares to impose the risk of
freedom, and cannot co-exist with the regressive 'flight from freedom'
into infantile expectations of being looked after by someone else. In
modern times these forms of democratic society have proved stronger
in the long run than all the various forms of dictatorship by way of
education, social welfare and military power.

But the relationship between person and community is not merely a political one. It is a personal one too, and in the personal sphere it is also sex-specific and has determined human civilization from time immemorial. Girls evidently feel themselves to be in continuity with their mothers, with whom they share the same gender; whereas from very early on boys are conscious of their difference. Because of this, the relationships of growing girls change organically, whereas growing boys have to come to terms with their difference from the mother, and that means with her autonomy.[47] On the other hand, at least in patriarchal societies, the mother has more pleasure in her differently sexed son than in her daughter. This too gives sons and daughters different starting conditions in life.[48]

These facts are conditioned by the different inborn constitutions of men and women; but the forms the constitutions assume are culturally conditioned. Boys are separated from the mother early on. They take the impress of the father, and are brought up 'to be men'. On the other hand, daughters imitate their mothers and are trained 'for womanhood'. At the two extremes we can easily detect the separated, solitary male individual, incapable of relation, who tries despairingly to be himself, and the female self, entangled in relation, self-dispersing in her flight from solitariness, who tries despairingly not to be herself. On the one hand we can talk about 'matricide' and on the other about the life-long dominance of the mother, and daughterly dependence. But 'ego-mania' and 'self-dispersion' are in fact really pathogenic symptoms in people whose selves are under-developed, rather than constitutive elements in the formation of personhood in sociality. We can even relate these two fundamental experiences positively to one another, if for a moment we forget the patriarchal impregnation of our society. Then the masculine experience of autonomy is just as much a human experience as is the profoundly human feminine experience of relation. It is this, ultimately, that makes it possible for men to learn from women, and women from men. The masculine experience of autonomy is shown pre-eminently in the man's orientation towards work, which every woman can understand. The feminine experience of relation is shown in her orientation towards people, which every man can understand. The masculine fear of the 'self-dispersion' which is termed 'feminine' is as unnecessary as the feminine fear of the 'ego-mania' which is termed masculine. Not the least important factor here is the question of age. When we are young, we seek the relationships which enrich life. Later on, women particularly have to learn to think of themselves, and to shape their own lives; and then contacts outside their jobs and families will become of vital importance.

On the level of the relations between women and men, mutual enrichment through their different experiences of life is conceivable. But when a culture is patriarchally impregnated, the emphases must be imposed in a critical spirit, and must come down on the side of feminine experiences of what it means to be human; for in a culture of this kind these experiences are notoriously undervalued. Criticism not only helps to set women free for their own experiences of life. It also serves to free men from the self-alienations and separations to which they have been brought up.

The self which becomes soluble in relations, and the self that remains separately and autonomously itself are not antitheses. Human life pulsates in both movements, and must not grow rigid and calcify in merely one of them. The life-giving Spirit finds expression in both the 'oceanic feeling of life' experienced through the warp and weft of all subjective life, and in the personal subjectivity of thinking and acting. The Spirit creates both the collective unconscious and the individual consciousness, and relates the two figurations of life to one another. It is understandable that – following the modern age, with its atomization of nature and its subjectivization of human beings – people should now seek for the 'New Age' of a cosmic feeling of community and a 'self' rich in relation. But this 'new age' would become a velvet-gloved conspiracy for the abolition of the human being if the inward experiences of human autonomy and personal initiative were to be condemned. Anyone who casts a slur on autonomy by calling it masculine ego-mania, and who fails to respect it as part of human dignity, is laying him or herself open to the suspicion of a thirst for power. For when all is said and done, the spider's web is not merely a symbol for the network of life, with its complex relationship; it is also an instrument for catching flies.

People experience themselves in the relationships of society, and society is made up of independent people. This polarity is part of life, and keeps life tense and expectant. The Spirit of life is the Spirit of love. Love unites what is separated, and separates what is united, and in this rhythm gives life its movement.

3. Open Friendship

The experience of friendship is an important stage on the way to the theology of social experience of God. 'A friend is someone who likes you.'[49] That is the simplest definition. The friend can be a man or a woman, an animal or a forest. Friendship is just there, and surrounds everyone from all sides. We do not have to seek or 'make' friends. Friendship is simply something we have to discover. It is there in the smile of a passer-by, in the play of the wind, or the rushing of a brook. It is 'the sympathy of the world' – the gentle power of attraction and participation, which holds together everybody and everything that lives. It is a vulnerable atmosphere of life. We can live in it without noticing it. We can live from it and continually destroy it. Open friendship turns the world into a home. That is why we are on the search for the traces of a friendlier world wherever we feel exiled and estranged. Friendship is a way of behaving that makes no claims. 'Friend' is not an official title, or a role we have to play, or a function in society. We have our brothers and sisters in the nature of things, and have to live with them. But friendships grow up out of free encounter. Friendship is a personal relationship between people who like one another. Friendship combines *affection with respect.*

Combining affection with respect does not mean wanting to serve the other person, or having to help him, or making use of him. It means simply liking someone for themselves, just as they are. The affection has to do with the *being* of other people, the respect has to do with their freedom. Friendship is the opposite of appropriation or the desire to possess. If we become aware of any such intention, we are put off, and the friendship withers. In friendship we sense that there is a wide space of freedom in which we can expand, because we are trusted and can lay aside the protective mechanism of mistrust.

Friendship combines this *respect* for the other person's freedom with deep *affection* for him or her as person. One can be a respected figure and enjoy esteem and admiration and yet not find anyone who 'likes one'. We do not need to bow down to a friend. We neither look up to him nor down on him. We can look a friend in the eye, for we feel that we are looked on with friendly eyes ourselves. Friendship like this frees people from the false pictures of themselves they build up out of their ego-mania or their self-dispersion. In friendship we do not have to present ourselves in any particular light. Selfcondemnations are forgotten. People who are friends sense the concord of the great harmony which makes life something living.

Friendship is not a temporary feeling of affection. It combines affection with *faithfulness*. We can rely on our friend, and as a friend we become someone on whom other people can rely. We are simply there, like a little star in the sky. Friends go on being there even in misfortune. Among friends there are no prejudices which pin the other person down, and no ideal pictures which are really a desire to make the other person someone different. So we do not constantly and anxiously have to assure ourselves of friendship. True friendship is not an association for mutual benefit like 'business friends'. It is a bond between people for their own sake. When people are personal friends, each of them is confident that the other will be a loving companion on the way. One trusts the other to be 'there'. This is a kind of faithfulness that has nothing to do with acting and having. It has to do with the person and the path they take through life.

Friendship comes into being out of *freedom*, it continues in freedom, and it safeguards mutual freedom. This is not the liberalism of ordinary civic life, which tolerates everything because it is interested in nothing. We are not free by nature. We only become free when someone likes us and affirms us with affection, as a mother affirms her child first of all. Friends throw open the free spaces of life for one another, and accompany one another in sympathy and immense interest. One element in this participation is being able to leave the other person in peace, like the brook that lets you sit still on its bank if you don't want to talk, as Joan Walsh Anglund puts it.[50] Hegel called friendship 'the concept of freedom in concrete form' and saw friendship as the interpersonal dimension of personal freedom.

Here the law of *quid pro quo* does not apply. People who are friends help one another without reward, but without a helper syndrome either. In friendship there is no question of 'services rendered'. We do not need friends only in some extremity. We need them most of all in order to share the joy of living and feel happiness in existence. Joy that is not communicated makes us melancholy. To rejoice with someone is as good as to suffer with them. Joy that is shared without envy and jealousy makes one ready to sympathize too without condescension.

Because friendship can only exist without outward coercion and without inward constraint, it is *lasting*, and its gentle power is victorious over the violent power of enmity, which never has time. In enmity we freeze, inwardly and outwardly; in friendship we open ourselves and come alive: 'Truly, what is rigid and unbending is the companion of death, while the soft and weak is the companion of life', says Tao te Ching rightly (Ch. 76); and this is true of enmity and friendship too. Because friendship is aligned towards permanence, it is ultimately stronger than enmity, which never has time.

In the long run, the future of the world will belong to *open friendship*. We experience this in personal relationships too. When in the family the relationship of parent to child comes to an end (because parental responsibility is finished, and the children have become independent), friendship remains. When in society professional relationships have ceased and people meet one another simply as people, and no longer in their social roles – then friendship can develop. When men and women overcome the privileges and slights of a patriarchal culture, then there can be friendship between them. The new human being, the true human being, the free human being is the person who likes to be with other people: the friend.

Can there only be friendship between people who are alike? Is friendship exclusive? Aristotle says that the foundation of a shared life is *philia*.[51] *Philia* presupposes identity of nature or community of interest. 'Birds of a feather flock together', because 'like draws to like'. Only what is lovable can be the object of love, and what counts as lovable is whatever is valuable, pleasurable or useful. This kind of love leads to friendship only where love can be returned, and that is impossible in the case of lifeless objects. Consequently there can only be friendship between living things. Where utility is the motive for friendship, people do not love each other for their own sake, but because of their mutual usefulness. Where pleasure is the aim, people love each other for the sake of the pleasure they give one another. Perfect friendship is only possible where people who are alike by nature love one another for what they are. People who are different can become friendly for utilitarian purposes or for pleasure; but when it is a matter of mutual esteem, only people who are alike can be friends: freemen with freemen, slaves with slaves, Greeks with Greeks, barbarians with barbarians, men with men, women with women, and so forth. It is true that there are 'darlings of the gods', says Aristotle, but no human being can seriously say that he loves Zeus. So friendship in this sense means the exclusive friendship of people who are the same: *philia*.

We find the opposite picture of friendship in the New Testament: *open friendship* with people who are different. In the Gospel of Luke Jesus had a name pinned on him as part of a smear campaign; but it actually describes with total accuracy the fellowship he gives to other people: he is called 'The friend of sinners and tax-collectors' (Luke 7.34). John the Baptist was an ascetic, and preached repentance. But Jesus received sinners and sat down at table with them. He got himself into 'bad company'. The innermost reason was his overflowing joy in the approaching kingdom of God. That is why he celebrated the messianic feast with the people who had been thrust out of society. In inviting joy, he opened himself for them, and respected both them and the poor, as the first children of the divine grace that creates everything afresh. He recognized their dignity as people. He bridged the gulf of their self-isolation, and did away with the social prejudice under which they suffered. Through speech and gesture, the divine 'friend of sinners and tax collectors' spread the encouraging and supportive atmosphere of open friendship among men and women.

In Jesus' Spirit, the community of his people later drew the proper conclusions and said: 'Accept one another as Christ has accepted you, for the glory of God' (Rom. 15.7). The basic law of the community of Christ is *acceptance of others* in their difference, for it is *this* experience of our neighbours, and only this, which is in line with Christian experience of God. Here other people's difference is not defined against the yardstick of our own identity, and our prejudice about people who are not like us. The difference is experienced in the practical encounter which mutually reveals what we are and what the other is.

It is the experience of God's affection and respect in the friendship of Jesus which shapes the Christian concept of open friendship. John 15.13–15 also makes this clear: Jesus' surrender of himself to death is presented as love for his friends. The men and women disciples are Jesus' friends. In the community of Jesus they are no longer God's servants. They are his friends. In Jesus's self-surrender God becomes the friend of men and women; and through Jesus, believers become friends of God. This gives believers the highest name which Israelite tradition has to give. The chosen who have 'seen' God count as 'God's friends'. James 2.23 calls Abraham 'the friend of God', for the very same reason that Paul calls him 'father of faith' (Rom. 4.1ff.): 'Abraham believed God, and it was reckoned to him as righteousness.' So it is not the exceptional ascetics and mystics who are 'God's friends'; it is all the men and women who are justified and believe. But in practical terms this means that they can talk to God as friends, knowing that it is as a friend that God listens to them.

Through Christian experience of God and the self in the friendship of Jesus, the barriers of the 'equality' principle break down: the friendship of the 'Wholly Other' God which comes to meet us, makes open friendship with people who are 'other' not merely possible but also interesting, in a profoundly human sense. The others are not just 'put up with'. They are welcome. The community of Christians can interpret itself not only as an assembly of believers, but also as a 'society of friends', as do the Quakers, who have proved their open friendship in the slums and in the struggle for the abolition of slavery. The motive for this is not the moral purpose of changing the world. It is festal joy over the kingdom of God which, with the name of Jesus and in his Spirit, has thrown itself wide open for 'the others'. In every true friendship we can experience God. It is the presence of his friendly Spirit which makes those who are friends so alive and their friendship so inexhaustible. They continually discover new things about one another. The wide space of the Spirit is the opening for their freedom, and in his trust, both self-trust and trust in one another grow.

There is a divine and a cosmic friendship which precedes personal friendship and invites us to personal friendship. In an environment viewed as hostile, we can only form exclusive friendships for mutual protection. In a community of creation experienced as friendly, we form open friendships. In open friendships we do not surrender our identity. We expand the relationships in which this identity can be experienced. If we believe in the community of creation in the life-giving Spirit of God, we discover the 'sympathy of all things', and make ourselves consciously a part of it.

4. Experiences of Love

The strongest and most intimate relationship between human beings is love. Love makes life worth living – it is the source of new life – it is as strong as death. Judaism and Christianity have put the double commandment of love at the centre of their life and faith. The Christian experience of God even says: 'God *is* love' (I John 4.16). What is the relationship between this experience of God and the experience of human love? What happens in the hermeneutical process which translates expressions for the experience of human love into the experience of God, and then comes back from the experience of God, interpreted in this way, to the experience of human love? In experiencing human love, are we not supposed to think of the experience of God? And in experiencing God, are we not supposed to think of the experience of love? In this case it would be wrong to use the same word for the two experiences. The meticulous theological distinctions between *eros* and *agape*,[52] *amor* and *caritas*,[53] sensual and spiritual love, are attempts to restrict the transference of the meanings. They have again severed the experience of God from the experience of love, and by doing so have really introduced a cleavage into the double commandment of love. But it is a *single love* which embraces God and our neighbour, just as according to the First Epistle of John it is a single love which is experienced *by* God and our neighbour.

A significant example of the way the one, single love has been split up into two different forms is the transferred, mystical intepretation of the Song of Solomon and its literal, erotic interpretation.[54] Does this wonderful love song really have a place in a religious book? People who were bothered by this, interpreted the poem allegorically, claiming that it referred to the soul's love for God. By so doing they abstracted sensual love from the love of God and banished it to 'the lower instincts', so that the transcendental love for God might be pure, spiritual, and confined to 'the heart'. But if the Bible is called – and rightly called – 'the book of life', then the life-giving experiences of love belong to this book, and in that case it is inadmissible to withdraw from this immanent experience of love its transcendent depths by abstracting from it a higher love. God – the quickening Spirit – can be experienced in the experience of human love. Even if his name is not explicitly mentioned in the Song of Solomon, his shining splendour radiates from every phrase with which the experience of love is described, for this experience is 'a flame of the Lord' (8.6). That is why the old Benedictine hymn maintains: 'Ubi caritas et amor, ibi Deus est' – where love is, there is God.

To find experiences of God *in* the experiences of love does not mean divinizing the experience of love, and elevating love into a cult. That would put too great a strain on the lovers, and would lead to destructive disappointments. To perceive the one *in* the other means being able to connect and to distinguish. Two spheres intersect, and two experiences deepen and shelter one another mutually. 'He who abides in love abides *in* God, and God abides *in* him' (I John 4.16). Like the Greek Fathers, we are here using a single expression for the one, single love: the word *eros*, and we shall avoid designations for a higher love, separate from this, such as *agape* and *caritas*. The New Testament uses the word ἀγάπη, and uses it for both divine and human love.[55] It is *one* love. The differences arise from the differences of the subjects and their relationships with one another.

The community of love is an *erotic community*: God's loving community with his beloved creation is erotic; the force which differentiates and unites all his creatures is erotic; the rapturous delight of lovers in one another is erotic. 'We call Eros divine and angelic, spiritual, of the soul and natural – we perceive it as a uniting and intermingling force.'[56] The creative Spirit of God is himself Eros, for out of his creations and in his creations his beauty shines forth and again awakens eros in its turn. The beloved is always the Beautiful and the Captivating – not yet the Good in itself, but the Good which shows itself to be beautiful, and the Beautiful which shows itself to be good, as Plato already knew. Even the divine grace shows itself in the loveliness of a person and in the unconscious sweetness and charm of a particular being. It was by no means a good idea to separate the morally good from the aesthetically beautiful, and to set morality above aesthetics, as did theological teachings about love in the middle ages. The radiance of the divine Spirit which emanates from created beings awakens the eros, and the eros sanctifies created life by loving and affirming it. Morality and aesthetics are one. This is the shared experience of human beings too. Love is quickening life. *Vita vivificans* is an ancient name for the Spirit of God who makes everything blossom and become fertile.

Of course eros is desire, and means the desire for union; but erotic love does not desire in order to subject and possess, but so as to participate in the life of the other person, and to communicate his or her own life. It was only in late antiquity and the world of Christian thought that sensual love was held cheap, as sinful concupiscence, eros accordingly being identified with greed and a thirst for dominance. In view of the patriarchal distortions of erotic love, this interpretation is not even wrong. But the original Greek concept of eros has nothing to do with self-love and self-complacent 'conquests'. It means passionate participation in the beautiful which has been glimpsed. Eros was neither an androcentric nor an anthropocentric concept. It was a cosmic expression for the divine mystery of the world. When someone is possessed by the power of eros he says 'I am so happy I could embrace the whole world'. This shows the fluid transitions from the personal to the cosmic eros, transitions which escape the reduced western and the limited modern interpretations of eros.

Erotic love is desire, but it is generous too, not merely in the material sense but even more in the personal one. It is only the person who wishes to degrade the other to his or her personal property who wishes to impose fetters. To love not oneself but the other person for themselves, means loving the other person's freedom too. Of course this does not mean their moods and caprice, but it does mean their liberty to develop themselves fully in all the wealth and beauty given to them. Like friendship, love unfolds only in the fragile and vulnerable sphere of freedom – indeed it is love itself which in the personal sense opens up freedom in the free spaces of life. True love opens vistas into that 'broad place where there is no cramping', and in this it is spirit of God's Spirit. It sounds paradoxical, but in the experience of love it is no contradiction to say that to desire and to liberate are one and the same thing.

In loving, the lovers are *counterpart and presence* for one another. The inclination of the Thou awakens a responding movement in the I, and vice versa. 'Primal distance and relation' in I-Thou relationships have been sufficiently, and sufficiently often, described. But in the experience of love there is more still: the beloved counterpart becomes the presence in which the lovers begin to live. They do not remain counterparts, standing over against one another. They become presence for one another, so that in this sense they begin to live in each other. This presence in its total immediacy is perhaps only comparable with the first, primal presence of the mother for the child, although it is quite different in kind. The child only slowly experiences that the motherly presence is also the mother as personal counterpart. In the experience of love the process is rather reversed: the personal counterpart becomes the encompassing presence. Counterpart and presence alternate in the rhythm of life, and must do so; for pure presence is imperceptible. In order to know one another, the lovers need not only union but detachment; not merely desire but also the setting-free; not solely the going out of the self but the withdrawal of the self too; not community alone, but also personhood. Being a counterpart is relation. Presence is encompassment. In love, to encompass one another and to be related to one another belong together.

The living interplay between presence and counterpart does not permit 'the other' to be turned into an object. It prevents us from making an objective image of the other person, and then pinning him or her down to that image. Love needs no image. It actually liberates us from the images which tie us down and which we make of ourselves. 'You shall not make for yourself an image or any likeness.' This commandment does not merely apply to the experience of God. It applies to the experience of love too.[57] Love fulfils the commandment, because it does not tie anything down to what was once reality, in the past. It throws open the new free spaces of the future. Anger nails other people down to what they once were or did. But love perceives the other person together with his or her future, and his or her still unawakened potentialities. Anger gives the other person no time and no chance. But love has time and can wait. That is why the apostle's advice is good advice for lovers: 'Do not let the sun go down on your anger' (Eph. 4.26).

5. The Body Language of Social Experience of God

There is no experience without its corresponding expression. This is true especially of the experience of love, which makes of life something living. Love's expression in look and word, the play of features and gesture, are as diverse and individual as the people and their circumstances, and as varied as the eras and civilizations in which these people live. And yet there are some forms and configurations which, at least in our culture, continually recur in different variations – forms and configurations which tell us something about the living power of love, and which have made their way into the community of Christians too.

First of all there are the beginnings of the experience of love, in which something stirs us without any act of our own: the look – the lightning flash – the kindling touch, the loving embrace, the heart-warming closeness. A spark, a flame, springs from the one to the other, sometimes of almost mystical immediacy, which then has first to create the mediating consonances and aquiescences. Erotic relational fields come into being, with their personal resonances and shared harmonies.

Experiences of God are often described in a corresponding way:

the electrifying touch of the Holy Spirit, the experience of faith which warms the heart, the thrust of energy which is called 'rebirth' to a new life, life's charismatic blossoming, and not least: the shining face of God which is invoked in every benediction and from which the Spirit comes to give life peace, and the illumined face of Christ from whom the life-giving Spirit comes to illuminate believers. In this sense the Spirit of God is like the divine Eros which pervades all created being with the power of its love:

> Steadfast may we cleave to Thee,
> Love, the mystic union be;
> Join our faithful spirits, join
> Each to each, and all to Thine.[57a]

The physical expressions of love take in all the senses: sight and hearing, smell and taste, and especially the sense of touch, which according to the mediaeval view is the fundamental human sense. Of all the physical ways of expressing the experience of love, we shall look at those which were carried over to the community born out of the shared experience of God, and shall confine ourselves to the Christian congregation.

The laying on of hands in blessing is general practice. An outward sign of encountering and greeting one another with peaceful intentions is *shaking hands*. This comes from early Germanic society and shows that the sword hand is unarmed. A more intimate sign is *the embrace* at the liturgical exchange of the 'peace' in the congregation. A counter-gesture here is the *proskynesis*, the 'kowtow' – prostration before another person, or falling on one's knees. All hierarchical ordinances require this gesture. It is the ritual with which the weaker put themselves at the mercy of the stronger and the subjugated offer their necks to the ruler for execution, in order to extol their sparing as an act of special magnanimity on the victor's part. In hierarchical forms of Christianity, this ritual is used towards bishops and the Pope. But in the early Christian, egalitarian community of 'brothers and sisters', this gesture was replaced by the *embrace*. In the service of worship, it was with a mutual embrace that people greeted one another with the 'peace'. A no less powerful gesture is the *foot-washing* (John 13.1–17). Jesus shows himself as 'master' by washing the feet of his friends; and in the same way 'you ought also to wash one another's feet' (v.14), performing this service of love for one another. A ceremonial foot-washing of the sick was part of the French coronation ritual. It is also celebrated by the Pope on Maundy Thursday. In some charismatic congregations there are occasionally spontaneous foot-washings. Feminist groups have also experimented with it. It can be the expression of a deep and loving community.

Finally, the most intimate sign of the bond of mutual love was '*the holy kiss*'.[58] For Paul this was evidently a matter of course in the Christian congregations (Rom. 16.16; I Cor. 16.20; II Cor. 13.12; I Thess. 5.26). I Peter 5.14 calls it 'the kiss of love'. This was not the proskynetic kissing of another's foot, nor did it mean kissing the hand in homage. What is meant is the warm kiss exchanged during the embrace. In other contexts the kiss signifies the awakening and communication of living energies, and an inward community of soul; so here too the 'the holy kiss of the communion of saints has its origin in the Holy Spirit' as the real communication and practical exchange of the love which, as the operation of the Spirit, is alive in believers. The holy kiss 'is an active form of the community of the Holy Spirit and has accordingly acquired a pneumatical imprint in the specific Christian sense'.[59] The kiss is alien to Asiatic and Indian societies, but in Jewish-Hellenistic civilizations it was general in families and friendships, as the Old Testament shows. It will have made its way into the Christian congregations as an extension of the kiss of greeting among relatives and friends. There has been much speculation about 'the Judas kiss'. But this cannot have been the sole connection between the 'holy kiss' in the Christian congregations and the person and history of Jesus. Perhaps the apocryphal tradition gives a hint here, when it tells us that Jesus often kissed Mary Magdalene, his κοινωνός, or companion, on her lips.[60]

The later development in the patristic church is interesting. According to Ambrose, since the kiss '*plenae caritatis fidelis exprimitur affectus*', it counted as the supreme sign of love and devotion (*caritas et pietas*). In the liturgy, it was exchanged after the eucharistic prayer. It was also called 'the kiss of peace'. The kiss of peace was exchanged at baptism too, and at the consecration of a bishop. Originally it was evidently also exchanged between men and women, for it was only after the third century that the Apostolic Constitutions II, 57, 17 separated the sexes from one another in the kiss of peace. Fear of erotic feelings made Clement of Alexandria recommend the *philema mysticon*, 'in which, as the word play suggests, the mouth is closed.'[61] It was probably the hierarchization of the church rather than a 'waning of brotherhood of heart'[62] which put an end to the kiss of peace, together with the embrace between sisters and brothers. The Protestant churches then laid all their stress on 'the hearing of the word', and suspended all the other senses in the service of worship. It was the Moravian Brethren who once again introduced 'the kiss of love' into the Agape meal. In today's ecumenical movement there is an enriching exchange and a new discovery of more varied ways of expressing fellowship and love.[63]

The way to the heart is through the stomach, says the proverb prosaically. An essential form of community is *the shared meal*. People who eat and drink together belong together like the family that sits down at the same table. There was always something sacred about a shared meal, especially according to the biblical traditions, and this sacred character was symbolized by the bread that was broken and the cup that was passed from hand to hand. The reverse is also true: experience of God led directly to the shared meal: 'And since they (Moses and Aaron) had beheld God, they ate and drank' (Ex. 24.11), this apparently being the natural reaction to the vision of the living God which was so supremely supernatual. According to Deut. 12.7 too, the people were to 'eat before the Lord and rejoice'. Whereas in Judaism the fellowship of the family table is at the centre, and the sabbath meal celebrated in the home is in the foreground, among Christians it is *the eucharistic fellowship*. Those who have eaten of one bread and drunk from one cup recognize one another in Christ's fellowship of love as children of the same Spirit. And through bread and wine they are brought into a natural community too. According to patristic and Moravian custom, the shared *Agape* meal is part of the eucharistic table fellowship (I Cor. 11.20ff.). This ensures that it does not remain symbolic but leads to community of life in the congregation. Again, experiences of the meal shared between human beings are transferred to the experience of God, and the experience of God is carried into the shared meal. Every shared meal can therefore be celebrated as a foretaste of the great Supper of the nations (Isa. 25.6ff.) and in anticipation of eating and drinking in the kingdom of God (Matt. 22.1ff.). If, with Jesus and in his Spirit, the kingdom of God is as close as the gospel says, then we have to celebrate, and the life of the senses becomes an Advent feast.[64]

Are these merely outward rituals for spiritual things, externals for what is an inward 'affair of the heart'? That is what we are often told, in intellectual disparagement of the body. But it is not the case.

We often perceive more with our senses than we realize, or than was intended. Sensory perception requires conscious interpretation, for often enough it precedes the conscious interpretation. That is why with our conscious minds we so often come back, wonderingly and interpretatively, to these sensory impressions.

The impression, the experience and the expression are all interwoven, and can be mutually deepening. The experiences of God must not be restricted to controlled religious forms of expressing these experiences. We experience God with our whole life, and can use all the ways of expressing life to express the experience of God. If God, the quickening Spirit, is love, then human experiences of love belong within the open space of this experience of God; and the experiences of God will intensify the experience of human love.

XII

The Personhood of the Spirit

A more precise discernment of the personhood of the Holy Spirit is the most difficult problem in pneumatology in particular, and in the doctrine of the Trinity generally. If we take the experience of faith as our starting point, then even in the New Testament it is already an open question whether God's Spirit was thought of as a person or a force. If we make the doctrine of the Trinity our point of departure, then the personhood of the Spirit is asserted rather than proved if, with Tertullian's principle *una substantia – tres personae*, the concept of person derived from God the Father is simply transferred to the Spirit, or if, for doxological reasons, the Spirit – as the Nicaeno-Constantinapolitan Creed declares – 'together with the Father and the Son is worshipped and glorified'. Simply to transfer like this a concept of person acquired elsewhere, obscures rather than makes apprehensible the special personhood of the Spirit. Consequently we have to reject any generalizing talk about the 'three Persons' of the Trinity.[1] The Spirit is different from the Father and the Son. Recent feminist analysis of the anthropological model for the trinitarian concept of person has shown the androcentric impress of the 'person' concept employed by Augustine, and then by Aquinas in the wake of Boethius. To define person as *rationalis naturae individua substantia* ('an individual substance rational in nature') certainly yields a concept reflecting the separated, no-further-divisible, self-sufficient masculine self of our Greek and Roman cultural history.[2] But applied to the Trinity, it is at best applicable to 'the origin of the Godhead who is himself without origin' – that is, the Father. But the Son and the Spirit exist *from* the Father, and even 'the origin without origin' can ultimately be called 'Father' only in his relation to the eternal Son.

It is true that in its later development of trinitarian doctrine, Christian theology has replaced this interpretation of 'person' in terms of substance by a relational and perichoretic understanding, and has hence, in the anthropological correspondence too, prepared the way for a self rich in relation and sociality.[3] But even this development has not yet arrived at the unique personhood of the Holy Spirit; it has merely socialized the Spirit relationally, so to speak, as 'the third in the bond'. Emphasis is then no longer on the divine Persons in themselves but on their relationality and their unique community. But then how are we to understand the person of the Spirit?

In this chapter we shall approach the personhood of the Holy Spirit without a previous concept of person, and we shall do so from two angles. First we shall draw on the help of the metaphors with which experiences of the Spirit have been described; second, we shall try to think through once more the relations of the Spirit in its origin, and in the consummated Trinity. We shall start from what the Spirit *effects*, and shall combine this with that which the Holy Spirit *is*, in his constitutive relations to the Father and the Son.

§1 METAPHORS FOR THE EXPERIENCES OF THE SPIRIT

In Chapters IV and V we used a whole series of metaphorical ways of describing the operation of the Spirit. We shall now try to sum up these systematically, in order to relate them to one another in such a way that they complement and deepen one another, though without excluding new and different experiences, and still other metaphors. For this, the dual complementarity for which models already exist would seem to suggest itself.[4] But I shall try instead to arrive at a triadic complementarity, and shall gather together four groups, each comprising three different metaphors:

1. the personal metaphors: the Spirit as lord, as mother and as judge;

2. the formative metaphors: the Spirit as energy, as space and as Gestalt;

3. the movement metaphors: the Spirit as tempest, as fire and as love;

4. the mystical metaphors: the Spirit as source of light, as water and as fertility.

After that I shall try to discover the inner relationships in these metaphors – the relations between subject and force, origin and field of energy, force and space, presence and counterpart. I should like to find patterns for the realities and experiences of life which are expressed in the astounding and still wholly uncomprehended assertion that 'God the Holy Spirit' is 'poured out' on all flesh.

It is hardly necessary to stress that this is not an attempt to arrive at a systematic structure. No limits are set to the power of the imagination to discover metaphors and to devise ways of expressing experience. But we should remember that nowadays the nature images employed – air, light, water, fire, and the rest – are images taken from an impaired life. Ever since Chernobyl, human confidence in nature too has been shaken. In many places the air and the water are poisoned. If we then still take these images to express the operation of the creating, preserving and life-giving Spirit of God, our intention is not romantic; it is critical and therapeutical. When we draw on images taken from biblical and Christian traditions, we are using metaphors derived from the pre-industrial era. We hardly ever choose metaphors drawn from technopolis and the experiences of 'the media landscape' deriving from it. That too is not romantically meant. It expresses the search for primal experiences, and for authentic and personal experiences of life in which the presence of eternity meets us.

1. *Personal Metaphors: Lord – Mother – Judge*

The third article of the Creed calls the Spirit 'the Lord who gives life' (the German version) or (in the more accurate English rendering) 'the Lord and giver of life' (*dominum et vivificantem*). Two metaphors springing from the experience of the Spirit are bound together so that they complement one another: the experience of liberation, and the experience of new life.

Behind the name 'Lord' is the idea of freedom which we find in II Cor. 3.17: 'The Lord is the Spirit; but where the Spirit of the Lord is, there is freedom.'[5] Paul means the Spirit of the resurrection, which takes possession of believers here and now, freeing them from the compulsion of sin and the power of death because it now already mediates to them eternal and imperishable life. In this Spirit they find direct and impregnable access to God, and begin to live with God, and in God. So the name 'Lord' has nothing to do with enslavement. Its context is liberation. This can only be explained from the first commandment: it is the Exodus experience which is Israel's revelation of God. When the Spirit is given the name Lord, Christian experience of the Spirit is being set within Israel's history with Yahweh. The End-time outpouring of the Spirit at 'Pentecost' is understood as a messianic Exodus experience. In the Nicene creed, this continuity is brought out by saying that it is the Holy Spirit 'who spake by the prophets'.[6] According to the messianic understanding of Christians, Israel's 'Lord' is the Holy Spirit, and 'the Old Testament' is the testimony of the history of the Spirit for the future of the kingdom of God; and as this testimony, it is present here and now, and must be heard as determinative for the present. There is nothing 'Old' about it, as the name falsely suggests. If 'Lord' is the name for the experience of liberation and for free life, then the name is misunderstood and brought into disrepute if it is interpreted in terms of masculine notions of rule. So it was good that this name should be complemented by the name of the One who gives and quickens life.

For Paul, it is the raised Christ who has become the 'life-giving Spirit' (I Cor. 15.45). For John, it is the Paraclete, who comforts as a mother comforts and from whom believers are 'born anew' (John 3.3–6). With the Syrian Fathers and Zinzendorf, we have apprehended these experiences through the metaphor of the Mother of life.[7] Human life is born, nurtured and accompanied by the life of the mother. So it is useful to use feminine metaphors for corresponding experiences of the Spirit. The mediaeval expressions for the life-giving Spirit, *fons vitae* and *vita vivificans*, clearly point to this. The rebirth to life corresponds to the conquest of sin, with its separation, and death, with its lack of relation. Freedom and life are the two key facts in experiences of the divine Spirit. Freedom without new life is empty. Life without freedom is dead.

But living freedom and free life can endure only in justice and righteousness. In justice, human freedom ministers to life – the life shared by all living beings. In justice, human life struggles for the freedom of everything that lives, and resists oppression. So justice brings the two key factors freedom and life down to a common denominator, just as, conversely, freedom and life prepare the broad place which the divine justice is to fill, so as to waken the hunger and thirst for righteousness and justice in all created beings. Only justice puts life to rights, and defines the content of liberty through 'the covenant of life'. It is only in justice that life can endure. The experiences of liberation and rebirth through the Spirit are joined by an inward necessity to the experience of the righteousness and justice of God which itself creates justice, justifies and rectifies.[8] The Spirit whom we are told 'convicts the world of its sins' (John 16.8), does not come to condemn but to save (John 3.17). That is why 'to convict of sin' becomes at the same time the conviction of sin's forgiveness.[9]

Because the Spirit is also called 'the Spirit of truth', sin is thought of pre-eminently as the lie, the obscuring of reality, and the deception of other people which is also a self-deception. It is only in truth that life comes to rest on a firm foundation and becomes dependable. This is true for the victims in one way and for the perpetrators in another – it applies to the people who have been deceived in a different way from the deceivers. That is why we distinguished the victims' experience of God's righteousness and justice which creates justice, from the perpetrators' experience of God's atoning and justifying righteousness and justice, although the two things cannot be separated. The two facets of the rectifying justice belong together, just as perpetrators and victims were brought together by the lie, the deception and the act of violence.

According to Old Testament ideas, to establish justice and to rectify are active functions performed by the judge, and this 'judging with righteousness' is expected to be a final and universal act on the part of the Messiah (Isa. 11), on whom 'the Spirit of the Lord rests'; so it is appropriate to call the Holy Spirit 'judge'. In the New Testament the word used for the Spirit is the 'Paraclete' – that is, the advocate and intercessor; but according to the Old Testament idea, the judge is the 'saviour' too, and his justice is a saving justice. In this sense the Spirit of God is invoked as 'Saviour'.

These three experiences, then – the experiences of 'being set free', of 'coming alive' and of being made 'just' – belong together and complement one another, making up the fulness of life in the experience of God; and in the same way the three names given to the source of these experiences also belong together and complement one another: the Spirit as lord, as mother and as judge. Every counter-check will at once discover how one-sided the viewpoint becomes if any one of these facets is left out, or if one term is reduced to something different.[10] This reduction already appears in the German translation of the third article of the Creed: '. . . and in the Lord, the Holy Spirit, who gives life'. The 'Lord' becomes the subject of 'giving life', whereas the Greek and Latin texts distinguish *between* the lordship and the giving of life. The German reduction robs the coming alive from the Spirit of its own special character, and suppresses the Spirit's motherhood. On the other hand, the opposite way of linking the designations is worth consideration: the Holy Spirit – the mother who liberates. Rebirth from the eternal divine life is also a liberation from the separations of sin and from the fate of death. According to the logic of the metaphor, only female life is capable of communicating physical life in the literal sense, not a 'lord' conceived of in masculine terms. The mother who gives life also frees the child for its own independent existence, and keeps that freedom alive through her nurturing commitment. The freedom of 'the liberating lord', on the other hand, as the Exodus motif tells us, is rather freedom from extraneous rule and self-imposed immaturity.

The use of masculine and feminine metaphors for these experiences of the divine Spirit open up different ways of access to human life. Theological language is impoverished if a linguistic strait-jacket is imposed at this point. Hildegard of Bingen has aptly and beautifully presented the multifarious, life-giving, judging, purifying and healing efficacy of the Holy Spirit in all its cosmic breadth:

Spiritus Sanctus vivificans vita,
movens omnia, et radix est in omni creatura,
ac omnia de immunditia abluit,
tergens crimina, et ungit vulnera,
et sic est fulgens ac laudabilis vita,
suscitans et resuscitans omnia.[11]

Finally, it is striking that these three metaphors should trace back experience of the operation of the divine Spirit to determining subjects who are thought of in personal terms. It is true that 'lord', 'mother' and 'judge' are functions, not personal names, but in each of them a transcendent subject is named for the efficacies which are immanently experienced. Because the experiences are contingent and cannot be 'acquired' or 'made', the Spirit is ascribed subjective freedom: 'The Spirit blows were it wills.' The metaphors are always born out of inferences drawn from these experiences – inferences about the things which allow themselves to be experienced in these particular ways.

The experience of freedom which we have not 'acquired' for our-selves, but which has 'befallen' us, lets us infer the transcendent power of liberation. The experience of the new life given to us lets us infer the womb or source of life from which that new life has come. The righteousness which puts us right lets us infer the just Judge who has acted on us. But this means that these descriptions for the divine Spirit apply only to his subjective relation to what he effects; they are not applicable to the inter-personal relations in which he himself exists.

2. Formative Metaphors: Energy – Space – Gestalt

I am giving the name 'formative metaphors' to the descriptions of the divine Spirit as energy, as space and as Gestalt, because these images are not talking about agents and their acts. They describe forces which impose a profound impress. We can observe these in nature too. Because they only express particular aspects of the experience of the Spirit in any given case, it is important to relate them to one another as complements. In themselves, they are even less able than the individual personal metaphors to express the operation of the divine Spirit adequately.

The experience of the divine Spirit as an *energy* and *vital power* goes back to the Hebrew *ruach* concept. This experience of the Spirit does not release those who are touched by it from this earth and their own earthly bodies, so that their souls can soar into the realms of spirits. It fills them with a new vitality entirely and wholly, body and soul.[12] We sense in ourselves the personal dynamic given to us, and then perceive it in everything else that lives. The experience of this vital power is as protean as living things themselves; and yet for all that it is a *single* vital power, which has gathered everything living into a great community of life, and sustains it there. The community of Christ's people can be a model for this, since it lives in the diversity of its different charismata and energies, and is united in the fellowship of the one energy of the Spirit – it *can*, that is, be such a model, provided that it relates itself to the diversity and the unity of everything living in the cosmos, and does not separate itself, withdraw into itself, and make itself poorer than it is.

We are mentioning the image of the charismatic community of Christ here so that we may ask about the forms and configurations assumed by the divine Spirit's torrent of energy. Neither in physics nor in love does energy exist as a pure thrust towards life. Through their frequencies, the electromagnetic fields acquire symmetrical structures which transpose their times and spaces into vibrations. There is no such thing as formless matter. Electrons, atoms, molecules and the higher structures are arranged in open systems. Open systems exist from the fluctuating exchange of energy. This does not mean that a calculable cosmos determines everything. There is chaos in nature too. Cosmos and chaos are evidently not merely destructively related to one another; they are creatively related as well. If we think about the personal levels, we find – in spite of all the dissimilarity – analogous energizing rhythms and fields of force in what goes on in relationships. What is 'between' people on the emotional level is like a field of attraction and repulsion – an order that soothes us and does us good, and a deranging chaos. The reciprocity of an energizing stimulus and an irritating sense of derangement frees new energies and awakens unguessed-of vitality; and this inspires life with new forms of expression. Joy in other people can be 'infectious'. That is the *vita vivificans*, and ultimately speaking all human beings lead a *vita vivificata*, since life is stimulated life *and* stimulating life, in living community. The counter-check is easy. If in the dynamic field between people only repulsion is conveyed and only rejection is experienced, then life is diminished and impaired, because it is thrown back on itself. The vital impulses then turn against themselves or wither away.

The experience of God is closely bound up with the experience of life between human beings, because the one is mediated through the other, because most of the images for experience of God are taken from the sphere of human relations and, finally but not least important, because experience of God is given in, with and beneath experience with other people.[13] To feel the closeness of the living God is to experience new vitality. To believe and sense the closeness of the risen Christ means that body and soul are lifted up by 'the power of the resurrection'. The mystics – especially the women mystics – have repeatedly described this closeness of God as illuminating and flowing waves of energy. Surrounded, flooded and interpenetrated by divine streams of energy, body and soul awaken like flowers in the spring and become fruitful – that is, they themselves become life that gives life.[14] Jeremiah and John already described the experience of the Spirit in just this way: God is 'the fountain of living water' (Jer. 17.13; John 4.14). If a person believes 'out of his heart [AV: out of his belly] shall flow rivers of living water' (John 7.38) –

that is to say, people touched by the Spirit will pass on the energies of the life that gives life, and apparently not only from soul to soul, but through their bodies too. The bodily zones that radiate energy are the glowing face, the shining eyes, the speaking mouth, the play of features and the gestures which show affection and commitment. It is these which supply and charge the metaphors for the life-giving, stimulating and electrifying closeness of God in the Spirit.

If it is to develop, every life needs its corresponding *living space*.[15] Vital power and energy are not enough by themselves. That is why the creation story already tells us that spaces for living were prepared first of all, before living things were created and put into them – the spaces of heaven and earth, air, land and water. The living spaces are the outward sides. They provide the spheres and 'elbow-room' for the different living things, and are just as important as the living things themselves. Indeed living things can even be viewed as the inner side of the spaces, and as the bodies that move in them – their embodiment, as it were. Modern, atomizing and individualizing thinking has viewed these living spaces as subsidiary, or has disregarded them, the intention being to integrate other living things into our own living space – the space of human beings – so that they can be utilized for human purposes. But anyone who destroys the living spaces of other living things destroys these things themselves, by destroying their chances for living. The progressive destruction of nature by modern society makes this as obvious as the 'burnt earth' strategy used in modern warfare. Economic competition too can mean disposing of people by 'cutting the ground' from under their feet. These negative examples show the importance of living space for the existence and development of the living thing. Between people it is essential to concede personal liberty. This liberty is given to children when parents withdraw – it is given through the trust which links affection with respect – it is given in the love whose desire is to set free, not to possess. In the warp and weft of social relationships we find the freedom to move freely, and in these free spaces we discover our potentiality for development. The free spaces sustain our freedom, and invite us to our full unfolding. In a merely competitive society, which guarantees personal liberty but offers no free spaces, personal liberty degenerates into a wolf-like, predatory liberty, and into the 'liberty' of the unemployed and homeless. That is the misery of a 'free world' which doubtless respects subjective liberties, but not the free spaces in social life.

Experience of God is bound up with these experiences between people in many different ways. According to Israel's seminal experience, experience of God means experiencing liberation from slavery in the Exodus, and experiencing the promised land into which it entered: 'Now the Lord has made room for us, and we shall be fruitful in the land' (Gen. 26.22). There is no liberation without the land of liberty. There is no liberation without the day of liberty which is the sabbath. Even the personal experience of God uttered in the Psalms embraces freedom from these two sides: 'Thou hast set my feet in a broad place' (Ps. 31.8). The divine Spirit is experienced as the Lord who sets free, and as the free space in which 'there is no more cramping'. That is why it can also be said that 'Thou encompasseth me from every side' (Ps. 139.5); and people who have this experience know that they are kept safe and set free in the broad place of the Spirit in which they can breathe deeply and unfurl their potentialities.

Out of the energies of life, and in the free spaces of life, the multifarious *configurations of life* come into being. A configuration or Gestalt is 'minted form which takes shape as it lives', to use a phrase of Goethe's.[16] In its Gestalt, the inward and the outward sides of a living being arrive at equilibrium. The contours of a Gestalt restrict, but its frontiers are open, communicative frontiers. That is why the individual configurations of life build communities for living with other living things, through an exchange of energy that sustains the life of them all. The wealth of species in nature, and the wealth of configurations in the species, show the wealth of possibilities in life itself.

In the human sphere, the individual Gestalt is made possible and given its impress by inner genetic conditions and by the frame of reference imposed by ecology and cultural history. Defined more closely, it is social conditions, and in particular the individual biography, which form the configuration of our lives. In the personal sphere, the important thing is always the way in which we mediate between our expectations of life and our experiences of life. The configuration or Gestalt of our body, soul and character is an expression of all the conditions we have mentioned, and yet in all these things the Gestalt is something unmistakably individual, and undeducible from the factors that contribute to it.

Experience of life in the experience of God also gives us form or Gestalt. If the experience of God is linked with life in the community of Christ, then it is never a general religious feeling or merely what Schleiermacher called 'a feeling and taste for the infinite'. The discipleship of Christ is a practical, personal way of living. On this path of discipleship we are 'formed' by God's Spirit – that is we are 'made like in form' to Christ, the 'first-born' of God's children (Rom. 8.29). We are 'conformed' to his messianic life and his healing, radiating, and loving way of living. We are conformed to his path of suffering in our conflicts with the powers of destruction. In his Spirit we already participate here and now in his resurrection, 'as dying, and behold we live' (II Cor. 6.9), and expect one day to be made 'like in form to his glorious body' (Phil. 3.21). Dietrich Bonhoeffer called this 'Christ's taking form in us'.[17] We would add: it comes about through the operation and guidance of the Holy Spirit.

Experience of the Spirit is experience of the divine life which makes our human life something truly living. That is why when we talk about the Spirit as vital energy, as living space and as the Gestalt of every community for living, these metaphors belong together. No one of them is enough by itself, but taken together they tell us something about the mystery of life – created life, life-giving life, and holy life. We can only talk about this life in metaphors such as these, because we are in it, and it is in us, and it is inexhaustible as long as we are here.

3. Movement Metaphors: Tempest – Fire – Love

The early Christian experience of Pentecost is presented with metaphors about the rushing of a great wind, and a flaming fire: 'And suddenly a sound came from heaven like the rushing of a mighty wind, and it filled all the house, and there appeared to them tongues as of fire . . . and they were all filled with the Holy Spirit and began to proclaim in other tongues, as the Spirit gave them utterance' (Acts 2.2–4). I am calling these metaphors *movement metaphors* because they express the feeling of being seized and possessed by something overwhelmingly powerful, and the beginning of a new movement in ourselves. They describe a movement that sweeps people off their feet, which possesses and excites not only the conscious levels but the unconscious depths too, and sets the men and women affected themselves on the move towards unsuspected new things. Deeply moved, we ourselves move, and go out of ourselves. The primal image is the Pentecost story, which tells how the experience of the

Spirit turns a crowd of Jesus' intimidated disciples into free witnesses to Jesus Christ, apostles of the gospel who carry the tidings 'to the ends of the earth' (Acts 1.8). I am relating the movement metaphors of tempest and fire to the experience of the life-affirming, life-giving love of God – that is, to the presence of the Holy Spirit.

The image of the *tempest* picks up once more the original meaning of Yahweh's *ruach*.[18] The divine is the living compared with the dead, and what is moving compared with the things that are petrified and rigid. God's Spirit is the breath of God's life, which gives life to human beings and animals. In the Old Testament, experiences of God are often presented with pictures of the rushing of wind or water. 'Thou makest the winds thy messengers, fire and flame thy ministers' (Ps. 104.4). 'And behold, the glory of the God of Israel came from the east; and the sound of his coming was like the sound of many waters; and the earth shone with his glory' (Ezek. 43.2). Elijah's experience of God on Mount Horeb is described in I Kings 19.11ff. with the help of all the natural elements: a mighty wind went before the Lord, tearing apart the mountains and breaking the rocks asunder. Then came earthquake and fire 'but the Lord was not in them'. After the fire came 'the voice of a hovering silence' (Buber's translation). When Elijah heard that, he covered his face and came forward and the Lord spoke to him. It is a comparable experience of God which the early Christian Pentecost story describes with 'the sound from heaven like the rushing of a mighty wind'.

From time immemorial, *fire* has been associated in many religions with the experience of God. It is especially central in Zoroaster. In the Old Testament, fire often accompanies the supernatural visions of God's glory. People experience the divine light like a devouring fire. For Moses, the burning bush which was not consumed was the sign of the presence of the holy God (Ex. 3.2). God went before the wandering people in a cloud by day and in a pillar of fire by night (Num. 9.15). The cloud in the form of fire covered the tabernacle, which was God's presence in the Exodus.[19] If we are eager about something we say that we are 'fired' with enthusiasm. Like fire, enthusiasm 'kindles' enthusiasm. Fire warms us, and we pass on the warmth. It lights us up, and we begin to shine. It consumes us, and we become a consuming flame for other people.

God's essential nature itself is described as a 'devouring fire' (Deut. 4.24), for he is a *passionate God*.[20] His 'jealous wrath' is like fire (Ps. 79.5; Ps. 89.46; Zeph. 1.18; Heb. 12.29). The awesome and mysterious God is graphically described in Ps. 18.8: 'Smoke went up from his nostrils, and devouring fire from his mouth; glowing coals flamed forth from him.' The God personified in these tremendous terms is the One who frees men and women from the fetters of hell and death. When the fire is called a 'devouring fire', it is describing *God's wrath*. But this wrath of God's is not the antithesis of his love. It is nothing other than his love itself, repulsed and wounded. It is not that the passionate love for the life of what he has created, and for his human children, is now transformed into deadly anger. On the contrary, this love assumes the form of such anger so that it may remain love. Only the withdrawal of God from his creation would be deadly. But his anger contains within itself his persevering and enduring love, and in his judgment is his grace. That is why in 'the devouring fire' of his anger the ardour of his love is manifested and experienced.

According to the Pentecost experience, the 'flaming fire' of the Holy Spirit makes those it touches incandescent in the presence of God. According to Luke 12.49, Jesus came 'to cast fire upon the earth'; but this does not mean the apocalyptic fire that consumes the world. It means the dawn of the kingdom of God, through the outpouring of the Holy Spirit on all flesh. This is what the messianic promise put into the mouth of John the Baptist is talking about too: 'He will baptize you with the Holy Spirit and with fire' (Matt. 3.11; Luke 3.16, following Mal. 3.2–3). It is the fire of purification in which everything is reforged: an image for the new creation of the world.

The images of the tempest and the raging fire are also images for the experience of the *eternal love* which creates life and energizes it from within, so that life can live. Why is love 'strong as death'? Because 'its embers are fiery' and it can itself be called 'a flame of the Lord' (S. of Sol. 8.6). If human love can become an experience of God, then the experience of God can be described as the experience of the divine love. Joy in one's own existence awakens in the experience of being loved. Human love and divine love are not identical, but the one can happen and confront us in the other. That is why human love becomes the 'real' symbol for eternal love – real in the sense that symbol and the thing symbolized partake of the same essence. The pentecostal hymns beseech the Holy Spirit to 'kindle a flame of sacred love' in us.[20a] This shows how close the fire metaphor is to love, and to the Holy Spirit. Hildegard of Bingen wrote:

> Fire thou and Comforter,
> Life of all creation's life,
> Holy art thou, quickening all forms of being.

> O ignis Spiritus Paracliti,
> vita vitae omnis creaturae,
> sanctus es vivificando formas.

She also directly called the Holy Spirit 'fire Spirit' and 'firebrand of love':

> O ignee Spiritus, laus tibi sit . . .
> O ignis caritatis . . . [21]

4. Mystical Metaphors: Light – Water – Fertility

The divine Spirit can be described as 'flowing light', 'living water' and 'fertility', and I am calling these descriptions *mystical metaphors*, because they are concepts charged by mystical experience, and because they express so intimate a union between the divine Spirit and what is human, and between the human spirit and what is divine, that it is hardly possible to distinguish the two. We shall again relate these images to each other, so that they complement one another in a meaningful way. The simplest prototype for this meaningful interplay is the plant, which builds up its life and becomes fruitful from the light of the sun and the water of the earth, through its leaves and through its roots.

The light metaphor for the divine Being is age-old. It is especially stressed in the biblical writings, although the sun is never turned into a deity. 'God is my light' (Ps. 27.1; Micah 7.8; I John 1.5). He is 'the Father of light' (James 1.17). Light is 'the garment' that he wears (Ps. 104.2). 'He dwells in unapproachable light' (I Tim. 6.16). This tells us that the radiance of the divine glory is for creaturely being unendurable, and yet that all creatures reflect it, and it that 'the light of God's countenance' shining on them (Ps. 4.6), is their salvation. It is just this shining radiance of God's glory which is said to have shone on the face of Christ (II Cor. 4.6; John 1.9; 8.12). But the same is said of the gospel too, and of the people who witness to it through their lives (Matt. 5.14). And it is this same radiance that is attributed to the Holy Spirit, who illuminates believers so that they are 'in the light', 'walk in the light' and 'abide in the light' (Eph. 5.8; I John 1.7; 2.9f.). Of course 'light' means the enlightenment of the eyes, for it is with the eyes that we see. But what we see is only that which shows itself to us. That is why in our experience God is both the object of our knowing and its source: 'In thy light do we see light' (Ps. 36.9). Because both the knowing and the knowledge proceed from God, in this context he also called a 'living fountain' (Ps. 36.9). This divine fountain of light illuminates the whole of creation, so that in its light we perceive what things are, and who we ourselves truly are. According to the mediaeval view, when the Creator floods his creation with his light, it appears as it is in his eyes, and we again see it in such a light that we can affirm and love it.

To say the same thing without metaphors: reality is characterized by a divine rationality, for it is created according to God's *ratio*, and his Spirit is within it. Our human rationality is capable of perceiving reality as far as this is intelligible. In the context of the created world, this means that created beings are able to know one another within their limits with their own rationality, because a divine rationality precedes them. If there were no congruences, however fragmentary, between the perceiving reason and the perceived reality, there could be no perceptions. But for finite human rationality, the reality of the world is of transcendent depth, since for human rationality the divine rationality is like 'a light that can never be drained to the lees'.[22] We have called this the concept of immanent transcendence.

But the divine light means more than merely perception through the eyes. It also means the streams of energy which we cannot see but sense, and which flood through us, transposing our life into vibrations and resonances. The divine light of the Spirit is not merely the cold light of rational knowledge. It is also the warm light of loving perception.[23] According to Mechthild of Magdeburg, the experience of 'the flowing light of the Godhead' is the beatific experience of the love of God.[24] The divine love draws the Deity out of itself, so to speak, so that the energies of the divine life brim over from the Godhead on to created beings, to transfigure them and make them eternally alive.[25] In this light and this love, the divine Spirit is so entirely all-embracing presence that he cannot be perceived as counterpart at all: we are in the Spirit, and the Spirit is in us.

The special thing about the metaphor of light for the experience of the Spirit is the fluid transition from the source of light to the emanating beam, and then to the radiance shed. It is one and the same light in the source, in the beam and in the shining. The difference is in the emanation. It would take us no further to reintroduce at this point the distinction between Creator and creature, eternity and time, infinity and finitude. In pneumatology we have to take up the concept of emanation, which has been falsely denigrated as neoplatonic; for through emanation, created being will be 'deified',[26] and God is glorified in what he has created.

The *water* metaphor is generally associated with the images of source, fountain and well. What is meant is the water which comes out of the earth. Whereas the light metaphor describes the operation of the Spirit 'from above', the metaphor of the source, spring, fountain or well sees it as coming 'from below'. The union of light and water is a necessity of life. Where light, water and warmth come together, the meadows become green and the trees blossom and bear fruit. In the Old Testament God himself is called 'the fountain of living waters' (Jer. 2.13; 17.13), or 'the fountain of life' (Ps. 36.9). 'The voice of the Father speaks in the song of praise: "I am an overflowing well which no one can drain dry" ', wrote Mechthild of Magdeburg.[27] In the Greek doctrine of the Trinity, God the Father was called 'the wellspring of the Godhead'. Out of God, blessing and the energies of life spill over on to the whole of creation (Ps. 65.9); from this fountain people receive 'grace upon grace' (John 1.16). In his conversation with the Samaritan woman, Jesus talks about the 'living water', using the remarkable turn of phrase: 'The water that I shall give him will become in him a spring of water welling up to eternal life' (4.14).[28] The 'well of life' is not in the next world, and not in the church's font: it is in human beings themselves. If they receive the life-giving water, they themselves become the wellspring of this water for other people. With this as background, Meister Eckhart painted the picture of God – the Spirit of life – as a great underground river which rises to the surface in the springs and fountainheads.[29] The image of the spring of water has two other important aspects as well: the water of life comes 'for nothing', and it is there 'for all' who are thirsty (Isa. 55.1ff.; Rev. 21.6).

The bond between the image and the Holy Spirit is symbolized by baptism. People are born again 'from water and Spirit' so that they may see the kingdom of God (John 3.5). If we do not take the birth 'out of the water' to be a merely fortuitous, outward sign of the inward new birth, then the water of baptism surely means not merely well-water, but also the nurturing waters out of which the new-born child comes. The symbolism of the fonts used in the ancient church frequently shows this motherhood of the life-giving Spirit. But this certainly does not exhaust the symbolism of the well-water. It reveals its meaning to us in the degree to which we 'thirst' for life and righteousness (Matt. 5.6).

There are many links in our language between light and water. We talk about sources of light and floodlight; about light streaming from a door or window; about light waves and ocean waves; and so forth. So it is just as appropriate to experience the operation of the divine Spirit as a 'flowing' or a 'flooding' light as it is to talk about the 'outpouring' of the Spirit on all flesh. In this metaphor too, it is one and the same water which wells up out of its source, allowing created being to live and be fertile. From time immemorial, the Roman fountain, which spills its water from basin to basin, has been an image for the doctrine of emanation.

Finally, the image of *fertility* emerges with inner logic from the link between the light and the water metaphors. As an image for the experience of God, it comes from the Old Testament: 'I am like an evergreen cypress, from me comes all your fruit' (Hos. 14.8). The 'tree of life' is a favourite expression in Hebrew. The divine Wisdom is a 'tree of life' (Prov. 3.18). Hope that has been fulfilled and 'a gentle tongue' are called 'a tree of life' (Prov. 13.12; 15.4). According to the Yahwist's creation account, a single 'tree of life' stood in the middle of paradise (Gen. 2.9). We meet this tree again at the end, as 'the tree of life' which will stand in God's paradise (Rev. 2.7) and in the city of Jerusalem which is to come down from heaven (Rev. 22.2) – an evergreen and uninterruptedly fruitful tree which gives eternal life. In John 15, Christ is compared with the vine, and believers with its grapes: 'He who abides in me, and I in him, he it is that bears much fruit' (15.5). According to Gal. 5.22, it is the Spirit whose 'fruits' are 'love, joy, peace, patience, kindness, goodness, faithfulness . . .' Because life is conceived by other life, and because it is life that makes life living, fertility is the quintessence of life in all its livingness.

Hildegard of Bingen chose 'fertility' as a way of expressing her experience of God, and she believed that the primal creation was always green and vital. It was only with the coming of sin that a kind of winter descended on creation, making it freeze and dry up. But

when the Spirit of flowing light and living water is experienced, the
eschatological springtime of the new creation of all things begins,
and the rebirth of the whole of life. So experience of the Spirit is the
experience of a new vitality which finds its truth in community with
the living God. In the experience of the Spirit, men and women sense
the creative breath of God and wake up, like nature in the spring.
What is eternal life? Meister Eckhart tells us that one of the attributes
of eternity is 'that in it Being and being-young are one'.[30]

In the mystical metaphors, the distance between a transcendent
subject and its immanent work is ended. The distinctions between
causes and effects disappear. In the metaphors of light, water and
fertility, the divine and the human are joined in an organic cohesion.
The result is a perichoretic interpenetration: you in me – I in you.
The divine becomes the all-embracing presence in which what is
human can fruitfully unfold. This implies a still closer relationship
than the one suggested by the concept of emanation.

§2 THE STREAMING PERSONHOOD OF THE DIVINE SPIRIT

Starting from the metaphors used to express the operation of the
Spirit and human experience of the Spirit, we shall now try to deduce
the contours of his personhood. This is only a deductive knowing,
derived from the operation experienced, not a direct knowing face
to face. But neither is it a speculative intrusion into the depths of the
triune Deity in an attempt to understand the primordial relationships
of the Spirit who proceeds from the Father and radiates from the
Son. In the primordial trinitarian relationships, the Spirit must appear
simply as he is. There, it is of course true that only the Father knows
the Spirit whom he breathes out, and only the Son knows the Spirit
whom he receives. But in the efficacies experienced and in the energies
perceived, this primal personhood of the Spirit is concealed from us,
and we paraphrase the mystery of his life with many metaphors. And
yet the operation of the Spirit is different from the acts in creation
which we ascribe to the Father, and different from the reconciling
sufferings which we ascribe to the Son; and from this difference in
kind of his efficacy and his energies, the unique character of his
personhood is revealed. If all God's activity in the world is pneumatic,
and hence every human experience of God too (since according to
the ancient 'trinitarian order' the Father always acts through the Son/
Logos in the Spirit, and the Son too acts in the name of the Father

through the Spirit who rests on him), then in the operation of the Spirit we experience the operation of God himself, and all the metaphors used for the Holy Spirit are metaphors for God in his coming to us, and in his presence with us. An understanding of the unique personhood of the Spirit is therefore decisive for the understanding of God in general.

When we call the Holy Spirit Lord, Mother or Judge, we are distinguishing between a determining subject and the acts which proceed from that subject. The subject remains transcendent to his acts. This means that he is also free in what he does, and his acts in their efficacies are experienced by us as contingent.

But then we of course have to differentiate. The 'Lord' is truly transcendent. As the Exodus happening from which he takes his name shows, he intervenes in Israel's history from outside, marvellously and 'with a strong arm', saving his people from their persecutors. The 'Mother' acts differently. She does not act outwards. She carries her child within herself, communicates her life to it, and gives birth to it with pain, so that she may hold it on her lap with joy. She is the archetypal image for the *vita vivificans*. The child's life grows in her, and then emerges from her. It is a giving of life in closest personal participation, with pain and with joy. The life that is born is life of her life and flesh of her flesh. It is a life differentiated from hers, a life of its own which grows up to autonomy; but the relationships are quite different from the relation between an author and his book, or an artist and his work. After it has been born, a life remains in life's relationships, whereas the work has to be able to exist on its own. Even in the case of the Judge who 'establishes justice' for the wretched and 'justifies' sinners through atonement, we found a profound inward participation through his solidarity and his atoning intervention; for it is out of the surrender of his own life that the justice emerges which gives new life to those without rights. Here the reciprocal operation of act and suffering can be clearly seen. The judge justifies by suffering the injustice. From this a shared life comes into being which becomes the source of inexhaustible vital energies. That, at least, is the way Paul experienced it: 'If God is for us, who can be against us? . . . Nothing can separate us from the love of God which is in Christ Jesus' (Rom. 8.31, 39). The notion of the determining subject and the act is complemented by the concepts of the one who gives birth to life, and the one who puts life right.

The formative metaphors and the mystical images paraphrase the experiences of the Spirit with ideas of emanation and perichoresis because they stress the immanence of God and attach no great importance to the aloofness of his transcendence. They describe a presence of God in which God as counterpart is not yet – or is no longer – discernible. The experience of 'flowing light' of course does not deny the transcendent source of light, and the experience of the 'living water' does not forget the inexhaustible wellspring; but the important thing is not the distinction between source and river. The whole weight lies on the connection. In this experience of God, the Spirit is known as a 'broad place' and a 'flooding light' in which those touched by it can discover themselves and develop. But we cannot make whatever encompasses us an object without moving out of it. We do not see the eyes we see with. We cannot perceive the place where we are standing unless we leave it. The same is true of experience of the Spirit. The Spirit is in us and round about us, and we are in him. In the Spirit, God is for us pure presence. In order to perceive him as 'object', we have to distance ourselves from his presence. But in the presence of the Spirit, can we perceive the Spirit as counterpart? Apparently the Spirit allows himself to be known as presence *and* counterpart, so that it is *only* in his presence that we can perceive him as counterpart at all: 'In thy light do we see light.'

There are analogies in the relations between people. A child grows *in* its mother and only become a counterpart *outside* the mother once it has been born and its umbilical cord has been cut. It experiences the mother first of all as 'encompassing presence',[31] before she becomes a 'person' and a recognizable counterpart, and thus a finite human individual. Lovers experience each other as counterpart and presence. Their subjectivity 'becomes soluble' in their relationships, and concentrates itself once again in their own individual being, and it is in this rhythm that their intersubjective shared life emerges. In mutual love they arrive at one another and themselves. They mutually come close to one another and to themselves. These experiences of personhood are different from the experiences of the solitary subject acting on objects, or from 'the individual and his property' as Max Stirner puts it. In the flow between counterpart and presence, a personhood comes into being with permeable frontiers, in energy-charged relationships. Selfhood is not arrived at by way of demarcations and differentiations. It comes to its full flowering through the power of life-giving relationships. 'Self-sufficiency' and 'self-dispersion' are simply frontier marks. Between 'closed' and 'open' lie the wide fields in which *im*pressions are absorbed and processed, and *ex*pressions are found for experiences.

If we take up this analogy as a way of understanding the experience of God, we then perceive the personhood of the divine Spirit in the flow between his presence and his counterpart, his energies and his essential nature. It is therefore no wonder that the people affected should talk about the Spirit as power and as person, as energy and as space, as wellspring and as light. This is not cloudiness in human thinking, or 'anonymity' on the divine side; it is wholly appropriate.

When the Spirit himself 'is poured out' on all flesh, this is a self-emptying through which he becomes present to all flesh in the force of his energies. Once men and women enter into his presence, in his light they perceive God, the fountain of light. According to the prophetic promise, the Spirit does not merely bring life and righteousness. He also brings the knowledge of God to all flesh. In the practice of Christian experience of the Spirit, this has led to a threefold prayer addressed to the Holy Spirit himself:

1. The *epikleses*: like most of the Pentecost hymns, these are simply prayers for 'the coming of the Holy Spirit' – that is, they are pleas for his parousia, his all-comprehending presence: 'Veni Creator Spiritus.' They are 'Maranatha' prayers. In this plea for the presence of the Spirit, the petitioners open themselves for the influence of his energies, for a new heart, and for the renewal of the face of the earth (Ps. 51.10f.; Ps. 104.30). The cry from the depths for the life-giving Spirit is already a sigh of the Spirit itself, and is one of his first signs of life.[32]

2. According to the ancient Christian order, it is in the Spirit that the Father is invoked through the Son, so that in this ancient Christian conception the Spirit carries prayers through the Son to the Father. What is important about this idea is that when people cry out in pain or in gratitude, they are then not just invoking a far-off God in heaven. Their cries are uttered in the presence of God on earth, and in their own situation. They cry to God, and experience that it is the Spirit of God himself who cries out in them and who, when they fall dumb, intercedes for them with groans that cannot be uttered.

3. In the experienced presence of the Spirit, individual and particular petitions to the Holy Spirit are then uttered too – prayers for the outpouring of his gifts, and for his charismatic endowment of life. This too is expressed in the ancient Whitsun hymn: 'Come down O Love divine . . .'

Boethius, as we saw (p. 268) defined 'person' as *'rationalis naturae individua substantia'*. According to what we have said here, we have to find a different definition for the personhood of the Holy Spirit, as it is experienced by men and women in its efficacies:

(*a*) It is not indivisible; it is self-communicating.

(*b*) It is not a 'self-existence' (*substantia*), cut off from all relationships; it is a social being, rich in relation and capable of relation.

(*c*) It does not manifest rational nature alone; it is also the disclosure of the eternal divine life, as wellspring of the life of all created being.

This brings us to the following definition:

The personhood of God the Holy Spirit is the loving, self-communicating, out-fanning and out-pouring presence of the eternal divine life of the triune God.[33]

§3 THE TRINITARIAN PERSONHOOD OF THE HOLY SPIRIT

It is one thing to work back from the operation of the Holy Spirit to his essential nature; it is quite another to perceive his essential nature from his constitutive relationships. The deduction from the deed to the doer of it begins with human experiences of the Spirit, and draws conclusions about his transcendent origin. But this knowledge is always an indirect knowledge, and remains tied to the experiences which are its point of departure. Only the energies of the Holy Spirit can be perceived from the Spirit's operation, not his Being as it exists in itself and is in itself. If we depend on the experiences of his operation, it will never be possible to do more than paraphrase the nature of the Spirit by way of metaphors. It was in this way that we arrived at the singular personhood of the Spirit as *presence and counterpart*.[34] But the question about the nature of the Holy Spirit cannot be answered only by pointing in this way to what he does.[35] It is true that scholars like to maintain that it is the unique character of biblical language to answer the question about God's Being by pointing to his acts. But this is true only of the stories about the divine history. It does not apply to the praise of God, and even less to the Being of God in the sabbath.

The nature of the Holy Spirit is perceived only in his relationships to the other persons of the Trinity, who are 'of like nature'.[36] His trinitarian inter-subjectivity illuminates his subjectivity, because his subjectivity is constituted by his inter-subjectivity. In his trinitarian inter-personhood he is person, in that as person he stands over against the other persons, and as person acts on them. With this we enter a different level from the level of experience, efficacy, and the inference about the primordial Trinity drawn from the economic Trinity in its work for salvation. But can we enter upon this level at all? Do not all our attempts to explore even the very depths of the Godhead remain fettered by our existence and our modes of experience, and therefore bound to the revelations of God? But what then actually happens when we forget ourselves and in doxological ecstasy praise and glorify the triune God for his own sake? Are we not then departing from his operations and adoring his essential nature? What we revere and love for itself, rests for us in itself and exists in itself even without us.

Let us try to approach the inner-trinitarian personhood of the Spirit with all due caution about speculation and over-hasty dogmatizations. We shall draw here on the previous doctrines of the Trinity held in the Western and Eastern churches, taking these as flexible conceptual frameworks. By relating them to various *movements* in the history of God, we shall relieve them of the rigid *in*flexibility they have assumed in the history of dogma.[37] We can then relate them to one another as complements, thereby resolving cruxes which have up to now seemed insoluble. We shall abandon the conceptual framework used hitherto – the pattern of essence and revelation, being and act, immanent and economic Trinity – because these dualities prove to be too wide-meshed a grid.[38] Instead we shall work with the patterns of the *monarchical Trinity*, the *historical Trinity*, the *eucharistic Trinity* and the *doxological Trinity*.[39]

1. The Monarchical Concept of the Trinity

The monarchical concept of the Trinity was developed pre-eminently in the West. It is meant to be applied to the economy of salvation, not to be used in an inner-trinitarian sense, as in the East. The starting point here is the event of the self-revelation (Barth's phrase) or self-communication (Rahner) of the One God: the unity of God precedes the triunity. It is a single movement in which the One God reveals himself through himself and communicates himself to men and women. This movement proceeds from the Father through the Son in the Spirit, and spreads out in creation through the manifold energies of the Spirit. The monarchical structure can be seen in all God's works: the Father always acts through the Son in the Spirit.

The Father creates, reconciles and redeems the world through the Son in the power of the Spirit. All activity proceeds from the Father, the Son is always its mediator, and the Holy Spirit the mediation. The Father is the revealer, the Son the revelation, and the Spirit God's revealedness.[40] The Son is God's self-revelation and also his self-communication.[41] As the Father's other Self, he is wholly related to the Father, and the same is correspondingly true of the Spirit. In this unified divine movement, the Spirit appears directly as 'Spirit of the Son' and mediates through the Son as 'Spirit of the Father'. But he himself is nothing other than the efficacy of the Son and Father. The Spirit is gift, not giver. Consequently everything that happens from God's side happens in the Spirit, every divine efficacy is effected by the Spirit. The divine energies flow from the Spirit into the world. Understood, then, as 'God's efficacious presence', no independent personhood can be perceived in the Spirit over against the Father or the Son.

According to this monarchical pattern for the Trinity, the 'economic Trinity' (as is always stressed) is bound to correspond to the 'immanent Trinity' – indeed must be identical with it; for if God is truth, then God corresponds to himself in his revelation, thereby making his revelation dependable.[42] How else are people to trust God's promises unless God himself promises his faithfulness in history and unless he is in his essential nature 'the faithful one'? For the sake of the dependability of revelation, we have to assume theologically that God is in himself as he appears to us: 'God remains faithful for he cannot deny himself' (II Tim. 2.13).

It follows from this that the 'trinitarian deduction'[43] from the revelation which is experienced and believed finds just that in God which revelation presupposes. God is 'beforehand in himself' (Barth's phrase*) what he is afterwards in his revelation. But what precedes revelation as its foundation is not 'the immanent Trinity'. If the doctrine of the Trinity describes only 'the transcendent primordial ground of salvation history', then it must infer the transcendent 'primordial ground' from the historical operations, and can naturally find nothing in the 'primordial ground' that fails to correspond to salvation history. This, however, means that 'the immanent Trinity' is related to 'the economic Trinity', and identified with it. But if this is the conclusion, then there is in actual fact no 'immanent Trinity'

* The English translation of Barth's *CD* uses the phrase 'antecedently in himself' [Trans.].

at all which could exist independently in itself. There is only a Trinity open and prepared for revelation and salvation. I am calling this the 'primordial Trinity'.

If in the history of salvation the Holy Spirit after Christ's cross and resurrection proceeds from the Father and from the Son, or from the Father through the Son, then this cannot be any different in God as he was 'beforehand in himself', or in 'the transcendent primordial ground' of this event. If we infer the primordial *processio* from the *missio* of the Spirit that has been experienced, we find only the correspondence; but then we have not yet talked about the Holy Spirit as he exists in himself in his relation to the Father and the Son; we have viewed him only as he shows himself to be as 'primordial ground' for salvation. But this means that the trinitarian inference does not take us outside the economy of salvation at all. We can infer the transcendent primordial ground, or God 'as he is beforehand in himself'; but this still does not bring us within reach of what is called the 'immanent Trinity'; we still invariably arrive only at the Trinity which destines itself, and opens itself, for the economy of salvation. We always reach only the 'God for us' and discern nothing of 'God in himself'.

In this monarchical divine movement we cannot know God directly in his essential nature, as God knows himself in his Word, and as the Son knows the Father.[44] This is not due to God's inaccessibility. It is due to the power of the divine movement into which we are impelled or drawn when we experience God's self-communication. In this divine movement we have God at our back, as it were, and in front of us the world, as field for the proclamation and for acts performed in God's Spirit. God is the one, single, mighty subject. He is sovereign in his revelation. Even our knowledge of his self-revelation is determined by him that is, through his Spirit – since he *permits* himself to be known to us, *gives* himself to be known, as German puts it. We might also call this monarchical trinitarian pattern the 'identity model', because it stresses the experience of identity: God's essential nature *in* his operations, God's Being *in* his revelation, God's revelation *in* our perception of it, God's Spirit *in* us. But this is the model of a functional doctrine of the Trinity.[45]

It was therefore quite logical that the monarchical concept of the Trinity should lead to the introduction of the *filioque* into the Nicene Creed. The Holy Spirit proceeds 'from the Father and the Son' because in salvation history he is sent by the Father and the Son, and is experienced in this way by human beings; and his eternal *processio* in the 'immanent' Trinity as transcendent primordial ground *must* correspond to his *missio* in the economic Trinity as this is experienced.[46]

At this point we shall not as yet criticize the logic of the Trinitarian inference, but shall first of all, with its help, remove the Filioque from the Nicene Creed again. For with the Filioque, the Holy Spirit is once and for all put in third place in the Trinity, and subordinated to the Son. But this makes it impossible to comprehend salvation history adequately. It is true that this order applies to the sending of the Spirit through Christ on the foundation of the resurrection, but it does not apply to Christ's own history in the Spirit. If Christ was conceived by the Holy Spirit, baptized with the Spirit, and ministered by virtue of the energies given him by the Spirit, then he presupposes the Spirit, and the Spirit precedes him. Christ comes from the Father in the Spirit. That is the truth of the synoptic Spirit christology which in the course of history was driven out by the christological pneumatology of Paul and John.[47] The relations in Israel's history with God cannot be seen in any other way either: it is through the liberating and guiding operation of the Spirit that Israel becomes God's first-born son.[48]

Moreover, the interactions of Son and Spirit, Spirit and Son are not in any way surprising, if we get straight in our minds the other trinitarian metaphor which is implicit in this interaction: the unity of Word and Breath for the unity of Son and Spirit. Where the Word of God is, there is also the breath of God in which it is uttered. Where God's breath calls created beings into life, there is also the Word which calls them by their names. So it is not correct to see everywhere in the monarchical order of the Trinity only the order: Father – Son – Spirit. We see the order: God – Spirit – Word everywhere too. God creates all things through the breath of his life in his creative words. Through the tempest of his Spirit he opens for Israel the path through the sea. The healing and life-giving Spirit comes upon Christ and 'rests' on him. If we perceive in salvation history the reciprocal co-efficacy of Spirit and Word, Son and Spirit, then we have to reject the one-sided definition of the Spirit in terms of the Son in the 'transcendent primordial ground', and hence the Filioque addition to the Nicene Creed. The idea of *the primordial Trinity* must open up a new possibility, also enabling us to talk about the procession of the Son from the Spirit, since this corresponds to the salvation history that can be experienced.[49]

Clericalism must be mentioned as a non-theological factor which led to the insertion of the Filioque and to the confining definition of the Spirit through the Son. If God is represented by Christ, Christ by the Pope, and the Pope by the bishops and priests, then – by way of the Filioque in the primordial relationships – the Holy Spirit, with all his charismata and energies in salvation history, is tied down to the operative acts of the priesthood. The Holy Spirit is then nothing other than the operation of 'the spiritual pastors', their ministerial grace, their proclamation, pastoral care and administration of the sacraments. The congregation turns into the passive recipient of the gifts of the Spirit mediated through the church. But in this way the Spirit does not make Christians their own determining subjects, or the rulers of their own lives.[50]

The doctrine of the Trinity traditionally held in the Western church can also be interpreted as a doctrine about *the Trinity in the sending*, since for this doctrine 'sending' is the quintessence of the relationships of the divine persons to one another and of their shared relationship to the world. 'The Father is always only the sender, sending both the Son and the Holy Spirit. The Son can be sent, but only by the Father, whereas he for his part can also send, but only the Holy Spirit. The Holy Spirit, finally, cannot send in any way at all, but can only be sent – and sent both by the Father and by the Son.[51] From the discerned sending of the Son Jesus Christ, and of the Holy Spirit through Christ, the eternal origin of these temporal sendings is inferred. Just because the eternal origin is the origin of just these particular temporal sendings, the economic Trinity always reveals merely an eternal Trinity which is already turned in commitment towards the world.

The *primordial* Trinity is from eternity an *open* Trinity. It is open for its own sendings, and in its sendings it is open for human beings and for the whole created world, so that they may be united with itself. The sending of the Son for the salvation of creation, and the sending of the Spirit to unite created being with the Son for the glory of the Father, reveal the love of God which goes out of itself. The Trinity which opens itself and goes out of itself can be termed *the threefold God*. The threefold God is open for human beings, open for the world, and open for time.

If the Trinity in the beginning goes out of itself in the sending of the Son and the Spirit, then God does not only reveal his love. He actually opens himself for the experience of the world and history. He does not merely act on the world. He invites created being to act on him as well, and in this way he 'experiences' his creation. This is not due to any deficiency of Being. It is the outcome of the rapturous abundance of his divine Being, which longs to communicate itself and is able to communicate itself. The history of the life of God, which communicates itself inexhaustibly and in unfathomable depth, is disclosed through the 'sending' Trinity. But for that very reason, this 'sending' Trinity cannot be the sole trinitarian concept of God to emerge from the contemplation of the history of Christ and from experience of the Holy Spirit.

2. The Historical Concept of the Trinity

The historical concept of the Trinity links on to the monarchical concept, transposing it from the vertical eternity-time relation to the sequence of the times of the Father, the Son and the Holy Spirit in salvation history. It is only possible to talk about an 'economic Trinity' if this is taken to mean the inner cohesion and dynamic thrust of all works of the Trinity in the economy of salvation. Although according to Augustine the *opera trinitatis ad extra sunt indivisa*, from earliest times the work of creating the world has been ascribed to the Father, the work of reconciling the world to the Son, and the work of sanctifying the world to the Holy Spirit. These 'trinitarian works' do not stand side by side, without any relation to one another. They belong within the context of salvation history, for the work of sanctification presupposes the work of reconciliation, and both have the work of creation as premise. The sense of time in salvation history is aligned towards the future of that history – that is to say, towards the eternal sabbath of the world in the kingdom of glory of the triune God: the work of creation is aligned towards the work of reconciliation, and the work of reconciliation is aligned towards the work of sanctification. The one thrusts forward to the other without supplanting it, and together they are all directed eschatologically towards the new creation of all things in the eternal kingdom.[52]

We are indebted to Joachim of Fiore for the historical interpretation of the doctrine of the Trinity in its bearing on the economy of salvation.[53] His historical periodization of salvation history, and his eschatological vision of its perfecting shaped the Western interpretation of history, particularly its modern form. The modern faith in progress grew up out of the messianic form Joachim gave to salvation history. Ever since Lessing, 'modern times' have been viewed as the fulfilment of the 'third kingdom of the Spirit' which history had prepared and heralded. This was the emotional thrust behind the Enlightenment. It knew itself to be the goal of history, and the revelation and solution of history's riddle. It was in this sense that Lessing wrote in *The Education of the Human Race*:

> Perhaps their 'Three Ages of the World' were not so empty a speculation after all, and assuredly they had no contemptible views when they taught that the New Covenant must become as much antiquated as the Old has been. There remained among them too the same economy of the same God. Ever, to let them speak my words, ever the self-same plan of the education of the race. Only they were premature. Only they believed that they could make their contemporaries, who had scarcely outgrown their childhood, without enlightenment, without preparation, all at once men worthy of their Third Age. And it was just this which made them enthusiasts. The enthusiast often casts true glances into the future, but for this future he cannot wait. He wishes this future accelerated, and accelerated through him.[54]

Lessing was convinced that with the age of Englightenment this future had come, and that he himself was its prophet. In the history of salvation, the law of the Old Covenant was succeeded by the gospel of the New Covenant, and this will be fulfilled in the kingdom of the Spirit, in which no one will have to teach the other because all will perceive the truth for themselves, and do what is good simply because it is good. But in expounding this view was Lessing really reproducing what Joachim of Fiore had taught in the thirteenth century?

Joachim's vision of the movement of the Spirit which thrusts forward in salvation history grew up out of his study of the relationship between the New Testament and the Old.[55] He discovered that the Old Testament outlines a history of promise which the New Testament neither fulfils nor abrogates, but endorses and expands. In this way he arrived at the conviction that in salvation history there was not only the one transition from 'the old law' of Moses to 'the new law' of Christ, as Aquinas taught, but that a further transition from the *nova lex Christi* to the *intelligentia Spiritus Sancti* was to be expected: 'the knowledge of all truth'. He associated with this expectation the apocalyptic hope for the coming of the *evangelium aeternum* before Christ's parousia; this, he believed, would bring Christians and Jews into the eternal kingdom.

Joachim drew up continually new lists of the periods of salvation history: the kingdom of the Father embraces, as order of the Father, the Mosaic Law. The liberty of human beings consists of their obedient bondage to this law. The kingdom of the Son is also the order of the Son, according to the gospel of Christ. Here the liberty of human beings is that they are the children of God. But after that will come the kingdom of the Spirit where, in the experience of the Spirit, God will be directly known. In the kingdom of the Father the order of marriage prevails, in the kingdom of the Son the order of priests, in the order of the Spirit the order of the spirituals. The first kingdom is dominated by effort and labour, the second by learning and discipline, the third by contemplation and praise; and so forth. The three ages are not on a par with one another, but are thought of in an ascending sequence. In each case they point typologically beyond themselves. The fulfilment of salvation history is found in 'the kingdom of the Spirit', for it is in the indwelling of the Holy Spirit that the gospel of Christ arrives at its goal. When the 'external' word of proclamation and doctrine finds inward assurance and personal comprehension, this is the beginning, in the Spirit and in a spiritual way, of the immediate seeing of God face to face.

The temporal concepts of anticipation and abrogation are misleading, however, if we disregard the trinitarian doctrine of appropriation to which Joachim of Fiore adhered, as his intricate diagram of the three intersecting rings shows.[56] If this is taken into account it is impossible to say that Joachim hoped for a coming of the Spirit 'without Christ'. Just as in the classic doctrine of appropriation the work of reconciliation is ascribed to the Son, without this meaning that the Father and the Spirit are thereby excluded, so in the same way the work of sanctification, illumination and enlightenment is ascribed to the Holy Spirit without exclusion of the Father and the Son. Just as the Father creates the world through the Son in the Spirit, so the Spirit illumines the world through the Son in the Father. The change of determining subjects in the sequence of works in the economy of salvation is a change within the Trinity, not a dissolution of the Trinity in history. By successively assuming the leadership, the Father, the Son and the Holy Spirit determine the eschatological dynamic of salvation history. What the Father begins, points forward to its consummation in the Spirit. The monarchical concept of the Trinity, according to which the Father always acts through the Son in the Spirit, and through the Spirit in the Son, describes *synchronically* what the salvation-history sequence of the kingdoms of the Father, the Son and the Spirit depicts *diachronically*. History begins with creation and ends with the transfiguration of the world. It begins in the Father and is consummated in the Spirit.

3. *The Eucharistic Concept of the Trinity*

The eucharistic concept of the Trinity is the logical consequence of the monarchical form of the Trinity, for the experience of grace arouses gratitude, and where God is known in his works, creation's song of praise awakens. Thanksgiving, prayer, adoration, praise, and the silent sinking into wonder, proceed from the energies of the Spirit who gives life, are directed towards the Son, and go with the Son to the Father. Here all activities proceed from the indwelling Spirit, all mediation takes place through the Son, and the Father is purely the recipient of the thanksgiving and songs of praise of his creatures. The Spirit glorifies the Son, and through the Son the Father. The Spirit unites us with the Son, and through the Son with the Father. This is expressed in the New Testament with the phrase: 'for the glory of God the Father' (Phil. 2.11). Here God's Being is described not through what he does but through the way he receives. From the God whom we wish to thank, sing and dance to, we await receptivity, not activity. We speak, and want him to hear. We live, and want him to experience us. The monarchical concept of the Trinity has its place in *the sending*, for the proclamation of the gospel and the accomplishment of Christian obedience in the world; but the situation in human life for this other concept of the Trinity – its 'Sitz im Leben' – is *the celebration of the eucharist* and the life which itself becomes a feast because it has been filled with grace and happiness. This concept was best developed by the Orthodox churches, whose centre is the celebration of the eucharist, and whose desire is to present themselves with the liturgy as the true public adoration of God.

If we look at the experience of God which men and women find in his works, then the monarchical 'sending' Trinity precedes the eucharistic Trinity: without *charis* there is no *eucharistia*. But if we ask about God's intention in his works of creation, reconciliation and redemption, then it is only in eucharistic form that the monarchical form of the Trinity arrives at its goal. For the intention of God's works is not that they should happen, but that they should awaken joy and thanksgiving, and the song of praise that returns to God. According to the first chapter of Genesis the completion of the works of creation, and hence their goal too, is the sabbath of creation and God's rest; and in the same way the end of all God's works in salvation history is the eternal sabbath in the kingdom of glory – what Athanasius described as 'the feast without end'.

In the sending of the Son and the Spirit, the primordial Trinity opens itself; it becomes open for the world and time, and experiences the history of creation. If this is the overflowing, *seeking love of God*, then the Trinity in the sending is vulnerable. We rightly talk about the suffering and pain of God's seeking love, for God himself is present wherever his love seeks out the beloved beings he has created. The passion history of Christ reveals the suffering of the passionate love of God. In this passion history, God suffers forsakenness and death in order to find the forsaken, the dying and the dead. This is the way God experiences human history. But in the eucharist of the Spirit, the homecoming of those who have been found begins, and that homecoming is also the beginning of God's love in its bliss. In the context of the history of the Spirit who 'is poured out on all flesh' so that it may be eternally living, the gospels rightly talk about God's joy (Luke 15.7, 10; Matt. 25.21), which leads to God's felicity, and finally to God's bliss.

God's suffering history in Christ's passion serves the history of God's joy in the Spirit over the homecoming of human beings and all other creatures into the kingdom of God. Athanasius summed this up in a statement which was accepted as authoritative in the patristic church: 'God became human so that human beings should be deified.'[57] The first phrase is talking about the divine *katabasis* or descent, the second about the human *anabasis* or ascent. The *katabasis* holds within itself the monarchical Trinity in the sending, the *anabasis* the eucharistic Trinity in glory. Basil also talked about these two movements of the Trinity, but he described the second more fully:[58] 'When, in a power that illumines us, we look unswervingly upon the beauty of the image of the invisible God, and through that image are led upwards to the vision of that Primal Image which is beyond all measure lovely, then the Spirit of knowledge is inseparably present . . . Just as no man knoweth the Father save the Son (Matt.

11.27), so no one can say Lord Jesus except in the Holy Spirit (I Cor. 12.3) . . . The way to the knowledge of God therefore proceeds from the one Spirit through the one Son to the one Father. Conversely, essential goodness and holiness and royal dignity proceed from the Father through the Only Begotten One to the Spirit. Thus we confess the hypostases without infringing that article of faith which speaks of the monarchy.'[59]

The eucharistic concept of the Trinity is the reversal of the monarchical concept. If in the monarchical concept the concerted divine movement is: Father → Son → Spirit, in the eucharistic concept it is: Spirit → Son → Father. In each case, the three hypostases arrive at their unity through their unified movement. If for the monarchical movement the expression 'the threefold God' would seem to suggest itself, for the eucharistic movement the most appropriate term is 'triunity'. The energies of the Spirit flow back to the Son and to the Father. But this means that both patterns are economic concepts of the Trinity – indeed that they really sum up the two sides of salvation history, which comes 'from God' and leads 'to God'.

But whereas in the monarchical 'sending' Trinity the foundation is *an experience of identity* which tells us that God himself is present *in* his revelation, in the eucharistic Trinity of glorification we discover *an experience of differentiation*. This makes it clear to us that our human and historical concepts can never grasp or apprehend God himself, and it therefore leads us to fathomless wonder over God, in apophatic silence and in eschatological hope for the beatific vision.[60] How should thanksgiving for salvation experienced in this life be expressed except with ideas and concepts impaired through our sickness? Isn't the song of praise sung by the liberated always still 'a song in a foreign land' (Ps. 137.4.)? The same is true of human theology in our historical condition. It can be the theology of *faith* but not yet the theology of *sight*. It is *theologia crucis* but not yet *theologia gloriae*. It can be *theologia viatorum*, but is not yet *theologia patriae*, it is *theologia ektypa* not *archetypa*, for the glory of God has not yet appeared, and not yet is 'the whole earth full of his glory' (Isa. 6.3).

The purpose of the Israelite prohibition of images is to preserve the mystery of God and at the same time to keep open the future of his glory. Religious symbols and metaphors are built up out of religious experiences. If they are dogmatized, these experiences become fixed, and their fixation makes them 'fixed ideas' – and that puts an end to the journey. The metaphors for experiences of God in history have to be flexible, so that they invite us to voyage into the future and encourage us to seek the kingdom of God. The true symbols of transcendence impel us to transcend. This applies to theological conceptions and terms too. If they are related to 'the wandering people of God', this eschatology relativizes them. They become signposts, and search images for God's future.

According to the messianic traditions of Judaism, when the messiah comes the idols and demons will disappear from the earth. In the messianic era the prohibition of images will be universally observed, for the messianic era will transform the world, making it so entirely and visibly God's world that the human mind can leave behind the world it has duplicated for itself through images, and hence alienated, and can experience the world directly. When the glory of God appears on earth 'a world without parables' will come into being, for the indwelling glory of God has no need of images and cannot be imaged.[61] The immediate, sensory nearness of God will make superfluous all the images, symbols and parables which we construct for ourselves in the foreign land, in order to bridge the distance. In the kingdom of God we shall no longer conceive or think even 'God' as we do in the history of alienation. And in the encompassing divine presence, God will also no longer be that hidden counterpart to whom we call here. The apophatic *experience of difference* arises of itself out of the human attempt to give God thanksgiving and praise. It leads inevitably to the eschatological relativization of the historical theology *of faith* in the love of God to the hoped-for eternal theology of *sight* in God's glory.

4. The Trinitarian Doxology

The trinitarian doxology leads beyond these three conceptions of the Trinity. This doxology is touched on in the Nicene Creed in the clause about the Holy Spirit 'who with the Father and the Son together is worshipped and glorified'. Anyone who is glorified 'together with' others cannot be subordinated to these others. He is their equal. 'Worship and glorification' go beyond the salvation that has been experienced and the thanksgiving that has been expressed. The triune God is worshipped and glorified *for his own sake*. The trinitarian doxology is the only place in Christian practice in which – at least in intention – our gaze passes beyond salvation history to the eternal essence of God himself, so that here we can talk about a doctrine of the Trinity in which the 'economic' themes play no part. Consequently trinitarian doxology is the *Sitz im Leben* for *the concept of the immanent Trinity*. How do we arrive at this conception?

It can come about quite simply as it does on the mystical ladder of love.[62] The beloved receives particular gifts of love and expresses thanks for them. But his thanks are not only for the gifts received but also for the loving hand from which they come. From this open hand he looks at the loving face that is turned towards him, and feels the heart that beats for him. But then the beloved forgets everything he has received, and everything that is related to himself, and marvels over his counterpart for her own sake. On this 'ladder of love', the human eros is turned aside from the objects of creation and the gifts of grace and drawn into the source from which they come, so that he no longer relates them to himself but to their origin. If he then begins to marvel over this origin, self-love stops and the wonderer sinks wholly into the selfless contemplation of God. He sees God as he really is, and no longer merely as he is for him, the created and beloved human being. At this point the eucharistic Trinity changes into the trinitarian doxology; thanksgiving is transformed into prayer, faith into sight and all self-concern is lost in selfless astonishment:

> Glory be to the Father and to the Son and to the Holy Spirit, as it was in the beginning is now and ever shall be, world without end.[63]

It is not that in his revelation God has not made himself present to human beings, or has not done so entirely. Nor is it true that God has revealed only his energies but not his essence. In the movement of the 'sending' Trinity we have to say with Hegel: 'Now there is no longer anything secret about God.'[64] God is *wholly* present, and present as *himself*, wherever people hear the voice that says 'I *am* the Lord your God . . .' There can be no question of half a revelation, let alone a merely fragmentary revelation. This is the truth behind modern talk about God's self-revelation. But we also saw that in the human eucharistic counter-movement we experience the infinite difference between men and women as historical beings, and the eternal God: 'We know in part and we prophesy in part . . . Now we see through a mirror in a dark word [Luther's translation], but then face to face' (I Cor. 13.9, 12). That is why with the eucharistic movement the eschatological hope for the 'seeing face to face' begins.

And the trinitarian doxology is the beginning of the seeing itself, for the seeing of God's glory is the goal of salvation history, and the trinitarian doxology anticipates this goal in the very midst of salvation history. But what can we say about this doxology if we are in the midst of history and not yet at its end, and as long as we are living in faith, not yet in sight?

The trinitarian doxology *interrupts* the liturgy which begins in the name of the triune God and ends with the blessing in his name, because it directs the senses to *the eternal present* in which we no longer remember the past and no longer wait for any other future. The doxology brings unutterable points of rest into the liturgical drama. Before the God who is 'for ever and ever', the things which concern us become petty. Even God's own works and God's salvation history recede behind God's eternal being.

So the trinitarian doxology brings into the liturgy something which is part of the experience of life itself; for after all, the aim of the church's liturgy is to reflect *the cosmic liturgy of creation*, and to correspond to the *divine liturgy of life*. It celebrates the feast of God. So we have to ask what corresponds to it in our experience of life. If we talk here about 'the feast of life', we are not merely thinking about life's special festive high-spots. We mean the life that is expressed in lament and grief as well as in laughing and dancing. Every life which finds a way of expressing itself is festal life. What corresponds in life to the trinitarian doxology in the divine liturgy is the perception of *the eternal moment*. I mean by that an awareness of the present which is so intense that it interrupts the flux of time and does away with transience. We call the moment in which life is as intensively experienced as this, *ecstasy*.[65] It is a momentary awareness of eternity, not a permanent one. Although every moment in life can be ecstatically lived in just this way, it is only the crowning ecstasies which interrupt everyday life; and we feel that these belong to a different category and that our everyday standards cannot grasp or judge them. We perceive these exceptional ecstasies of life with all our senses, and yet they reach beyond our sensory perceptions – not as if they were 'supersensory', but because they are so intensive that the distance we need if we are to perceive them is taken from us, and we ourselves become wholly present and wholly living in the ecstasy of life.

In trinitarian doxology the linear movements end, and the *circular* movements begin. This is objectively expressed in the co-equality axiom of the Nicene Creed: if the Holy Spirit 'together with' the Father and Son is 'at the same time (*simul*) worshipped and glorified', then the Spirit is seen in the perichoretic fellowship he shares with the Father and the Son, and this puts an end to his position as 'third Person' in the Trinity; for 'at the same time' permits to 'pre-' and no 'post-'. Spirit – Father – Son are now no longer in the linear monarchical movement of God's self-communication to human beings, nor are they any more in the eucharistic movement of the self-communication of human beings to God; this is now the self-circling and self-reposing movement of *perichoresis*. Of course the circular movement too is no more than a temporal symbol for eternity, but its source is not historical time but the time of the natural cycles which regenerate life – even if theologically the cyclic concept of time is ascribed rather to the angels, whose existence is neither transitory like nature, nor historical like human beings, but who exist aeonically.

In the trinitarian doxology we adore God for himself and glorify him because he is what he is. The trinitarian figure for this is therefore 'the immanent Trinity'. Of course in human doxology the Trinity becomes an unfathomable mystery which excels all imaginings and concepts. For anyone who enters into the wonder, the be-wondered counterpart becomes an inexhaustible source of always wider and ever deeper wonderment. How could we ever stop and where could we ever come to an end of the marvelling?

It is not enough to draw on the metaphysical distinction between God's accessible energies and his non-accessible essence, as a way of describing this doxological experience of never being able to plumb the fathomless dimensions, and of never coming to an end.[66] To describe this happening by way of the distinction between act and person (as Western theology has done ever since Augustine) does not lead into the unsearchable depths of doxology either, although the personal concepts are more appropriate than concepts drawn from the metaphysics of substance. According to the patterns of thinking used in this account, the trinitarian doxology and the eternal moment of ecstasy which it expresses liturgically really have to do with the 'seeing face to face'. Here we would interpret it by saying that God's countenance emerges from its hiddenness and begins to 'shine', as the Aaronic benediction says. The erotic, life-giving energies of the Spirit begin to flow, renewing 'the face of the earth' (Ps. 104.30) and filling human hearts (Rom. 5.5). The result is radiance, and response to these energies. 'Now we all, with unveiled face, reflect the glory of the Lord, and shall be transfigured into his likeness from one degree of glory to another; for this comes from the Lord who is the Spirit' (II Cor. 3.18). Men and women too emerge from the hiddenness in which they become a riddle and a mystery for themselves and one another. *Homo absconditus* becomes *homo revelatus*. In the light of glory, people become clear and comprehensible to themselves and each other, because they stand in the divine light and are flooded by it, through and through. In the relationship to God it is a single glory which pervades both God and human beings, so that they can look upon one another. The perfecting and consummation of love is always this 'seeing face to face': '*Fruitio Dei et se invicem in Deo*', said Augustine.

If in the trinitarian doxology God is worshipped and glorified for his own sake, and if this is the beginning of the 'seeing face to face', then the divine Trinity comes to *rest* in the eternal presence of its glory, and reposes in itself, so that it is perceived by human beings in its eternal presence as eternal counterpart. This is especially important when we are thinking of the Holy Spirit, for in his presence among human beings he is perceived by human beings as eternal counterpart 'together with the Father and the Son'. He is a counterpart that joins and does not divide. He is a counterpart in his presence, not in the remoteness of his absence. The trinitarian doxology is directed in the presence of the Spirit to the counterpart of the Spirit, who is perceived in his eternal fellowship with the Father and the Son. Every wondering admiration requires not merely the embrace but also the distance, so that we can look the other in the eyes, face to face. The same is true of wonder over the triune God: eternal presence becomes eternal counterpart. This does not put an end to the eternal presence; it merely deepens it. The person who worships and adores becomes in his self-forgetfulness part of the worshipped and adored counterpart. Adoration and worship are the ways in which created beings participate in the eternal life and the eternal joy of God, and are drawn into the circular movement of the divine relationships.[67]

Trinitarian doxology does not put an end to the monarchical Trinity, the historical and the eucharistic Trinity; it completes their movements. That is why it can also be viewed as presupposition for the origin of these divine movements. Its underlying conception of the 'immanent Trinity' must preserve the ideas in the other trinitarian conceptions. Even if it excels these, nothing can emerge in its own concepts which could contradict any of the other movements of the Trinity.

5. Is the Filioque Addition to the Nicene Creed Necessary or Superfluous?

The ecumenical deliberations on this subject at the Klingenthal conferences in 1978 and 1979[68] showed, in my view, that the addition to the Nicene Creed which maintains that the Holy Spirit proceeded from the Father and from the Son is *superfluous*. Let me sum up the sequence of ideas which leads to this conclusion:

1. If the Spirit is said to proceed from the Father, this also says that he proceeds from the Father of the Son, for it is only in relation to the Son that the first Person of the Trinity has to be called 'Father'.

2. If the Spirit proceeds from 'the Father of the Son', then he has his origin in the Father's relation to the Son. He proceeds not only from the Father, but also from his fatherhood.

3. The fatherhood of the Father cannot be thought without the sonship of the Son. If the Spirit proceeds from the fatherhood of the Father, then the Son is not uninvolved. His sonship participates indirectly in the direct procession of the Spirit from the Father. The Son accompanies the procession of the Spirit from his Father.

4. The procession of the Spirit consequently presupposes the existence of the Father and the Son, as well as the reciprocal relationship of the Father and the Son: 'As soon as God is called Father, he is thought of as having a Son.'[69]

5. Even though the primordial relations have to be distinguished from the perichoretic relations in the life of the Trinity, the Spirit's hypostatic existence is nevertheless given its imprint by the Father and by the Son: from the Father, as origin of the Godhead, the Spirit receives his hypostatic divinity, from the Son and from the Father and from their reciprocal relationships he receives his inner-trinitarian configuration or Gestalt.

The Filioque addition therefore contributes nothing new to the statement about the procession of the Spirit from the Father. It is superfluous, not required, and it can consequently be struck out.

Is the Filioque addition wrong in itself and pernicious in its historical effects? With this addition the Holy Spirit is sent to third place in the primordial relationships of the Trinity. In the light of his origin, he is subordinated to the Son; and it is consequently impossible for him to appear in any other way in the economy of salvation. The relationships between the Son and the Spirit can then no longer be understood as reciprocal relationships. The way always leads from the Son to the Spirit, no longer from the Spirit to the Son. But this hard and fast conclusion is mistaken. In the eternal simultaneity of the Trinity, the begetting of the Son does not take priority over the procession of the Spirit. The Orthodox theologians are right when they talk about a reciprocal 'accompaniment' – the Spirit accompanies the begetting of the Son, and the Son accompanies the procession of the Spirit. They are then admittedly changing the metaphor for the Trinity and are no longer talking about the Son and the Spirit, but about God's Word and his Breath.

Every person of the Trinity has two names because there are these two metaphors. The first Person is Father/Utterer, the second Person is Son/Word, the third Person is Spirit/Breath. From these two metaphors we can immediately see that Word and Breath proceed simultaneously from God, and that the Spirit accompanies the Word, and the Word the Spirit.

The Spirit's accompaniment of the eternal begetting of the Son by the Father is also called the 'manifestation' of the Spirit through the Son.[70] The birth of the Son is so intensively accompanied by the procession of the Spirit from the Father that we have to say: the Son is begotten by the Father through the Spirit. If this is true in the eternal origin of the Son, then the Spirit is present in the Son in all eternity. The hypostatic Persons of the Spirit and the Son remain so united with one another that they exist indivisibly in one another in eternity. The Son is just as inconceivable without the Spirit as the Spirit is inconceivable without the Son.

This leads to the second important idea: the Spirit who proceeds simultaneously from the Father with the birth of the Son, *rests* in the Son. The Son is the recipient of the Spirit and his eternal resting place. The Son is born from the Father as dwelling place for the Spirit, and the Spirit proceeds from the Father in order to dwell eternally in the Son. Whereas with the Filioque addition the primordial relationships within the Trinity end with the Spirit, without this addition their completion in the Son is conceivable: the Spirit proceeds from the Father and rests in the Son.

This makes the third idea possible: The Spirit who rests in the Son and indwells him, *shines* from the Son and through the Son. He sheds his eternal light *from the Son* on to the mutual relations between the

Father and the Son, bringing into God's eternal Being and God's eternal love *God's eternal light*. This eternal light brings *eternal joy* into God's Being and his love. This is the transfiguration within the Trinity itself which proceeds from the Spirit. The glory of God is an inner-trinitarian energy too, not merely an energy turned outwards. It illumines God's eternal essence with God's eternal light. But then the Spirit also shines *through the Son* on whom he rests – shines, that is, in revelation, making the men and women touched by it 'children of light' (Eph. 5.8ff.).

According to these conceptions, then, the Spirit *accompanies* the Son, *rests* in the Son, and *shines* from the Son; and this corresponds much better to the Spirit-history of Christ and the Christ-history of the Spirit about which the New Testament talks than the one-sided definition which pins the Spirit down to his procession from the Father and the Son; for this corresponds only to the kairos after Christ's resurrection and since Pentecost. In fact it does not even correspond to this kairos properly, since there too the Son makes the Spirit accessible to us, and the Spirit procures for us access to the Son. So the reciprocal relationship between Son and Spirit is the only remaining conclusion. This is the most important theological objection to the Filioque.

The Nicene Creed talks about the Holy Spirit in his primordial relation to the Father and in his *fellowship in glory* together with the Father and the Son. It is important to distinguish origin from completion. Whereas in the constitutive hypostatic primordial relations the Son is eternally 'born' from the Father, and the Spirit eternally 'proceeds' from the Father, these 'proceedings' have no meaning in the glorification. The hypostatic Persons of the triune God are seen and contemplated in their eternal perichoresis and their eternal simultaneity. Through their reciprocal relationships they indwell one another, forming their unity through their unique community, no longer through their unilinear movement. Their unity is constituted by their 'togetherness'. Their eternal 'simultaneity' makes them equal in rank, so that even the Father, for whose glory everything in salvation history takes place, is no longer the First, but One among the Others. The original hypostatic differentiations are ended and consummated in the eternal perichoresis, and it is this that is extolled in the trinitarian doxology. In 'the transcendent origin' of salvation history, we see the primordial, self-opening Trinity; in its eschatological consummation we find the Trinity resting in its glory.

In the passage through the monarchical and the historical forms of the Trinity and its eucharistic configuration, there come into being what we can perceive to be the patterns of the Trinity in its final consummation.

Finally, *the trinitarian doxology* is paralleled by *the social analogy* of the triune God. The perichoretic unity of the divine Persons who ek-sist with one another, for one another and in one another, finds its correspondence in the true human communities which we can experience – experience in love, in friendship, in the community of Christ's people which is filled by the Spirit, and in the just society.[71] The correspondences are called to life through the fascinating attraction of the triune God who rests in himself and revolves in himself. In the monarchical Trinity the unity of the three Persons comes into being through the unified movement of *God's sovereign rule*. In the historical Trinity the unity comes into being through the direction of time, which thrusts towards *the future*. In the eucharistic Trinity the unity of the divine Persons comes into being through the unified movement of *thanksgiving*. It is through the trinitarian doxology that we first perceive the immanent Trinity as it rests and revolves in itself, and whose unity lies in the eternal *community* of the divine Persons. The essential nature of the triune God *is* this community. The unity of God also appears as the community of the three Persons who exist with one another, for one another and in one another. The Spirit who is glorified 'together with' the Father and the Son is also the wellspring of the energy which draws people to one another, so that they come together, rejoice in one another and praise the God who is himself a God in community:

Let's get together and be alright,
one love, one heart.
Give thanks and praise to the Lord
and be alright.[72]

VENI CREATOR SPIRITUS

Hymn for the Feast of Pentecost by Rabanus Maurus

Veni, creator Spiritus,
mentes tuorum visita,
imple superna gratia,
quae tu creasti, pectora.

Come, O creator Spirit, come,
And make within our hearts thy home;
To us thy grace celestial give,
Who of thy breathing move and live.

Qui diceris Paraclitus,
donum Dei altissimi,
fons vivus, ignis, caritas
et spiritalis unctio.

O Paraclete, that name is thine,
Of God most high the gift divine;
The well of life, the fire of love,
Our souls anointing from above.

Tu septiformis munere,
dextrae Dei tu digitus
tu rite promissum Patris
sermone ditans guttura.

Thou dost appear in sevenfold dower
The sign of God's almighty power;
The Father's promise, making rich
With saving truth our earthly speech.

Accende lumen sensibus,
infunde amorem cordibus,
infirma nostri corporis
virtute firmans perpeti.

Our senses with thy light inflame,
Our hearts to heavenly love reclaim;
Our bodies' poor infirmity
With strength perpetual fortify.

Hostem repellas longius
pacemque dones protinus;
ductore sic te praevio
vitemus omne noxium.

Our mortal foe afar repel,
Grant us henceforth in peace to dwell;
And so to us, with thee for guide,
No ill shall come, no harm betide.

Per te sciamus da Patrem
noscamus atque Filium,
te utriusque Spiritum
credamus omni tempore.

May we by thee the Father learn,
And know the Son, and thee discern,
Who art of both; and thus adore
In perfect faith for evermore.[73]

V Emitte Spiritum tuum, et creabuntur.

R Et renovabis facium terrae.

V Send forth thy Spirit and all will be newly created.

R And thou wilt renew the face of the earth.

NOTES

Introduction

1. O. Dilschneider, 'Die Geistvergessenheit der Theologie', *ThLZ* 86, 1961, 261; M. Kwiran, 'Der Heilige Geist als Stiefkind? Bemerkungen zur Confessio Augustana', *ThZ* 31, 1975, 223–236.

2. K. Barth, postscript to *Schleiermacher-Auswahl*, ed. H. Bolli, Munich 1968, 310ff.

3. For literature in German, cf. U. Gerber, postscript to H. Berkhof, *Theologie des Heiligen Geistes*, 2nd ed., Neukirchen 1988, 141–178 (German expanded trans. of *The Doctrine of the Holy Spirit*; cf. n.29); for literature in English, cf. A. Heron, *The Holy Spirit in the Bible, in the History of Christian Thought and in Recent Theology*, Philadelphia and London 1983.

4. J. Moltmann, review of Y. Congar, *Der Heilige Geist* (German trans. of *Je crois en l'Esprit Saint*; cf. n.32), *ThLZ* 108, 1983, 624–627.

5. The first thrust in this direction can be found in L. Vischer (ed.), *Spirit of God, Spirit of Christ: ecumenical reflections on the filioque controversy*, London 1981 (Faith and Order paper No. 103), published after the Klingenthal conferences of 1978 and 1979.

6. Cf. W. Hollenweger, *The Pentecostals*, trans. R. A. Wilson, London and Minneapolis 1972, which is still a standard work. Also S. M. Burgess and G. B. McGee (eds), *Dictionary of Pentecostal and Charismatic Movements*, Grand Rapids 1988.

7. Cf. C. Schütz, *Einführung in die Pneumatologie*, Darmstadt 1985, 114ff.

8. This is how S. Kierkegaard characterizes sin in *The Sickness Unto Death* (1849), trans. W. Lowrie, London, Toronto and Princeton 1941.

9. One of the finest interpretations of the ecumenical vision is given by E. Lange in *Die ökumenische Utopie oder was bewegt die ökumenische Bewegung?*, Stuttgart 1972.

10. G. Müller-Fahrenholz, *Heilsgeschichte zwischen Ideologie und Prophetie. Profile und Kritik heilsgeschichtlicher Theorien in der ökumenischen Bewegung zwischen 1948 and 1968*, Freiburg 1974. For the old, Swedenborgian vision of the 'Johannine church', which was deeply influenced by Joachim of Fiore, cf. F. W. J. Schelling, *Philosophie der Offenbarung* (1841/2), ed. M. Frank, Frankfurt 1977, 316ff. The Johannine church is supposed

to follow the 'Pauline' and the 'Petrine church' as the Spirit is supposed to follow the Word and the ministry: 'Peter, Paul, John! In this succession they are representatives of the three ages of Christian development . . . Peter is the law-giver, what is fundamental and stable. Paul broke out like a fire and is the Elijah, representing the principle of development, of movement, of freedom in the Christian church. John is the apostle of the future . . . The true church is neither of these two; it is that which proceeds from the foundation of Peter by way of Paul into the church of St. John . . . Peter is the apostle of the Father, and sees most deeply into the past; Paul is the apostle of the Son, and John of the Spirit . . . Peter is Christ's direct successor, John his successor only at the time of his coming.'

11. H.-G. Link (ed.), *Gemeinsam Glauben und Bekennen. Handbuch zum apostolischen Glauben*, Neukirchen-Vluyn 1987; *CREDO IN SPIRITUM SANCTUM*, I-II, Vatican City 1983.

12. In England there was a similar controversy between H. Wheeler Robinson, who inclined towards liberalism (cf. his book *The Christian Experience of the Holy Spirit*, London 1928), and the Barthian F. Camfield (*Revelation of the Holy Spirit. An Essay in Barthian Theology*, London 1933). Cf. here Heron, *Holy Spirit*, 124. From the Catholic aspect, cf. *Revelation and Experience*, ed. E. Schillebeeckx and B. Van Iersel, *Concilium* 113, 1978.

13. K. Barth and H. Barth, *Zur Lehre vom Heiligen Geist*, Beiheft 1, *Zwischen den Zeiten*, Munich 1930.

14. Ibid., 47.

15. Ibid., 48.

16. Ibid., 94.

17. Cf. W. Schmidt, *Zeit und Ewigkeit. Die letzten Voraussetzungen der dialektischen Theologie*, Gütersloh 1927; G. Oblau, *Gotteszeit und Menschenzeit. Eschatologie in der Kirchlichen Dogmatik von Karl Barth*, Neukirchen-Vluyn 1988.

18. Cf. here K. Blaser, *Vorstoss zur Pneumatologie*, Zürich 1977. The question about the relation between revelation and experience is dealt with in chs I to III.

19. P. Tillich is correct in this. Cf. his *Systematic Theology* III, Chicago 1963, 11ff.: 'Life and the Spirit'.

20. Thus rightly W. Joest, *Dogmatik* I: *Die Wirklichkeit Gottes*, Göttingen 1984, 302. Cf. also M. Beintker, 'Creator Spiritus. Zu einem unerledigten Problem der Pneumatologie', *EvTh* 46, 1986, 178–196.

21. Thus C. Schütz, *Einführung in die Pneumatologie* (cf. n. 7), as his table of contents shows.

22. Cf. my criticism in *ThLZ* 108, 1983, 628ff.

23. Cf. L. Dabney, *Die Kenosis des Geistes. Kontinuität zwischen Schöpfung und Erlösung im Werk des Heiligen Geistes*, dissertation, Tübingen 1989.

24. G. Altner (ed.), *Ökologische Theologie*, Stuttgart 1989; P. Joranson

and K. Butigan (eds), *Cry of the Environment, Rebuilding the Christian Creation Tradition*, Santa Fé 1984.

25. Cf. A. D. Galloway, *The Cosmic Christ*, New York 1951; P. Teilhard de Chardin, 'Christology and Evolution' in his *Christianity and Evolution*, trans. René Hague, London 1971; W. Beinert, *Christus und der Kosmos*, Freiburg 1974.

26. E. Moltmann-Wendel, *Wenn Gott und Körper sich begegnen*, Gütersloh 1989, following D. Kamper and C. Wulf, *Die Wiederkehr des Körpers*, Frankfurt 1982.

27. Cf. Lin, Hong-Hsin, *Die Person des Heiligen Geistes als Thema der Pneumatologie in der Reformierten Theologie*, dissertation, Tübingen 1990.

28. Thus H.-J. Kraus, *Systematische Theologie im Kontext biblischer Geschichte und Eschatologie*, Neukirchen-Vluyn 1983, 449; also his *Heiliger Geist. Gottes befreiende Gegenwart*, Munich 1986; similarly G. Sauter, 'Geist und Freiheit', *EvTh* 41, 1981, 212ff.; Sauter calls the Spirit 'God's becoming-present'.

29. H. Berkhof, *Theologie des Heiligen Geistes*, Neukirchen-Vluyn 1968, 134 (this book being the expanded German trans. of *The Doctrine of the Holy Spirit*, The Warfield Lectures 1963–64, Richmond, Va., 1964; London 1965).

30. See Ch. II, § 3.

31. V. Lossky, *In the Image and Likeness of God*, London 1974, 92.

32. Y. Congar, *Je crois en l'Esprit Saint*, Paris 1979–80, III, 29 (*I Believe in the Holy Spirit*, trans. D. Smith, New York and London, 1983).

33. I have criticized the generalizing concept of person in the doctrine of the Trinity with the argument that in the primal trinitarian relationships everything is unique because it is *ipso facto* for the first time. Cf. J. Moltmann, *The Trinity and the Kingdom of God*, trans. Margaret Kohl, London 1981 (=*The Trinity and the Kingdom*, New York 1981), Ch. V, § 5, 188ff.

34. Berkhof, *Heiliger Geist*, 134.

35. Ibid., 135.

36. H. Mühlen, *Der Heilige Geist als Person. In der Trinität, bei den Inkarnation und im Gnadenbund: ICH – DU – WIR*, Münster 1963.

37. K. Rahner, 'Der dreifaltige Gott als transzendenter Urgrund der Heilsgeschichte' in *Mysterium Salutis* II, Einsiedeln 1967, 317–401.

I *Experience of Life – Experience of God*

1. H. G. Gadamer, *Wahrheit und Methode*, Tübingen 1960, 329 (*Truth and Method*, trans. and ed. G. Barden and J. Cumming, 2nd corrected ed., London and New York 1979). I am drawing on the excellent article 'Erfahrung', *TRE* X, 83–141, with contributions by H. Wissmann, U. Köpf, E. Herms and J. Track, as well as on F. Kambartel's article 'Erfahrung', *HWP* II, 609–617. G. Ebeling, *Dogmatik des christlichen Glaubens* I-III, Tübingen 1979, has cautiously carried the concept of experience into

dogmatics. Cf. also G. Ebeling, 'Die Klage über das Erfahrungsdefizit in der Theologie als Frage nach ihrer Sache' in *Wort und Glaube* III, Tübingen 1975, 3–28 (not in ET *Word and Faith*). Y. Congar's great book, *I Believe in the Holy Spirit*, trans. D. Smith, London and New York 1983, also has as its sub-title: *Revelation and Experience of the Spirit*.

2. E. Hennecke and W. Schneemelcher (eds), *Neutestamentliche Apokryphen* II, Tübingen 1964, 154: Johannesakten, Der Hymnus Christi (ET *New Testament Apocrypha*, ed. R. McL. Wilson, II, London 1965: Acts of John, the Hymn of Christ).

3. With this we are taking up one of the key concepts in W. Dilthey's philosophy. 'The experience receives an expression. This expression represents the experience in all its fullness. It brings out what is new' (*Gesammelte Schriften* VI, 4th ed., Stuttgart 1962, 317). 'For the expression can contain more of the spiritual context than any introspection can give, raising it from depths which the consciousness illuminates' (ibid., VII, 206). Dilthey distinguishes three classes in the expression of life: the linguistic and logical expression; the appropriate act; the Gestalt, bodily mime and gesture. Cf. O. F. Bollnow, *Die Lebensphilosophie*, Berlin 1958, 37ff.

4. E. Dirscherl, *Der Heilige Geist und das menschliche Bewusstsein. Eine theologiegeschichtlich-systematische Untersuchung*, Würzburg 1989, 714.

5. B. Quelquejeu and J.-P. Jossua, 'Erfahrung', *NHThG* I, 231.

6. J. Moltmann, *God in Creation*, trans. Margaret Kohl, London and New York 1985, Ch. X, § 1: 'The Primacy of the Soul', 247ff.

7. Cf. J. Track, 'Erfahrung' III/2, *TRE* X, 116f.

8. D. Riesman, *The Lonely Crowd*, New York 1950; also his *Individualism Reconsidered*, New York 1954.

8a. *West-Eastern Divan*, trans. Edward Dowden, London 1914. The German text is as follows:

Suleika: Volk und Knecht und Überwinder,
          Sie gestehn zu jeder Zeit:
          Höchstes Glück der Erdenkinder
          Sei nur die Persönlichkeit . . .

Hatem: Kann wohl sein! so wird gemeinet;
          doch ich bin auf anderer Spur:
          Alles Erdenglück vereinet
          find ich in Suleika nur.

          Wie sie sich an mich verschwendet,
          bin ich mir ein wertes Ich:
          Hätte sie sich weggewendet,
          Augenblicks verlör ich mich   (VIII, 21).

9. In §3 of the introduction to his *Glaubenslehre*, F. Schleiermacher

equated 'immediate self-consciousness' with a 'certainty of feeling', in order to distinguish it from an objective consciousness of itself. What he says suggests that this is a negative description of the self-consciousness determined by God. If this is so, then psychological attempts at verification of the 'immediate self-consciousness' are superfluous. Cf. *Glaubenslehre*, 1821/2, 2nd revised ed. 1830 (*The Christian Faith*, trans. of 2nd ed. by H. R. Mackintosh and J. S. Stewart, Edinburgh 1928; Philadelphia 1976).

10. Gadamer, *Wahrheit*, 340ff., on the experience of the Thou (for ET cf. n.1).

11. S. Crites in 'The Narrative Quality of Experience', *JAAR* 39, 1971, 291–311.

12. Cf. J. Moltmann, 'Die Entdeckung der Anderen. Zur Theorie des kommunikativen Erkennens', *EvTh* 50, 1990, 400–414.

13. For this concept cf. H. Küng, *Existiert Gott?*, Munich 1978, 490ff. (*Does God Exist?*, trans. E. Quinn, London and Garden City, NY, 1980, 442ff.).

14. M. Polanyi introduced the term 'tacit dimension' into the discussion; cf. his *Personal Knowledge*, Chicago 1958, and *The Tacit Dimension*, New York 1966.

15. B. Brecht, preface to *Leben des Galilei*, Frankfurt 1962 (*The Life of Galileo*, trans. D. I. Vesey, London 1967).

16. B. Pascal, *Oeuvres* II, Paris 1908, reprinted 1965, 133. Cf. here J. Pieper, *Über den Begriff der Tradition*, Cologne and Freiburg 1958; G. Krüger, *Freiheit und Weltverwaltung*, Freiburg 1958.

17. J. Moltmann, 'Zur Bedeutung des Petrus Ramus für Philosophie und Theologie im Calvinismus', *ZKG* 68, 1957, 295–318; W. J. Ong, *Ramus, Method, and the Decay of Dialogue*, Cambridge, Mass., 1958.

18. R. Descartes, *Discourse on the Method of Rightly Conducting the Reason* in *The Philosophical Works of Descartes*, trans. E. S. Haldane and G. R. T. Ross, revised ed. Cambridge 1931, reprinted 1979, 119. For comment, cf. K. Jaspers, *Descartes und die Philosophie* (1937), Berlin 1948.

19. W. Leiss, *The Domination of Nature*, New York 1972; C. Merchant, *The Death of Nature*, San Francisco 1980.

20. Cf. Herms, 'Erfahrung' II, 89f.

21. Jaspers, *Descartes*, 42f.

22. I. Kant, Preface to the second edition of the *Critique of Pure Reason* (1787).

23. C. Lasch, *The Culture of Narcissism. American Life in an Age of Diminishing Expectations*, New York 1978.

24. Herms, 'Erfahrung' II and IV.

25. Ibid., 97.

26. Ibid., 99.

27. Ibid., 131.

28. See Ch. XI.

29. A. N. Whitehead, *Process and Reality, An Essay in Cosmology* (1929),

New York 1960, with the comment by M. Welker, *Universalität Gottes und Relativität der Welt*, Neukirchen-Vluyn 1981.

30. J. Moltmann, *Experiences of God*, trans. Margaret Kohl, London and Philadelphia 1980; also *God in Creation*, 205f.; G. Greshake, *Gott in allen Dingen finden. Schöpfung und Gotteserfahrung*, Freiburg 1985, 44ff. The encyclical 'Dominum et Vivificantem' (1986) III, 54, says rightly: God is spirit who '*in himself* is *wholly transcendent* with regard to the world . . . For he is absolute Spirit, "God is spirit"; and also, in such a marvellous way, he is not only *close to this world* but *present* in it, and in a sense *immanent*, penetrating it and giving it life from within . . . [Only the Spirit] can be "*closer* than my inmost being" . . . Only the Spirit can be so immanent in man and in the world, while remaining inviolable and immutable in his absolute transcendence.' Cf. also the *Bagavadgita*, 6, 30: 'He who sees me in the universe / And also sees the universe in me / From him will I never more be removed / And he will never more be removed from me.'

31. For John Wesley the perception of God 'in all things' was a necessary part of faith in God. For him the 'separation' of things from God was 'practical atheism'. See 'Upon our Lord's Sermon on the Mount', Discourse III, I. 11 (1742) in *Standard Sermons*, ed. E. H. Sugden, London 1921, 5th ed., 1964, No. 23: 'But the great lesson which our blessed Lord inculcates here, and which he illustrates by this example, is *that God is in all things*, and that we are to see the Creator in the glass of every creature; that we should use and look upon *nothing as separate from God*, which is indeed a kind of *practical atheism*, but, with a true magnificence of thought, survey heaven and earth and all that is therein, as contained by God in the hollow of His hand, who by His intimate presence holds them all in being, who pervades and actuates the whole created frame and is, in a true sense, the soul of the universe.'

32. That is in my view the truth of the well-known penultimate sentence in R. Bultmann's *History and Eschatology* (Gifford Lectures 1955; Edinburgh 1957): 'In every moment slumbers the possibility of being the eschatological moment.' But I would not agree with Bultmann's coda: 'You must awaken it'; for in reality 'the eschatological moment' awakens us, we do not awaken it.

33. Descartes took over this conclusion from Augustine, *De Civitate Dei* XI, 26.

34. Quoted in M. Grabmann, *Die Grundgedanken des Heiligen Augustinus über Seele und Gott* (1929), Darmstadt 1957, 12.

35. M. Luther, WA 40, II, 328.

36. For the facts cf. L. R. Brown (ed.), *State of the World 1989. A Worldwatch Institute Report on the Progress toward a Sustainable Society*, New York 1989. For the interpretation, B. McKibben, *The End of Nature*, New York 1989.

II *Historical Experience of the Spirit*

1. Cf. 'Geist' in F. Kluge, *Etymologisches Wörterbuch der deutschen Sprache*, 13th ed., Berlin 1963, 242; also R. Albertz and C. Westermann, 'ruah', *THAT* II, 726–753; W. H. Schmidt, P. Schäfer and K. Berger, 'Geist', *TRE* XII, 170–196. Cf. also H. Gunkel, *Die Wirkungen des heiligen Geistes nach der populären Anschauung der apostolischen Zeit und nach der Lehre des Apostels Paulus*, 3rd ed., Göttingen 1909.

2. Thus rightly J. Daniélou, quoted in Y. Congar, *Je crois en l'Esprit Saint*, Paris 1979–80, vol. I, 20 (*I Believe in the Holy Spirit*, trans. D. Smith, New York and London 1983). H. Gunkel, *Genesis*, 9th ed., Göttingen 1977, 104, already called the *ruach* 'the life-giving, formative divine power'.

3. A. Heron, *The Holy Spirit in the Bible, in the History of Christian Thought and in Recent Theology*, Philadelphia and London 1983, 3. Cf. also C. Westermann, 'Geist im Alten Testament', *EvTh* 41, 1981, 223–230; Silvia Schroer, 'Der Geist, die Weisheit und die Taube. Feministisch-kritische Exegese eines neutestamentlichen Symbols auf dem Hintergrund seiner orientalischen und hellenistisch-frühjüdischen Traditionsgeschichte', *FZPhTh* 22, 1986, 197–225.

4. Helen Schüngel-Straumann, 'Ruah (Geist-, Lebenskraft) im Alten Testament' in Maria Kassel (ed.), *Feministische Theologie. Perspektiven zur Orientierung*, 2nd ed., Stuttgart 1988, 59–73, esp. 61.

5. H.-J. Kraus, *Systematische Theologie im Kontext biblischer Geschichte und Eschatologie*, Neukirchen-Vluyn 1983, 449.

6. H. Schüngel-Straumann, 'Ruah', 63.

7. Thus H.-J. Kraus's definition (*Systematische Theologie*, 449), citing M. Kähler. Similarly Heron, *Holy Spirit*, 9: 'The *ruach* as divine presence.'

8. As for example in M. G. Büchner, *Biblische Real- und Verbal-Hand-Concordanz oder Exegetisch-homiletisches Lexikon*, 18th ed., Brunswick 1888, 458.

9. H. Schüngel-Straumann stresses this point, 'Ruah' 64: 'The power of life given by God is at the same time the breath, the power of life from which created beings live.'

10. This means that the fear of pantheism, which Heron expresses (*Holy Spirit*, 9), is without foundation.

11. H. Schüngel-Straumann gives this excellent definition, 'Ruah', 61.

12. Cf. M. Jammer, *Concepts of Space*, Cambridge, Mass., 1954; Oxford 1955, 26ff.

13. In the following passage I am following the summaries in *THAT* (cf. n.1), as well as Y. Congar, *L'Esprit Saint*, and A. Heron, *Holy Spirit*, but I see a different pattern in the different dimensions of experience of the Spirit.

14. Cf. E. Berkovits, 'Das Verbergen Gottes' in M. Brocke and H. Jochum (eds), *Wolkensäule und Feuerschein. Jüdische Theologie des Holocaust*, Munich 1982, 43–72.

15. Cf. Kraus, *Systematische Theologie*, 449.

16. G. von Rad, *Weisheit in Israel*, Neukirchen 1970, 204 (*Wisdom in Israel*, trans. J. D. Martin, Nashville 1972; London 1975). Cf. also G. Schimanowski, *Weisheit und Messias. Die jüdischen Voraussetzungen der urchristlichen Präexistenzchristologie*, Tübingen 1985, esp. 75ff.

17. Congar, *L'Esprit Saint*, vol. I, 29.

18. E. Sjöberg, '$\pi\nu\epsilon\tilde{\upsilon}\mu\alpha$', *TDNT* VI.

19. P. Schäfer, *Die Vorstellung vom Heiligen Geist in der rabbinischen Literatur*, Munich 1972.

20. A. M. Goldberg, *Untersuchungen über die Vorstellung von der Schechina in der frühen rabbinischen Literatur*, Berlin 1969, 455ff.: 'Schechina und Heiliger Geist'.

21. B. Janowski, ' "Ich will in Eurer Mitte wohnen." Struktur und Genese der exilischen Schechina-Theologie', *JBTh* 2, 1987, 165–193.

22. P. Kuhn, *Gottes Selbsterniedrigung in der Theologie der Rabbinen*, Munich 1968, 89.

23. G. Scholem, *Von der mystischen Gestalt der Gottheit*, Frankfurt 1973, 135ff.

24. F. Rosenzweig, *Der Stern der Erlösung*, Heidelberg 1971, II, Buch 3, 192ff. (*The Star of Redemption*, trans. W. W. Hallo, London 1971).

25. Cf. Kuhn, *Gottes Selbsterniedrigung*, 23ff.

26. J. Moltmann, *The Crucified God*, trans. R. A. Wilson and J. Bowden, London and New York 1974, 267ff.

27. E. Wiesel, 'Der Mitleidende' in R. Walter (ed.), *Die hundert Namen Gottes*, Freiburg 1985, 70ff.

28. Scholem, *Von der mystischen Gestalt*, 146.

29. Rosenzweig, *Stern*, 192ff. Cf. also J. Jonas, *Zwischen Nichts und Ewigkeit. Zur Lehre vom Menschen*, Göttingen 1963; also his 'Der Gottesbegriff nach Auschwitz' in O. Hofius (ed.), *Reflexionen finsterer Zeit*, Tübingen 1984, 61–86. But Jonas relates his dream of 'the adventure of divinity and the odyssey of time' to evolution as the modern world view rather than to the experience of God in Auschwitz.

30. Rosenzweig, *Stern*, 194.

31. Rosenzweig took over the term from Hegel. It does not imply assent to the Christian doctrine of the Trinity.

32. Scholem, *Von der mystischen Gestalt*, 194, with a quotation from Judah ben Barzillai of Barcelona, in the period before the development of the Spanish Kabbalah.

33. L. Dabney, *Die Kenosis des Geistes: Kontinuität zwischen Schöpfung und Erlösung im Werk des Heiligen Geistes*, dissertation, Tübingen 1989.

34. S. Mowinckel, *He That Cometh*, Oxford 1956.

35. G. Scholem, 'Zum Verständnis der messianischen Idee im Judentum', *Judaica* I, Frankfurt 1963, 227f.

36. J. Moltmann, *The Way of Jesus Christ. Christology in Messianic Dimensions*, trans. Margaret Kohl, London and New York 1990, Ch. VII: The Parousia of Christ, 313ff.

37. C. Westermann, 'Geist im Alten Testament', *THAT* II, 224.

38. Cf. W. Zimmerli, *Ezekiel: a Commentary*, trans. R. E. Clements, vol. 2, Hermeneia, Philadelphia 1983.

III Trinitarian Experience of the Spirit

1. For more detail cf. J. Moltmann, *The Way of Jesus Christ. Christology in Messianic Dimensions*, trans. Margaret Kohl, London and New York 1990, Ch. III.

2. E. Käsemann, *Essays on New Testament Themes*, trans. W. J. Montague, London 1964, 15ff., and *New Testament Questions of Today*, trans. W. J. Montague and Wilfred F. Bunge, London 1969, 23ff.

3. Thus R. Scheffbuch, 'Mit Ernst Christ sein', *EK* 9, 1989, 527ff.

4. N. Nissiotis, *Die Theologie der Ostkirche im ökumenischen Dialog*, Stuttgart 1968, 72ff.' D. Staniloae, *Orthodoxe Dogmatik*, Zürich and Gütersloh 1985 and 1990, vol. I, 46ff.; vol. II, 31ff.

5. H. Berkhof, *Theologie des Heiligen Geistes*, Neukirchen-Vluyn 1968, 18f. (German expanded trans. of *The Doctrine of the Holy Spirit*, The Warfield Lectures 1963–64, Richmond, Va., 1964, London 1965).

6. L. Vischer (ed.), *Geist Gottes – Geist Christi*, Frankfurt 1981 (*Spirit of God, Spirit of Christ. Ecumenical Reflections on the Filioque Controversy*, WCC, Geneva 1981), where it is stated that this mutual relationship must be viewed as 'a fundamental principle of Christian theology'. Thus also A. Heron, *The Holy Spirit*, Philadelphia and London 1983, 127ff.; J. D. G. Dunn, *Christology in the Making*, London and Philadelphia 1980, 136ff.; K. Blaser, *Vorstoss zur Pneumatologie*, Zürich 1977, 23ff.; W. Kasper, 'Christologie von unten? Kritik und Neuansatz gegenwärtiger Christologie' in L. Scheffczyk (ed.), *Grundfragen der Christologie heute*, 2nd ed., Freiburg, Basel and Vienna 1975, 169; also John Paul II, Encyclical *Dominum et Vivificantem*, 1986, I, 4.

7. Cf. J. D. G. Dunn, *Jesus and the Spirit. A Study of the Religious and Charismatic Experience of Jesus and the First Christians as reflected in the New Testament*, London and Philadelphia 1975.

8. D. Bonhoeffer, *Letters and Papers from Prison*, ed. E. Bethge, trans. R. H. Fuller, [4th] enlarged ed., London and New York 1971, 361 (letter of 16.7.44): 'The Bible points people to the helplessness and suffering of God; only the suffering God can help.'

9. O. Michel, *Der Brief an die Hebräer*, 13th ed., Göttingen 1974, 24.

10. Ibid., 314.

11. J. Calvin, *Corpus Reformatorum* LV, 111: 'Nunc clare ostendit unde aestimanda sit mors Christi, non ab externo actu scilicet, sed a Spiritus virtute.'

12. Cf. above all M. R. Mansfield, *Spirit and Gospel in Mark*, Peabody, Mass., 1987; R. Pesch, *Das Markusevangelium*, 3rd ed., Freiburg 1980.

13. Cf. Moltmann, *The Way of Jesus Christ*, 137ff.

14. J. Jeremias, *Neutestamentliche Theologie* I, Gütersloh 1971, 70 (*New Testament Theology*, trans. J. Bowden, London and New York 1971).

15. L. Dabney, *Die Kenosis des Geistes, Kontinuität zwischen Schöpfung und Erlösung im Werk des Heiligen Geistes*, dissertation, Tübingen 1989, 151.

16. Thus E. Vogelsang, *Der angefochtene Christus bei Luther*, Berlin 1932, 66, following Luther, WA V, 58, 18.

17. Moltmann, *The Way of Jesus Christ*, Ch. V, §4.1: The Rebirth of Christ from the Spirit, 247ff.

18. W. Thüsing, *Per Christum in Deum. Studien zum Verhältnis von Christozentrik und Theozentrik in den paulinischen Hauptbriefen*, Münster 1965, 153. Cf. also I. Hermann, *Kyrios und Pneuma. Studien zur Christologie des paulinischen Hauptbriefe*, Munich 1961.

19. J. Calvin, *Corpus Reformatorum* XLVII, 48. Cf. W. Krusche, *Das Wirken des Heiligen Geistes nach Calvin*, Göttingen 1957, 137ff.

20. *Dominum et Vivificantem* II, 41.

21. Berkhof, *Theologie des Heiligen Geistes*, 18.

22. Ibid.

23. Ibid., 19.

24. *Lasst Euch vom Geist bewegen. Enzyklika über den Heiligen Geist von Papst Johannes Paul II. mit einem Kommentar von Hans Urs von Balthasar*, Freiburg 1986.

25. The event of faith is evidently also trinitarian: 'No one can say "Jesus is Lord" except by the Holy Spirit' (I Cor. 12.3) and 'No one can come to me unless the Father draws him' (John 6.44).

26. Vischer (ed.), *Geist Gottes – Geist Christi*, 15 (*Spirit of God – Spirit of Christ*, op. cit., cf. n. 6).

27. J. Moltmann, *The Trinity and the Kingdom of God*, trans. Margaret Kohl, London 1981 (= *The Trinity and the Kingdom*, New York 1981), 178ff.

28. D. Staniloae, 'Der Ausgang des Heiligen Geistes vom Vater und seine Beziehung zum Sohn als Grundlage unserer Vergöttlichung und Kindschaft' in L. Vischer (ed.), *Geist Gottes – Geist Christi*, 159ff. (cf. n. 6), with appeal to John Damascene and Gregory Palamas.

29. Vischer (ed.), *Geist Gottes – Geist Christi*, 14. At the Klingenthal conferences in 1979 and 1980 Eastern and Western church theologians agreed on this point. Cf. also Nissiotis, *Theologie der Ostkirche*, 68: 'A pneumatological christology can save us from the dangers of Christomonism.'

30. Gregory of Nyssa, PG 44, 377.

31. Berkhof, *Theologie des Heiligen Geistes*, 124.

32. *Dominum et Vivificantem*, III, 65.

Notes for the Introduction to Part Two

1. H. Schmid, *Die Dogmatik der Evangelisch-Lutherischen Kirche, darge-stellt und aus den Quellen belegt*, 7th ed., Gütersloh 1893, Pars III, ch. III, 294–365. Cf. here O. Weber, *Grundlagen der Dogmatik* II, Neukirchen-Vluyn 1962, 378ff., which includes a thorough working-through of the earlier literature.

2. H. Heppe and E. Bizer, *Die Dogmatik der Evangelisch-Reformierten Kirche, dargestellt und aus den Quellen belegt*, Neukirchen-Vluyn 1958, Loc. XX-XXIII, 404–467.

3. This is demonstrated in detail in H. E. Weber, *Reformation, Orthodoxie und Rationalismus*, I and II, Gütersloh 1940 and 1951.

4. J. Moltmann, *The Way of Jesus Christ. Christology in Messianic Dimensions*, trans. Margaret Kohl, London and New York 1990. D. Bonhoeffer had already worked out very clearly the interlocking of Christ's representative 'being for others' and the 'being in Christ' of these others; cf. his *Sanctorum Communio* (1927), trans. R. Gregor Smith, London 1963, and *Act and Being* (1931), trans. B. Noble, London 1962.

IV *The Spirit of Life*

1. Cf. C. Schütz, 'Spiritualität' in *Praktisches Lexikon der Spiritualität*, Freiburg 1988, 1170–1180. A turn towards political sanctification out of the experience of the people can be found today in Latin American liberation theology. Cf. G. Gutiérrez, *We Drink from Our Own Wells: the spiritual journey of a people*, trans. M. J. O'Connell, Maryknoll, New York, and London 1984; J. Sobrino, *Spirituality of Liberation*, ET Maryknoll, New York, 1988.

2. Cf. O. F. Bollnow, *Die Lebensphilosophie*, Berlin 1958.

3. D. Bonhoeffer, *Ethik*, München 1949, 97 (*Ethics*, trans. N. H. Smith, London 1955).

4. P. Tillich, *Gesammelte Werke* XI, Stuttgart 1969, 64ff.

5. Ibid., 66.

6. Ibid., 68.

7. N. O. Brown, *Life against Death. The Psychoanalytical Meaning of History*, New York 1959, esp. Ch. XVI: 'The Resurrection of the Body', 307–322.

8. R. Bultmann, *Theology of the New Testament* I, trans. K. Grobel, London 1952, 232. For the apocalyptic correction of his existential interpretation of Paul, cf. E. Käsemann, 'On Paul's Anthropology' in *Perspectives on Paul*, trans. Margaret Kohl, London and Philadelphia 1971, 1–31.

9. Bultmann, *Theology*, 235.

10. Ibid., 236.

11. The discovery of the significance of the comma was of decisive

significance for Kohlbrügge. Cf. H. F. Kohlbrügge, *Römer 7*, BSt 28, Neukirchen-Vluyn 1960.

12. Bultmann, *Theology*, 237.

13. Ibid., 238 (altered).

14. Ibid., 244f.

15. G. Sauter, 'Geist und Freiheit', *EvTh* 41, 1981, 214.

16. M. Grabmann, *Die Grundgedanken des Hl. Augustinus über Seele und Gott in ihrer Gegenwartsbedeutung*, Darmstadt 1957.

17. G. Tersteegen, *Geistliches Blumengärtlein inniger Seelen oder: Kurze Schlussreimen, Betrachtungen und Lieder über allerhand Wahrheiten des inwendigen Christenthums, zur Erweckung, Stärkung und Erquickung in dem verborgenen Leben mit Christo in Gott* (1768), 13th ed., Elberfeld 1826, No. 39, 28.

18. B. Pascal, *Pensées*, 434 E.

19. Augustine, *Confessions*, I, 1.

20. B. Groethuysen, *Philosophische Anthropologie*, Berlin 1928, 78ff.

21. Though following Augustine, I am presenting in my own way the consequences of a love for God that has miscarried, drawing on modern psychological analyses. Cf. N. O. Brown, *Life against Death*, 77ff.; T. Moser, *Gottesvergiftung*, Frankfurt 1976; H. E. Richter, *Der Gotteskomplex. Die Geburt und die Krise des Glaubens an die Allmacht des Menschen*, Reinbek 1979.

22. S. Kierkegaard, *The Sickness unto Death* (1849), trans. W. Lowrie, London, Toronto and Princeton, NJ, 1941.

23. H. E. Richter, *Gotteskomplex*, (cf. n.21).

24. M. Luther, WA V, 128, 36: 'Humanitatis seu (ut Apostolus loquitur) carnis regno, quod in fide agitur, nos sibi conformes facit et crucifigit, faciens ex infoelicibus et superbis diis homines veros, idest miseros et peccatores. Quia enim ascendimus in Adam ad similitudinem dei, ideo descendit ille in similitudinem nostram, ut reduceret nos ad nostri cognitionem. Atque hoc agitur sacramento incarnationis. Hoc est regnum fidei, in quo Crux Christi dominatur, divinitatem perverse petitam deiiciens et humanitatem carnisque contemptam infirmitatem perverse desertam revocans.'

25. Augustine, *Ep. Joh. ad Parth*. Tract. IV, 6.

26. Bernard of Clairvaux, *Die Botschaft der Freude*, texts selected and trans. into German by P. J. Leclercq, Neusiedeln 1953, reprinted Zürich 1977. Cf. also E. Albrecht, *Meister Eckhardts sieben Grade des schauenden Lebens*, Aachen 1987.

27. Teresa of Avila, *The Interior Castle* (1577), trans. E. Allison Peers, London 1974.

28. T. Merton, *The Seven Storey Mountain*, New York 1948.

29. Dorothee Sölle, *The Inward Road and the Way Back*, trans. D. L. Scheidt, Philadelphia 1978, London 1979.

30. William of Saint-Thierry, quoted in Grabmann, *Grundgedanken des Hl. Augustinus* (cf. n.16), 12.

31. Bernard of Clairvaux, from *Jesu, dulcis memoriam* in the translation by Ray Palmer ('Jesus thou joy of loving hearts'). Cf. also the eighteenth-century Gerhard Tersteegen:

> Der Geist, ein Wunderding,
> könnt er gleich alles kriegen,
> was Erd und Himmel hat,
> es würd ihm nicht vergnügen.
> Sobald er Gott im Grund gefunden hat,
> hätt er auch gar nichts mehr,
> so spricht er: ich bin satt.

32. N. O. Brown, *Love's Body*, New York 1966.
33. Cf. A. Heschel, *The Sabbath. Its Meaning for Modern Man*, New York 1951; J. Moltmann, *God in Creation*, trans. Margaret Kohl, London and New York 1985, Ch. XI: 'The Sabbath: The Feast of Creation', 276ff.

V *The Liberation for Life*

1. My previous contributions to the concept of freedom are: 'Die Revolution der Freiheit' (1967) in *Perspektiven der Theologie*, Munich 1968, 189–211 (*Hope and Planning*, selection trans. Margaret Clarkson, London and New York 1971); 'The Hope of Resurrection and the Practice of Liberation' (1974) in *The Future of Creation*, trans. Margaret Kohl, London and Philadelphia 1979, 97–114; *Menschenwürde, Recht und Freiheit*, Stuttgart 1979 (one of these essays, on 'Christian Faith and Human Rights', is printed in *On Human Dignity*, trans. M. D. Meeks, Philadelphia 1984); 'Die Befreiung der Unterdrücker', *EvTh* 38, 1978, 527–537; 'The Kingdom of Freedom' in *The Trinity and the Kingdom of God*, trans. Margaret Kohl, London 1981 (= *The Trinity and the Kingdom*, New York 1981), 191–222.
2. For this the distinction between *imperium* and *dominium* is often cited. Cf. E. Jüngel, *Wertlose Wahrheit. Erörterungen* III, Munich 1990, 202ff.
3. Barmen Theological Declaration, 1934, Thesis 2.
4. Cf. Lactantius, *De ira Dei* (*c.* 314). For a critical view cf. A. N. Whitehead, *Process and Reality*, New York 1929, 519ff. He calls it the idolatry 'of the fashioning of God in the image of the Egyptian, Persian and Roman imperial rulers'. The Galilean origin of Christianity on the other hand, rests upon 'the tender elements in the world, which slowly and in quietness operate by love'.
5. Cf. H.-J. Kraus, *Systematische Theologie im Kontext biblischer Geschichte und Eschatologie*, Neukirchen-Vluyn 1983, § 57, 146ff.
6. From 1981 onwards prayers for peace were held every Monday evening in the Nikolaikirche in Leipzig, the congregation joining together in saying the Beatitudes from the Sermon on the Mount. The congregation was very

small and without any influence. In 1989 these prayers for peace suddenly spread to other Protestant churches in Leipzig. In October 1989 thousands of people who were demonstrating for democratic change streamed out of the churches on to the streets. On November 9 the Berlin wall fell and the dictatorship disappeared. This is a good example of the way the Word and Spirit of Christ, and the Spirit and providence of God work together.

7. Citing Ernst Bloch, 'Kann Hoffnung entäuscht werden?' in *Verfremdungen* V, Frankfurt 1962, 219.

8. E. Fromm, *The Fear of Freedom*, London 1942, reprinted 1984.

9. J.-P. Sartre, *Existentialism and Humanism*, trans. P. Mairet, London 1948.

10. E. Bloch, *Das Prinzip Hoffnung*, Frankfurt 1959, 1413 (*The Principle of Hope*, trans. N. and S. Plaice and P. Knight, Cambridge, Mass., and Oxford 1986).

11. E. Bloch, *Atheism in Christianity*, trans. J. T. Swann, New York 1972.

12. B. Groethuysen, *Die Enstehung der bürgerlichen Welt- und Lebensanschauung in Frankreich* I and II, Halle 1929, reprinted Frankfurt 1978.

13. Harvey E. Cox, *The Secular City*, New York 1965.

14. I, Kant, *Kritik der praktischen Vernunft, Werke*, ed. W. Weischedel, IV, Darmstadt 1956, 254ff. (*Critique of Practical Reason*, trans. T. K. Abbott, London 1979).

15. G. W. F. Hegel, *Lectures on the Philosophy of World History, Introduction: Reason in History*, trans. H. B. Nisbet, Cambridge 1975. Also the comment in I. Ritter, *Hegel und die französische Revolution*, Cologne 1957.

16. K. Marx, *Die Frühschriften*, ed. S. Landshut, Stuttgart 1953, 207.

17. Cf. R. Strunk, *Politische Ekklesiologie im Zeitalter der Revolution*, Munich and Mainz 1971.

18. A. Kuyper, *Reformation wider Revolution. Sechs Vorlesungen über den Calvinismus*, trans. into German by M. Jaeger, Berlin 1904, 80ff.

19. Jon Sobrino, *Sterben muss, wer an Götzen rührt. Das Zeugnis der ermordeten Jesuiten in San Salvador: Fakten und Überlegungen*, trans. into German by F. Flohr, Fribourg 1990. Cf. also M. Lange and R. Iblacker, *Christenverfolgung in Südamerika. Zeugen der Hoffnung*, Freiburg 1980.

20. Here I am drawing especially on G. Gutiérrez's classic book on liberation theology, *Theologie der Befreiung*, Mainz and Munich 1973 (*A Theology of Liberation*, trans. C. Inda and J. Eagleson, Maryknoll, New York, 1973); also his *Die historische Macht der Armen*, Mainz and Munich 1984 (*The Power of the Poor in History*, Maryknoll, New York, 1984).

21. Cf. Norbert Greinacher's extensive documentation in his *Konflikt um die Theologie der Befreiung. Diskussion und Dokumentation*, Zürich 1985.

22. Gutiérrez, *Theologie*, 20f. (ET *A Theology of Liberation*, see n. 20; all quotations are translated from the German.)

23. Ibid., 173ff.

24. Ibid., 179.

25. This is made very clear in E. Cardenal, *Love in Practice: the Gospel in Solentiname*, trans. D. D. Walsh, London 1977, and in the handbook *Vamos Caminando*, Lima 1979 and London 1984. Cf. also, G. Gutiérrez, *We Drink from Our Own Wells: the spiritual journey of a people*, trans. M. J. O'Connell, Maryknoll, New York, and London 1984; J. Sobrino, *Spirituality of Liberation*, Maryknoll, New York, 1988.

26. Gutiérrez, *Theologie der Befreiung*, 151ff., esp. 162f.

27. Ibid., 140.

28. Ibid., 148.

29. John Paul II, 'Die Gefahren gebührend einschätzen. Predigt bei der Messe in Managua am 4. März 1983' in *Predigten und Ansprachen von Papst Johannes Paul II. bei seiner apostolischen Reise nach Mittelamerika.* Verlautbarungen des Apostolischen Stuhls 46, Bonn 1983, 35–46, esp. 38f.

30. The European peace movement was confronted with the same reproaches. Cf. J. Moltmann (ed.), *Friedenstheologie – Befreiungstheologie. Analysen, Berichte, Meditationen*, Munich 1988.

31. For the theological side cf. G. Schrenk, *Gottesreich und Bund im älteren Protestantismus vornehmlich bei Johannes Coccejus*, Gütersloh 1923, reprinted Giessen and Basel 1985. For the political side, cf. E. Reibstein, *Johannes Althusius*, Karlsruhe 1955.

32. G. Oestreich, 'Die Idee des religiösen Bundes und die Lehre vom Staatsvertrag', in *Zur Geschichte und Problematik der Demokratie, Festschrift für H. Herzfeld*, Berlin 1958, 11–32. For the American development cf. W. J. Everett, *God's Federal Republic. Reconstructing Our Governing Symbol*, New York 1988, and C. S. McCoy, 'The Federal Tradition of Theology and Political Ethics: Background for Understanding the U.S. Constitution and Society' in *The Annals of the Society of Christian Ethics*, 1988, 113–132.

33. H. Languet, *Wider die Tyrannen (Vindiciae contra tyrannos*, 1580), together with C. B. Hundeshagen, *Calvinismus und staatsbürgerliche Freiheit*, trans. and ed. by L. Wyss, Zürich 1946.

34. Cf. I. Fetscher, *Karl Marx und der Marxismus*, Munich 1967, 33ff: 'Liberaler, demokratischer und marxistischer Freiheitsbegriff.'

35. For the term 'possessive individualism' cf. C. B. Macpherson, *The Political Theory of Possessive Individualism. Hobbes to Locke*, Oxford 1962.

36. R. Garaudy points this out very clearly; cf. *The Alternative Future: a vision of Christian Marxism*, trans. L. Mayhew, New York 1975, Harmondsworth 1976.

37. See R. Musil, *The Man without Qualities*, trans. E. W. Wilkins and E. Kaiser, London 1953.

38. Cf. here E. Jüngel, *Zur Freiheit eines Christenmenschen. Eine Erinnerung an Luthers Schrift*, Munich 1978; J. Moltmann (ed.), *Religion der Freiheit. Protestantismus in der Moderne*, Munich 1990.

39. J. Bohatec, *England und die Geschichte der Menschen- und Bürger-rechte*, Graz 1956.

40. Cf. M. Theunissen, *Sein und Schein. Die kritische Funktion der Hegelschen Logik*, Frankfurt 1978; also W. Huber, *Folgen der Freiheit*, Neukirchen-Vluyn 1983, 118ff.

41. F. Kluge, *Etymologisches Wörterbuch der deutschen Sprache*, 19th ed., Berlin 1963, 216.

42. Cf. here V. Genovesi, *Expectant Creativity. The Action of Hope in Christian Ethics*, Philadelphia 1982.

43. F. Lang, *Die Briefe an die Korinther*, NTD 7, Göttingen 1986, 275.

44. I. Hermann, *Kyrios und Pneuma*, Munich 1961, 38ff.

45. Jon Sobrino has worked this out particularly clearly in his *Spirituality of Liberation* (cf. n.25).

VI *The Justification of Life*

1. I am developing here what I have already written about justification: 'Justification and New Creation' in *The Future of Creation*, trans. Margaret Kohl, London and Philadelphia 1979, 149–171; 'Die Befreiung der Unter-drücker', *EvTh* 38, 1978, 527–537; 'Spirit as Affirmation of Life' in *God in Creation*, trans. Margaret Kohl, London and New York 1985, Ch. X, § 2.6, 268–270; 'Righteousness from the Sufferings of Christ' in *The Way of Jesus Christ. Christology in Messianic Dimensions*, trans. Margaret Kohl, London and New York 1990, Ch. IV, § 4, 181–196.

2. I am here adhering to the form of the doctrine of justification maintained by my Göttingen teachers H.-J. Iwand, E. Wolf and E. Käsemann: H.-J. Iwand, *Glaubensgerechtigkeit und Luthers Lehre*, ThEx 75, Munich 1941; E. Wolf, 'Die Rechtfertigungslehre als Mitte und Grenze reformatorischer Theologie' in *Peregrinatio* II, Munich 1965, 11ff.; E. Käsemann, ' "The Righteousness of God" in Paul' in *New Testament Questions of Today*, trans. W. J. Montague et al., London 1969, 168ff.

3. To base the righteousness of faith one-sidedly on the theology of the cross, as does the Augsburg Confession in its Fourth Article, is non-Pauline. It reduces the justification of life to the forgiveness of sins. A. Schlatter already criticized this in *Luthers Deutung des Römerbriefes*, Gütersloh 1917, 53ff. E. Käsemann, ' "Righteousness of God" ', developed his criticism further by interpreting the righteousness of God as 'power' (173f.), as 'gift and service' and as 'freedom and obedience' (171).

4. L. Ragaz recognized this and brought out the point with admirable clarity: *Die Gleichnisse Jesu. Seine soziale Botschaft*, Bern 1944, 106ff. Cf. also G. Eichholz, *Gleichnisse der Evangelien. Form, Überlieferung, Auslegung*, Neukirchen-Vluyn 1971.

5. L. Ragaz, *Gleichnisse*.

6. F. M. Dostoievesky, *The Brothers Karamasov*, Book 6, Ch. III: Conversations and Exhortations of Father Zossima. This concept of universal

guilt is only the reverse side of the Russian Orthodox concept of universal forgiveness. It comprehends not only the world of human beings but the world of nature too: 'Beg the animals for forgiveness!' The divine love is all-comprehensive, for 'all is like an ocean, all is flowing and blending; a touch in one place sends up movement at the other end of the earth' (trans. C. Garnett, London 1913, 339).

7. Dorothee Sölle, *Politische Theologie. Auseinandersetzung mit Rudolf Bultmann* (1971), Stuttgart 1982, has convincingly shown the transference of the metaphysical concept of sin ('existential' in Bultmann) into the concrete political concept of sin, thus documenting her own progression from existential theology to political and liberation theology.

8. Cf. the declaration of the World Missionary Conference in Bangkok in 1973 on salvation and social justice. K. Viehweger (ed.), *Weltmissionskonferenz Bangkok. Sarmudhprakam – Kilometer 31*, Munich 1973, 146–149.

9. N. Greinacher, *Die Kirche der Armen. Zur Theologie der Befreiung*, Munich 1980, 79–109: 'Von Medellin nach Puebla'.

10. A praiseworthy exception is F. Herzog, *Justice Church. The New Function of the Church in North American Christianity*, New York 1980; also his article 'Dogmatik IV', *TRE* IX, 1983, 115: 'He makes the sinner righteous and creates justice for those without rights.'

11. L. Boff and V. Elizondo (eds), *Option for the Poor: Challenge to the Rich Countries, Concilium* No. 187, 1986.

12. J. H. Cone, *The Spirituals and the Blues*, New York 1972, 53f.: 'Because black slaves knew the significance of the pain and shame of Jesus' death on the cross, they found themselves by his side. "Were you there when they crucified my Lord?" '

13. E. Wolf, 'Die Christusverkündigung bei Luther' in *Peregrinatio* I, Munich 1954, 72ff.; E. Vogelsang, *Der angefochtene Christus bei Luther*, Berlin 1932.

14. D. Bonhoeffer, *Letters and Papers from Prison*, ed. E. Bethge, trans. R. H. Fuller, [4th] enlarged ed. London and New York 1971, 361 (letter of 16.7.44). K. Rahner took the contrary view: 'Only the *Deus impassibilis* consoles me'; quoted in H. Vorgrimler, *Karl Rahner verstehen*, Freiburg 1985, 152 (ET *Understanding Karl Rahner*, London and New York 1986).

15. Bonhoeffer, poem 'Christen und Heiden' (see 'Christians and Pagans', in *Letters and Papers from Prison*, p. 349).

16. On the question about forgiveness and atonement 'after Auschwitz', cf. S. Wiesental, *Die Sonnenblume. Eine Erzählung von Schuld und Vergebung*, Stuttgart 1981; A. and M. Mitscherlich, *The Inability to Mourn*, New York 1975.

17. R. Schwager, *Brauchen wir einen Sündenbock? Gewalt und Erlösung in den biblischen Schriften*, Munich 1978.

18. H. Gese, 'Die Sühne' in his *Zur biblischen Theologie*, Munich 1977, 85–106; B. Janowski, *Sühne als Heilsgeschehen*, Neukirchen-Vluyn 1982.

19. This is convincingly shown by N. Hoffmann, *Sühne. Zur Theologie der Stellvertretung*, Einsiedeln 1981.

20. P. Stuhlmacher, *Reconciliation, Law, and Righteousness*, ET Philadelphia 1986.

21. Thus rightly N. Hoffmann, *Kreuz und Trinität. Zur Theologie der Sühne*, Einsiedeln 1982, 30, with much of whose book I find myself in agreement.

22. Vogelsang, *Der angefochtene Christus*, 30ff.; W. Maas, *Gott und die Hölle. Studien zum Descensus Christi*, Einsiedeln 1979, 211ff.

23. Cf. Hoffmann, *Kreuz und Trinität*, 17ff.

24. This was shown by H. Gollwitzer, *Von der Stellvertretung Gottes*, Munich 1969, supplementing and in criticism of Dorothee Sölle, *Christ the Representative*, trans. D. Lewis, London and Philadelphia 1967.

25. E.-M. Bachmann, *Machet herrlich sein Lob. Gebete der Ostkirche*, Neukirchen-Vluyn 1987, 57.

26. On structural sin, cf. Rosemary R. Ruether, *Sexism and God-Talk. Toward a Feminist Theology*, Boston and London 1983, Ch. 7, 159ff.

27. U. Duchrow and G. Liedke, *Schalom. Der Schöpfung Befreiung, den Menschen Gerechtigkeit, den Völkern Frieden*, Stuttgart 1987.

28. J. Moltmann, *The Crucified God*, trans. R. A. Wilson and J. Bowden, London and New York 1974, Ch. 8: 'Ways towards the Political Liberation of Man', 317ff.

29. B. McKibben, *The End of Nature*, New York 1989.

30. L. R. Brown, *State of the World 1989. A Worldwatch Institute Report on Progress Toward a Sustainable Society*, New York 1989.

31. C. Gestrich. *Die Wiederkehr des Glanzes in der Welt. Die christliche Lehre von der Sünde und ihrer Vergebung in gegenwärtiger Verantwortung*, Tübingen 1989, 284ff., goes into the questions about 'collective guilt', but in his criticism of what he calls 'political theologies' (294) does not recognize the non-symmetry of unjust and just conditions. If he had studied the Christian-Marxist dialogue, which was the starting point for European 'political theology', this recognition would not have escaped him.

32. K. Barth, *Christengemeinde und Bürgergemeinde*, Munich 1946.

33. For more detail cf. J. Rawls, *A Theory of Justice*, Boston 1971, and J. Moltmann, *Politische Theologie – Politische Ethik*, Mainz and Munich 1984.

VII *The Rebirth of Life*

1. Cf. E. Cremer, *Rechtfertigung und Wiedergeburt*, Gütersloh 1907, 14.

2. Thus rightly O. Weber, *Grundlagen der Dogmatik* II, Neukirchen-Vluyn 1962, 400. Cremer, *Rechtfertigung*, 82, had already pointed this out.

3. E.g., 'Wiedergeburt', *RGG*[3] IV, 1698f.

4. Rom. 4.25. Also Augsburg Confession IV.

5. Thus also L. Christenson, *Komm' Heiliger Geist. Informationen*,

Leitlinien, Perspektiven zur geistlichen Gemeindeerneuerung, Neukirchen-Vluyn 1989, 173: 'Justification makes clear the thing on which our relationship *rests* . . . Sanctification on the other hand comprises everything that happens in the relationship.'

6. M. Fox (ed.), *Illuminations of Hildegard of Bingen*, Santa Fé 1985, 30ff. *Viriditas* means 'the greening power'.

7. Cremer, *Rechtfertigung*, 163.

8. A. Schlatter in his criticism of the Reformers' doctrine of justification, *Luthers Deutung des Römerbriefs*, Gütersloh 1917. The Apology of the Augsburg Confession IV, 251, does at least call faith 'a divine power in the heart through which we are born anew'.

9. K. Barth, *CD* IV/2, 291, 369.

10. See Barth's account of Kohlbrügge in *Die protestantische Theologie im 19. Jahrhundert*, Zürich 1947, 579–587 (*Protestant Theology in the Nineteenth Century*, trans. B. Cozens et al., London 1972, New York 1973).

11. K. Barth, *CD* IV/2, 291 (slightly altered).

12. Ibid., 511. Cf. O. Weber's critical comment in *Grundlagen*, 382f.

13. Weber, *Grundlagen*, 400.

14. Ibid., 401.

15. Cf. E. Schweizer, *Heiliger Geist*, Stuttgart 1978 (*The Holy Spirit*, trans. Reginald H. and Ilse Fuller, Philadelphia 1980, London 1981).

16. N. Nissiotis, 'Die österliche Freude als doxologischer Ausdruck des Glaubens' in M. Welker et al. (eds), *Gottes Zukunft – Zukunft der Welt, Festschrift für J. Moltmann*, Munich 1986, 78–88.

17. Cf. J. W. Fowler's important investigations, *Stages of Faith. The Psychology of Human Development and the Quest for Meaning*, San Francisco 1981.

18. J. Moltmann, *Prädestination und Perseveranz. Geschichte und Bedeutung der reformierten Lehre 'de perseverantia sanctorum'*, Neukirchen-Vluyn 1961; J. M. Gundry Volf, *Paul and Perseverance. Staying In and Falling Away*, Tübingen 1990.

19. Moltmann, *Prädestination und Perseveranz*, 176ff., against 'decisionism and actualism in the doctrine of faith'.

19a. *Solida Declaratio* XI, 50.

20. Cf. W. Cramer, *Der Geist Gottes und des Menschen in frühsyrischer Theologie*, Münster 1979, 28.

21. E. Hennecke and W. Schneemelcher, *Neutestamentliche Apokryphen* I, 4th ed., Tübingen 1984, 107 (ET *New Testament Apocrypha*, Philadelphia 1963–65); cf. here also M. Buber, *Werke* II, Heidelberg 1964, 483.

22. Hennecke/Schneemelcher, 29 (for ET cf. n.21 above).

23. Ibid., 36.

24. Cf. also Elaine Pagels, *The Gnostic Gospels*, London and New York 1981, Ch. III: 'God the Father/ God the Mother', 57ff.

25. Cramer, *Geist Gottes*, 68ff.: Die Muttergestalt des heiligen Geistes.

26. H. Dörries, *Die Theologie des Makarios/Symeon*, Göttingen 1978.

27. Cf. A. S. Outler, *John Wesley*, New York 1964, 9 n. 26.

28. Following a remark of Zinzendorf's, quoted by M. Meyer in *EvTh* 43, 1983, 423 (cf. n.29 below).

29. N. Graf Zinzendorf, *Hauptschriften* II, Hildesheim 1963, 33ff.: 'Die erste Rede in Pennsylvanien.' Comment, with extensive material, in M. Meyer, 'Das "Mutter-Amt" des Heiligen Geistes in der Theologie Zinzendorfs', *EvTh* 43, 1983, 415–430. Zinzendorf even declared later: 'It was not appropriate that the motherly office of the Holy Spirit should have been made plain, not by a sister but by me, among the sisters.' See H.-C. Hahn and H. Reichel (eds), *Zinzendorf und die Herrnhuter Brüder. Quellen zur Geschichte der Brüder-Unität*, Hamburg 1977, 293.

30. Meyer, 'Das "Mutter-Amt" des Heiligen Geistes', 423.

31. Ibid., 425.

32. P. Tillich, 'Protestantismus und politische Romantik' (1932) in *Gesammelte Werke* II, Stuttgart 1962, 209–218.

VIII   *The Sanctification of Life*

1. The hymn 'Veni Creator Spiritus . . .' includes the petition: 'Accende lumen sensibus' – let thy light kindle our senses. It is not only the heart and the inward being that are wakened to life by the Spirit of life. It is the outward being and the senses too. We become aware of life in a new way and feel it once more. Cf. here C. Schütz, *Hüter der Hoffnung. Vom Wirken des Heiligen Geistes*, Dusseldorf 1987, 18, with a reference to R. Guardini.

2. J. Wesley, Sermon on 'The New Birth' in *Standard Sermons*, ed. E. H. Sugden, 5th ed., London 1964, II, 232. Cf. also Sermon 19 on 'The Great Privilege of those that are born of God': 'The Spirit or breath of God is immediately inspired, breathed into the new-born soul; and the same breath which comes from, returns to God. As it is continually received by faith, so it is continually rendered back by love, by prayer, and praise, and thanksgiving – love and praise and prayer being the breath of every soul which is truly born of God. And by this new kind of spiritual *respiration*, spiritual life is not only sustained but increased day by day.' Cf. T. Runyon, 'A New Look at "Experience" ', *The Drew Gateway* 57, 1987, 3, 44–54, with reference to John Wesley.

3. J. W. Fowler, *Stages of Faith. The Psychology of Human Development and the Quest for Meaning*, San Francisco 1981; K. E. Nipkow, *Grundfragen der Religionspädagogik* III, Gütersloh 1982; also his *Bildung als Lebensbegleitung und Erneuerung*, Gütersloh 1990; F. Schweitzer, *Lebensgeschichte und Religion*, Munich 1987.

4. G. Eichholz, *Die Theologie des Paulus im Umriss*, Neukirchen-Vluyn 1972, 279.

5. A. Köberle, *Rechtfertigung und Heiligung*, 3rd ed., Tübingen 1930.

6. O. F. Bollnow, *Die Lebensphilosophie*, Berlin 1958, 37ff.

7. J. Baur, *Salus Christiana. Die Rechtfertigungslehre in der Geschichte*

des christlichen Heilsverständnisses, Göttingen 1968; O. H. Pesch, *Theologie der Rechtfertigung bei Martin Luther und Thomas von Aquin. Versuch eines systematisch-theologischen Dialogs,* Mainz 1967.

8. W. Joest, *Gesetz und Freiheit. Das Problem des Tertius Usus Legis bei Luther,* 4th ed., Göttingen 1968; also his *Dogmatik 2: Der Weg Gottes mit dem Menschen,* Göttingen 1968, 453ff.

9. J. Calvin presents the *vita christiana* in a more balanced way: *Institutio* III, 14. According to his view, sanctification means progressing in the gospel – and not in the moral but in the eschatological sense, by virtue of the *meditatio resurrectionis,* which Calvin sets over against the Platonic *meditatio mortis.* 'Quaere ille demum solide in Evangelio profecit, qui ad continuam *beatae resurrectionis meditationem* assuefactus est' (*Inst.* III, 25, 1).

10. A. S. Outler, *John Wesley,* New York 1964; M. Schmidt, *John Wesley* I-III, 2nd ed. Zürich 1987; H. Lindström, *Wesley und die Heiligung,* 2nd ed., Stuttgart 1982; W. Klaiber and M. Marquardt, *Heiligung aus biblischer und evangelisch-methodistischer Sicht,* Stuttgart 1987.

11. The inner experience of the Holy Spirit is for Wesley more than a hope and more than a beginning, however: 'It is termed "the kingdom of God", because it is the immediate fruit of God's reigning in the soul . . . It is called "the kingdom of heaven", because it is (*in a degree*) heaven opened in the soul.

> Everlasting life is won,
> Glory is on earth begun.

. . . For this we also pray in those words, "Thy kingdom come". We pray for the coming of his everlasting kingdom, the kingdom of glory in heaven, which is the continuation and perfection of the kingdom of grace on earth. Consequently this, as well as the preceding petition, is offered up for the whole intelligent creation, who are all interested in this grand event, the final renovation of all things, by God's putting an end to misery and sin, to infirmity and death, taking all things into his own hands, and setting up the kingdom which endureth throughout all ages' (*Works,* ed. T. Jackson, London 1829–31, V: 81, 336).

12. See J. Wesley, rules of the united societies (1739). Today cf. also *Soziale Grundsätze der Evangelisch-methodistischen Kirche (1984),* Stuttgart 1985.

13. W. J. Warner, *The Wesleyan Movement in the Industrial Revolution,* New York 1930; M. Weber, *The Protestant Ethic and the Spirit of Capitalism,* trans. T. Parsons, foreword by R. H. Tawney, London and New York 1930; R. H. Tawney, *Religion and the Rise of Capitalism,* London 1926.

14. T. Jennings, *Good News for the Poor. John Wesley's Evangelical Economics,* Nashville 1990.

14a. J. Wesley, *Works,* bicentennial edition, ed. R. P. Heitenrater and F. Baker, vol. 19 (*Journal,* ed. W. R. Ward), 211ff., Nashville 1990. The translation from Latin into English there printed is by Henry Moore.

15. A. Schweitzer, *Die Ehrfurcht vor dem Leben. Grundtexte aus fünf Jahrzehnten*, 5th ed., Munich 1988; cf. also *Reverence for Life* (Strassburg sermons), trans. R. H. Fuller, New York 1969, London 1970; also *The Teaching of Reverence for Life*, trans. R. and C. Winston, London 1966.

16. *In Defense of Creation*, The United Methodist Council of Bishops, Nashville 1986.

17. G. Freudenthal, *Atom und Individuum im Zeitalter Newtons*, Frankfurt 1982.

18. J. Moltmann, *Creating a Just Future*, trans. J. Bowden, London and Philadelphia 1989.

19. W. Joest, 'Heiligung', *RGG*³ III, 180–181.

20. M. Luther, *Heidelberger Disputation*, zu These XXVIII: 'Peccatores sunt pulchri, quia diliguntur, non ideo diliguntur, quia sunt pulchri' [Sinners are beautiful because they are loved; they are not loved because they are beautiful], in E. Vogelsang (ed.), *Luthers Werke in Auswahl* V, Berlin 1933, 392.

21. F. Kluge, *Etymologisches Wörterbuch der deutschen Sprache*, 19th ed., Berlin 1963, 298; also 'Holy', in *Oxford English Dictionary*.

22. R. Kaiser, *Gott schläft im Stein. Indianische und abendländische Weltansichten im Widerstreit*, Munich 1990, 23f.

23. J. Calvin, *Institutio* III, 1, 3.

24. M. Beintker, 'Creator Spiritus', *EvTh* 46, 1986, 12–26.

25. E. Käsemann, *Essays on New Testament Themes*, trans. W. J. Montague, London 1964, 65.

26. J. Moltmann, *The Passion for Life*, Philadelphia 1978.

IX The Charismatic Powers of Life

1. I am following E. Käsemann's essay 'Ministry and Community in the New Testament' in *Essays on New Testament Themes*, trans. W. J. Montague, London 1964, 63–94. Cf. also U. Brockhaus, *Charisma und Amt. Die paulinische Charismenlehre auf dem Hintergrund der frühchristlichen Gemeindefunktionen*, Wuppertal 1972; A. Bittlinger, *Im Kraftfeld der Heiligen Geistes. Gnadengaben und Dienstordnungen im Neuen Testament*, Marburg 1968; H. Mühlen, *Geistesgaben heute*, Mainz 1982; H. Baumert, *Gaben des Geistes Jesu. Das Charismatische in der Kirche*, Graz 1986. Cf. also *EvTh* 49, 1989, 1, which is devoted to the theme 'Charisma und Institution'.

2. Käsemann, 'Ministry and Community', 71f.

3. Ibid., 72.

4. Ibid., 75.

5. Cf. here L. Christenson, *Komm Heiliger Geist*, Neukirchen-Vluyn 1989, 246ff.

6. Ibid., 29.

7. E. Fromm, *The Art of Loving*, New York 1956, London 1957; B. Welte,

Dialektik der Liebe, Frankfurt 1973; J. Pieper, *Über die Liebe*, Munich 1974; N. Luhmann, *Liebe als Passion. Zur Codierung der Intimität*, Frankfurt 1982.

8. Christenson, *Komm Heiliger Geist*, 262ff.: (on the healing ministry of the church today). Cf. also B. J. Hilberath, *Heiliger Geist – heilender Geist*, Mainz 1988.

9. E. Peterson, 'Was ist der Mensch?' in *Theologische Traktate*, Munich 1951, 225ff.

10. J. Moltmann, *The Way of Jesus Christ. Christology in Messianic Dimensions*, trans. Margaret Kohl, London and New York 1990, 104ff.

11. Christenson, *Komm Heiliger Geist*, 266, draws express attention to 'the healing of memories'.

12. A. Lowen, *Körperausdruck und Persönlichkeit. Grundlagen und Praxis der Bioenergetik*, Munich 1981.

13. Käsemann, 'Ministry and Community', 84.

14. J. Moltmann, *Diakonie im Horizont des Reiches Gottes*, 2nd ed., Neukirchen-Vluyn 1989, esp. 52ff.; S. D. Govigi, *Strong at the Broken Places. Persons with Disabilities and the Church*, Louisville 1989.

15. J. Moltmann, *The Church in the Power of the Spirit*, trans. Margaret Kohl, London and New York 1977, 289ff.

16. *Die Frau in Familie, Kirche und Gesellschaft. Eine Studie der EKD*, Gütersloh 1979, 29.

17. Agnes Berner-Hürbin, *Eros – die subtile Energie. Studie zur anthropologischen Psychologie des zwischenmenschlichen Potentials*, Basel 1989; Catherine Keller, *From a Broken Web: Separation, Sexism, and Self*, Boston 1986, Ch. I: 'The Separate and the Soluble', 7ff.

18. G. Hocquenghem and R. Schérer, 'Formen und Metamorphosen der Aura' in D. Kamper and C. Wulf (eds), *Das Schwinden der Sinne*, Frankfurt 1984, 75–89.

X *Theology of Mystical Experience*

1. M. Luther, *Randbemerkungen zu Tauler* (1516) in O. Clemen (ed.), *Luthers Werke in Auswahl*, Bonn 1912–33, V, 306: 'Unde totus iste sermo procedit ex theologia mystica, quae est sapientia experimentalis et non doctrinalis.'

2. E. Cardenal, *Das Buch der Liebe*, German trans. by A. Schwarzer de Ruiz of *Vida en al amór*, 4th ed., Hamburg 1976; *To Live and to Love*, ET by K. Reinhardt, New York 1971; trans. D. Livingstone under the title *Love*, London 1974.

3. Cf. H. U. von Balthasar, 'Aktion und Kontemplation' in *Verbum Caro*, Einsiedeln 1960, 245–259; T. Merton, *Contemplation in a World of Action*, New York 1973. On Merton cf. E. Ott, *Thomas Merton – Grenzgänger zwischen Christentum und Buddhismus. Über das Verhältnis von Selbsterfahrung und Gottesbegegnung*, Würzburg 1977. On the ancient Greek

concept of theory cf. K. Kerenyi, *Antike Religion*, Munich 1971, 97ff.; for the modern concept of theory, cf. M. Horkheimer, *Critical Theory*, selected essays trans. M. J. O'Connell et al., New York 1972.

4. On the following section cf. K. Tilmann, *Die Führung zur Meditation* I, 6th ed., Einsiedeln 1974; *The Cloud of Unknowing*, ed. P. Hodgson, Early English Text Society, Oxford 1958; this fourteenth-century Middle English work has also been translated into modern English in many editions; W. Johnston (ed.), *The Cloud of Unknowing and the Book of Privy Counselling*, New York 1973; J. V. Taylor, *The Go-Between God. The Holy Spirit and the Christian Mission*, London and Philadelphia 1972, has developed the idea of the perception of perception as an experience of the Holy Spirit.

5. Cf. as exemplary from Protestant life the devotion to the cross of Count Zinzendorf, the founder of the Moravian Brethren, and from Catholic life the devotion to the passion of St Paul of the Cross, the founder of the Passionist order; cf. M. Bialas, *Das Leiden Christi beim Heiligen Paul vom Kreuz (1694–1775). Eine Untersuchung über die Passionszentrik der geistlichen Lehre des Gründers der Passionisten*, dissertation, Regensburg 1977.

6. This has been shown and described by H. Heppe, *Geschichte des Pietismus und der Mystik in der reformierten Kirche, namentlich der Niederlande*, Leiden 1879, and H. E. Weber, *Reformation, Orthodoxie und Rationalismus* II, Gütersloh 1951. My own contributions to the subject of Protestant mysticism can be found in 'Grundzüge mystischer Theologie bei Gerhard Tersteegen', *EvTh* 16, 1956, 205–224, and 'Geschichtstheologie und pietistische Menschenbild bei Johann Coccejus und Theodor Undereyck', *EvTh* 19, 1959, 343–361.

7. Thus for example J. Arndt, *Vier Bücher vom wahren Christentum*, 6th ed., 1857, 18: 'The man who is like in form to God is born of Christ' and 11: 'The image of God in man is the human soul in its likeness in form to God'. In Protestant theology, this *imago* christology goes back to Osiander's teaching about essential righteousness.

8. E. Schäfer, *Meister Eckharts Traktat 'Von Abgeschiedenheit', Untersuchung und Textausgabe*, Bonn 1956, 210ff.

9. Meister Eckhart, *Deutsche Predigten und Schriften*, ed. J. Quint, 4th ed., Munich 1977, 214. There are a number of English translations of Eckhart, e.g., *Selected Treatises and Sermons*, trans. J. M. Clark and J. V. Skinner, London 1963.

10. Eckhart, ed. Quint, 308, 309. The idea about the abolition of the mediations of God through the love for God of the human being brings Christian mysticism astonishingly close to Zen Buddhism. Cf. T. Merton, *Zen and the Birds of Appetite*, New York 1968 (with reference to Eckhart in the opening chapter, 17ff.) and *Mystics and Zen Masters*, New York 1967.

11. John of the Cross wrote his 'dark night of the soul' in a prison cell in the Carmelite monastery in Toledo. Cf. his *Complete Works*, trans. E. Allison

Peers, reissued Wheathampstead 1974; W. Herbstrith, *Therese von Lisieux. Anfechtung und Solidarität*, 2nd ed., Frankfurt 1974. H. Urs von Balthasar describes this night very soberly in *Wer ist ein Christ?*, Einsiedeln 1965, 82f. (*Who is a Christian?* trans. J. Cumming, London 1968). He says that 'the way of contemplation, honestly and consistently pursued, normally issues in a night: in no longer seeing why one is praying, or why one has given up so much, no longer knowing whether God is even listening, still desires the sacrifice, and still accepts it . . .'

12. On the following passage cf. J. Moltmann, *The Crucified God*, trans. R. A. Wilson and J. Bowden, London and New York 1974, 45ff.

13. On the relationship between apostles and martyrs, the best study is still E. Peterson, *Zeuge der Wahrheit*, Leipzig 1937.

14. W. Schrage, 'Leid, Kreuz und Eschaton. Die Peristasenkataloge als Merkmale paulinischer theologia crucis und Eschatologie', *EvTh* 34, 1974, 141–175. Christian action and Christian contemplation lead inescapably to Christ's passion. That is their common point of reference, however else one may wish to relate the *vita activa* and the *vita contemplativa* to one another.

15. J. B. Metz, *Zeit der Orden? Zur Mystik und Politik der Nachfolge*, Freiburg 1977.

16. *Theologia Deutsch*, ed. H. Mandel, in *Quellenschriften zur Geschichte des Protestantismus*, No. 7, Leipzig 1908, 88f.; Cardenal, *Liebe*, 21ff., 34ff., 101ff. (for ET cf. n.2).

17. Meister Eckhart, ed. Quint, 60.

18. No one has described this better than C. E. Rolt in *The World's Redemption*, London 1913. Independent of him, very similar ideas are to be found in N. Berdyaev, *The Meaning of History*, trans. G. Reaves, London and New York 1936. In his dogmatics (posthumously published by Gertrud von le Fort, Leipzig 1925, § 14, 212ff.: 'God as Love'), E. Troeltsch talks about the 'suffering of God' which begins with creation and only ends when God returns to himself. The 'breakthrough of finite souls into the divine life' is a step on this way, 'God's way to himself'.

XI *The Fellowship of the Spirit*

1. F. Tönnies, *Gemeinschaft und Gesellschaft*, 2nd ed., Darmstadt 1988.

2. P. Kropotkin, *Mutual Aid: a factor of evolution* (1902), ed. P. Avrich, London 1972.

3. This was the original foundation and beginning of Calvin's theology, *Institutio* I, 1, 1: 'All our wisdom, if it really deserves the name of wisdom and is true and reliable, really comprehends two things: the knowledge of God and our knowledge of ourselves. These two things are connected in many ways, and so it is not so easy to say which of them comes first and then itself affects the other.'

4. F. Schleiermacher, *Glaubenslehre*, 1821/2; 2nd revised ed. 1830; ET of

2nd ed., *The Christian Faith*, ed. H. R. Mackintosh and J. S. Stewart, Edinburgh 1928, Philadelphia 1976, § 121, 2.

5. Ibid., § 121.

6. Ibid., § 121, 2.

7. Ibid., § 121, 3.

8. *Glaubenslehre*, 1st ed., § 144.

9. M. Tetz (ed.), *Fr. Schleiermacher und die Trinitätslehre*, Gütersloh 1969, 80. I am indebted here to W. Brandt, *Der Heilige Geist und die Kirche bei Fr. Schleiermacher*, Zürich 1968, 253f.

10. J. Ratzinger, *Einführung in das Christentum*, Munich 1968, 194f. (*Introduction to Christianity*, trans. J. R. Foster, London 1969); also his essay 'Theologie und Kirche', *Communio* 15, 1986, 518ff.

11. Cf. T. Litt, *Das Bildungsideal der deutschen Klassik und die moderne Arbeitswelt*, Bonn 1955; Y. Spiegel, *Theologie der bürgerlichen Gesellschaft. Sozialphilosophie und Theologie bei Fr. Schleiermacher*, Munich 1968.

12. Psalm 104 expresses the all-embracing 'community of creation'. The reconciliation of the cosmos through Christ, about which Col. 1.20 speaks, restores it.

13. J. Moltmann, *God in Creation*, trans. Margaret Kohl, London and New York 1985, 203ff.

14. Thus E. Jantsch, *Die Selbstorganisation des Universums*, Munich 1984, 412.

15. I. Prigogine, *From Being to Becoming: time and complexity in the physical sciences*, San Francisco 1980.

16. W. Heisenberg, *Der Teil und das Ganze*, Munich 1969, 324f. (*Physics and Beyond*, trans. A. J. Pomerans, London and New York 1971).

17. M. Scheler, *Die Stellung des Menschen in Kosmos*, Munich 1949, 44; ET *Man's Place in Nature*, Boston 1961, 42f. But here the passage has been translated directly from the German.

18. Cf. F. Dostoievsky, *The Brothers Karamazov*, trans. C. Garnett, London 1913, Book 6, Ch. III: Conversations and Exhortations of Father Zossima, g) of prayer, of love (339): 'Love all God's creation, the whole and every grain of sand in it. Love every leaf, every ray of God's light. Love the animals, love the plants, love everything. If you love everything, you will perceive the divine mystery in things. Once you perceive it, you will begin to comprehend it better every day. And you will come at last to love the whole world with an all-embracing love. Love the animals: God has given them the rudiments of thought and joy untroubled. Do not trouble it, don't harass them, don't deprive them of their happiness, don't work against God's intent. Man, do not pride yourself on superiority to the animals; they are without sin, and you, with your greatness, defile the earth by your appearance on it, and leave the traces of your foulness after you – alas it is true of almost every one of us! . . . Brothers . . . love is dearly bought, it is won slowly by long labour . . . Every one can love occasionally, even the wicked can. My brother asked the birds to forgive him; that sounds senseless, but it is right; for all is

like an ocean, all is flowing and blending; a touch in one place sends up movement at the other end of the earth. It may be senseless to beg forgiveness of the birds, but birds would be happier at your side . . . and children and all animals, if you yourself were nobler than you are now. It's all like an ocean, I tell you. Then you would pray to the birds too, consumed by an all-embracing love, in a sort of transport, and pray that they too will forgive you your sin. Treasure this ecstasy, however senseless it may seem to men.'

19. I am presupposing what I have already written in *The Church in the Power of the Spirit*, trans. Margaret Kohl, London and New York 1977, and confine myself here to the concept of 'the fellowship of the Spirit'.

20. Irenaeus, III, 24, 1 (SC 211, 474, 27–29, ed. A. Rousseau and L. Dontreleau, Paris 1943ff.).

21. K. Barth, *Christengemeinde und Bürgergemeinde*, Munich 1946, 36: 'The true state must have its prototype and model in the true church. The existence of the church is therefore exemplary . . .'

22. Pastors and preachers often like to present the community of Christians as a 'model' for the culture of society.

23. D. Staniloae, *Orthodoxe Dogmatik* I, Zürich 1985, 67.

24. Athanasius, *De incarnatione verbi*, cap. 8, PG 26, col. 996 C.

25. Staniloae, *Dogmatik* I, 48.

26. Ambrose, *De Spiritu Sancto* III, 1, 8 and 3, PL 16, col. 811f.

27. Staniloae, *Dogmatik* I, 51.

28. Gregory of Nazianzus, Oration 31, 26f., PG 36, col. 161.

29. O. Weber, *Versammelte Gemeinde*, Neukirchen-Vluyn 1949.

30. J. Moltmann, *Theology of Hope*, trans. J. W. Leitch, London and New York 1967, 329ff.

31. According to Luther's preface to his Smalcald Articles of 1537, 'our churches are through God's grace illumined and furnished with the pure Word and right use of the sacrament, with the perception of all kinds of callings and estates and right works'. Awareness of the calling to worldly vocations is accordingly the third main perception of the Reformation.

32. J. Zizioulas, *Being as Communion. Studies in Personhood and Church*, London and New York 1985, 218.

33. J. Moltmann, *History and the Triune God*, trans. J. Bowden, London and New York 1991, 63f.

34. H. Luther, 'Bildung durch wechelseitige Begleitung der Generationen' in R. Strunk (ed.), *Schritte zum Vertrauen. Praktische Konsequenzen für den Gemeindeaufbau*, Stuttgart 1989, 142ff.

35. R. Strunk, *Vertrauen. Grundzüge einer Theologie des Gemeindeaufbaus*, Stuttgart 1985, 20ff.

36. J. Beck, 'Konfliktbearbeitung und Vertrauensbildung in der Gemeinde' in R. Strunk (ed.), *Schritte zum Vertrauen*, 213.

37. H. Falcke, 'Kirche und christliche Gruppen – ein nötiges oder unnötiges Spannungsfeld?' in R. Strunk (ed.), *Schritte zum Vertrauen*, 164–178. I am

following his analysis but am proposing a different pattern of theological interpretation.

38. Christel Becker-Kolle, 'Grenzen überwinden im diakonischen Handeln. Aus der Arbeit einer Aids-Beratungsstelle' in R. Strunk (ed.), *Schritte zum Vertrauen*, 118ff.

39. L. Feuerbach, *Grundsätze der Philosophie der Zukunft* (1843), 60, PhB 227, 169.

40. J. Ratzinger, 'Liebe', *LThK*, 2nd ed., VI, 1031–1036.

41. Ibid., 1033; cf. also C. Yannaras, *Person und Eros. Eine Gegenüberstellung der Ontologie der griechischen Kirchenväter und der Existenzphilosophie des Westens*, Göttingen 1982.

42. This is also stressed, though also in a one-sided way, by A. Nygren, *Eros und Agape*, 2nd ed., Gütersloh 1957 (trans. P. Watson, London 1983).

43. M. Buber, *Einsichten. Aus seinen Schriften gesammelt*, Wiesbaden 1953, 10.

44. M. Buber, *Urdistanz und Beziehung*, Heidelberg 1951; F. Ebner, *Das Wort und die geistigen Realitäten. Pneumatologische Fragmente* (1921) in *Schriften* I, Munich 1963, 75–342.

45. G. J. Dorrien, *Reconstructing the Common Good. Theology and Social Order*, New York 1990.

46. W. J. Everett, *God's Federal Republic. Reconstructing Our Governing Symbol*, New York 1988.

47. Catherine Keller, *From a Broken Web. Separation, Sexism, and Self*, Boston 1986. I am taking up her observations and cautiously correcting her interpretations on the male side.

48. Valerie Saiving, 'The Human Situation: A Feminist View', *Journal of Religion* 1960; Margarete Mitscherlich, ET *The Peaceable Sex*, New York 1987.

49. Joan Walsh Anglund, *A Friend is Someone who Likes you*, London 1958. Cf. here J. Moltmann, 'Open Friendship' [trans. Martha Corcoran] in *The Open Church*, ed. M. D. Meeks, Philadelphia and London 1978.

50. J. Walsh Anglund, *A Friend*.

51. Aristotle, Nicomachean Ethics VIII.

52. Nygren, *Eros und Agape*, H. Gollwitzer's wonderful and sensitive interpretation of the Song of Solomon, *Das Hohe Lied der Liebe*, Munich 1978, suffers somewhat from the distinction between eros and agape, and the Christian restriction of eros. Here I am following the psychoanalytical approach of Agnes Berner-Hürbin, *Eros – die subtile Energie*, Basel 1989.

53. Cf. here J. Pieper, *Über die Liebe*, Munich 1972; J. B. Lotz, *Die Drei-Einheit der Liebe: Eros – Philia – Agape*, Frankfurt 1979.

54. Cf. F. Ohly, *Hohelied-Studien. Grundzüge einer Geschichte der Hoheliedauslegung des Abendlandes bis zum 1200*, Wiesbaden 1958; G. Krinetzki, *Kommentar zum Hohelied. Bildsprache und Theologische Botschaft*, Frankfurt 1983; G. Gerlesmann, BKAT XVIII, Neukirchen-Vluyn 1965.

55. E. Stauffer, '*ἀγαπέν*', *ThWNT* I, 20–55, whose antithesis between eros and brotherly love (55) does not follow from his biblical exposition. A wholly positive Christian evaluation of eros is given by H. Haag, *Du hast mich verzaubert. Liebe und Sexualität in her Bibel*, Zürich 1980. Cf. also H. Haag and Katharina Elliger, *Stört nicht die Liebe. Die Diskriminierung der Sexualität – ein Verrat an der Bibel*, 2nd ed., Freiburg 1986.

56. Maximus Confessor, quoted in Yannaras, *Person und Eros*, Göltingen 1982, 122f.: 'The first cause of the heavenly Eros is God, limitless and without Cause as he is. For if this Eros be truly love, and if, as it is written *God is love*, then it is clear that the all-uniting Eros – that is to say love – is God. From God, Eros now descends to the angels, so we may also call Eros angelic, and this divine Eros is discovered as a love which leads to unity. For among the angels, all is harmony, and there is no strife between one thing and another. From this follows the spiritual Eros among those men of the church who know God, of whom Paul says that they should all speak in harmony with one another (I Cor. 1.10). The Lord says also "they should be one as we also are one". But this he says of those who are Christians because of truth; but further also of all men among whom the law of love rules. The souls who are endowed with reason he called spiritual, since they are moved by his heavenly Spirit. But he called [spiritless] Eros, the Eros of those without reason, sensual love, and this is certainly without Spirit. For out of the force of this love the birds all flock into the air, the swans, geese, cranes, ravens or similar creatures. But terrestrial beasts are also thus – the deer, the cattle and all others, and also the beasts which live in water – tuna fish, grey mullet and their kind. Hence even those who do not live in flocks and herds are led to others of their kind. He called natural Eros that which dwells as attribute in creatures without soul and reason; for such creatures love the Creator because He has given them existence. In the movement of their lives, that is to say the movement of their nature, these beings too are aligned towards God' (PG 4, 268 CD – 269 A).

57. Max Frisch, *Tagebuch 1946–1949*, Frankfurt 1950, 31f.: 'Love frees us from every image. This is the intoxicating, risky, really exciting thing, that we never come to the end of the people we love: because we love them; as long as we love them.' (Cf. also Max Fritsch, *Sketchbook, 1946–49*, trans. G. Skelton, New York and London 1977).

57a. C. Wesley.

58. W. Stählin, 'Der kuss im Neuen Testament', *ThWNT* IX, 136–144 (ET in *TWNT* IX).

59. K. M. Hoffmann, *Philema Hagion*, Gütersloh 1938, 91. Cf. also A. Wünsch, 'Der kuss in Talmud und Midrasch' in *Festschrift für I. Lewy*, Breslau 1911, I–XXXIV; I. Löw, 'Der Kuss' (1921) in K. Wilhelm (ed.), *Wissenschaft des Judentums im deutschen Sprachbereich* II, Tübingen 1967, 641–675.

60. Thus the Gospel of Philip discovered in Nag Hammadi says: 'The companion of the [Savior is] Mary Magdalene. [But Christ loved] her more

than [all] the disciples and used to kiss her [often] on her [mouth].' Cf. Elaine
Pagels, *The Gnostic Gospels*, London 1980 and New York 1981, 15.

61. Quoted in Stählin (cf. n. 58).

62. G. Büchner, *Real – und Verbal-Hand-Concordanz oder exegetisch-homiletisches Lexikon*, 18th ed., Brunswick 1888, 678.

63. It is also interesting that in the theology of the Trinity, the kiss of love
could be used as metaphor for the procession of the Spirit 'from the Father
and the Son'. M. J. Scheeben, *Handbuch der Katholischen Dogmatik* II, 3rd
ed., Freiburg 1948, 379: 'The Latin Fathers on the other hand stress in a
masterly way that the Holy Spirit, as effusion of the love between the two,
is the link, or a formal bond, vinculum, *osculum*, amplexus between the
Father and the Son.'

64. Cf. here now Maria Caterina Jacobelli, *Risus paschalis e il fundamento
teologico del piaceve sessuale*, 3rd ed., Brescia 1991.

XII *The Personhood of the Spirit*

1. I have called this way of speaking modalistic, and have instead postulated
the 'trinitarian principle of uniqueness' in the original relations. Cf. J.
Moltmann, *The Trinity and the Kingdom of God*, trans. Margaret Kohl,
London 1981 (= *The Trinity and the Kingdom*, New York 1981), 188ff. H.
U. von Balthasar agreed; cf. *Theodramatik IV. Das Endspiel*. Einsiedeln
1983, 148ff. The following comments on the unique personhood of the Holy
Spirit are a reply to the justifiable questions of Regina Radlbeck, *Der
Personenbegriff in der Trinitätslehre der Gegenwart – untersucht am Beispiel
der Entwürfe Jürgen Moltmanns und Walter Kaspers*, Regensburg 1989.

2. Thus rightly Catherine Keller, *From a Broken Web, Separation,
Sexism, and Self*, Boston 1986, 163ff., following Nancy J. Chodorow, *The
Reproduction of Mothering: Psychoanalysis and the Sociology of Gender*,
Berkeley 1978.

3. Cf. *The Trinity and the Kingdom*, 171ff.

4. Thus Karl Barth, for example, summed up God's attributes as com-
plementing one another; cf. *CD* II/1, 351ff. A very fine account of unusual
metaphors for the operation of the Spirit is given by C. Schütz, *Hüter der
Hoffnung. Vom Wirken des Geistes*, Düsseldorf 1987.

5. See Ch. V, § 4.

6. See Ch. II, § 4.

7. See Ch. VII, § 4.

8. See Ch. VI, § 5.

9. This is rightly stressed in Section II of the encyclical *Dominum et
Vivificantem* (1986).

10. P. Rosato, *The Spirit as Lord. The Pneumatology of Karl Barth*,
Edinburgh 1981.

11. Hildegard von Bingen, *Lieder. Nach den Handschriften herausgegeben
von Pudentiana Barth OSB, M. Immaculata Ritscher OSB and J. Schmidt-*

Görg, Salzburg 1969, 229. Cf. also *Symphonia armonie celestium revelationum*, ed. B. Newman, New York 1988, 141.

12. See Ch. IV, § 1. Thus also K. Stendahl, *Energy for Life, Reflection on the Theme 'Come Holy Spirit – Renew the Whole Creation'*, Geneva 1990. W. Pannenberg, *Systematische Theologie* I, Göttingen 1988, 414ff., (ET *Introduction to Systematic Theology I*, Grand Rapids and Edinburgh 1991) wishes to understand not only God's Spirit but also God's life, and hence the Godhead itself, as 'field of force'. I cannot follow him in his conclusion here. Highly inspiring for cosmic pneumatology, on the other hand, is J. C. Maxwell, *Dynamical Theory of the Electromagnetic Field*, ed. T. F. Torrance, Edinburgh 1982. Cf. J. Moltmann, *God in Creation*, trans. Margaret Kohl, London and New York 1985, 9ff.

13. J. V. Taylor stresses this particularly emphatically in *The Go-Between God. The Holy Spirit and the Christian Mission*, London and Philadelphia 1972.

14. For Hildegard of Bingen the power of the Holy Spirit is *viriditas*, the power of greening. She called God 'purest springtime'. Cf. *Lieder*, 243/245. Cf. here also M. Fox, *Illuminations of Hildegard of Bingen*, Santa Fé 1985.

15. Cf. Moltmann, *God in Creation*, Ch. VI: 'The Space of Creation', 140ff., and in the present book Ch. VIII, § 5.

16. On the Gestalt concept, cf. *God in Creation*, Ch. X, § 2, 255ff.

17. D. Bonhoeffer, *Ethik*, Munich 1949, 23ff. (*Ethics*, trans. N. H. Smith, London 1955).

18. Cf. Ch. II.

19. C. Hinz, ' "Feuer und Wolke im Exodus." Kritisch-assistierende Bemerkungen zu J. Moltmanns "Theologie der Hoffnung" ', *EvTh* 27, 1967, 76–109.

20. Cf. A. Heschel, *The Prophets*, New York 1962, 247ff., who talks about the pathos of God.

20a. C. Wesley.

21. Hildegard of Bingen, *Lieder, Carmina* No. 19 (cf. n.11), 232f.

22. J. Pieper, *Das unaustrinkbare Licht. Das negative Element in der Weltansicht des Thomas von Aquin*, Munich 1953.

23. Especially illuminating here is the feminist theology of Catharina Halkes, *Das Anlitz der Erde erneuern. Mensch – Kultur – Schöpfung*, Gütersloh 1990, 70ff.

24. Mechthild of Magdeburg, *Das fliessende Licht der Gottheit*, ed. P. Gall Morel, Darmstadt 1976; *'Ich tanze wenn du mich führst'. Mechthild von Magdeburg. Ein Höhepunkt detuscher Mystik*, selected, translated and introduced by Margot Schmidt, Freiburg 1988, 77:

'O du giessender Gott in deiner Gabe!
O du fliessender Gott in deiner Minne!
O du brennender Gott in deiner Sehnsucht!
O du verschmelzender Gott in der Einung mit deiner Liebe.'

Also 90: 'Der heilige Geist berührt sie mit seiner fliessenden Flut.'

25. F. Kronseder, *Im Banne der Dreieinigkeit*, Regensburg 1954, 26: '*Amor extasim facit*, Love thrust outwards. Love does not permit the lover to rest in himself; it draws him out of himself in order that he may be wholly in the beloved (Dionysius Areopagita).'

26. I understand 'deification' here in the sense of Orthodox theology. Cf. D. Staniloae, *Orthodoxe Dogmatik* I, Gütersloh 1985, 291ff.: 'The world is destined to be deified.'

27. Mechthild of Magdeburg, '*Ich tanze . . .*', (cf. n. 24), 92.

28. Elisabeth Moltmann-Wendel, 'Johannes 4, 5–14', Evangelische Kirche im Rheinland, Landessynode 1991, Düsseldorf 1991, 35–41.

29. Fox, *Illuminations of Hildegard of Bingen*, (cf. n. 14), 32.

30. Meister Eckhart, *Schriften und Predigten* I, Leipzig 1903, 164.

31. Thus Dorothy Dinnerstein, following Catherine Keller, *From a Broken Web*, 118ff. I have derived suggestions from Catherine Keller for the following passage. On the concept of feminine personhood, cf. Carol Gilligan, *In a Different Voice: Women's Conception of the Self and of Morality*, Cambridge, Mass., 1982; Anne Wilson Schaef, *Weibliche Wirklichkeit*, Wildberg 1985.

32. Cf. Ch. III, § 4, 2.

33. From this point the personhood of the Son and the personhood of the Father also have to be defined afresh. But this is not required in the framework of this pneumatology. I shall return to it in later work.

34. Cf Ch. VII, § 4.

35. Thus, for example, H. Hübner, 'Der Heilige Geist in der Heiligen Schrift', *KuD* 36, 1990, 182: 'Still, in the framework of the Bible's way of speaking and arguing, the question about God's Being is for the most part answered by pointing to what he does. In other words, in biblical thinking *essence* and *function* are to a very large extent not conceptually distinguished, not only in respect of God.'

36. For more detail cf. J. Moltmann, *The Trinity and the Kingdom*, Ch. V, § 3: 'The Immanent Trinity', 161ff.

37. Cf. J. Moltmann, 'Die trinitarische Geschichte Gottes', *EvTh* 35, 1975, 208–223.

38. These distinctions derive from general metaphysics, not from specifically Christian theology. They grasp the mystery of God merely exoterically, not esoterically, and are therefore at most applicable to God's relation to the world generally, but not to the inner self-distinctions in God himself. Cf. here already K. Barth, *CD* II/1, 257ff.

39. J. Moltmann, *History and the Triune God*, trans. J. Bowden, London and New York 1991, 68ff.

40. K. Barth, *CD* I/1, § 8, 295ff.

41. K. Rahner, 'Der dreifaltige Gott als transzendenter Urgrund der Heilsgeschichte', *Mysterium Salutis* II, Einsiedeln 1967, 317–401.

42. This is Rahner's thesis: ' "The economic Trinity" is "the immanent

Trinity" and vice versa', 328. This postulate identifies that which in Barth's theology is called 'correspondence'. For critical comment cf. B. Wenisch, 'Zur Theologie K. Rahners', *MThZ* 28, 1977, 383–397, and F. X. Bantle, 'Person und Personbegriff in der Trinitäteslehre K. Rahners', *MThZ* 30, 1979, 11–24. Y. Congar writes very pertinently: 'The economic Trinity thus reveals the immanent Trinity – but does it reveal it entirely? There is always a limit . . . The infinite and divine manner in which the perfections that we attribute to God are accomplished elude us to a very great extent. This should make us cautious in saying "and vice versa" ' (*I Believe in the Holy Spirit*, trans. D. Smith, London and New York 1983, vol. III, 16).

43. K. Barth, *CD* I/1, summary headings to §§ 10–12, 384, 399, 448.

44. Cf. here J. Moltmann, 'Gottesoffenbarung und Wahrheitsfrage' (1966) in *Perspektiven der Theologie*, Munich 1968, 13–35.

45. K. Barth, *Christliche Dogmatik im Entwurf*, Munich 1927, 164, talked about the 'monarchical word of God' because what it communicated was: 'God reveals himself as the Lord' (172). The monarchical identification proceeds along the following lines: God *in* his Word, his Word *in* the biblical testimony, the biblical testimony *in* the preached Word.

46. G. S. Hendry, *The Holy Spirit in Christian Theology*, London 1965, 42ff., in criticism of Barth.

47. J. Moltmann, *The Way of Jesus Christ. Christology in Messianic Dimensions*, trans. Margaret Kohl, London and New York 1990, Ch. III, § 1, 73ff.

48. The Wisdom of Solomon, chs 9–11.

49. I agree with D. Staniloae, who therefore talks about an 'accompanying of the birth of the Son through the manifestation of the Spirit'. Cf. L. Vischer (ed.), *Geist Gottes – Geist Christi*, Frankfurt 1981, 160 (*Spirit of God – Spirit of Christ*, London 1981, Faith and Order paper 103).

50. Cf. here the Old Catholic theologian H. Aldenhoven, 'Der Zusammenhang der Frage des Ausgangs des Heiligen Geistes mit dem Leben der Kirche' in L. Vischer (ed.), *Geist Gottes – Geist Christi*, 134–143, esp. 140f. (cf. n.49 above).

51. J. Pohle and J. Gummersbach, *Lehrbuch der Dogmatik* I, Paderborn 1952, 464.

52. For more detail cf. J. Moltmann, *The Trinity and the Kingdom*, Ch. IV: 'The World of the Trinity', 97ff.

53. Cf. here J. Moltmann, 'Christian Hope – Messianic or Transcendent? A Theological Conversation with Joachim of Fiore and Thomas Aquinas', *History and the Triune God*, 91ff.

54. G. E. Lessing, *The Education of the Human Race*, trans. F. W. Robertson, London and New York 1927, §§ 88–90 (slightly altered).

55. *Concordia novi et veteris testamenti*, Venice 1519.

56. Critics of Joachim and his influence on the European view of history have overlooked this; cf. K. Löwith, *Weltgeschichte und Heilsgeschehen*, 2nd ed., Stuttgart 1953, and H. de Lubac, *La postérité spirituelle de Joachim*

de Fiore, 2 vols, Paris 1979. The diagram is printed in *Storia e Messagio in Gioacchino da Fiore. Atti del i Congresso Internazionale di Studi Giocchimiti Fiore 1984*. Cf. also J. J. Ferreira de Farias, SJ, *O Espírito e a História. O Pneuma Divino no recente debate sobre as pessoas da Trinidade*, dissertation, Rome 1989.

57. Athanasius, *De incarnatione*, cap. 54.

58. Basil of Caesarea, *De Spiritu Sancto*, 31d, 41a.

59. Ibid., 39d and e.

60. G. Wainwright, *Eucharist and Eschatology*, London 1971 and New York 1981.

61. G. Scholem, *Judaica* I, Frankfurt 1963, 72f.

62. Cf Ch. X, § 3.

63. D. W. Hardy and D. F. Ford, *Jubilate, Theology in Praise*, London 1984 (= US title *Praising and Knowing God*, Philadelphia 1985), esp. 71ff. Cf. also L. Boff, *Der dreieinige Gott*, Düsseldorf 1987, 227ff., 247ff.; B. Forte, *Trinität als Geschichte*, Mainz 1989, 211ff., who calls this 'the trinitarian home'.

64. G. W. F. Hegel, *Sämtliche Werke*, ed. H. Glockner, vol. 15, 3rd ed., Stuttgart 1959, 100.

65. M. Heidegger, *Über den Humanismus*, Frankfurt 1965, 15f., has used the term ecstasy ontologically: 'The ecstatic nature of the human being rests on his ek-sistance . . . Ek-sistance means substantially going outside, to stand in the truth of being.' Cf. here also C. Yannaras, *Person und Eros*, Göttingen 1982, 28f. I am using the term ecstasy here in the sense of the 'philosophy of life' (*Lebens philosophie*).

66. Thus G. Florovsky, *Collected Works*, vol. III: *Creation and Redemption*, Nordland's Belmont 1976; V. Lossky, *In the Image and Likeness of God*, New York 1974, 54; also his *Die mystische Theologie der morgenländischen Kirche*, Graz 1961, 104ff. Cf. here Dorothea Wendebourg, *Geist oder Energie. Zur Frage der innergöttliche Verankerung des christlichen Lebens in der byzantinischen Theologie*, Munich 1980. The Jewish theologian A. Heschel, *The Prophets*, 55ff., also distinguishes between God's presence and his essential being: God is unapproachable in his holiness and at the same time present in what he does in the world. But if this were so, then God's holiness would be inviolable, and there would be no need for us to 'hallow' or sanctify it.

67. F. Kronseder puts it very finely in *Im Banne der Dreifaltigkeit*, Regensburg 1954, 45: 'To open up for human beings the circle of the divine relationships and to draw the soul into God's own stream of life: that is the quintessence of revelation and redemption.'

68. Cf. Vischer (ed.), *Geist Gottes – Geist Christi*, 12–23 (cf. n.49). Cf. also Congar, *I Believe in the Holy Spirit* (cf. n.42), who tries to find a position that mediates between East and West. I am here taking up the train of thought pursued in Ch. III, § 3, and developing it further.

69. B. Bolotov, 'Thesen über das Filioque', *Revue internationale de Théologie* 24, Berne 1898, 692.

70. This idea derives from John Damascene and Gregory of Cyprus. It has been further developed by D. Staniloae in *Orthodoxe Dogmatik* I, Gütersloh 1985, 46ff. Cf. also his contribution to Vischer (ed.), *Geist Gottes*, 158ff. I am taking up his ideas here. Cf. also P. Evdokimov, *L'Ésprit Saint dans la Tradition orthodoxe*, Paris 1969, 70ff.

71. On the social doctrine of the Trinity and its concept of person, cf. J. Moltmann, *The Trinity and the Kingdom of God* (cf. n.1); L. Boff, *Der dreieinige Gott* (cf. n.63) B. Forte, *Trinität als Geschichte. Der lebendige Gott – Gott der Lebenden*, Mainz 1989; Dorothea Wendebourg, 'Person und Hypostase, Zur Trinitätslehre in der neueren orthodoxen Theologie' in *Vernunft des Glaubens, Festschrift für W. Pannenberg*, Göttingen 1988, 502–524.

72. Bob Marley.

73. English version by Robert Bridges.

INDEX

INDEX OF NAMES

INDEX OF CONFESSIONS, CREEDS AND OTHER DOCUMENTS

INDEX OF BIBLICAL REFERENCES